LYTTON STRACHEY AND THE
BLOOMSBURY GROUP

Michael Holroyd, who was born in London in 1935, studied science at Eton and read literature in Maidenhead Public Library. He is the author of *Hugh Kingsmill: A Critical Biography* (1964), and *A Dog's Life*, a novel (1969). He spent over six years working on the life of Lytton Strachey, during which he read over thirty thousand letters and trunkfuls of other documents. In 1968 the biography was awarded the Yorkshire Post Book of the Year Prize. At present Michael Holroyd is at work on a life of Augustus John.

MICHAEL HOLROYD

Lytton Strachey
and the Bloomsbury Group:

His Work, Their Influence

PENGUIN BOOKS

Penguin Books Ltd, Harmondsworth, Middlesex, England
Penguin Books Inc., 7110 Ambassador Road, Baltimore, Maryland 21207, U.S.A.
Penguin Books Australia Ltd, Ringwood, Victoria, Australia

—

The contents of *Lytton Strachey: A Biography* and *Lytton Strachey and the Bloomsbury Group: His Work, Their Influence* were originally published by William Heinemann Ltd in two volumes under the title: *Lytton Strachey: A Critical Biography* in 1967-68. They were first published in the U.S.A. by Holt, Rinehart & Winston, Inc., under the titles *Lytton Strachey; the Unknown Years, 1880-1910*, and *Lytton Strachey; the Years of Achievement, 1910-1932*.

—

Lytton Strachey and the Bloomsbury Group: His Work, Their Influence published in Penguin Books 1971

—

Copyright © Michael Holroyd, 1967, 1968, 1971

—

Made and printed in Great Britain
by Cox & Wyman Ltd.,
London, Reading and Fakenham
Set in Intertype Lectura

CONTENTS

Preface   7

Acknowledgements   13

1. Bloomsbury: The Legend and the Myth   17
2. Independent and Spectatorial Essays   55
3. Landmarks in French and English Literature   129
4. Eminent Victorians   161
5. The Great Panjandrum   243
6. Elizabeth and Strachey   289
7. Books, Characters and Commentaries   338

Appendix   375

Select Bibliography   379

Index   388

LYTTON STRACHEY'S reputation has been likened to a meteor, hurrying across the skies to its extinction, and leaving behind it only a whiff of incandescent sulphur. When his posthumous collection of papers, *Characters and Commentaries*, was published, a reviewer in *The Granta*, S. Gorley Putt, made it the occasion for a cautionary lesson, advising future critical scriveners to conserve sufficient energy for a deathbed destruction of miscellaneous essays, lest the piety of less squeamish survivors should later assemble them into a book. This fierce reaction of attitude against his work, which had started at his own university, Cambridge, quickly gathered momentum after his death, spreading to London where it impressed itself strongly upon the metropolitan centre of English culture, and then across the Atlantic to America where in 1936 Douglas Southall Freeman described the author of *Eminent Victorians* and *Queen Victoria* as 'one of the most pernicious influences in modern biography'.

His biographies, however, continued to sell, in Britain and especially in America, though his literary stock in both countries has remained for the last quarter of a century at a relatively low ebb. Only recently has it looked like making a recovery. Readability was his forte, a readability which delighted the public and dismayed the pundits who saw in it only a reflection of the author's shallowness as a thinker and interpreter of human actions. In an age that has eulogized needless and often clumsy obscurantism, narrative power has been perversely misrepresented as a literary vice, whereas, if not an absolute virtue, it is at least a condition of virtue, a by-product of creative literature which does not render a bad book good but enhances the value of an otherwise fine literary achievement. Famous throughout the world as the most readable of biographers, Strachey was fundamentally an essayist;

but his critical essays – so compact and self-contained, yet always elegant and beautifully shaped – are unread by the public and out of fashion with many of the critics. And so it has come about that his rightful place on the literary stage has been usurped by other writers without a tithe of his technical skill, his wit or his genius for narrative.

Unlike a number of his contemporaries, Strachey has received scant attention from biographers, and this omission has tended to encourage some critical misunderstanding. Naturally not all that has been held against him is untrue. But thirty-five years of . posthumous literary criticism, unsupported by any significant amount of biographical information, produced a popular impression considerably distorted and removed from actuality. For most people the name of Lytton Strachey probably conjured up an image of that stale old gingerbread figure, the sardonic and cynical *dix-huitième-siècle* debunker. Mistakes like that made by Mr Ivor Brown who, in support of his view that the sedentary and enfeebled Strachey underestimated the physical energies of Queen Victoria, presumed that he had never beheld her beloved Cairngorms – which rose, in point of fact, almost out of his back garden in Rothiemurchus – are perhaps slight in themselves. Yet cumulatively they have served to manufacture the myth of a flippant, clever, wholly superficial character, without deep emotions in himself and without an understanding of them in other people, with a restricted appreciation for what is 'polished, pregnant and concise' in the field of art, and with no appreciation whatever of the important facts of real life.

The facts of Strachey's life tell another story. At the age of twenty-five he already seems to have had some premonition of what posterity might be tempted to say of him. He saw himself as a romantic. Do not, he warns his future biographer, write that

> 'He lives outside the world.' Or 'This remark,
> Did I not know his goodness very well,
> Would make me guess that some red imp of Hell
> Had served him with a quill to burn and sting,

Twisted from out a fallen seraph's wing.*
No! Neither give your pity; . . . .
. . . . But strive thus to think of me. –
'He has drunk far too deeply of love's wine
Ever to fear or ever to repine.
His spirit, calmed with that fierce opiate,
Sees, and despises, and submits to Fate.
He knows how wise he is, and by that rule
He knows without pretence that he's a fool.*

I do not see Lytton Strachey exactly as he saw himself at that early age. But that he was a highly emotional man, with catholic sympathies, is undeniable. For psychological reasons, and owing in part to immediate practical considerations, he was unable adequately to communicate his most passionate feelings in his writings, and this deficiency has misled critics of his prose style to deduce that he was passionless and cold. That he is not among the very great figures in English literature must, for this same reason, be admitted. The purpose of this book, besides drawing readers' attention to his various literary accomplishments, for long so fashionable, is to persuade them to turn back to his works and re-interpret them in a fresh and more personal light.

A minority of critics, often personal friends, have continued loyally to uphold Strachey's literary reputation through these lean times. The most thorough and scholarly of these, Professor C. R. Sanders, too anxious, it may be, to silence the loud chorus of denigration, has lavished on his subject a volume of generous and unstinted praise which unfortunately has done little to restore Strachey's position. It seems unlikely, in any case, that Lytton Strachey himself would have welcomed a hagiographer. 'Discretion', he once wrote, 'is not the better part of biography.' And, by the same token, sentimentality – the deplorable result of suppressed knowledge – is not the better part of literary criticism. But before now a definitive examination of his life and work has not been practical. 'About Strachey's life there is little to say', reported André Maurois in 1936. 'The biography of the biographer has not yet been written.' A quarter of a century later, when I started on this book and its companion volume *Lytton Strachey: A Biography*, it had still not been written. Clive Bell, in an essay on Strachey, has indicated some of the problems which rendered such a biography impossible. 'Lytton could love, and perhaps he could hate', he explained. 'To any-one who knew him well it is obvious that love and lust and that mysterious mixture of the two which is the heart's desire played in his life parts of which a biographer who fails to take account will make himself ridiculous. But I am not a biographer; nor can, nor should, a biography of Lytton Strachey be attempted for many years to come. It cannot be attempted till his letters have been published or at any rate made accessible, and his letters should not be published till those he cared for and those who thought he cared for them are dead. Most of his papers luckily are in safe scholarly hands.'

Now, over thirty years after Lytton Strachey's death, his friends and family have combined to put those papers at my disposal without any form of embargo as to how they should be used. The reasons for this necessary delay – an unusually long one in modern times – have been more specifically dealt with by Lytton's younger brother and literary executor James Strachey in the course of an interesting letter to Professor Martin Kallich (2 October 1956). 'As is generally known,' he wrote, 'my brother was to a very large extent homosexual. Traces of his views on that subject are to be found in his published works; but in those days nothing more open would have been permissible. His attitude was strongly in favour of open discussion. But he was never inclined to undue solemnity. There is a large amount of unpublished material – including a very great deal of delightful correspondence – which I hope will become accessible with the gradual advance of civilized opinion. For this advance we owe a good deal, I believe, to Lytton's own influence (though this is not gen-erally known) on his contemporaries, and, of course, more than anything to that of Freud.'

It may seem ironic that, after all this time, the life and work of Lytton Strachey should finally be commemorated by two volumes – that standard treatment of the illustrious dead that he was so effective in stamping out. Yet the irony is more apparent than real – no more incongruously relevant, say, than the fact that Lytton Strachey himself should have been jointly responsible for *The Greville Memoirs* – a work in eight fat volumes. He did not, moreover, censure *all* two-volume biographies – admiring, for example, Sir Edward Cook's excellent *Life of Florence Nightingale* – but derided only those which were slipshod and ill-digested, written without detachment or humour, and drenched in a tone of tedious panegyric.

Strachey, of course, worked almost entirely from published sources which he re-fashioned aesthetically and re-interpreted. I have worked almost entirely from unpublished sources which pose quite a different problem – inspecting over thirty thousand letters from, to, and about my subject, in addition to trunks full of miscellaneous papers, diaries, essays, speeches, autobiographical pieces, poems and so on. In putting together my narratives, I have drawn particularly freely from the letters, since it seems unlikely that any comprehensive selection of these – scattered pretty widely over England and America – will be a practical publishing proposition in the foreseeable future. Lytton was not a ready or eloquent conversationalist, and seems to have been allergic to the telephone. On the other hand he was a copious and very good correspondent, whose letters communicate uniquely his subtle and peculiar personality. 'No good letter was ever written to convey information, or to please the recipient', he wrote in an essay on Horace Walpole's letters: 'it may achieve both these results incidentally; but its fundamental purpose is to express the personality of the writer.' Where his own letters merely convey information I have paraphrased and blended them in with other sources of information; where the pleasure of the recipient has been the main purpose I have either omitted them altogether or offered some elucidation of this purpose; where I have judged his personality to be best expressed, I have quoted.

11

ACKNOWLEDGEMENTS

My book has been made possible by the kindness and cooperation of the late James Strachey, who, besides making accessible a formidable mass of unpublished material, answered the many questions which I put to him during the course of my work and also checked all the biographical facts of my typescript, though he is not to be held responsible for any of the opinions that I have expressed. Among others who have helped me in one way or another and to whom I would like to acknowledge my gratitude and indebtedness are: The Dowager Lady Aberconway, the late J. R. Ackerley, Mr Harold Acton, Lord Annan, the late Baroness Asquith of Yarnbury, Mrs Barbara Bagenal, the late Thomas Balston, the late Bishop Lumsden Barkway, Mr and Mrs J. L. Behrend, the late Clive Bell, Professor Quentin Bell, Mr Gerald Brenan, the Hon. Dorothy Brett, Mr Richard Carline, Mr Noel Carrington, Lord David Cecil, Lady Diana Cooper, Lord Cottesloe, Dr Lissant Cox, the late John Davenport, Mr James Dicker, Professor Bonamy Dobrée, Mr and Mrs Guy Elwes, the late E. M. Forster, Mr Roderick W. B. Fraser, Mr Roger Fulford, Mr David Garnett, Mrs Angelica Garnett, the Hon. Robert Gathorne-Hardy, Mr William Gerhardie, Mrs Marjorie Gertler, Mrs Julia Gowing (*née* Strachey), Mr Duncan Grant, Mrs Karin Hall, Sir Roy Harrod, the late Christopher Hassall, Mr R. A. Hodgkin, Mr Basil Holroyd, the late Mr and Mrs Kenneth Holroyd, Mr Richard Hughes, Mrs Mary Hutchinson, the late Aldous Huxley, Miss Elizabeth Jenkins, Sir Caspar John, the late Dorelia John, the late C. H. B. Kitchin, Lady Pansy Lamb, Mr John Lehmann, Miss Rosamond Lehmann, Mr Robert Lescher, the late E. B. C. Lucas, the late F. L. Lucas, the late André Maurois, the late Professor H. O. Meredith, Mr Gabriel Merle, Mrs Dorothy Moore, Mr Raymond Mortimer, Lady Mosley, Lord Moyne, Dr A. N. L. Munby, Mrs U. Nares, the late Sir Harold Nicolson, Miss Lucy Norton, Mrs Frances Partridge, the late Hesketh Pearson, Professor Lionel Penrose, Mr Alfred H. Perrin, the Hon. Wogan Philipps (Lord Milford), Mr William Plomer, Mr Peter Quennell, Mrs Nancy Rodd, Sir John Rothenstein, Sir Steven Runciman, the late Lord Russell, Mr George Rylands, the late Lord Sackville, Miss Daphne Sanger, the late Siegfried Sassoon, Mr

Alan Searle, Roger Senhouse, the late Sir John Sheppard, the late the Reverend F. A. Simpson, Professor George Kuppler Simson, Professor W. J. H. Sprott, Mrs Alix Strachey, the late Evelyn John St Loe Strachey, M.P., Mr John Strachey, the late Philippa Strachey, Mr and Mrs Richard Strachey, Sir Charles Tennyson, Dame Sybil Thorndike, Miss Marjorie H. Thurston, the late Iris Tree, Mrs Igor Vinogradoff, the late Boris von Anrep, the late Arthur Waley, Sir William Walton, Mrs Ursula Wentzel, Mrs Amabel Williams-Ellis (*née* Strachey), the late John Dover Wilson, the late Leonard Woolf, Mr Wayland Young (Lord Kennet).

I should also like to record my thanks to the following: Chatto & Windus Ltd, the Chelsea Public and Reference Library, King's College Library, Cambridge, the National Book League, the Royal Society of Literature, the Society of Authors, and the Slade School of Fine Art.

I must also express my indebtedness to Mr David Machin for his unfailing patience and support over three long years; to Mr Roger Smith for his meticulous checking and preparing of my typescript for the printers; to Miss Jennifer Holden who helped to correct each page of my work and gave me many valuable suggestions; and to Mr Herbert Rees for his expert assistance at proof stage.

The writing of this book was largely made possible by the award, in 1963, of the Eugene F. Saxton Memorial Fellowship for the composition of the first volume; and, in 1965, for the second volume, of a Bollingen Foundation Fellowship.

I am grateful to the following for kindly granting me permission to quote from copyright sources: Lord Annan for *Leslie Stephen* (MacGibbon & Kee); the late Bishop Barkway for unpublished writings; Rupert Crew Ltd for *The Wandering Years* by Cecil Beaton (Weidenfeld & Nicolson); Professor Sir J. D. Beazley for unpublished writings; the Administratrix of the Estate of Sir Max Beerbohm for letters and *Mainly on the Air* (Heinemann and Alfred A. Knopf, Inc); Professor Quentin Bell, Chatto & Windus Ltd and Harcourt, Brace & World, Inc. for *Old Friends* by Clive Bell, also Professor Bell for unpublished writings; A. P. Watt & Son for *Queen Victoria* by E. F. Benson (Longmans); A. M. Heath & Co. Ltd for *My Restless Years* by Hector Bolitho (Max Parrish); George Weidenfeld & Nicolson Ltd for *Memories* by C. M. Bowra; Hamish Hamilton Ltd for *South from Granada* by Gerald Brenan, also the author for unpublished writings; William Collins Sons & Co. Ltd for Ivor Brown's Introduction to *Queen Victoria* by Lytton Strachey (Collins Classics edition); Mrs Frances Partridge for unpublished writings by herself, the late Ralph

Partridge and Carrington; Lord David Cecil, C.H., for an article in the *Dictionary of National Biography*; Mr John Stewart Collis for *An Artist of Life* (Cassell); Routledge & Kegan Paul Ltd and The Macmillan Company for *Enemies of Promise* by Cyril Connolly (copyright 1948 by Cyril Connolly); William Collins Sons & Co. Ltd for *Two Flamboyant Fathers* by Nicolette Devas; the Society of Authors for unpublished letters by Norman Douglas; Mrs T. S. Eliot for a review and unpublished letters by the late T. S. Eliot; Curtis Brown Ltd for *General Gordon* by Lord Elton (Collins); the late E. M. Forster, C.H., for unpublished writings; Sigmund Freud Copyrights Ltd for an unpublished letter by Sigmund Freud; Mr Roger Fulford for unpublished writings; Mr David Garnett for *The Flowers of the Forest* and *The Familiar Faces* (Chatto & Windus); Mr William Gerhardie for *Resurrection* (Cassell) and unpublished writings; Mrs Marjorie Gertler for *Selected Letters* by Mark Gertler (Hart-Davis) and for unpublished letters by Mark Gertler; Mr Duncan Grant for an extract from an article and for unpublished writings; Professor G. B. Harrison for unpublished writings; Sir Roy Harrod for *The Life of John Maynard Keynes* (Macmillan); Mrs Dorelia John for *Chiaroscuro* by Augustus John (Cape); Martin Secker & Warburg Ltd and Farrar, Straus & Giroux, Inc. for *The Bloomsbury Group* by J. K. Johnstone (copyright © 1954 by Noonday Press); Sir Geoffrey Keynes for letters by J. M. Keynes; Associated Book Publishers Ltd for *Progress of a Biographer* (Methuen) and *The Return of William Shakespeare* (Eyre and Spottiswoode) by Hugh Kingsmill; the late C. H. B. Kitchin for unpublished writings; Laurence Pollinger Ltd (acting for the Estate of the late Mrs Frieda Lawrence) and The Viking Press, Inc. for letters by D. H. Lawrence (copyright 1932 by the Estate of D. H. Lawrence, 1960 by Angelo Ravagli and C. Montague Weekley) and Laurence Pollinger Ltd and Alfred A. Knopf, Inc. for 'None of That' by D. H. Lawrence; David Higham Associates Ltd for *The Whispering Gallery* by John Lehmann (Longmans); Mr Michael MacCarthy for *Memories* by Desmond MacCarthy (MacGibbon & Kee); Hamish Hamilton Ltd and Alfred A. Knopf, Inc. for *Forty Years with Berenson* by Nicky Mariano; Doubleday & Co. Inc. for *archy's life of mehitabel* by don marquis (copyright 1933 by Doubleday & Company Inc.); the late Kingsley Martin for *Father Figures* (Hutchinson); the late Professor H. O. Meredith for an unpublished letter; Mrs Igor Vinogradoff for *Ottoline: The Early Memoirs of Lady Ottoline Morrell* (Faber & Faber); Mr Raymond Mortimer for *Channel Packet* (Hogarth Press) and *Duncan Grant* (Penguin); Mr Beverley Nichols for unpublished writings; the late Sir Harold Nicolson for *The Development of English Biography* (Hogarth Press); Mrs Hesketh Pearson for *Beerbohm Tree* (Methuen) and *Modern Men and Mummers* (Allen & Unwin) by Hesketh Pearson; Mr William Plomer for *At Home* (Cape) and a letter; William Collins Sons & Co. Ltd for *The Sign of the Fish* by Peter Quennell; Mr Kerrison Preston for *Letters from Graham Robertson* (Hamish Hamilton); Hamish Hamilton Ltd for *Summer's Lease* by John Rothenstein; Mr S. de R. Raleigh for letters by Sir Walter Raleigh; Dr A. L. Rowse for a review; the late Bertrand Russell (Earl Russell, O.M.) for *Portraits from Memory* and *The Autobiography of Bertrand Russell* (Allen & Unwin and Little, Brown) and for unpublished letters; Mr Alan Searle for unpublished writings; Mr Roger Senhouse for unpublished writings; the Reverend F. A. Simpson for unpublished writings and *Louis Napoleon and the Fall of France* (Longmans); David Higham Associates Ltd for *Laughter in the Next Room* by Osbert Sitwell (Macmillan); David Higham Associates Ltd for *The Autobiography of Alice B. Toklas* by Gertrude Stein (The Bodley Head); Mr Frank Swinnerton for *The Georgian Literary Scene* (Dent); Professor Robert H. Tener for a letter; Dame Sybil Thorndike for unpublished writings; Sir Stanley Unwin for *The Truth About a Publisher* (Allen & Unwin); Longmans, Green & Co. Ltd for *Our Partnership* by Beatrice Webb and the Trustees of the Passfield Trust for Beatrice Webb's *Diary*; Mr Edmund Wilson for 'Lytton Strachey' from *The Shores of Light* (Farrar, Straus & Giroux, Inc. and W. H. Allen); Professor John Drover Wilson, C.H., for an article and an unpublished letter; Mr Leonard Woolf for his own published and unpublished writings and those of Virginia Woolf.

ONE

Bloomsbury:
The Legend and the Myth

'For those too young to have known it, the Bloomsbury world is like the memory of a legendary great-aunt; a clever, witty, rather scandalous great-aunt, who was a brilliant pianist, scholar and needlewoman, who could read six languages and make sauces, who collected epigrams and china and daringly turned her back on charity and good works. The influence of Bloomsbury can still be found in the adulation of France; in the mixture of delicious food with civilized values, and in "saying what you mean". Religion was covered by a belief in the importance of human relationships, and the belief seems reasonable enough, though one gets the impression that the milk of human kindness was kept in the larder and that the tea was usually served with lemon. But Bloomsbury, at least in its own eyes, stood for something more important; it stood for tolerance and intelligence, for seriousness about art and scepticism about the pretensions of the self-important, and it carried on a crusade about the conscious philistinism of the English upper classes. Lytton Strachey displayed all these aspects better than any other writer connected with Bloomsbury, and its faults and virtues reflect and explain his own.' *Times Literary Supplement* (17 June 1949)

1
THE VISIGOTHS

THE five years, 1906–1911, that immediately follow Lytton Strachey's time at Cambridge form the most unsettled and indeterminate period of his adult life. Everything was speculative, uncertain, fluctuating. He had plenty of plans, but they were all vague and impractical, so that he pursued them only with faint heart. After quitting the one society of which he had managed to become an integral part, he had been pitchforked back to London, to his family, to nothing. His environment was still largely that of his childhood days, which he had partly outgrown and from which he alternately longed and feared to cut free. At the same time he felt his most urgent need was to merge with – perhaps to create – another congenial society where he could lay the foundations of a successful career; a society that would help to assuage his longing, minimize his sense of fear. 'Oh dear me!' he had written to Maynard Keynes six months after coming down from Trinity, 'when will my Heaven be realized? – My Castle in Spain? Rooms, you know, for you, Duncan [Grant] and Swithin[1], as fixtures – [Leonard] Woolf of course, too, if we could lure him from Ceylon; and several suites for guests. Can you conceive anything more supreme! I should write tragedies; you would revolutionize political economy, Swithin would compose French poetry, Duncan would paint our portraits in every conceivable combination and permutation, and Woolf would criticize us and our works without remorse.'

Such was the dream; and reality approximated to it only haphazardly. Three years later a substitute community for Cambridge, something along the lines Strachey envisaged, had already taken shape in the purlieus of unfashionable Bloomsbury. It was not, of course, the ideal, Castilian concourse of Strachey's yearnings, nor did he succeed in planting within it the seeds of his own propitious future. In a sense it held him back from realizing his ambitions sooner, for Bloomsbury took the edge off his discontent, making discomfort and obscurity almost endurable. It mitigated, too, a little the claustrophobia of family life. In a letter to his sister, Dorothy Bussy (25 February 1909), he confesses to a wish that he had achieved something spectacular, 'but I seem to be as far off from even starting as ever. My condition is not encouraging. With this damned *Spectator* every week I see no hope of ever doing anything. It's pretty sickening. On Monday I shall be in my 30th year, and if I happened to die there'd be precious little to show for them all – perhaps one or two poems of highly doubtful taste, et voilà tout. It's sickening and occasionally I'm absolutely in despair. If I had decent health I should go into

1. B. W. Swithinbank. See *Lytton Strachey: A Biography*, p. 255–7.

a garret and starve until I'd done something, but that's impossible. The only consolation is that as it is I lead a very tolerable life.

'At the present moment, as usual, I take more interest in Duncan [Grant] than in anyone else. He's a genius and charming, but I think he's still rather younger than his age, so that what he does seems to me immature. But I suppose there's no harm in that. Otherwise the people I see and like most are two women – viz. Vanessa [Bell] and Virginia [Stephen], with neither of whom I'm in love (and vice versa).'

As Duncan Grant gradually faded from the forefront of Strachey's life, these two custodians of the so-called Bloomsbury Group began to figure more prominently. While at Cambridge he had sometimes been invited by Thoby Stephen, nicknamed 'The Goth', to 22 Hyde Park Gate, where the two girls lived and cared for their invalid father. Deaf, suffering from internal cancer, almost completely helpless, Sir Leslie Stephen was wholly dependent upon his daughters. On 22 February 1904 he died, and the four children, Vanessa and Virginia, Thoby and Adrian, left their old home to set up house together at 46 Gordon Square.

Strachey's visits to the Stephens had now grown more frequent. 'On Sunday I called at the Gothic mansion', he wrote to Leonard Woolf (21 December 1904) not long after they had moved into their new home, 'and had tea with Vanessa and Virginia. The latter is rather wonderful, quite witty, full of things to say, and absolutely out of rapport with reality. The poor Vanessa has to keep her three mad brothers and sister in control. She looks wan and sad.'

At this time, however, the two sisters existed in Strachey's mind as little more than spectral adjuncts to the magnificent Goth, and he used to refer to them collectively as the 'Visigoths'. After Thoby's tragic death in 1906, they had not vanished from his life, but slowly asserted themselves as separate individuals, full of their own interest and fascination. When Clive Bell married Vanessa, Virginia and Adrian moved to a house near by previously occupied by Bernard Shaw, 29 Fitzroy Square, so as to allow the newly-married couple to live alone in Gordon Square. Their circle of friends, of which Thoby's Cambridge contemporaries formed the nucleus, was not broken up by this move, but enlarged. 'If ever such an entity as Bloomsbury existed,' wrote Clive Bell,[2] 'these sisters with their houses in Gordon and Fitzroy Squares, were the heart of it. But did such an entity exist?' To offer anything like a coherent answer to this deceptively simple question, it is necessary to disentangle the origins of Bloomsbury from its retrospective reputation.

The group of friends surrounding Strachey, Leonard Woolf and Thoby Stephen were in a sense the original source of Bloomsbury. To most of them, any girl (who was not also a sister) might, for all they knew, have been a species of creature belonging to some other planet; and when Thoby had first introduced them to Vanessa and Virginia – shy and alarming in their long white Victorian dresses with lace collars and cuffs, their large hats, delicately balancing parasols and looking as if they had stepped out of some romantic painting by Watts or Burne-Jones – this double apparition took away their breath. They were nonplussed. Leonard Woolf recalls that 'it was almost impossible for a man not to fall in love with them, and I think I did so at once. It must, however, be admitted that at the time they seemed to be so formidably aloof and reserved that it was rather like falling in love with Rembrandt's picture of his wife, or Velasquez's picture of an infanta, or the lovely temple of Segesta.'[3]

After Thoby's death, Strachey had got to know the two sisters more intimately, to see some way behind the aloofness. In his opinion, and probably in the opinion of most other people, Vanessa was the more beautiful. Her figure was tall and imposing, her face perfectly oval with grey-blue eyes, hooded lids and a full sensitive mouth. In these days she radiated a sense of mature physical splendour, moving with an attractive, undulating walk that later earned her the nickname of 'the Dolphin'. Though often severe in the judgements she fixed upon people, her manner was usually gay and spontaneous. At the same time there was also something magis-

2. *Old Friends*, pp. 129–30.   3. *Sowing*, p. 186.

terial about her presence, a quality of quietude that befitted the eldest child of Leslie Stephen's second marriage. This element increased with the years and is vividly conveyed by Duncan Grant's portrait of her[4] – a sensitive yet uncompromising figure seated imperiously upon a high-backed Victorian chair. Despite being the member of a new, determindly enlightened set of artists and writers, she still liked to segregate the human race into two elementary classes – those who basked within the charmed circle of her youthful friends, and those who, possibly through no fault of their own, had been born into a less privileged stratum of society. To one side of this division, she erected a third tiny kingdom within which not all her emancipated principles were allowed to operate – her children. Over them she watched with a jealous and possessive eye. When Julian, her son was killed during the Spanish Civil War, she broke off for life her friendship with the painter Wogan Philipps (Lord Milford), who had travelled with him to Spain. And when her daughter Angelica wanted to marry David Garnett, she opposed the match violently, even though Garnett was a personal friend and member of Bloomsbury.

Though his relationship with her was made a little confused by her far more intimate association with Duncan Grant, Strachey did experience some mild flutter of physical attraction towards Vanessa. Her collapsed and dreamy attitudes, however, and her wild inconsequence often exasperated him. Her nature was entirely feminine, and she seemed to have a special relationship with homosexuals who felt safe with her and confided in her. She enjoyed entering into men's discussions and even making bawdy jokes, but she had no interest in current affairs. An artist of considerable talent, she scanned only the illustrations in the newspapers, seldom bothering to read through the dull grey columns of print; and on one notable occasion, seated next to a man whose features were intolerably familiar to her, she innocently asked Asquith, then prime minister, whether, unlike herself, he was interested in politics.

4. This portrait, which is reproduced in the Penguin volume *Duncan Grant* by Raymond Mortimer, now hangs in the Tate Gallery.

In spite of a natural, unselfconscious humour and gaiety, Vanessa's thoughts were largely disconnected from everyday affairs. She often seemed in the dark over the most common-place matters, and in casual conversation her metaphors were delightfully mixed. Her best and most original remarks, David Garnett observed, were vaguely experimental. 'When she coined an epigram it was often because she had forgotten a cliché.

' "In that house you meet a dark horse in every cupboard," she exclaimed with some indignation. And of Maynard: "It runs off his back like duck's water." But of all her sayings the most withering was: "Ah, that will be canker to his worm." '[5]

The same spirit of vagueness seems to have informed her painting, some of which is disquietingly sentimental. Though at one time or another she was influenced by Post-Impressionism – in particular Cézanne – and by the Fauvists, she retained an overall detachment from the stylistic movements of her day. Possibly her finest painting was to be a self-portrait done in 1958. Here there is no dreamy uncertainty: the face under its almost comically wide-brimmed hat is steeped in wistful sadness and resignation, the once sensuous mouth now tired and tremulous, the eyes from behind the large spectacles focused beyond the limits of the surrounding world.[6]

Early photographs of Virginia Stephen show her as less robust and comely than Vanessa, rather anaemic and ethereal. From out of a thin anxious face, her enormous green eyes gaze fearfully at the cold, slow terrors of the universe. There was always something impalpable about her. She appeared to glide below the turbulent sea of life as in a dream that would pitch without warning into the terrifying troughs of nightmare. The mystic aura that during her life enveloped her fragile being like a cocoon has caused many of her friends' retrospective memories to take on the illusion of reverie. For though she could be as animated as her sister – when her haunted expression suddenly lighting up with a smile, made her face look oddly different – yet her nature was perpetually

5. *The Flowers of the Forest*, p. 40.
6. This painting is now in the collection of Sir Kenneth Clark.

clogged with morbid self-obsession, the intensity of which would recurrently build up and explode, leaving her in a shattered state of collapse. Even in lighter moments, her compulsive fits of vitality seemed to come not from her physical resources, but through a painful, electric system of nerves.

Tall and slender, with a noble forehead and narrow, aquiline features, she radiated an ascetic, sexless charm which contrasted strangely with her vivid enthusiasm when excited by the curiosity of some discussion. Leaning forward in her chair, a cigarette held limply in her long fingers, her head cocked to one side like an intelligent dog, she would talk in her throaty, deepish voice with a keen sensibility, wit and an inquiring passion that was altogether dissimilar to Vanessa's balanced, judicial tone. Her mental animation mounted rapidly as she spoke, but if someone dared stupidly to interrupt her in full flight she would all at once grow fierce, flashing back some scathing repartee and then reverting to her sullen posture of aloofness.

At her most sympathetic, most relaxed, Virginia displayed a warmth and power of direct friendship that hinted at the deep burden of loneliness from which she was always endeavouring to escape. In convivial surroundings, among trusted friends, she gave the impression of brittle high spirits that might at any second '"leave the ground" and give some fantastic, entrancing, amusing, dreamlike, almost lyrical description of an event, a place, or a person', or alternatively snap and in a trice capsize her frail being into unexpected, imponderable gloom. The peculiar remoteness of personality which manifested itself amusingly in Vanessa's social gaffs and off-beat colloquialisms was present in a far more terrifying form in Virginia. And whereas Vanessa's vagueness exasperated Strachey, Virginia's asexual, twilight elusiveness he found psychologically curious. The one jarred upon his matronly sense of order and proportion; the other, the consequence of a strange and original emphasis of concentration, chimed in with his own mystical apprehensions, running to some extent parallel with that ever-present desire of his to find release from the prison of his physical self. He admired her; but her novels were not to his taste. Virginia's strong, masculine intelligence and heightened feminine sensibility seemed almost to cancel each other out, producing a sort of eddying cross-current, a bleak no-man's-island that is reproduced in the aseptic, vestal texture of her fiction – a literary quality that dismayed Strachey. Bi-sexuality would have fascinated him; but he abhorred a vacuum.

Despite Virginia's militant feminism and Strachey's radical passivism, neither of them was well-suited to the sort of conscious Fabian worrying that was then forming so great a part of intellectual discussion. But whereas Strachey's pensive silences were rather stylized, Virginia's were more distracted and impenetrable. She seemed oddly isolated from it all, at once half-eager and half-frightened of breaking free from the coiling meshes of her absorbed and tortured self-preoccupation. This spirit of sharply alternating animation and reserve had been conditioned by her father. Leslie Stephen was an enlightened man, but sexually repressed and maladjusted, so that although his children had benefited from his literary tolerance, they had also suffered grievously under the meanness and dogmatic puritanism of his household. Perhaps the pathos of such a man's life could only be appreciated by his friends, most of whom thought him very lovable. The contrast between Vernon Whitford in Meredith's *The Egoist* and Mr Ramsay in Virginia Woolf's *To the Lighthouse* underlines Leslie Stephen's opposing roles as friend and father. Virginia herself was directly affected by this duality. In her obituary notice of him in *The Times* she pays tribute to his vigour of mind, his honesty, and endearing eccentricities. But her fictional portrait of him depicts a man essentially unimaginative, joyless, tyrannical. However she might respect his various gifts and achievements objectively, she still felt in an organic sense that his dominating presence had squeezed the very life-blood from her veins. Somehow he had taken away from her the ability to nourish her ravenous appetite for life. As she helped to nurse him through his long, last appalling illness she must already have known that her hopes of liberation of spiritual release, centred upon his death. The consciousness of this had filled her with a dreadful sense of guilt, and in May 1904, not long after her father's death, she suffered a mental breakdown. Both of them could no longer continue that half-life in such close proximity. He died and she recovered. From him she had inherited a strong egoism together with a neurotic and demanding conscience; from her mother, a fine, artistic delicacy and sensitivity. These diverse elements were not to be resolved, but waged within her a tangled and exhausting conflict. Her increasing obsession with death indicated a growing awareness that a part of her father still lived on in her. While she breathed, his alien spirit continued to enshroud her. She could not wash it off. So death became for her the ultimate release, the resurrection through patricide by *felo de se.*

Though she had been well cared for as a child, the comfort of her early years had been punctuated by a series of traumatic shocks – madness, senility and death itself. Before she was ten years old, her first cousin, the handsome and talented J. K. Stephen, had begun to show alarming symptoms of a worsening mental instability. His eccentricities were so unpredictable and extreme that he was soon expelled from his club, and later, after making violent advances to Virginia's half-sister, Stella Duckworth, he was committed to an asylum where in 1892 he died. His father – Virginia's uncle Fitzjames – was inconsolable. He retired; his health rapidly deteriorated; he became within a few short months an old man, and died not long afterwards. The following year had brought the greatest disaster of all, when Julia Stephen, Virginia's mother, died. The shock of this had led to a complete breakdown, and she tried to commit suicide by throwing herself out of a window. It was from this time, too, that her father's health had steadily worsened, and when in 1898, within a year of her marriage, Stella Duckworth died, the old man came to rely entirely on his two daughters. Although Virginia's life was never inactive, the environment at Hyde Park Gate, especially when her brothers were away at school or university, had grown overcast. She longed for the sunlit holidays by the sea;

and the sea became for her a symbol of freedom. Her poetic genius needed stimulus from the outside world, yet she felt an even stronger need for protection against the ruthless, unheeding cruelty of which the world was so full. Her wraith-like spirit seemed never completely drawn into her body, never entirely possessed by it. In consequence, the probing, innocent curiosity she felt about all human activity, though often passionate, remained peculiarly bloodless and trivial. In place of direct personal involvement, she continued with unanswerable childlike persistence to pose strings of improbable questions. What must it feel like to be a king? A newly-married bride? A bus conductor? Craving to be set free from her egomania by something or someone stronger and altogether dissimilar to herself, she speculated endlessly upon the unknown: and for her the unknown was frequently the commonplace. Thoby might have rescued her, but he too had died. And there was no one else.

What temporary respite from introspection she did find, came not through the composition of her books – as was the case with Strachey – which were merely intricately charted extensions of this process of self-examination, but in appraising a sequence of vicarious sensations, and in screwing her concentration round upon diverse happenings which, by their very lack of all personal connection, seemed to diminish the status of the individual and his subjective agonies. In such piecemeal fashion did she hope to reconcile her yearning for poetic experience without personal immolation. Like a bat, relying on sound waves alone to tell it the geography of its surroundings, she put together a vision of the world full of wisps and fragments – a shadow, a silhouette, a twig in the wind, the mark on a wall. If Strachey was like some theatrical director and producer rolled into one, passionately excited not only by the professional décor and costume, but also by the positioning of the *dramatis personae* upon the stage and the synchronization of their rehearsed speeches, Virginia was the special freelance correspondent who, unconcerned by the event-plot, lies concealed in the dark recesses behind the stage and spies on the actors as they retouch or take off their make-up between the acts. Her novels, which involved much anguished self-observation, are delvings into the sick, neurasthenic depths of her nature, which, like that of Coleridge, was subterranean. As an ordinary, open-air land-animal she was inexplicable. 'Virginia is I believe a more simple character than appears on the surface,' Strachey wrote many years later to Ralph Partridge (1 September 1920). 'Her cleverness is so great that one doesn't at first see a kind of ingenuousness of feeling underneath.' He saw her, and rightly, as some deep sea-creature, whose habits and moods could not be properly understood on the hard matter-of-fact surface of things. There are many exquisite vignettes scattered through her work that convey her unique sensibility with a lyrical, muted radiance, which seems to tremble from the refracted rays of a sunlight playing far below the green waves to the soundless bed of the ocean. She breathed in the oxygen of life and gave out in her novels only carbon dioxide. Her view of the universe was somnambulistic; she felt remote from waking reality, and indulged in few of the ordinary adult appetites, eating only a bare minimum and shying hysterically away from sexual intercourse. Though she saw humanity through a glass lucidly, she seemed paralysed from translating her interests into active participations, so that she remained a connoisseur of feeling rather than a lover of life. Her observation of human relationships is always subtle and accurate, but sometimes comes little nearer to the wonder of real love than, as William Gerhardie has said, a medical analysis of the menstrual cycle.

Although she resented his superior education, mistrusted his cynical tendency to gossip, and later, for a time, rather envied his meteoric rise to fame, Virginia always felt a peculiarly warm affection for the sickly, hypochondriac Strachey. She was often at her most enchanting, most self-forgetful, with those who were ill. Invalids, with their impaired vitality and excessive self-preoccupation, she welcomed as fellow creatures in her dimly-lit underworld. In company with Thoby's other Cambridge friends, several of whom had found asylum in Bloomsbury, she was as relaxed, as whimsically amusing as her difficult temperament permitted. But her moods were unpredictable, and behind her brilliance there was always some hint of stress. These moods were dependent not on people but on her writing. Proof correcting was especially perilous. Yet despite the terrible risks involved, she continued to work all her life with the greatest courage. She had really no alternative. Writing *was* her life. Deep beneath her sensitive geniality were sown the seeds of suspicion and envy. In self-protection she assumed an air of wariness, treating everyone as a potential rival. Touchy and mistrustful, she held herself for the most part in check. But when someone happened casually to mention that Vanessa must find it very tiring to stand long hours at her easel, she was at once outraged, and promptly stalked off to buy herself a tall desk at which, for the rest of her life, she made a point of standing while writing her novels. It was characteristic of her deep-seated neurosis that she should read into some harmless remark a non-existent slight, and then set about punishing herself because of it.

Her nervous sensibility could be easily inflamed into a burning sense of persecution. If one congratulated her on looking well she interpreted one's remark as meaning she appeared red and coarse. Should one praise her latest novel, she might read into it a dislike of her last but one. When the Germans bombed London, she calculated the serious damage in terms of decreased book-sales. Tense and shy in company, she could turn bitter and malicious behind her friends' backs in order to repay imaginary aspersions and grievances. She was jealous, too, of their achievements, at one time expressing a wish that Duncan Grant had followed his father into the army, and at another announcing that Strachey should have been an Anglo-Indian Civil Servant. T. S. Eliot also, she once observed, had he stayed in banking, might well have ended up as a branch manager! She can be, and has been, put down as a textbook example of a leptosome whose neurosis was schizophrenic though, most probably, her condition was that of a manic depressive. Yet (curiously, since Leonard Woolf was an early enthusiast of Freud's) she was never psychoanalysed, merely treated by doctors, as each medical crisis arose.

The atmosphere within the two Bloomsbury salons at Vanessa's and Virginia's houses was in several respects quite different, and reflected to some degree their differing personalities. The Bells 'are a wild sprightly couple', Strachey wrote to Duncan Grant soon after they had married and set up house together (2 June 1907). 'The drawing-room has no carpet or wall-paper, curtains some blue and some white, a Louis XV bed (in which they lie side by side), two basket chairs, a pianola, and an Early Victorian mahogany table!' Number 46 was a spacious house set in the centre of the east side of Gordon Square. Clive Bell's hospitality was warm and jovial, reminding his guests of the hunting and shooting milieu in which he had been brought up, and contrasting oddly with the pictures of Picasso and Vlaminck which hung on the walls. His exuberance, which overlaid a morbid fear of illness and pain, lent muscle to the bleak and fastidious gatherings of his intellectual companions, and went some way to prevent the Bloomsbury Group from turning into another Clapham Sect. 'When the door was opened,' wrote David Garnett, who was to join this circle of friends at the beginning of the war, 'a warm stream of Clive's hospitality and love of the good things of life poured out, as ravishing as the smell of roasting coffee on a cold morning.'

Some affinities there still were, however, with the Claphamites. Bloomsbury, like Clapham, was a coterie, Noël Annan points out in his *Leslie Stephen*.

It was exclusive and clannish. It regarded outsiders as unconverted and was contemptuous of good form opinions. Remarks which did not show that grace had descended upon the utterer were met with killing silence. Like the Claphamites they criticized each other unsparingly but with affection. Like Clapham, Bloomsbury had discovered a new creed: the same exhilaration filled the air, the same conviction that a new truth had been disclosed, a new Kingdom conquered . . .

. . . the fourth generation of the Clapham Sect naturally repudiated the moral code of their forefathers. The doctrine of original sin was replaced by the eighteenth-century belief in man's fundamental reasonableness, sanity and decency. They violently rejected Evangelical notions of sex, tossed overboard any form of supernatural belief as so much hocus-pocus, and set their sails in the purer breezes of neo-Platonic contemplation. And yet one can still see the old Evangelical ferment at work, a strong suspicion of the worldly-wise, an unalterable emphasis on personal salvation and a penchant for meditation and communion among intimate friends.

For Strachey, at least, the Bloomsbury atmosphere represented primarily an invitation to congenial friendship. Though he found sympathetic companions hard to come by, he was never an outcast in Bloomsbury. For there the tables were turned, and it was the ordinary proletariat, the 'unconverted', who found themselves out of place, who were encouraged to feel ill-at-ease and rather inadequate. Outsiders were apt to be particularly disconcerted at Virginia and Adrian's house in the south-west corner of Fitzroy Square. The large drawing-room on the ground floor was decorated in a quite different style from the interior of Gordon Square. There were no cubist paintings, only a Dutch portrait of a lady and Watts's portrait of Sir Leslie Stephen. Soon after the two of them had settled down there, Lady Strachey came to have tea with Virginia and look over the house where Lytton was to spend so much of his time. During the early part of the meal Hans, the Stephens' dog, made a large, conspicuous mess on the carpet directly between the two women; but such was the impeccable self-control laid upon them by the pressure of late-Victorian etiquette that the ceremony of afternoon tea proceeded on its unhurried way without either of them alluding to the disaster.

Guests would encounter a more dismaying welcome here than at Clive Bell's home. Virginia, especially, reacted with the *gaucherie* of an awkward child; but it was a *gaucherie* tempered into what was later to be recognized as the perfect Bloomsbury manner. None of them, for instance, would smile as they shook hands, a habit which proved extremely effective in unsettling strangers. Adrian, then studying Law, was moreover a confirmed and celebrated practical joker. Led on by his accomplice Horace de Vere Cole, a kindly but clownish retainer to Augustus John, he helped to perpetrate a number of daring, widely publicized hoaxes – digging up Piccadilly as a navvy, and at another time arranging a party for all the citizens of Birmingham whose names – beginning with 'Row', 'Ram', 'Side', Higgin' or 'Winter' – ended with 'bottom', and who, finding their unknown host had failed to arrive, were obliged to introduce themselves to one another. Probably the most notorious of all these practical jokes took place on board H.M.S. *Dreadnought*, one of whose officers was persuaded that the Emperor of Abyssinia together with his retinue desired to be officially shown round the ship. Cunningly disguised with thick make-up and extravagant theatrical costumes, and countering all questions with the same mumbled phrase, 'Bonga-Bonga', Duncan Grant, Virginia and Adrian Stephen, Horace Cole and two friends were welcomed aboard the Admiral's flagship with magnificent pomp and formality. There, despite a number of narrow escapes, the masquerade was brought off with the dexterity and finesse of a professional ballet performance: the band struck up with the anthem of Zanzibar, the mariners were paraded and inspected, innumerable salutes were exchanged, several decorations proffered. Only later, to the great scandal of the press and embarrassment of the authorities, was the true identity of the visitors revealed. Questions were asked in Parliament: the joke was complete.

Besides the live-wire hoaxes of Adrian and Horace Cole, who was at any moment apt to put salt in the cocoa or to spit in the whisky, an unwary guest might also have to contend with the inner ferocity of Virginia's character, concealed under a delusive, diffident manner, at once subversive and inexorable. 'Upon an unforeseen introduction, for instance,' wrote Duncan Grant, 'there was an expression of blazing defiance, a few carefully chosen banalities and a feeling of awkwardness.' Those whose wish to proceed further had not been successfully quenched by this welcome would then be shown into Adrian's or Virginia's study. Adrian's was on the ground floor, well ordered, neat and handsomely lined with books. Virginia's workroom was directly above, untidy, books littered all over the floor and furniture, her tall desk –

at which she stood writing for two hours each day – positioned near the window.

It was in Adrian's ground-floor study that their friends assembled on Thursday evenings – 'a continuation', Duncan Grant explains[7], 'of those evenings which began in Gordon Square before Thoby died and Vanessa married. It was there that what has been called "Bloomsbury" for good or ill came into being.

'About ten o'clock in the evening people used to appear and continue to come at intervals till twelve o'clock at night, and it was seldom that the last guest left before two or three in the morning. Whisky, buns and cocoa were the diet, and people talked to each other. If someone had lit a pipe he would sometimes hold out the lighted match to Hans the dog, who would snap at it and put it out. Conversation; that was all. Yet many people made a habit of coming, and few who did so will forget those evenings.

'Among those who consistently came in early days were Charles Sanger, Theodore Llewelyn Davies, Desmond MacCarthy, Charles Tennyson, Hilton Young (later Lord Kennet), Lytton Strachey.'

The mood and atmosphere of these Thursday-night congregations were an extension to those of the Cambridge Conversazione Society[8], and Strachey soon found in Fitzroy Square a tolerable substitute for the delights of Trinity and King's. This was better than he had expected. Less than four years ago he had crept away from the divine amenities of Cambridge into 'the limbo of unintimacy', prepared for a silent and wretched exile. But Bloomsbury had taken him in, soothed and warmed him a little. There was a strong affinity between the scheme of things in Gordon and Fitzroy Squares, and the courts of Trinity and King's. The rooms were different, but the same tobacco-smoke stole up the windows against the night sky, the same talk of Greeks and Romans – mostly Greeks – sped on around him. 'Talking, talking, talking', sighed Virginia Woolf in recollection of those days, ' – as

7. *Horizon*, June 1941, vol III, no. 18.
8. The Cambridge Conversazione Society, sometimes called 'the

if everything could be talked – the soul itself slipped through the lips in thin silver discs which dissolve in young men's minds like silver, like moonlight. Oh, far away they'd remember it, and deep in dullness gaze back on it, and come to refresh themselves again.'

Though the routine of his life, divided between his family and friends, Hampstead and Bloomsbury, was less well arranged than before, though perhaps he was less contented inwardly than as an undergraduate, Strachey did not appear to languish in greater despair. No longer, surrounded by kindred spirits, did his emaciated form crouch in odd and angular shapes on sofas, tables, basket-chairs, wrapped for hours in deep imponderable silence. For now that he and his friends were less absurdly young, their methods of communal conviviality, if still idiosyncratic, had grown more relaxed and mature. The infiltration of feminine society into the circle also did something to lighten the intensity of austere scholasticism that had typified their Cambridge dialectics. The Cambridge garrison of Bloomsbury, a civilized fortress, as they saw themselves, isolated amid the hostile, native population of London, was inevitably less immune than the university itself from the vulgar assaults of ignorant masses. Life was necessarily composed of less subdued and even tones, less prim and exclusive conduct, less absolute free thinking, less rigid informality, now that they were no longer sequestered from everyday human activity in the dingy, antiquarian charm of a few literary backwaters. 'In exchange for the peace of Cambridge,' J. K. Johnstone acutely comments, 'the traffic of London clattered by on the pavements just outside. The world was closer, and there was certain to be a new awareness of it.'

What passing references there are in Strachey's essays to the boom and bombast of twentieth-century living show his deeply ingrained dislike and even horror of it. 'He was quite definitely,' wrote Max Beerbohm in his Rede Lecture, 'and quite impenitently, what in current jargon is called an escap-

---

Apostles' or simply 'the Society' was a secret fraternity to which Strachey had been elected early in 1902. See *Lytton Strachey: A Biography*, pp. 179–91.

ist.' Bloomsbury society was for him a quiet oasis in this desert of loud loneliness. Yet he was always conscious of those vast, unplanned areas of city life which began only a few steps away and sprawled in all directions for so many hideous miles. He dreamed of an ordered, reasonable, unrespectable, tidy, refreshingly simple world, where happiness, beauty and companionship were not stigmatized as immoral – the very antithesis of sophisticated London. The seven consecutive years he spent there after coming down from Trinity served to widen that fissure in his nature which he was later to dramatize so successfully.

This peculiar dualism was at the same time echoed in his strange, carefully modulated speech. He used two strikingly different types of voice. One, high-pitched and tinny, was employed deliberately to deflate pomposity; to express astonished disagreement with some opinion (when it was often accompanied by a raising of the eyebrow); to introduce either an element of clowning or baiting into the conversation; or to tease someone he liked. 'Sometimes in this mood,' recalled E. B. C. Lucas,[9] 'his splendid, architectural nose would appear larger than usual, presumably owing to an angle of the head. The high voice, then, was an affectation. Lytton would not have denied this. The comment on a friend's narrative: "*Too* ghastly, my dear" was an affectation so transparent that it constituted a sort of musical phrasing, part of a style. Like all "Bloomsberries", he disliked pretension and silliness – the former much more than the latter, which after all could be a trait in youth, and so, forgivable; and in order to show up pretension, he would assume the high voice and the high brows, and so prick the bubble.' Occasionally, to parody or ridicule some attitude, he would chant whole sentences in a feeble, monotonous falsetto. At other times – in moments of intimacy or when reading out loud – he would employ a rather deep, bass voice, which with a strange inversion of

9. E. B. C. Jones, the novelist, the first wife of F. L. Lucas of King's College, Cambridge. Known to her friends as 'Topsy', she had a rather arch way of referring to herself, in a deep voice, as 'Monkey' – 'Monkey doesn't read Shakespeare', etc. Living in Cambridge, she exerted a considerable influence on some of the most gifted undergraduates there.

stress might all at once rise to a reedy crescendo in emphatic termination of his sentence. As shown by his letters, he was much affected by the weather, and in rain and cold was apt to fall silent for long stretches. He did not often laugh. But an expression which was not exactly a smile would slip over his face, his eyes gleaming and fixed on whoever was speaking, and the mental climate grew warm and sunny. His two celebrated voices were, then, not entirely natural, but a contrived over-emphasis of a natural idiosyncrasy. In 1909, this dual voice was still something of a novelty, adopted to help establish for himself the *persona* which he wished others to accept and remember. But later in his life these voices, together with other distinctive appendages to his new Bloomsbury image – the beetroot-brown beard, the attenuated fingers, and a variety of runcible hats and cloaks – worked themselves into the recognized fabric of his highly stylized personality. They were no longer put on, but came as it were spontaneously to him, just as lines do to a good actor. In the opinion of Ralph Partridge, who knew Strachey only during the last twelve years of his life, 'these two voices of his were not an affectation but a natural gamut of expression – and the top notes were an echo of Voltaire's "high cackle" from the eighteenth century'.

In spite of his involuntary contact with a wider, more cosmopolitan world than Cambridge, Strachey's demeanour could still be as rigidly uncompromising as ever. When Clive Bell invited some French friends of his to Gordon Square, the francophil Lytton, resenting the intrusion of strangers, and uncomprehending foreigners at that, stubbornly pretended to be incapable of understanding a word of the French language, and retreated into one of his grim spells of non-communication. Like Virginia Stephen he tended to distrust people whom he did not know well, and was supremely anxious not to fail in any attempt to impress them. But then again, if they were not handsome, or quick-witted, what, in any case, could possibly be the point in impressing them? They hardly existed. All the same he detested obscurity, and dreamt of being welcomed on his own terms by a society that he scorned. This feeling was shared by several of his friends, and it was on a superfine mixture of arrogance and diffidence, of ambitious talent and crippling shyness, that the Bloomsbury Group was largely founded. Such were some of its biographical and psychological origins; the various and conflicting myths which were erected round the group during later years were vaguer and vaster. But since the sociological and literary legends of Bloomsbury have gained a wide acceptance despite only random approximation to the truth, they can no longer be set aside simply, but call for some rather more detailed re-examination.

2

HOME THOUGHTS ON HUMAN GROUPS

About 1910 or 1911, Molly MacCarthy, the wife of Desmond MacCarthy, in the course of a letter to Frank Swinnerton, described the Stephen family and their associates as 'Bloomsberries'. The word caught on, and it was not long before Arnold Bennett and other writers outside this tiny oligarchy were referring to Virginia Woolf, as she had then become, as 'the Queen of Bloomsbury'. The phrase, used mostly in a derogatory sense, was intended to convey a meaning similar to 'highbrow', the leader of a semi-precious, brittle form of mock-Hellenic culture, encased in a Gallic frame. But, as Vanessa Bell pointed out in a paper entitled 'Old Bloomsbury', the original circle, which had started to meet in 1904 and broke up at the beginning of the war, had really ceased to exist several years before the term became fashionable, and other people inherited its name and reputation.[10]

10. Vanessa Bell lists the original members of Bloomsbury as herself, her sister Virginia, Thoby and Adrian Stephen, Clive Bell and Leonard Woolf, Maynard Keynes, Duncan Grant and Roger Fry, Desmond and Molly MacCarthy, Lytton, Oliver, Marjorie and James Strachey, Saxon Sydney-Turner, Harry Norton, E. M. Forster and Gerald Shove. In the opinion of Leonard Woolf, Bloomsbury 'came into existence in the three years 1912 to 1914', after he himself had returned from Ceylon. Thoby, therefore, who died in 1906, was not, in his version, a member. There were, he states, thirteen of them in all. He excludes from the above roll-call Gerald Shove, Harry Norton and Lytton's brothers and sister. Of the ten men in this group, MacCarthy, Lytton, Saxon Sydney-Turner, Forster,

In the years that followed, two divergent fables of Bloomsbury arose and were given wide controversial publicity. Though opposite in many respects, both fostered one common and fundamental fallacy – that the Bloomsbury Group was a strategically planned and predetermined literary movement, starting in about 1905 and continuing on with various alterations in membership and in emphasis of sacred doctrine until the early 1930s. In much authoritative French, German and Russian criticism of early twentieth-century literature in England, the Bloomsbury myths were, and still are, strongest, perhaps because the individuals involved are less well known. Yet even in England numerous essays and theses have been produced which imply or state categorically that the work of Clive and Vanessa Bell, David Garnett, Duncan Grant, Maynard Keynes, Leonard and Virginia Woolf, E. M. Forster, Lytton Strachey and several others, shares an identical system of aesthetics, the same philosophy and values, all of which stem from *Principia Ethica* and that unsuspecting innocent, G. E. Moore.

Despite their superficial contradictions, the twin concepts of Bloomsbury were closely related to each other, and seem to have taken root from a variety of human motives. Those contemporary writers who were not admitted to the select band thought they saw in it a dangerous organic unity which it did not really possess. Others disliked these eminent late-Victorians for their socially secure antecedents and inherited financial independence. And for still others again, Bloomsbury represented a new exclusive movement, an avant-garde fashion of superior, voluntary ostracism from life – 'life' so often meaning a mixture of politics and cricket. At the same time, the more obscure rank and file on the fringe of the set lent currency to this damaging mystique so as to attract unto themselves a reflected glory from the luminaries of W.C.1.

Keynes and himself had been 'permanently inoculated with Moore and Moorism'. The basis of this assembly, however, was simply friendship. James Strachey, who denied belonging to Bloomsbury, also disagreed with Leonard Woolf, believing that the group came into existence precisely during his absence in Ceylon, that is in about 1907.

Then more recently, studious literary critics, who appear to comprehend next to nothing of the isolated way in which a work of art is evolved, have prolonged the legend to a point where it threatens to become established tradition. With the result that now, what had initially been useful as a quick, rough-and-ready term of classification to the journalist, has been built up into a very real obstacle in the labours of the literary historian and biographer.

The two imaginary Bloomsburies are in amusing disaccord. For many years the Press notices which this largely fictitious coterie drew were unfavourable. An over-serious, self-important Bohemia, Bloomsbury was said to be composed of highly pretentious, ill-mannered dilettanti, who derived a masochistic excitement from casting themselves in the role of super-sensitive martyrs to the coarse insensitivity of the barbarian world of twentieth-century London. Arrogant, squeamish pedagogues, their desire to take in people whom they affected to consider their antipodean inferiors in every way belied their assumption of conceit. It was all a sham. Their pseudo-Greek culture, their overriding contempt for the less well educated, at whose head they placed D. H. Lawrence, their insularity and the uncertain grimaces, mock-frivolity and infantile practical hanky-panky which passed among them for humour, were in fact outlets of a rigid and reactionary class system such as, perhaps, only England could boast of. Under their wincing, spinsterish mannerisms these world-shunners were immensely, ruthlessly ambitious. They possessed, however, little potent imagination and to attain their aims they formulated a set of restricting artistic rules which had the effect of substituting phoney aestheticism for genuine creative talent. Exclusive not by virtue of any extraordinary ability, but mainly through a supercilious, studiously cultivated priggism, they were too clever by half to perform ordinary services on behalf of the community, yet too 'arty' and unreliable to find places in the universities where they might otherwise have been usefully employed.

Strange rites, sinister rituals and unmentionable initiation ceremonies were soon attributed to those who tended the dark flower of Bloomsbury. Beside this exotic growth, the green carnation was a very pallid cosmetic. According to the pugilistic poet Roy Campbell, the Bloomsbury equivalent to shaking hands was a pinch on the bottom accompanied by a mouse-like squeak – a salutation that does not appear to have varied with the sexes. Yet in spite of many such emphatically sub-normal and heterologous characteristics, no one seemed able to agree as to who precisely made up this queer tribal faction. Everyone, of course, knew the chieftains – Lytton Strachey, Virginia Woolf, Clive Bell and so on – but after them, as Osbert Sitwell put it, there 'followed a sub-rout of high-mathematicians and low-psychologists, a tangle of lesser painters and writers'. Taking a census of these lesser breeds was no easy matter since, as another wit explained, 'all the couples were triangles and lived in squares'. Free speech, of course, abounded. They held forth in the mixed company of their late-night cocoa parties with the greatest freedom about sexual generalities, but, in the words of E. M. Forster, 'would have shrunk from the empirical freedom which results from a little beer'. According to Frank Swinnerton, Strachey's level of free speech was somewhat in advance of that of the others, and he dangled before them 'the charms of lasciviousness, the filth of Petronius, the romance of the Arabian Nights'. Love, too, so the rumour went, was uninhibitedly free; and yet there seemed little enough ebullience:

> 'Here verse and thought and love are free;
> Great God! Give me captivity.'

despairingly cried E. W. Fordham in the *New Statesman*. Second to no one in the violence of his hostility towards Bloomsbury was Percy Wyndham Lewis, who depicted it as a select and snobbish club comprising a disarray of catty, envious and shabby potentates, collectively bent upon getting the better of himself. Making a cultural stronghold of the Victorian hinterland where they resided, these freakish monsters of his imagination had managed to set up a *societification* of art, substituting money for talent as the qualification for membership. Private means, he explained, was the almost invariable rule. 'In their discouragement of too much unconservative originality they are very strong. The tone of "society" (of a spurious donnish social elegance) prevails among them. ... All are "geniuses" before whose creations the other members of the Club, in an invariable ritual, must swoon with appreciation.' There was another rather curious way in which they differed – namely in their dress. 'For whereas the new Bohemian is generally as "mondain" and smart, if a little fantastic, as he or she can be, this little phalanstery of *apes of god* went the length of actually dressing the part of the penniless "genius".' They presented, Lewis affirmed, a curious spectacle of a group of financially secure men and women, 'drifting and moping about in the untidiest fashion'.

And then, of course, there was the Bloomsbury voice, an appendage of the Strachey clan – 'bringing to one's mind', Wyndham Lewis commented, 'the sounds associated with spasms of a rough Channel passage' – which further cut off this abominable company of citizen-intellectuals from the commonplaces of burgess life. Modelled on the infectious Strachey falsetto – in whom it was doubtless the result of some unfortunate malformation – this rare dialect was taken up and soon spread from Cambridge to Bloomsbury and thence to the outlying regions of Firle and Garsington. 'The tones would convey with supreme efficiency the requisite degree of paradoxical interest, surprise, incredulity', observed Osbert Sitwell; 'in actual sound, analysed, they were unemphatic, save when emphasis was not to be expected; then there would be a sudden sticky stress, high where you would have presumed low, and the whole spoken sentence would run, as it were, at different speeds and on different gears, and contain a deal of expert but apparently meaningless syncopation.' By this manner of communication, Osbert Sitwell continues, were the true adherents to the cult of Bloomsbury to be recognized. 'The adoption by an individual of the correct tones was equivalent, I apprehend, to an outward sign of conversion, a public declaration of faith, like giving the Hitler salute or wearing a green turban.'

The great exemplars of Bloomsbury remained for a long

time unrecognized by the general public, who are always indifferent to such cliques and juntas unless they are represented as having other than artistic significance. But in the First World War, the Bloomsbury Group was advertised as a left-wing pressure organization which aimed at taking over the Labour Party and establishing an intellectual dictatorship that had little or nothing in common with the ordinary working man. It was hinted darkly that they had built up a sinister hold over the Press, though no one, it seems, thought of asking why, with such a powerful underground network of public relations, they were not depicted by journalists in a rather more attractive light. In the latter part of the war, when most of Bloomsbury came out as agricultural pacifists and rustic conscientious objectors, hostility towards them greatly intensified, and ardent-eyed patriots, who had hitherto dismissed the group as a bunch of harmless prigs, now pointed with alarm to the explosive danger, in the very centre of London, of an obviously militant pro-German force. During the twenties, this hysterical enmity abated: some critics, feeling themselves prematurely outdated, still poured out derision, but many more expressed admiration qualified only by envy. *Queen Victoria*, for example, was greeted with almost universal approbation, and from America Hugh Walpole reported that Lytton Strachey was worshipped, 'the God of the moment everywhere'.[11]

Probably the chief cause for aversion still felt by some outsiders was the overblown approbation which members of the élite exchanged among themselves in books, and reviews — the most notorious example being Clive Bell's *Te Deum* sung in joint praise of Duncan Grant and Vanessa Bell, which was especially interesting in the light of these artists' very close relationship. But for the most part this reciprocal, closed-shop admiration was greatly exaggerated by outsiders. For in England, where the creative artist is regarded as an anti-social delinquent, writers and painters inevitably turn to one another for the warmth and reassurance with which to lighten their unenviable task, and dispel the cold climate of alien

11. *Figures in the Foreground* by Frank Swinnerton, p. 106.

indifference that envelops them. This sympathy – often rather
hypocritical and amply compensated for by the adverse
criticism expressed to third parties – which members of
Bloomsbury extended to one another was interpreted by the
less favoured as a peculiarly unhealthy, almost incestuous
outbreak of mutual patronage and self-admiration – a view
which was neatly summed up in Roy Campbell's narcissistic
epigram, 'Home Thoughts on Bloomsbury':

> Of all the clever people round me here
> I most delight in me –
> Mine is the only voice I hear,
> And mine the only face I see.

The other popular and complementary version of Bloomsbury may be briefly defined as a counter-interpretation of the
same abstract assumptions. The group is said to have comprised an alert and original band of men and women whose
splendidly unfashionable and undemocratic enlightenment
proved too strong for our universities and too idiosyncratic
for our uncultured society. The much derided Bloomsbury
voice, believed to symbolize in some mysterious way all that
the movement stood for, came naturally to Lytton Strachey
in whom it was so delightful that it charmed everyone and
soon spread equally naturally to his friends. Occasionally it
might be put on a little to tease – for there was perpetual
gaiety in Bloomsbury – and sometimes, by the sly cadence of a
single word – *Really?*' or 'Extra*ordi*nary!' – an outsider's
truism was horribly crushed – for Bloomsbury could never
gladly suffer fools. But there was more to it than this. By
certain bold inflections of emphasis, they could induce rather
conventional people, who would have resented direct opposition, to question and revalue their long-cherished principles.

During the war, the Bloomsberries were said to have
displayed marked moral courage by resisting the attractions
of armed combat, and by persisting in their rational aversion
to senseless avoidable slaughter. In a time of crass barbarism
they alone retained their sanity. When an angry old pullover-
knitting lady asked an elegant young man-about-Blooms-
bury whether he wasn't ashamed to be seen out of uniform

while other young men were fighting for civilization, the reply was confident and characteristic: 'Madam, *I* am the civilization they are fighting for.' That their united pacifism was practical and common-sense, not cowardly, was proved in the Second World War − a very different affair involving different points of Moorish ethics − when many of them came out as staunch and active patriots. In the opinion of many, including Roy Harrod and Rosamond Lehmann, Strachey also might have come out strongly in favour of war in 1939 had he been alive. David Garnett is more assured and surprising in his suppositions. 'Lytton was maturing and developing', he wrote. 'The rise of Hitler, the abominations carried out in Germany before the war and in almost all countries of Europe and Asia during it, the legacy of evil that the Germans have left behind them in France, would have been to him what the Calas affair was to Voltaire.

'Lytton, if he had lived, would have spoken for mankind on Auschwitz, Hiroshima, the nuclear bomb and torture in France with a clarity and force with which the political leaders of the world would have had to reckon. He could not have been neglected as Russell and Forster are.'[12]

In between these wars we are to picture Strachey and other brave Bloomsbury spirits with their copies of *Principia Ethica* debating how best to translate its message into the various realms of art, economics, literature (subdivided into fiction and non-fiction), painting and politics. All members chose or were allocated particular fields in which to work, and spent the remainder of their careers running this specialized school for higher philosophical propaganda.

Such, in essence, is the view of Bloomsbury projected recently, in particular by J. K. Johnstone in his closely reasoned study, *The Bloomsbury Group* (1954).[13] Treating the individual

12. *The Familiar Faces*, p. 130.
13. *The Bloomsbury Group*, written as a thesis at the University of Leeds by J. K. Johnstone, was undertaken at the suggestion of Professor Bonamy Dobrée, and read in typescript by Noël Annan. It was published in 1954 by Secker and Warburg, under the supervision of one of the firm's directors, Roger Senhouse, himself on the fringe of Bloomsbury during the 1920s and 1930s.

differences between the novels of Virginia Woolf and E. M. Forster, the biographies and essays of Lytton Strachey, and the aesthetic criticism of Roger Fry as being merely superficial variations on a generic pattern, he set out to discover some basic agreement between their work and the ethical pronouncements of G. E. Moore. And in the Conclusion at the end of his book, the author recapitulates his findings.

There is [he declares] a common respect for things of the spirit; a belief that the inner life of the soul is much more important than the outer life of action or the outer world of material things; an admiration for the individual and for the virtues of courage, tolerance and honesty; a desire that man shall be whole and express himself emotionally as well as intellectually; a love of truth and of beauty. And the integrity and careful composition of their books demonstrate a profound respect for art, and a conviction that form is as important to a work of art as content; that, indeed, the two are inseparable since the artist cannot express emotions and ideas adequately except in significant form.

But are these really the qualities by which we recognize the characteristic output of Bloomsbury? Surely in so far as they apply to each and every member of the group they may be said to apply equally to nearly *all* artists – a fact which perhaps explains why so many dissimilar writers working in the first part of the twentieth century, and ranging haphazardly at one time or another from William Gerhardie to F. R. Leavis (who hold nothing in common except their complete independence from the clan) have quite erroneously been classified in print by various ill-informed critics as 'typical Bloomsbury'. Besides which, not all Bloomsbury did hold these values. A number of them, being devout atheists, cherished little respect for the inner, immortal life of the soul.[14] And if this inner life was counted so very much more import-

14. I have presumed from the wording that he employs that J. K. Johnstone used the word 'soul' as meaning the immaterial part of man 'regarded', in the words of the *Oxford Dictionary*, 'as immortal or as subject to salvation and damnation or as animating the body or as existing independently of it or as the true self . . .' It is possible, however, that he used it simply in its subsidiary meaning as the organ of emotion, thought and will.

ant than the life of action, why was it that Strachey chose two queens, a general and a dynamic woman of action as subjects for his biographies? The all-embracing importance which he himself certainly attached to significant form was by no means shared by all the others – Desmond MacCarthy, for example, whom Johnstone mentions as another member of the sect.

Some attempt to interweave these two fables of Bloomsbury into a convincing, comprehensive pattern has been made by the poet Stephen Spender. In setting about this he has been obliged to treat as indivisible 'Old Bloomsbury' and the new-look Bloomsbury of the 1920s. The plausibility of his version springs from the literary skill with which it is presented and from his wisdom in not regarding Bloomsbury as a proselytizing body, but simply as a tendency. To qualify for membership, Spender explains, one had to be agnostic, responsive to French impressionist and post-impressionist painting, and in politics a liberal with slight leanings towards socialism. The group represented 'the last kick of an enlightened aristocratic tradition'. Setting their standard at five hundred pounds a year and a room of one's own (in Virginia Woolf's words), they sought to entrench themselves within an impenetrable, class-conscious ring against the social revolution advancing on all sides. Their tolerant, scrupulous, cerebral flirtation with left-wing politics was an indication of the guilt which they felt at their own inborn and untouchable snobbery. In short, Stephen Spender's Bloomsbury is chiefly sociological – the symbol of a cultured, intelligent, politically naïve era, as seen by a representative of the 1930s – a less aesthetic but more serious and politically responsible decade.

In the sinking of unique differences beneath a general classification, critics have incorrectly assumed that, in matters of taste and judgement, the writers and artists whose names are linked with Bloomsbury were in accord with one another, and that they presented to the world a united if not easily definable front. The danger of seeking common trends within any set of people is that one is obliged to misrepresent, now slightly, now more drastically, the actual individual truth in order to preserve an even façade. In the case of Bloomsbury this has been particularly noticeable, for often the opinions and inclinations of its members were very far from being uniform. Leonard Woolf was always passionately interested in politics; Strachey, though he inclined to become more leftish under his brother James's persuasion during the war, was largely indifferent to political questions of the hour. Clive Bell enthused over the most abstract art; Roger Fry held aloof;[15] while Strachey himself was even more conservative and dismissed Clive Bell's *Art,* in a letter to James Strachey, as 'utter balls' (22 February 1914). Though he had learnt at Cambridge to enjoy a literary appreciation of the visual arts, Strachey considered that both Clive Bell and Roger Fry were downright silly in their highflown admiration of Matisse and the early Picasso, and he made some attempt through Vanessa Bell to discourage Duncan Grant from the post-impressionist and cubist influences under which he was falling. As for Maynard Keynes, Strachey maintained that he possessed no aesthetic sense whatever; and Clive Bell held a similar opinion of Harry Norton. Despite his tenuous friendship with E. M. Forster, who was certainly no atheist or even agnostic, Strachey found his novels quite unreadable – a view similar to that which Virginia Woolf affected to hold of his own biographies – while his aesthetic differences with Roger Fry,[16] who injected a mood of earnest Quakerism into the group, effectively stifling the movement towards sybaritic pleasure, were, according to

15. Clive Bell has generally been put down as a popularizer of Roger Fry's aesthetic theories; and while there is much truth in this, it is not wholly true. After the failure of the Omega Workshops in 1919, Fry grew much less concerned with contemporary art. He had, in any case, from the first felt doubts about Clive Bell's theory of 'significant form', and wondered whether 'it might be possible', Professor Quentin Bell writes, 'that some paintings were "operatic" in the sense of being a perfect fusion of two different kinds of art. It was towards a solution of this nature that he was looking in his last years.' When, in 1925, I. A. Richards published his *Principles of Literary Criticism,* a work which strongly attacked Fry's standpoint, Strachey welcomed this new attitude.

16. Of another of the Bloomsbury literary critics, Fry seems to have held a distinctly mediocre opinion. 'I don't mind a weather-cock,' he once remarked of him, 'but a weather-cock that crows is too much.'

Gerald Brenan, enlivened by personal antipathy. Nor had Strachey much in common with Arthur Waley whose scholarship he respected – though it does not seem to have inspired him as did the work of the non-Bloomsbury Professor Giles – but whose unremitting shyness exasperated him. Several of the so-called group he hardly knew at all! Sir Charles Tennyson, whom Duncan Grant names as one of the original intimate circle which met at Fitzroy Square, wrote to the present author: 'I was fairly often in the same room with him [Strachey], but never really knew him. He was a good many years younger than me and in a more highbrow set, so that I really have nothing beyond a quite superficial and useless impression.' Another critical mistake has been to assume that all Bloomsbury was nourished on Moore's ethics. The two Stephen sisters seldom if ever discussed questions of academic moral philosophy, while some later recruits to the group, Raymond Mortimer, Ralph Partridge and Roger Senhouse who were all at Oxford, and Gerald Brenan, who did not go to Cambridge, never burnt the midnight oil over the complicated pages of *Principia Ethica*. Roger Fry, whose aesthetic principles J. K. Johnstone claims were closely integrated with Moore's work, and in a sense completed it, actually dismissed *Principia Ethica* as 'sheer nonsense'.

According to the Freudian definition, 'two or more people constitute a psychological group if they have set up the same model-object (leader) or ideals in their super-ego, or both, and consequently have identified with each other'.[17] If one accepts this conception, then clearly Bloomsbury was not strictly a group at all. But it did comprise something – an atmosphere, a mood, a culture which today can be detected in those who have inherited its tradition, Noël Annan, Quentin Bell, Kenneth Clark, Cyril Connolly and others. Although it accepted part of the Apostolic severity – a then idiosyncratic belief in good moral values, true personal relationships, free and more or less reasonable thinking and speech – it was permeated with other qualities that made it very unlike the

17. This definition is given by S. Scheidlinger in *Group Dynamics* (1954), p. 56, edited by D. Cartwright and A. Zander.

original Cambridge Conversazione Society. Maynard Keynes and Harry Norton, two Apostles of the highest-grade intellect who belonged to Bloomsbury, were rather despised by most of the others. For Bloomsbury was deficient in purely intellectual interests, being strongly dominated by the visual arts and literature. Science was unheard of, and even music was almost absent.

Fry's influence on the whole climate of English painting was unrivalled. Many of his theories, as Kenneth Clark has written, were 'assimilated by those who had never read a word of his writings . . . in so far as taste can be changed by one man, Fry changed it'. Ironically, this change in taste may have been more beneficial to painters with whom he was not closely associated than to the 'Bloomsbury Court Painters', Vanessa Bell and Duncan Grant. The work of Ben Nicholson, for example, approached theoretically far closer to the Bloomsbury ideal of the significant relationships of line and colour divested of all reference to life and its emotions, than that, say, of Vanessa Bell who, while proclaiming that Fry did not go far enough in his denunciation of representational art, drew inspiration for her best work from the emotional content of the places and people she knew most intimately.

Latterly neither Fry nor Clive Bell much liked the purely abstract art to which their theories so logically led. Fry was seldom interested in people, or the relation of theories to people. He relied for personal insight on the opinions of the three women he loved – Vanessa Bell, Virginia Woolf and Helen Anrep. His influence on the work of Duncan Grant may well have been particularly inappropriate. Grant was a lyrical painter in the English tradition of Constable, a natural impressionist in his handling of paint, and a born decorator with a flair for inventive designs, for rich and original colour harmonies. His participation in the Omega Workshops gave much scope to these gifts, though the Bloomsbury insistence on amateurishness led to an almost deliberate use of nondurable materials, so that few of his delightful Omega products now survive. But in the 1920s he became a victim to 'significant form', following Fry's vehement commitment to the more austere traditions of Cézanne and away from the decorative surface of Matisse and Gauguin from whom he had most to gain. Already by 1923, Fry seems to have appreciated that Formalist principles were not conducive to bringing out the best in Grant's work. With his usual honesty, he confessed to a fear that Grant's preoccupation with solid form and the third dimension was harming the expression of his rhythmic sense and exquisite taste in colour and decoration, all of which were geared most successfully to the flat surface.

Today the name of Bloomsbury is respectable – perhaps too respectable – while at the same time remaining unfashionable. Its collective reputation had declined with that of Strachey's individual status, for its present comparatively low quotation is felt by many to be due to its characteristic Stracheyesque shortcomings – in particular a fondness for exaggeration leading to distortion of truth and a fake aestheticism which was already beginning to bring the author of *Elizabeth and Essex* into some disfavour by 1930 and which has helped to prolong the usual widespread denigration after death – a recognition, David Garnett believes, of the influence he would have exerted had he lived. Of his two Cambridge idols, Lowes Dickinson had devoted his life to the task of interpreting, for the benefit of his compatriots, Plato and the Greek ideals of civilization; while G. E. Moore, in the words of Maynard Keynes, was even 'better than Plato'. The Apostles who immediately succeeded Moore, and who were led by Keynes and Strachey, modified these ideals, which were later transferred to Bloomsbury, making them more worldly and sophisticated. There these ideals were translated into a neo-Greek cult of friendship, donnish rather than Hellenic. In his book *Civilization: An Essay*, Clive Bell echoed a recurrent theme of Bloomsbury writers: that to be completely civilized a human being must be liberated from material cares and vexations. Indisputably the best example of such a scheme in practice was given by Plato. The Greeks, he pointed out, because they had slaves who freed the citizens from everyday chores so that they might concentrate on worthier affairs, had attained a standard of civilization that came nearer the heart's desire than was conceived possible by any other people in history. And so it should be with Bloomsbury, which took its inspiration from the Greek example. Virginia Woolf's celebrated 'five hundred a year each of us and rooms of our own' is anticipated by Strachey in a letter to Duncan Grant (23 August 1909): 'Good God! to have a room of one's own with a real fire and books and tea and company, and no dinner-bells and distractions, and a little time for doing something! – It's a wonderful vision, and surely worth some risks!'

Independence founded on the Hellenic model – that was what so many of them aspired to. Strachey had no very scholarly knowledge of the Greek language, but he saw in the élite at Cambridge the centre of a new and expanding civilization, sweetened by the free, venturesome flavour of ancient Greece and the sentiment of Athens. Having shed the dry Victorian ectoderm, the world seemed solid and fruitful, and he and his friends felt convinced that fresh progress would now start up, and that they would contribute something of value to this advancement. It was this undefined, hopeful, reforming spirit of 'neo-Platonism' which spread from Trinity and King's to the literary salons of London that later became recognized as the distinctive religion of Bloomsbury. 'A strange thing – when you come to think of it – this love of Greek,' Virginia Woolf reflected in her novel, *Jacob's Room*, 'flourishing in such obscurity, distorted, discouraged, yet leaping out, all of a sudden, especially on leaving crowded rooms, or after a surfeit of print, or when the moon floats among the waves of the hills, or in hollow, sallow, fruitless London days, like a specific; a clean blade; always a miracle.'

The inevitable reaction to this 'civilization' came, ironically, from Cambridge itself, starting with I. A. Richards, whose *Principles of Literary Criticism* (1925) aimed at exploding the aesthetic approach to literature, and declared the concepts of 'beauty' and 'pure aesthetic value' to be myths. From then on literary criticism was to be led by precept rather than example, and under the new dictatorial authority, impressionistic writing lost favour. The disciples of this new 'scientific' criticism were irritated by the extreme aestheticism of Bloomsbury, which, they proclaimed, accentuated strangeness and fascination at the expense of heart and conscience, and which had tended to evolve a flippant society where, to use the words of Lord David Cecil, 'it is more important to be clever than good, and more important to be beautiful than to be either!'

This new wave of criticism subsequently gained in strength and reached its full impetus under the redoubtable leadership of Dr F. R. Leavis, whose dislike of Strachey – the Mephistopheles of the Bloomsbury World – rested on his antipathy to what he saw as an immature valuation of life masquerading under an air of detached irony, a ruthless sacrifice of truth for literary purpose, and a puny, irresponsible assertion of personal prejudice over serious sociological scrutiny. That divine confluence of Cambridge amenities, hymned by E. M. Forster in his Life of Goldsworthy Lowes Dickinson, was denounced by Leavis as: 'Articulateness and unreality cultivated together; callowness disguised from itself in articulateness; conceit casing itself safely in a confirmed sense of sophistication; the uncertainty as to whether it is serious or not taking itself for ironic poise; who has not at some time observed the process?'

The narrowly blinkered Leavis could observe little else. His assumption that good ends could not conflict clothed him in a strait-jacket which prevented him from reaching much that was valuable in literature. To him the charmed circle of Bloomsbury and Strachey's lucid interval of prestige, both of which dominated temporarily the metropolitan centres of taste and fashion, were an unforgivable departure from the great tradition of powerful representative Cambridge men of their time – Sidgwick and Leslie Stephen, Maitland and Dr Leavis. 'Can we', he asked with rather Stracheyesque rhetoric, 'imagine Sidgwick or Leslie Stephen or Maitland being influenced by, or interested in the equivalent of Lytton Strachey?' Can we imagine Dr Leavis being so interested? And this same derisory question is, by implication, repeated again and again and again throughout his writings. For as the conviction of personal persecution thickened round his critical faculties and choked his turgid prose style, so he laid greater and greater emphasis on the inessential trappings of literature, its civic importance and tutorial status.

Despite this low grading from Downing College, many of the King's and Trinity members of Bloomsbury were undoubtedly perfect representatives of the Cambridge culture of their generation. They were passionately attached to the beauty and emotional flavour of the place, and in London looked for what most resembled it. If the Bloomsbury Group has to be treated as a homogeneous entity, then it can in no manner be dissociated from Cambridge, and all Cambridge stood for. The best features in their environment of privileged culture – the play of mind with mind on literary and other topics, and a sane and humane morality – Strachey with his sensitive intelligence and irregular deviations was well qualified to absorb and enjoy. Nor was Bloomsbury the wholly desiccated intellectual unit it is so often depicted as being, but was bound together by intense and enduring personal relationships, which for all their complexity were managed in a very civilized way. For a number of years, however, after going down from Cambridge – years of self-discontent and aimlessness – Strachey also exemplified the limitations of the over-cultivated. By a perversion of language, good taste came to mean not the taste of persons with healthy appetites, but of persons with weak digestions. The collective literary voice – described by F. L. Lucas in a letter to Irma Rantavaara as 'shepherd's piping in Arcadia' – is distinctive in its thinness and its clarity. Moreover, the superhuman detachment and remoteness on which they sometimes prided themselves did sever them from the deeper sources which stem out of a raw and vulnerable contact with reality. Romantic academics and quietists, deeply allergic to the humdrum, many of them were, to use the words of E. M. Forster, full of the wine of life without having tasted the cup – the teacup – of experience.

The myths which have billowed up round the name of Bloomsbury are like voluminous clouds arising from a small central flame. For although these friends who met on Thursday evenings before the war shared no fixed and common values germinating from an original gospel, they may be said to have been permeated with similar intuitions. The keystone to these intuitions was a desire for partial independence from the parochial and pretentious fog of Victorianism. They were alike in their determined opposition to the religious and moral standards of Victorian orthodoxy; and in their work they represented more truly than anything else the culmination and ultimate refinement of the aesthetic movement. Essentially they were reformers rather than revolutionaries. Virginia Woolf's concept of a proper financial and domestic standard, no less than Strachey's Preface to *Eminent Victorians*, was a declaration of this spirit of partial independence, a wish to cut herself off from the immediate past by escaping from the family sitting-room to another, unopened wing of the same house – not to a new house or town or country.

And if they looked back to the example of ancient Greece, in the modern world they turned their eyes towards the Continent. Under the delusion that things were ordered differently in France, they made an attempt to establish on French lines a society fit for the discerning minority. 'A time had come', wrote Virginia Woolf in her biography of Roger Fry, 'when a real society was possible. It was to be a society of people of moderate means, a society based on the old Cambridge ideal of truth and free speaking, but alive, as Cambridge had never been, to the importance of the arts. It was possible in France; why not in England? No art could flourish without such a background. The young English artist tended to become illiterate, narrow-minded and self-centred with disastrous effects upon his work, failing any society where, among the amenities of civilization, ideas were discussed in common and he was accepted as an equal.'

But Bloomsbury did not transform the naturally isolated and painful process of artistic creation. Once 'Old Bloomsbury' had lost its bloom and become moribund, the new Bloomsbury Group flowered into a gayer, more pleasure-loving and fashionable clique, tripping in quicker, high-stepping time to the light fantastic twenties. But, like all rather self-conscious 'modern' movements, this phase was destined, as surely as the coming of death itself, to dwindle and wither into an extinct relic in the history of artistic taste. For all their elegant and ingenious tinkerings, most of the Bloomsbury writers and artists were unable finally to sever the umbilical cord joining them to the inherited traditions of the past. Theirs was a tenuous transitory mood, largely barren and inbred, a suspension bridge that now forms our authentic link back to the solid cultural traditions of the nineteenth century. They modified, romanticized, avoided those traditions with varying degrees of success. But rather than being the real founders of a new and originally conceived civilization as Virginia Woolf supposed, they were, in the words of Roger Fry himself, 'the last of the Victorians'.

TWO

Independent and Spectatorial Essays

'I shouldn't mind being a journalist if it really paid; but does it? I'd rather be a cabin boy on a sailing ship, whether it paid or no. Romance is the only thing worth living and dying for. . . . Romance! What visions, what excitements, what smells! Our poor imaginations are tired out with the construction of worlds so different from our own, we are exhausted, we give up, we take to journalism, we are contented, we are rich, we exist no more.' *Lytton Strachey to John Sheppard* (11 October 1903)

'It's a pity that writing should be nearly always such an intolerable process.' *Lytton Strachey to B. W. Swithinbank* (13 August 1908)

'I suppose I shall worry through somehow – but how I loathe writing for money and against time!' *Lytton Strachey to David Garnett* (23 August 1915)

1

BALLADS AND COUNTERBLASTS

STRACHEY's knowledge of literature had already expanded enormously while he was at Cambridge. He read widely and was continuously writing poems, epigrams, essays. The strange dichotomy of his character found an interesting parallel in the contrast that soon developed between his susceptibilities as a reader and his performance as a writer. 'My ideal in writing is the non-flamboyant – unless one's Sir Thomas Browne,' he wrote to his sister Dorothy (1905), 'but I'm annoyed to find that every time I write I become more flamboyant than before. It's so difficult to be amusing unless one does plunge into metaphors, "paradoxes", "brilliant epigrams", etc., etc., etc. – unless one's Swift.'

For Strachey, Swift was always one of the absolute masters

of English prose. Sober, unemphatic and simple, 'the only ornament in his writing', he later wrote[1], 'is the rhythm, so that, compared to the decorative and imaginative prose of such a writer as Sir Thomas Browne, it resembles the naked body of an athlete beside some Prince in gorgeous raiment'. On the whole he preferred the stark vigour of nudity to the splendour of glowing colour and elaborate form. The classical authors were his natural favourites. Yet his persistent dread of boring others, and of being bored himself, drew him some way towards the more facile entertainment of romantic literature. In his response both to the classical and romantic, the same wish to minimize or embellish the disorder of real life is clearly present. He loved the Elizabethans for their verbal felicity and dazzling variations upon formal, as opposed to subjective, sentiments. Sir Thomas Browne, with his flaring opulence which overlaid the strange mystic murmurs of his spirit, was at this time his best-loved seventeenth-century prose writer; while the eighteenth century with its infinite delicacies and refinements of social intercourse, seldom disturbingly profound, unruffled as yet by the invention of a communal conscience, fascinated him more completely than any other single epoch. Among Victorian men of letters, Swinburne was undoubtedly now his choice, preaching a paganism less offensively muscular than Meredith, less despairing than Edward FitzGerald, but at the same time more excitingly romantic and alive than Walter Pater. On those early Sunday mornings as the Midnight Society at Trinity was breaking up and its members wandering back to their rooms, the cloisters of Nevile's Court would re-echo to the wild, masochistic rhapsodies, the inspired efflorescence which Swinburne had poured out to those erotic phantoms, his imaginary mistresses.

On a different level was Strachey's youthful interest in Donne and Henry James. In neither did there exist this highly coloured romanticism, sensuous appeal or vivid, visual imagery; but instead an intricate stylistic technique that absorbed his intellect. The mental processes of Donne were erected

1. 'Jonathan Swift', *Spectator*, 102 (27 February 1909), 341–2. Collected in *Spectatorial Essays*, 141–6.

over and above the emotional content of his poetry, and so far from clarifying the poet's inner feelings, tended to abandon them altogether in a cerebral labyrinth. For Donne, like Strachey, had been at odds with his age and sought in these metaphysical acrobatics some relief from the oppression of his emotional self-interest. The attraction of Henry James was of a similar nature. 'I have been reading Henry James in large quantities', he notified his mother (2 May 1901). Just as, when a child, he had lost himself in the disentangling of complicated puzzles, so now he quickly became fascinated in pursuing James's eternally qualified meditations.[2] In June 1901 he composed a long and amusing parody of James's style entitled 'The Fruit of the Tree'. Taken as a whole, the danger of such a parody is that it reflects only too faithfully the fearful tedium of the prose which it attempts to caricature. Something of its quality however may be seen in an extract taken from the preamble:

'For you who understand there can (with one exception) be nothing in what follows there ought not to be. My story, if I have one (and in that very speculation there seems to be so much of it), must, after all, be clarity itself to those from whom it is written, who are so exactly not those who would hesitate or boggle at a meaning. It's as right as anything – to you; for the one exception to its rightness, which may be, precisely, my way of telling it, I must make, in advance, both an apology and an explanation. If I could leave on you just the impression it left on me, oh! I should be thoroughly contented. It was deep; deeper, you know, a good deal than I was, or even am; so that, in the end, I found and perhaps still find

2. Throughout his life, Strachey persisted in admiring, and in being puzzled by his admiration for, Henry James. On 28 May 1920, for example, he wrote to Middleton Murry: 'What's puzzling is that, quite apart from art, one does somehow feel, in spite of everything, that there was something distinguished about him [Henry James] – something big; but one doesn't see what. On the artistic side, one of the strangest things, I think, is that re-writing of his early novels in his later style. What *did* he mean by it? In one of the letters he positively says that he's not making any substantial changes – merely writing every other sentence over again! Is it possible that he supposed that substance and style were separable? It's very odd indeed.'

myself swimming upon an ocean whose profundity it is altogether impossible to gauge. What he found – or whether he found anything at all – are questions which, though they add immensely to the complication – might perhaps eventually lead to a solution of the whole thing. At any rate it is certain that whatever interest my story has centres round just two persons, two characters, two phases. Its fascination is that it holds a perpetual antithesis between two such wonderful contraries. That one of them was he and one of them was I is really the least that can be said; there was (and I want to show it you) such a great deal more underneath. If I succeed you may have a glimpse of a conflict; the powers of good and the powers of evil you may see ranged as in *Paradise Lost* upon the one hand and the other: if I show you that I shall be happy; what I shall never show you, and what, even more, I shall never show myself, is, in the clashing of opposites, exactly which was which.'

Through a rigid application of such abstract literary devices, Henry James was able to transform normal people into extraordinarily involved psychological specimens, in which inanimate condition they might be examined with the mind alone. His characters were no longer living men and women, but cold entities, without the terror of flesh and blood. In reading his novels Strachey entered a world of emasculated beings incapable, unlike those around him, of causing real pain. What he gained, both from the recondite abstractions of Donne and the plots and subterfuges of Henry James, from the prolonged formalities of the Elizabethans and the involved mannerisms of the nineteenth century, was always a diminution of his own internal apprehensions and sense of conflict. Like crossword puzzles, like the higher ethical dilemmas of G. E. Moore, such literature was removed alike from the humdrum and the vulgar, and posed an absorbing complex of abstract equations. To some extent literature was, and remained for him, a window closed tight against the racket, the noisome fumes and pandemonium of rushing and shuddering which, as he could clearly see from his snug retreat, filled the outside thoroughfare from end to end in one loud, excruciating traffic-stream. But though literature was to act partially as a refuge from, rather than a revelation of, reality, his sharp eye for salient facts and his needle of delicate feline malice, which are freely displayed in his most characteristic writing, were to pierce the soft cushioning of literary conventions and bring the reader momentary peeping glimpses of actuality and pathos. He was a born artist, but one who sometimes played for safety and directed his gifts to the professional task of becoming a perfect craftsman. Sometimes the mere hack-work of verbal carpentry, however accomplished, loses its power to hold him, and he produces a tiny gem of creative sculpture. But the revolt is followed, as it were, by a recoil of fear; and like a diver who has sunk too far into the gloomy depths of the ocean, he returns quickly and with palpitating heart to the smooth bright surface of things.

Another writer of whom Strachey became very fond at Cambridge was Pope, whose appeal was more directly personal. As a result of his pronounced bodily infirmities, Pope had nursed throughout his life a hypersensitivity most often reserved for himself and his own misfortunes. Though also extremely sensitive, Strachey, especially in his later years, was of a rather more kindly disposition than Pope, whose feelings, he once commented, 'were far more easily roused into expression by dislike than by affection'[3]. Because Strachey was particularly appreciative of Pope's similar vein of feminine delicacy and wit, and responded to his painting of the more subtle undercoats of fervent emotion, he seems at this time to have over-rated the quality of Pope's more obscure poems, so many of which show off malicious triviality that can hold no great interest for today's reader. But there was a special lesson to be learnt from the proper study of this miserable little man who as potentate of letters, overcame his physical disadvantages to such a degree that even the most eminent members of the cultured classes came to live in fear of him.

Strachey's own wit, like that of many celebrated humorists, had been cultivated in private as a defence against anticipated hostility in public. While at Cambridge he sharpened up his

3. 'English Letter Writers', *Literary Essays*, p. 245.

style by formulating nearly a hundred aphorisms. 'I occupy myself by writing Réflexions in the manner of the French', he wrote to Leonard Woolf in July 1903. 'It is a very pleasant summer amusement, I find, and you shall see the result. The advantage is that one need never think about one subject for more than 5 minutes at a time, and one need never give one's reasons.' Many of these aphorisms point to Strachey's obsessive preoccupation – most fully exhibited in his letters – with the genital and excremental functions of the human body. Perhaps the best are concerned with the problems of literary style and contemporary manners. Others are avowals of his paganistic objections to Christianity. Among the least successful are those which assume a cynical mood of worldliness. A number of examples, taken from his notebooks, will convey the variety and quality of these 'Réflexions'.

'It is as impossible to talk of a lady as if she were a man as to talk of her as if she were a prostitute.'

'It is always easier for a lady to fall in love with her footman if she is deaf.'

'A woman sometimes gives her love to her husband only when she has nothing else left to give him.'

'Our vanity is sometimes hurt even more by the admiration of those we disdain than by the disdain of those we admire.'

'It is easier to believe in reason than to be reasonable.'

'The excitement in conversation which is given by champagne is present of its own accord in the most exciting conversations.'

'It is possible to have good manners and to be vulgar; and it is possible to be refined and to have no manners at all.'

'We find it easier to reflect on the actions we have performed than to act on the reflections we have made.'

'We are never given time to think of the great things we have done by the little things we are doing.'

'It is a point of difference between prose and poetry that prose demands perfection of form and poetry can do without it.'

'There are a few common words – *rose, moon, star, love* – which are so beautiful both in themselves and in what they express that their presence insensibly heightens a bad piece of writing, but makes a good one more difficult to compose.'

'Civilization loves the truth and Barbarism tells it.'

'Some people are as much ashamed of their God as of their genitals, and blush when you mention either.'

'When a Christian is dying it is not the fear of Hell that disturbs him, but the fear of Death.'

Strachey also gave epigrammatic expression to that inverted Wordsworthian feeling of self-obliteration which, in all his passions, brought with it such a sense of unburdening relief: 'We are so unimportant that whether we think we are or not hardly matters.' Many of his aphorisms are elaborately unspontaneous, concocted in the form of parables too long and commonplace to quote, and carrying with them the faint, musty aroma of Oscar Wilde's more affected fairy tales. Others are shorter and more trite. To become fully aware of the flatness of the worst of these one has only to contrast the urgent cry for companionship uttered in his Liverpool diary[4] with a corresponding Cambridge aphorism: 'Our best and most beautiful pleasure is love.' In general, these maxims consist of rather self-conscious experiments in style which convey much of the waxed inefficacy that he himself found so deathly in Walter Pater. Some, however, are acute and one or two aptly sum up the whole business of writing epigrams:

'A witty thing is sometimes said by accident, but never a stupid one.'

'The maxims we write in our youth we correct in our maturity, and burn in our old age.'

'There are few things more difficult to write than a good aphorism; and one of them is to write a true one.'

In contrast to the artificial refinement of many of these aphorisms, Strachey was fond of expressing a degree of grossness in his verses which, like the indecencies of Swift, had its origin in the disgust felt by a confined, frustrated spirit at the dual nature of man. 'The best and worst parts of us are the secrets we never reveal' runs one of his aphorisms. On the whole, these love poems reveal the worst part of Strachey. There is little pathos in them, little tenderness and almost no

4. 'The truth is I want *companionship*.' See *Lytton Strachey: A Biography*, pp. 116-17.

humour.[5] The ones which he himself prized most highly make up a sonnet sequence and were probably addressed to (Sir John) Sheppard. Written at a time when the Oscar Wilde scandal was still very much present in many people's minds, they are experimental in stated emotion rather than in any literary form, and their interest is mainly psycho-sociological. Strachey's compulsive preoccupation with the male reproductory and excretory organs was the outcome of and reaction to an age of excessive prejudice against sex – and in particular homosexuality – and while ostensibly these poems look forward to an epoch unfettered by puritanism, they convey above all else the intense morbidity of Strachey's mind during these years. Nevertheless, he remained convinced that his – as opposed, say, to R. C. Trevelyan's – was the only method of writing real poetry; that is, without an immediate eye to publication. It was, he felt, the only way of telling the whole truth; yet in moments of depression he was forced to concede that his poems were too wordy, too unintellectual.

What Professor Charles Sanders, with romantic sang-froid, has described as 'the abandonment and ribaldry of a young satyr', consists of little more than various frequently reiterated expressions of hopeful, melancholy lust (more often than not depressingly rhymed with 'dust'), of vain invocations to 'Cruel Fate', and elegiac descriptions of 'laughing limbs', 'purple locks', 'cold lips', etc., and a truly phenomenal amount of copulation. What strikes one about these poems is the incongruity between their highly respectable form, and their obsession with sex, which Strachey refers to again and again as if in the mere repetitious penning of those unspoken words which describe the ordinary biological activities of mankind he was automatically thrown into some ravishing intoxication. 'But it's the extraordinary question of the naked body which really fascinates and absorbs', he explained to Leonard Woolf. 'Heavens! it's mysterious and splendid! Terrible, melancholy and divine – those strange, inevitable, silent operations of nature! The lust and the strength of youth! Death!' Such moments of ecstatic delirium were usually followed by a

5. For one that does contain some humour, see Appendix.

sickening return to inescapable common sense, when he seems to have comprehended in full the discrepancy which lay between the happiness he really sought and the dead quality of his versifying.

> My love is larger than the universe
> Yet lies for ever coffined in my verse
> As in a pompous ineffectual hearse.[6]

Among the published verses belonging to this period, one of the earliest, completed on 24 October 1899, was entitled 'I like the maiden of the Farm', and comprises a more or less formal rendering of the self-contempt which so often overwhelmed him:

> She cannot hear me when I speak
> She thinks that I'm absurdly weak;
> She thinks that I'm a dreadful fright
> On all occasions – and she's right.

Others of his poems, a number of which appeared in the *Cambridge Review* and elsewhere, show that he was already most proficient at imitating the metaphysical school of poets, as well as Pope, Dryden, Swinburne and Tennyson – 'a concoction of pretty verses', as he subsequently described the more sentimental compositions of the latter, 'flavoured to the taste of atrophied females'. Because his verse is so derivative, one of his most successful achievements was in direct parody. 'After Herrick', which came out in the *Cambridge*

6. With the author's treatment of Lytton's Cambridge poems in the above two paragraphs, James Strachey was in vigorous disagreement. 'I have been positively staggered by some of your ethical judgements on the subject of sex and religion,' he wrote. 'Your remarks about Lytton's poems astound me. I can quite understand your saying that they're very poor poems and also that you can't quote them. But the impression you give of holding up your hands in shocked horror at their fearful obscenity makes me wonder whether you've ever come across a young human being. ... When I read these passages I wonder why on earth you ever set out to write this book – and I feel inclined to want the whole thing thrown out of the window. The whole of Lytton's life was entirely directed to stopping critical attitudes of the sort that you seem to be expressing ... in order to account for Lytton's quite ordinary youthful excesses, you have to cook up over and over again your stale Adlerian explanation. Things are really more complicated than that ...'

Review on 12 June 1902, has a neatness and simple control of metre that his more ambitious pieces often lack:

> Wheneas I walk abroad by Night
> And Heavens-ward cast up my sight,
> The Luminaries of the Skies
> Make me think on Julia's Eyes.
>
> But when I take my walks by Day
> In flower-deckt field or garden gay,
> I see the flaming of the rose,
> And straightway think of Julia's Nose.

A number of his compositions are cast in song or ballad form, with a repeated chorus at the end of each stanza. Others are more terse and epigrammatic, and lead on to a contrived twist held back to the last line to give point to the whole piece. The following two examples illustrate well his degree of proficiency in this field. The first is dated January 1900; the second, undated and without name, was probably written in 1903.

By the Pool

> Love, your body's very white,
> May I touch it with my finger?
> (See, the day sinks into night)
> Softly, softly shall we linger
> By the pool we love so well.
> Mirabel, oh Mirabel,
> Let me touch you with my finger.
>
> Love, your mouth is very red,
> May I pluck it like a cherry?
> (See, the day is nearly dead)
> Who would be or sad or merry
> By the pool we love so well?
> Mirabel, oh Mirabel,
> Let me pluck you like a cherry!
>
> Love, your eyes are very blue
> May I gaze on them forever?
> (Bid the day a last adieu)
> No rough hand us twain can sever

> By the pool we love so well,
> Mirabel, oh Mirabel
> Let me gaze on you forever.
>
> Nature in jewels is so rich
> She fills with diamonds every ditch,
> Bright pearls o'er all her flowers she flings,
> Gives the small beetle emerald wings,
> With amber drops she decks the trees,
> Adorns with sapphire the broad seas,
> And so, complete in every part,
> She fashioned out of jade your heart.

In his last two years at Cambridge, Strachey began to write book reviews, contributing half a dozen to the *Spectator* and rather fewer to the newly formed *Independent Review*. He also composed for various occasions a number of interesting essays – the literary form which above all others suited his peculiar talent. One of the earliest of these pieces, about thirteen thousand words in length, was 'Warren Hastings', a subject which attracted him by virtue of his family's association with India, and their traditional defence of Clive's and Hastings's colonial administration. He completed this essay on 26 September 1901, and submitted it for a Trinity award, the Greaves Prize. Despite the enthusiasm of Stanley Leathes, who thought it the best composition of its kind that he had ever seen, it did not win the award. There were, it would appear, several valid reasons for this failure. Though it is undoubtedly a knowledgeable and thorough piece of work, as an essay it is disappointing. The rather concentrated historical commentary – full of dates and information concerning the size of armies – which forms the backbone of the paper does not fit in with the romantic biographical portraiture and interpretation which is arbitrarily grafted on to it. As so often when he set out to conform wholeheartedly to the familiar traditions of the Stracheys, there was something forced about his performance. In his anxiety to vindicate Hastings, he bombarded his enemies with a surfeit of abuse, inflating the principal figures to the outsize proportions of Hollywood villains. For all his rhetoric and indignation they remain celluloid concoctions, beings without real substance.

The blackest of these knaves, and Hastings's evil genius, we are told, was Philip Francis, who 'could boast of a great reserve of malignity, of meanness, and of unscrupulous ambition. His personal enmities were distinguished by a ferocious and relentless cruelty, and his public opponents usually became his private foes. He was as crafty as he was false, as arrogant as he was selfish. In his private life he gambled and drank and seduced his neighbour's wife.'

In short he was thoroughly *bad*.

Like Iago, Francis, as depicted by Strachey, is little more than a puppet, whose dramatic function is to force the unqualified idealist, the tolerant and enlightened hero – in this case Hastings himself – to see his conduct from the opposite standpoint, which explains every action in terms of self-interest. In this he is aided by a band of ignorant political enthusiasts among whom 'the figure of Burke is a supreme one, towering in all its superb error, in all its deluded grandeur, far above the stage sentimentality of Sheridan or the forced-up furies of Fox'.

But it is in its direct interpretation of Hastings as the best-abused personage in the whole course of history that the weakness of this total vindication becomes obvious. He will hear no word of censure against his hero, a man of fine deeds rather than empty words, of practice rather than quibbling theories, who brings out in him his own most romantic and unreasonable literary vein. Hastings was one of the gods, an ideal figure set in the same imperishable mould as the magnificent Thoby Stephen. The concluding paragraph of 'Warren Hastings' brings unblushingly into the open that all-consuming admiration which flared up within Strachey, like a schoolboy's infatuation, at the spectacle of this deathless, immaculate being:

'The final word on Hastings must perhaps be that he was a superman. What weaknesses, besides the physical, he had in common with the mass of mankind, it is difficult to see. His very passions took the form of devotion to the public weal; he never descended to a fault or even to a foible; he was perfection as a statesman, a husband, a friend; he soared.'

Most of the essays which Strachey wrote at Trinity were composed for the Sunday Essay Society which met every week in the rooms of Professor Bevan. The most notorious of the papers he read out to this Society was entitled 'The Ethics of the Gospels'[7] (February 1905), an attack on Christianity which delighted some and outraged others, and which in later years he was sometimes prevailed upon to deliver again. It is a painstaking and well-finished piece of work, but its tone of detached clinical inquiry is very obviously sham – a stylistic device employed so as to exaggerate the devastating effect of the paper. Its main aim purports to be an impartial consideration of the value of Christ's teaching, chiefly through a detailed examination of His commandments. By means of a rigidly austere, literal interpretation of meaning, and by ingeniously setting scripture against scripture, he leads his audience logically and infallibly on, deeper and deeper into a bewildering tangle of obscurities and confusions from which it can only reasonably conclude that Christ, as represented in the Bible, put forward 'no statement of the principles upon which feelings and actions ought to be guided'.

Another, earlier disquisition, entitled 'The Colloquies of Senrab', was on approximately the same theme, and also created something of a sensation. 'Senrab' was the backward spelling of Barnes, a brother of the future bishop of Birmingham, who had previously delivered a paper on 'Intellectual Snobs', directed against Strachey and the other members of the Midnight Society[8]. Written as a parody of the stereotyped sermon, Strachey's scathing rejoinder was regarded by many – including

7. In a letter to G. E. Moore (21 February 1905), Lytton wrote: 'I read a paper at the Sunday Essay last Sunday on the Ethics of the Gospels. It was considered unfair – a mass of quibbles, etc. [D. H.] MacGregor was heard to say something at lunch next day about the difference between Philosophy and Casuistry. [F. E.] Bray and A. C. Turner maintained a strict silence after the paper was read, until [Erasmus] Darwin begged some Christian to give his point of view. Bray's was that Harnack did not come to the same conclusion as the writer of the paper, also that the love of beauty was not good. A. C. Turner embarked on an enormous sentence, which no one ever heard the end of.'

8. The Midnight Society, founded at Trinity College, Cambridge, dur-

Maynard Keynes, a member of the audience, at that time personally unknown to Strachey – as 'a most brilliant satire on Christianity'. Strachey himself grew a little apprehensive at the rumpus to which it gave rise. 'I read yesterday (to the Sunday Essay Society) a scurrilous paper on the subject of Christianity', he wrote to his mother (10 November 1902). 'I hope I shall not be sent down like Shelley in consequence. But the world has changed – and even Shelley was not at Cambridge.'

Some of these early lucubrations anticipate, in argument, the artistic theories which he was later to put into practice in his own books. In 'Art and Indecency' he makes a witty and impassioned plea – reminiscent once again of Oscar Wilde[9] – for the divorce of ethics from aesthetics: 'It would be absurd to praise a locomotive for its virtue, or to condemn a soup as immoral; and it seems no less absurd to discuss the ethics of a symphony. Conversely, it is ridiculous to introduce aesthetic considerations into moral questions; the Kaiser's delinquencies have really nothing to do with his moustaches; and, while it is probable that some at any rate of the 11,000 virgins of Cologne were not good-looking, their holiness remains unimpeachable.'

Another paper, 'The Historian of the Future', may be regarded as a forerunner to the celebrated Preface Strachey wrote many years later to *Eminent Victorians*. But what is perhaps most noticeable about all these pieces is their distinctive style, which speaks eloquently of the great personal influence exerted over him at Cambridge by the philosopher, G. E. Moore. A single quotation taken from the last-mentioned essay will show readers of the *Principia Ethica* that Strachey's manner of argument reads in places like an unintentional parody of Moore's minutely detailed question-and-answer method of breaking down statements into their component parts in order to discover what they *really* meant and what

---

ing Strachey's second term there, consisted of (besides Strachey himself) Clive Bell, A. J. Robertson, Saxon Sydney-Turner and Leonard Woolf. In the opinion of Clive Bell, who was never elected to the Apostles, the Midnight Society was a precursor of the Bloomsbury Group.

9. See the Preface to *The Picture of Dorian Gray*.

evidence existed to support their meaning: 'The theory I want at present to discuss is, briefly, the theory that History is a science. What that phrase precisely means is certainly doubt-ful, and it is just this very doubt which makes me particularly inclined to discuss it. What do we mean by History? What do we mean by science? What, if you like, do we mean by "is"? These are all interesting questions, and questions which, con-sidering their importance in any discussion of this sort, are singularly rarely asked, and even more rarely answered. Never-theless it seems to me that to answer them is in reality a quite simple matter, and that having once accomplished this the true answer to the more complex question "Is History a Science?" will follow naturally and of its own accord.'

By far the best of Strachey's Cambridge essays are ap-preciations of English literature. From these, two stand out as supreme. 'Shakespeare's Final Period', originally delivered to the Sunday Essay Society on 24 November 1903, and pub-lished the following August in the *Independent Review*[10], was written as a counterblast to the theory, made fashionable by several respected critics of the day, that Shakespeare's last years – during which he wrote *Cymbeline*, *The Tempest* and *The Winter's Tale* – were passed in a saint-like state of tran-quillity, ultimately benign and docile, and infused with a joyous spirit of universal forgiveness bordering on the senile. By the ample use of quotations which display a coarseness and brutality of language totally incongruous with the cosily idealistic fancies of Professor Dowden, Sir Israel Gollancz and a number of other noted Shakespearian commentators, Stra-chey demonstrated convincingly that there was little real evi-dence to sustain so improbably academic an interpretation. These critics, he pointed out, had naïvely relied on the happy endings to Shakespeare's last plays, those final scenes of 'for-giveness, reconciliation and peace', and Strachey is at his most assured in refuting this particular contention. Set in the style of traditional fairy tales, the conclusions of which were pre-ordained by ageless convention, these plays, he believed,

10. Later collected in *Books and Characters* and in *Literary Essays* (1—15)

really illustrated Shakespeare's lessening hold on reality. He is in his second childhood, and his eyes, no longer fixed unblinkingly upon the actual world, are filled with a fairyland vision of wonder and enchantment. Yet this felicitous dream only holds him intermittently. Each time it fades and the shadows of his turbulent nature sweep across to darken the smooth unruffled surface of his fantasy, the dream plunges into nightmare, and Shakespeare's sudden terror bursts out in childish rage and petulance.

Strachey's understanding of Shakespeare's character had deepened since he wrote in his Liverpool diary five years previously that Shakespeare was 'a cynic in his inmost heart of hearts'. He makes good use of the unabashed sentimentality of the established Victorian critics as a lens through which to bring his own contradictory view of Shakespeare into focus, to sharpen the contours of his figure. But once he strays from the perversely guiding commentaries of these critics and relies on his own unaided perception, a measure of his assurance falters, he confesses his lack of confidence in reconciling the work of any author with his personal character, and concludes that Shakespeare was 'bored with people, bored with real life, bored with drama, bored, in fact, with everything except poetry and poetical dreams'. As a piece of literary criticism this statement is hardly less sentimentalized in its own way than the theories of Dowden and Gollancz. What Strachey chose to call boredom was almost certainly complete exhaustion. It is at least as difficult to equate such an abyss of ennui as he imagines with the rage and fury of Shakespeare's outbursts (alternating with that pathetic, flickering unreality of his last wistful day-dreams) as it is to discover in these passages the ordered workings of a pedagogic mind conditioned to some state of serene and elderly self-possession. Boredom, which comes from a deficiency in imaginative and emotional experience, is a malady most incident to youth; exhaustion, the cumulative outcome of a surfeit of personal experience and physical activity, generally afflicts the old. The outward symptoms of both maladies may often appear similar, and Strachey's confusion of one with the other provides an interesting pointer towards his own state of mind.

The longest and best of all the prose pieces he wrote at this time was on the 'English Letter Writers'[11], which he completed shortly after his twenty-fifth birthday and submitted in the hope of winning the Le Bas Prize for an English essay[12] – though that year no award was finally made. Over twenty thousand words in length, Strachey composed it, almost in its entirety, during a single week. The subject was well chosen and suited admirably his literary temperament. 'Perhaps', he was to write some fifteen years later, 'the really essential element in the letter writer's make-up is a certain strain of femininity'. In 'English Letter Writers' his own feminine strain of elegance and directness was consequently working in an ideal medium, and can be seen at its most enjoyable. In their mixture of triviality and intimacy the letters with which he dealt formed an expression not of the innermost complexities of human nature – with which Strachey was seldom quite at his ease – but of the glamorous highlights and flourishes of the individual personality, the odd historical quirks and vivid characteristics which chiefly diverted him. His theme was therefore not too exacting, and required just that blending of literary susceptibility and intellectual shrewdness with which he was so well equipped.

The essay is divided into six chronological chapters. In the first of these, which examines the Elizabethans, Strachey wrote: 'The Elizabethan age was pre-eminently an age of action, and some of the finest of its letters were written with the object of forwarding some practical end.' Elsewhere, too, the letters are analysed less as reflections of their correspondent's personal temperament than as microcosms of the age in which they were written. Strachey's sense of history, a subject which he had been officially studying now for many years at two schools and two universities, is as sure as one would expect. 'An eighteenth-century letter', he explains in his

11. Later collected in *Characters and Commentaries* and in *Literary Essays* (234–89).

12. This essay was not printed during Lytton's lifetime, but was first published posthumously by James Strachey in *Characters and Commentaries* (1933), and later reprinted in *Literary Essays* (1948).

second chapter, 'is the true epitome of the eighteenth century.' His reading of character throughout succeeding epochs is less fluent. Of Pope's letters we are told simply that they do not reveal his true nature as does his poetry. The correspondence of Addison shows us merely a 'charming, polished, empty personality'; that of Steele, only an exhibition of fine manners; while we are introduced to Swift with the bland announcement that 'it is not our purpose, however, to discuss the colossal mind of the great Dean of St Patrick's'.

Passing on to his third chapter, Strachey considers first the letters of Lady Mary Wortley Montagu, whose 'wit has that quality which is the best of all preservatives against dullness – it goes straight to the point', but to whom life seemed little more than a game of whist; and secondly the redoubtable figure of Lord Chesterfield, whose correspondence with his son provides a fitting counterpoint tó Lady Mary Wortley Montagu's with her daughter. He is especially good when discussing Lord Chesterfield's letters, immediately putting himself in the place of the shy, bullyable, gawkish Philip Stanhope, with whose unremitting persecution by post he feels a profound commiseration. To Strachey's mind the scheme of conduct propounded by Chesterfield in these classic manuals of deportment was wholly odious – blindly, vulgarly, patronizingly, absolutely conventional. The fanatical earnestness with which he strove to implant culture and an accomplished code of manners in his lonely, inarticulate son, only succeeded in stimulating to an unnatural extent a perfectly natural tendency to boorishness – a reaction which so incensed Chesterfield that he himself soon forgot his own manners and a number of those other social virtues he felt such an ungovernable desire to promote in his stuttering, ungainly pupil. Though Strachey's indignation clouded in places the humorous relish he felt for this ludicrous tragi-comedy, the curious nature of Chesterfield's relationship with his illegitimate son greatly interested him, and he saw quite simply what so many more pretentious and masculine critics have missed: that Chesterfield was a bore of gargantuan proportions.

The fourth chapter of the essay is devoted entirely to the letters of Horace Walpole, to whom Strachey was often to return in the course of his career. His enduring interest in Walpole underlies much that was similar in their lives. As a result of their persisting fear of insecurity, they each remained emotionally immature, morbidly vulnerable to the least pin-prick of ridicule. They subsisted as eternal though un-orthodox bachelors, preoccupied for much of the time with escaping 'into centuries that cannot disappoint one'. Both, in their later life, were reassured by comfortable surroundings, a leisured and not too exacting routine, disliking, as shy, caustic and fastidious eccentrics, the rowdy presence of children. Above all, they practised the art of letter-writing with a grace and wit seasoned with a dash of sharp, cat-like malice. But of the two, Strachey's absorption in the soothing shades of the past was far less complete. For he possessed a finer intelli-gence and humanity than Walpole, and, having once attained a measure of critical detachment, could never be so easily satisfied by purely historical meditation. At the same time, he felt a particular gratitude to Walpole for having produced, through the years, an encyclopedic correspondence so per-fectly composed. In these letters there were no terrifying heights, no resounding chasms; everything was reduced to an evenly chiselled alabaster surface. The wilderness of nature had been tamed, and in its place Walpole had laid out the symmetrical precision of a formal garden. Strachey's response to this type of writing points, once again, to the duality of his temperament, for he never quite approves intellectually of what, he admits, attracts him emotionally. Each time he picked up these letters he was allured and fascinated, fol-lowing the figure of Walpole as he minced upstairs and down-stairs and no further, daintily rearranging the china cups in the closets of Strawberry Hill. But then, on closing the book, the spell dissolved; and he would reflect critically on how little all this exquisite frippery amounted to.

The correspondence of Cowper and Gray was more per-sonal, yet also more reticent. He probably read Cowper only in selection, for he misses altogether those lowering undertones of his style, the tortured pessimism of his subconscious apprehensions. As far as Cowper's letters go, he wrote, 'they are perfect, but they hardly go anywhere at all. Their gold is absolutely pure; but it is beaten out into the thinnest leaf conceivable. They are like soap bubbles – exquisite films surrounding emptiness, almost too wonderful to be touched.' In the case of Gray, Strachey experienced a deeper appeal. Was it, he asks, Gray's refinement, the breadth of his sympathies, or perhaps his quiet, compact sense of humour that so charmed his devotees? On reflection he decides that it was chiefly none of these qualities, but Gray's deep and abiding melancholy which sounded in his own heart such a sure echo. Had he himself been seduced into remaining all his life at Cambridge, it is possible that he might have come to share with Gray something of that same subdued note of tender regret, instead of developing that peculiar, off-beat countertenor, the straining, over-contrived exclamatory voice which can be heard in his more romantic writing. Strachey seems to have realized that he and Gray were partly of the same mettle, and their latent similarity is nowhere more implicit than in his final paragraph: 'His spirit seems still to hover about Cambridge. Those retired gardens, those cloistered courts, are as fitted now for his footstep and his smile as they were a hundred years ago. It seems hardly rash, when the midnight fire has been piled up, when sleep has descended upon the profane, when a deeper silence has fallen upon the night, when the unsported oak still stands invitingly ajar, to expect – in spite of the impediments of time and of mortality – a visit from Gray.'

The sixth and final chapter covers the letters of Byron, Shelley, Keats and Lamb. Of these Strachey appreciated the last three most. He offers neat epistolary quotations to display the individual merits of each correspondent, but has little really illuminating to say about any of them as human beings. With Byron, on the other hand, whom he disliked, the rays of his imaginative insight converged and focused upon the man who stood behind the letters. He is not blind to Byron's vivid appeal – 'The cumulative effect of Byron's vigour', he wrote, 'acts upon the reader like a tonic or a sea-breeze; he himself begins to wish to throw his ink bottle through the window, to practise pistol-shooting in bed, to scatter his conversation with resounding oaths' – but he found what he describes as 'the peculiar masculinity of his style' highly uncongenial. Though he knew only too well that all good letter-writers are egoists at heart, only Byron is taken to task for his egoism. 'Unfortunately,' he wrote, 'Byron's character was marred by a defect only too common to men of this particular type: he was a complete egoist. And round this fault a multitude of others naturally clustered – narrowness of interests, lack of real enthusiasms, vulgarity, affectation. His letters are concerned with one subject and one alone – himself.' Yet Strachey's aversion did not rest simply with this general condition of egoism as he maintained, but sprang largely from one particular manifestation of it which he instinctively believed was the whole truth behind the wicked Byronic myth – the sordid, unaffectionate and incestuous affair he carried on with his sister. The contrast between Strachey's picture of Byron and the vaguer, more blurred impressions of Shelley and Keats is convincing evidence of how, in much the same manner as Pope, disfavour could sharpen up his sense of reality. His discriminative powers crystallize round Byron and produce not just the embodiment of a romantic age or movement, but the living outline of a real if rather distasteful human being.

What makes 'English Letter Writers' such a good essay is the very authentic appreciation which Strachey obviously feels for his subject-matter, and which he charmingly conveys in a prose that is for the most part economical but never austere, and studded throughout with short, well-chosen quotations. Himself an extraordinarily prolific correspondent, he is well qualified to show us that, though the best letters may have many distinguishing qualities – a deftness of touch, ease of expression, an unforced brilliance and gentle pervading amiability – yet, for true excellence, they must always succeed in suggesting that the personality of the letter-writer is even more attractive than the correspondence itself.

2

BIOGRAPHIA LITERARIA

On 3 March 1903, Strachey had written to his mother: 'I have taken 5 shares in Trevelyan and Co's Review, feeling (1) it was the least I can do, and (2) that I rather wanted to as he [G. M. Trevelyan] says, every time he sees me, "There is a majority of Apostles on the Editorial Committee!" So there's room for hope at least that it won't be as fearful as its prospectus. They haven't yet thought of a name.'

Later that same year, this new intellectual liberal monthly was christened the *Independent Review*, and its first issue came out in October. The aspirations of its subscribers ran high, and when E. M. Forster purchased the initial number, he felt convinced that 'a new age had begun'. As it turned out, the review did not enjoy a particularly long life, though it elicited in its time many good articles. The consumptive Nathaniel Wedd, Lowes Dickinson and George Trevelyan were all associated with the paper's foundation and the laying down of its political policy – which was to combat militant imperialism, protectionism and Joe Chamberlain, and to advocate what they considered to be a constructive domestic programme. 'They are violent free traders – much more violent, I feel, than I could ever be', Strachey wrote to John Sheppard. 'On the whole I don't think I shall ever hate Chamberlain as much as I hate (say) Robert Bridges.' Since the type of qualified radical humanism which it favoured has always been a popular line among English middle- and mupple-class intellectuals, the *Independent Review* soon attracted some of the most able men of letters of the day, including Lascelles Abercrombie, Hilaire Belloc, Wilfrid Blunt, H. N. Brailsford, G. K. Chesterton, Ramsay MacDonald and H. G. Wells. In April 1907 the name of the periodical was changed to the *Albany Review*, and several further distinguished persons were added to the list of contributors, among them William Archer, A. C. Bradley, Thomas Hardy, Andrew Lang, Gilbert Murray, G. W. E. Russell and Sidney Webb. Under both names the review ran from the autumn of 1903 to the spring of 1908, bringing out altogether some fourteen volumes, ten numbers of which include papers by Strachey. Yet though he remained a faithful contributor, Strachey did not wholeheartedly go along with the official policy,[13] which he considered to be still too reactionary. Several of his pieces which appeared in the review's columns were intended to be veiled attacks on the Liberal Party.[14] By adopting a controlled, diplomatic tone he contrived to jam over his powder so that even the editor would not notice the political import of what he was saying. But it was a tiresome business, and perhaps, he sometimes reflected, once it was successfully achieved the efficacy of the powder had almost gone.

These essays, together with those which were printed in the *New Quarterly* from 1907 to 1910, were written ostensibly as reviews of current books, and may be divided into three different categories: those in which Strachey indulged his liking and wide knowledge of French literature; those which may be regarded as an overflow from his original Cambridge essay, 'English Letter Writers'; and finally a few miscellaneous pieces set in eighteenth-century England – his favourite period in English history.

It was when contributing to this first category that Strachey seems to have felt at his most assured. The opening issue of the *Independent Review* carried in it his very first published prose work entitled 'Two Frenchmen'[15]. For an undergraduate of only twenty-three it is an astonishingly impressive essay, displaying not just literary promise, but mature achievement. 'The greatest misfortune that can happen to a witty man', the essay begins, 'is to be born out of France.' And with his own style Strachey clearly exhibits his personal preference for aphoristic neatness. Each sentence is beautifully balanced and

13. 'I think "the Phenomenal Review" would have been the right name', Strachey wrote to John Sheppard (15 September 1903). 'Trevy would be furious if he knew I'd said that; he'd even be hurt. But he wouldn't see that though I'd said it, I'd meant it only half.'

14. See, for example. 'The First Earl of Lytton', *Independent Review*, XII, March 1907, and included in *Literary Essays*.

15. *Independent Review*, I (October 1903), 185–9. Later collected in *Characters and Commentaries* and in *Literary Essays*, (100–105).

the whole composition flows with perfect smoothness. But in places his fondness for the epigrammatic is overstrained to the verge of triviality, as, for example, when he announces: 'La Rochefoucauld, there can be no doubt, was the cleverest duke who ever lived.'

Dealing not only with the two Frenchmen of the title, Vauvenargues and La Bruyère, but also with a third, La Rochefoucauld himself, the essay is particularly interesting for the split it shows between Strachey's purely impressionistic criticism and his more analytical method of examination. 'Two Frenchmen' reads almost like the product of two men in good working collaboration. While one of them is intoxicated by the sheer minstrelsy of elegant literary variations, the other evidently stands in need of strong drink in order to face up with equanimity to the petty self-interest of the human beings who chant these mellifluous songs. Thus he compares La Rochefoucauld's writing to 'a narrow strip of perfectly polished parquet whereon a bored and aristocratic dancer exquisitely moves'. But a little farther on, when he is evaluating the achievement of Vauvenargues and no longer under the hypnotic spell of La Rochefoucauld's literary performance, he notes with aversion his (La Rochefoucauld's) 'paradoxical cynicism', and condemns him for his 'portrait of humanity restricted and distorted to the extent of being (for all the sobriety of the presentment) really nothing more than an ingenious caricature'.

That Strachey's partiality for French literature did not overwhelm his critical faculties – even where his heroes were involved – is convincingly demonstrated by his paper on 'Voltaire's Tragedies', published in April 1905[16]. As with 'Two Frenchmen', the piece starts off with a pithy epigram: 'The historian of Literature is little more than a historian of exploded reputations.' There can be little doubt that during these first years of writing criticism, Strachey, with his heightened sense of the ridiculous, was acutely conscious of

16. The original title was 'The Tragedies of Voltaire,' *Independent Review*, V (April 1905), 309–19. Later collected in *Books and Characters* and in *Literary Essays* (106–19).

how easy it is to be ludicrously mistaken in one's literary pronouncements. The effect of this constant awareness was to promote that inbred caution which held pretty firmly in check his more romantic flair. Here he telescopes into a dry, tightly-knit résumé, the complex and unrealistic plot of Voltaire's *Alzire, ou Les Américains*, revealing as if almost by accident the fatuity of the whole counterfeit concoction. In its ironic compression, with all the emphasis and foreshortening of caricature, 'Voltaire's Tragedies' stands out as an early miniature example of Strachey's biographical technique.[17]

Also anticipating the form of his later books is the fine biographical pen portrait he drew of 'Mademoiselle de Lespinasse'. This was the eighth of his articles to appear in the *Independent Review*[18], by which time the struggle between his sober reliance on known facts and the attraction which he always felt for romantic speculation is more jauntily presented: 'Who was her father? According to the orthodox tradition, she was the child of Cardinal de Tencin, whose sister, the famous Madame de Tencin, was the mother of d'Alembert. This story has the advantage of discovering a strange and concealed connection between two lives which were afterwards to be intimately bound together; but it has the disadvantage of not being true.' All the same, such disadvantageous truth was not to frustrate altogether the expression of romanticism, and where Strachey was unable to interweave it unobtrusively with the main thread of his narrative, he falls back on personal asides which stick out at intervals like frayed and gaudy strands. His overblown comment, for instance, on one of Mademoiselle de Lespinasse's letters, is pure romantic rhetoric belonging, in mood, to his

---

17. This essay provides also what is perhaps the first example of what austere persons would consider an atrocity. '[Voltaire] is capable, for instance, of writing lines as bad as . . .', Strachey explained, and gave three quotations, the last of which – 'Vous comprenez, seigneur, que je ne comprends pas' – was never in fact written by Voltaire at all, but was a parody invented by Strachey's sister Marjorie. But then, of course, Strachey only says that Voltaire was *capable* of writing lines as bad as this.

18. *Independent Review*, X (September 1906), 82–3. Later collected in *Characters and Commentaries* and in *Biographical Essays* (153–64).

Elizabeth and Essex period: 'Who does not discover beneath these dreadful confidences', he asks darkly, 'a superhuman power moving mysteriously to an appointed doom?'

But if Strachey's imagination was intermittently romantic, seeking to evolve fanciful mysteries in preference to solving real and tedious problems, his critical intelligence remained strictly classical, paring the wings of his more conjectural flights, and saving him from the risk of flopping into rich absurdity. This classicism is best exemplified by his unrivalled ability to describe and reconstruct a highly involved factual situation with compact lucidity. In this task he is never wearisome, never superfluous or dull, since he always goes straight to the point, sharply illuminating what hitherto had been merely shadowy. It seems quite evident, too, that realizing how adept he was in this sphere, his enjoyment was proportional to his self-confidence. Today, his style still retains all its sparkle and power to enliven the reader. He is, for instance, sympathetic to Mademoiselle de Lespinasse, and depicts her as an undeserving victim of circumstance – the way in which he sometimes saw himself. Her life and adventures are sorted out and narrated with such vividness that a stronger impression of her true likeness is conveyed to one than can be directly accounted for by the slightly sentimental estimate of her which this essay specifically puts forward.

Written at a time when he was still searching for some home from home – an idealized, amiable community where he could rediscover the joys of Cambridge – Strachey evokes the salon of Julie de Lespinasse in language, the sad, breathless intensity of which suggests that he already had in mind some notion of the then gradually emerging Bloomsbury Group. 'Oh! It was a place worth visiting – the little salon in the rue Saint-Dominique. And, if one were privileged to go there often, one found there what one found nowhere else – a sense of freedom and intimacy which was the outcome of real equality, a real understanding, a real friendship such as have existed, before or since, in few societies indeed.'

This fascination which Strachey felt to disentangle the complex impulses that lay behind a love affair revolving so close to the vortex of some glittering social scene had affinities with his attraction to the stage, and is equally pronounced in his essay 'Lady Mary Wortley Montagu'[19]. The self-deceit, the appeal of social reputation masquerading as profound human love, the welter of ambition and egotism so deftly intermixed with protestations of selfless devotion, all this emotional machinery conducted at the forefront of fashionable society was aggrandized, for Strachey, from something sordid and mean into the rich and forgivable flamboyance of a picturesque spectacle. The aristocratic sugar icing sweetened and made deliciously appetizing to his palate the whole messy, tasteless dish; the action on the platform was transformed from a rude conflict of ruthless impulses into a carnival decked with fine regalia. Written two years after his 'English Letter Writers', 'Lady Mary Wortley Montagu' reveals a rather deeper, more intricate understanding of human nature. In the Cambridge essay Strachey had been too greatly swayed by Horace Walpole's portrait of Lady Mary as 'Moll Worthless' and was content to represent only the superficial truth. But in this later composition he shows that there existed another side to her, and he is at pains to emphasize the bitter disillusionment which underlay her sterile eccentricities and which gave humanity to the 'old, foul, tawdry, painted, plastered personage' whom Walpole saw in the last dreadful years of her life.

The occasion of this article was a newly published biography, *Lady Mary Wortley Montagu and her Times* by George Paston. In referring specifically to this book, Strachey states in strong and unqualified terms the disgust he felt at the quality of contemporary biography – which he was soon enough to alter so fundamentally by the example of his own work. 'The book,' he wrote, 'with its slipshod writing, its uninstructed outlook, its utter lack of taste and purpose, is a fair specimen of the kind of biographical work which seems to give so much satisfaction to large numbers of our reading public. Decidedly, "they order the matter better in

19. *Albany Review*, I (September 1907), 708–16. Later collected in *Characters and Commentaries* and in *Biographical Essays* (34–42).

France", where such a production could never have appeared.'

Another of his essays produced as a corollary to his 'English Letter Writers' was 'Horace Walpole'[20]. Walpole, of course, was one of Strachey's favourite literary figures, and here he defends him convincingly from Macaulay's brilliant caricature – 'mopping and mowing, spitting and gibbering, dressed out in its master's finery, and keeping an eye upon the looking-glass'. Ironically enough, some of the features which are depicted in this gloriously burlesque portrait might be said to resemble Strachey himself. In a passage which Strachey ignores, Macaulay had written of Walpole's literary capacities in words which some later critic might apply to the essays of Lytton Strachey with almost equal justification: 'What then is the charm, the irresistible charm of Walpole's writings? It consists, we think, in the art of amusing without exciting. He never ... fills the imagination or touches the heart; but he keeps the mind of the reader constantly attentive and constantly entertained. ... If we were to adopt the classification, not a very accurate classification, which Akenside has given of the pleasures of the imagination, we should say that with the Sublime and Beautiful Walpole had nothing to do, but that the third province, the Odd, was his peculiar domain.'

By his mastery of graceful decoration and the perpetual process of his sparkling imagery, Walpole banished that arid sense of boredom to which Strachey was so acutely susceptible that he had attributed it to Shakespeare. He felt a special affinity with Walpole's deceptive and subtle character, and liked to see the incongruity between his own private and public self reproduced in the double personality of Walpole. So much is evident from a passage which comprises the whole essence of his defence against Macaulay's soaring banalities: 'But the truth seems to be, in spite of "those glaring and obvious peculiarities which could not escape the most superficial observation" – his angry, cutting sentences, his constant mockery of his enemies, his constant quarrels with his friends, and his perpetual reserve – that Walpole's nature was

20. *Independent Review*, II (May 1904), 641–6. Later collected in *Characters and Commentaries* and in *Biographical Essays* (187–93).

in reality peculiarly affectionate. There can be no doubt that he was sensitive to an extraordinary degree; and it is much more probable that the defects — for defects they certainly were — which he showed in social intercourse, were caused by an excess of this quality of sensitiveness, rather than by any lack of sincere feeling. It is impossible to quarrel with one's friends unless one likes them; and it is impossible to like some people very much without disliking other people a good deal. These elementary considerations are quite enough to account for the vagaries and the malice of Walpole.'

There is plain autobiographical interest, too, in 'Sir Thomas Browne'[21], which was the first major piece of criticism Strachey composed after coming down from Cambridge. The swelling nostalgia he feels rises raw and undisguised near the conclusion of the essay, when he suddenly breaks in to exclaim: 'In England, the most fitting background for his [Browne's] strange ornament must surely be some habitation consecrated to learning, some University which still smells of antiquity and has learnt the habit of repose. The present writer, at any rate, can bear witness to the splendid echo of Browne's syllables amid learned and ancient walls; for he has known, he believes, few happier moments than those in which he has rolled the periods of the *Hydriotaphia* out to the darkness and the nightingales through the studious cloisters of Trinity.'

A less direct indication of the sense of loss that afflicted Strachey at this time is provided by the general tone and manner in which 'Sir Thomas Browne' is written. It is one of the most purely academic of all his literary essays. After cursorily admitting that Browne was a physician who lived in Norwich, Strachey quickly absorbs himself into a close study of his style, and except for a single oblique reference to the amount of self-confidence needed to indulge such a wealth of allusion and unrestrained ornamentation, he nowhere seeks

---

21. *Independent Review*, VIII (February 1906), 158–69. Later collected in *Books and Characters* and in *Literary Essays* (35–46). See also Strachey's unsigned review of Edmund Gosse's *Sir Thomas Browne*, 'A New Book on Sir Thomas Browne', *The Speaker, 13* (3 February 1906), 441.

to associate the extraordinary stylistic qualities of Browne's prose with the personality of its author. The esoteric vocabulary, the Latinisms, the 'elaboration of rhythm, wealth and variety of suggestion, pomp and splendour of imagination', which he describes with such awe are connected with nothing but themselves, and make up a self-contained world full of sound and extraordinary charm, of abstract and elliptical patternings, half-grotesque, half-romantic and wholly imaginary. The 'subtle blending of mystery and queerness' which characterizes Browne's prose is the dreamland of Caliban, and, like Caliban, Strachey is comforted in his loneliness by the sweet airs which fill the place of his captivity, which promise to carry him elsewhere, and which, pending this paradise, compensate for those deficiencies in himself and in the hideous actuality of London where, as an exile from Cambridge, he was forced to go on living.

The groves of Academe in London could offer Strachey precious little shelter to hold him absolutely *in statu quo* as a Chekhovian perpetual student – 'Why is it', he once asked David Garnett (May 1915), 'that we are *not* Tchekhoff characters?' Despite his initial withdrawal under the shell of abstract literature, the biographical element was soon reintroduced into his method of criticism. Published in the *Independent Review* during March 1907, and composed shortly after Thoby Stephen's death in the previous year, 'The First Earl of Lytton'[22] contains a passage on the correspondence between Sir James Fitzjames Stephen and Lord Lytton – his own godfather 'Owen Meredith' – which very obviously reflects on Strachey's past friendship with Thoby: 'The friendship', he writes, 'is remarkable for something more than its swift beginning: it was a mingling of opposites such as is a rare delight to think upon. Sir James Stephen was eminently unromantic. His qualities were those of solidity and force; he preponderated with a character of formidable grandeur, with a massive and rugged intellectual sanity, a colossal com-

22. *Independent Review*, XII (March 1907), 332–8. Also in *Living Age*, 253 (20 April 1907), 153–6. Later collected in *Characters and Commentaries* and in *Literary Essays* (202–7).

monsense. The contrast is complete between this monolithic nature and the mercurial temperament of Lord Lytton, with his ardent imagination, his easy brilliance, his passionate sympathy, his taste for the elaborate and the coloured and the rococo. Such characteristics offended some of his stiff countrymen; they could not tolerate a man to whom conventions were "incomprehensible things", who felt at home "in the pure light air of foreign life", whose dress was original, as nearly all about him", and who was not afraid to express his feelings in public. But the great lawyer judged differently. . . .

'The story which the letters tell has much of the attractiveness of a romance.'

In all these papers, a natural caution, enhanced by his awareness of the easy fallibility of critics, is in conflict with a desire to create some novel and striking effect. The greater part of his review of Austin Dobson's *Fanny Burney*, entitled 'The Wrong Turning'[23], is given over to expounding and amplifying the paradox of Fanny Burney's immense reputation among the greatest intellects of her own day as a creative novelist – a reputation that, after her death, fell like a stone into insignificance. Again, in 'The Lives of the Poets', these two opposing strains are neatly brought together and crystallized into a single sentence: 'Johnson's aesthetic judgements are almost invariably subtle, or solid or bold; they have always some good quality to recommend them – except one: they are never right.'[24] This criticism, with its carefully manipulated opening which appears actually to add emphasis to the apparently audacious conclusion is largely just. For it is surely undeniable that Johnson's piety warped his sense of literature, that his avowed intention to furnish his readers with moral instruction stifled any eloquent expression of the beauties he could sense but not interpret in the poetry of Shakespeare and Milton. Yet Strachey's generalization, from which springs the whole theme of his essay, is again a deliberately narrow one,

23. *Independent Review*, XII (February 1904), 169–73. Later collected in *Characters and Commentaries* and in *Literary Essays* (120–6).

24. *Independent Review*, X (July 1906), 108–13. Later collected in *Books and Characters* and in *Literary Essays* (94–9).

giving only the illusion of breadth. What of Dr Johnson's more positive attributes? After his defence of Warren Hastings and Horace Walpole, one might reasonably have expected Strachey to attempt a rescue of Johnson from Macaulay and Carlyle's one-sided portraiture, and to develop the view propounded by Leslie Stephen and Walter Raleigh that, notwithstanding the merits of Boswell's magnificent *Life*, a great deal of Johnson's character lay outside the biography's scope. Instead, he swallows this version whole, and can offer only one feeble answer as to why such a John Bullish personality could still be read with pleasure. It was, he explains, Johnson's *wit* which sanctified all his copious errors. 'He has managed to be wrong so cleverly, that nobody minds.'

This basic lack of appreciation of Johnson's salient qualities is the obverse of Strachey's relish for the elaborate architectonics of Sir Thomas Browne. In these immediate post-Cambridge days his interest in Johnson was restricted to an evaluation of him as a skilled exponent of English prose style who, like Horace Walpole, had found his exemplar in Browne. Yet in the essential dissimilarity between Johnson's relationship with life and letters, and his own, lay Strachey's real cause for disapproval. For though Johnson's writings contain less artistic organization than Strachey's, less response to the more recondite beauties of the English language, less dramatic balance, one can feel in their rough, abiding texture what is absent from so much of Strachey's work – the free gust of life itself, moulded into its own most natural form, which outlasts even the cleverest and most fluent of sterile, literary techniques. Strachey's offspring are elegantly proportioned, but they are still-born in comparison with the very best of Johnson's, which, like himself, might be deformed, but through which the erratic pulse of life beats strongly.

At the same time Strachey cannot be dismissed by any means simply as an appalled and curious spectator of life. He was a partial participant. As a spectacle the world fascinated him. As an experience it filled him with a mixture of enthralment and revulsion. The ironic detachment which is spread over his prose style had a real purpose. It was something of a protective mantle – like Walpole's mannerisms – assumed so as to disguise his febrile and erotic vulnerability, his predisposition to unhappy, undignified infatuation. His unsteady and emaciated frame, so finely attuned, trembled on the brink of perpetual disaster. Cerebrally and emotionally he responded with a nervous, phrenetic abandon to life; physically he responded less. And in this partial restraint, he sometimes felt, lay his saving factor. Although he had too much sense of humour to set up as an important personage, he flattered himself that, publicly, he could establish an impressive, even formidable figure, of which his oddly reticent and rapid prose style was to form a destructive feature.

This peculiarly segmented taste for living conditioned his appreciation and practice of writing. Strachey's response to the greatest poets and men of letters was real and sincere. His relation to their work touched the most profound springs of his being; yet he could not always hammer into words what that relationship was. The sharp abrasive bisection between his emotion and thought manifested itself as an artificial barrier which was erected between his obvious literary enjoyment and his powers of interpretation, a barrier which ran almost straight across the entire corpus of his criticism. Like the old Cavalier in *Woodstock*, he loved 'to hear poetry twice, the first time for sound, the latter time for sense'[25], and the separation of these two qualities impeded his own depth of critical penetration. 'Words are to the poet', he once wrote, 'as notes are to the musician'[26]; and he saw his first duty as a critic to point out what was best worth hearing in an author, supported by some testimony from the work under discussion. 'Hear how melodious such a passage sounds!' he exclaims with rapture, and plays a few bars for us to listen to. Then to this illustration he appends a rather pedagogic appraisal which seeks to analyse the properties of each note or phrase in isolation. Since, however, the sum of the properties of each isolated note seldom approximates to the cumulative effect of the completed passage, Strachey is left to conclude

25. 'Comus at Cambridge', *Spectator*, 101 (18 July 1908), 94–5.
26. 'Milton's Words', *Spectator*, 99 (14 December 1907), 991–2.

that art is magic, a fabulous sleight-of-hand produced by the unconscious instinct of the artist-conjurer. Again and again he points in hopeless wonder and exaltation at the mysterious processes of literary creation. For so long as it remained inexplicable, literature could not be demeaned by common-sense definitions and made subject to the ordinary laws of the empirical world. Art, therefore, was removed from actuality, and far from irradiating the humdrum and painful everyday with fresh meaning and beauty, constituted a universe of its own, a land of fantasies and day-dreams which conferred on one the same benefits as falling in love.

Like a boy, Strachey expected and desired the marvellous and mythological in what he read. Much of his favourite reading was for him a spicy concoction, an opiate in the drinking of which the encircling, documentary view of life faded back into a blurred oblivion. He shrank from relating art too directly with the natural order of things – a divorce which automatically gave rise to the mystery of its immaculate conception. Because the greatest poems in the language are not autobiographical, in the sense that though rooted in intense personal experience they rise to an impersonal significance, Strachey maintained that they were not to be associated with the 'particular griefs or joys or passions which give birth to them'. Poetry was a world on its own, self-contained, self-sufficient and safe, into which one might escape for short intervals whenever the pressure of outside events rose too high. But it follows that, if the actual source and original context of a work is cut off altogether from its literary qualities, then there remains little for the critical faculty to grapple with except the mechanics of literature – the grammar, the punctuation, the peculiarities and conventionalities of style – all of which is about as relevant as an analysis, in the appreciation of a piano sonata, of the wood from which the piano has been constructed. Strachey's two-stage critical formula, applied to all sorts and conditions of poets, led to a wide deviation in values, and synchronized with perfect harmony only when matched with the highflown, romantic writers so beloved of academics – the rich, colourful prose-world of Sir Thomas Browne, or the wild rhapsodies of Swinburne, so languorous, dreamy and unreal. But in its application to men who drew their inspiration more directly through personal experience, the defects of this critical method, the incongruity between his passionate enjoyment and the dry, scholastic comment, is often striking. Thus, with due seriousness, Strachey balances the merits and demerits of an adjustment of the time sequence in *Othello*[27]; Gloucester's eyes are torn out in *King Lear*, he observes elsewhere, 'as a contributory means towards a general artistic purpose'[28]; and again, after quoting some timeless, transcendental lines from Wordsworth, he adds: 'Who can doubt that the vague and vast sublimity of this wonderful description depends upon the Latinized vocabulary?'[29]

Nowhere can the apprehension of ridicule that helped to spread this disharmony of heart and mind be more palpably felt than in 'The Poetry of Blake', an essay which Strachey contributed to the *Independent Review* in the spring of 1906.[30] The sense and melody of Blake's poetry is uniquely compacted together. Nevertheless, Strachey, rather hesitantly, tried to separate them. As one might expect, he is fully sensitive to the awful loneliness and power of Blake's lyrics, but the essence of these incomparable utterances, he goes on to explain, partly depends 'upon subtle differences of punctuation and of spelling'. Surely criticism of this nature is as narrow and unavailing as the most preposterous of Johnson's aesthetic precepts?

'It often happens', Strachey wrote in one of his *Spectator* reviews, 'that criticism is mainly interesting for the light it throws on the critic[31].' This dictum holds good for his own

27. See 'The Praise of Shakespeare', *Spectator*, 92 (4 June 1904), 882.

28. 'King Lear', *Spectator*, 100 (23 May 1908), 830–31. Later collected in *Spectatorial Essays* (66–70).

29. 'The Grandiloquence of Wordsworth', *Spectator*, 100 (2 May 1908), 746–7. Later collected in *Spectatorial Essays* (160–65).

30. *Independent Review*, IX (May 1906), 215–26. Later collected in *Books and Characters* and in *Literary Essays* (139–50).

31. 'Shakespeare on Johnson', *Spectator*, 101 (1 August 1908), 164–5. Later collected in *Spectatorial Essays* (59–65).

criticism of Blake. On first acquaintance, these pure, ecstatic lyrics seemed to open up regions of strange imagination and mysterious romance, a fancied world of fable and delight. But closer knowledge disclosed that such attractive surface qualities were singularly deceptive. Beneath the childlike charm there lay a forbidding austerity; the far-off fairyland proved to be a mirage which, on dissolving, uncovered a horizon of unearthly remoteness. For Blake's universe was not make-believe, but real: a visionary interpretation of human destiny. His short poems shoot like fearful stabs of lightning across the darkness of the sky, illuminating momentarily the quagmires and shifting sands of our sad, twilight existence. But these were sights that remained shrouded from Strachey's eyes. 'Nothing', declared Blake, 'can withstand the fury of my course among the stars of God and the abysses of the Accuser.' To Strachey the ring of such a sentiment was superb; but it was not practical politics. He almost preferred the cosier simplicity of Mary Coleridge[32], or even the pastoral mysticism of Wordsworth, whose spiritual tenderness was more countrified than Blake's 'inspired ravings', and whose habitual caution – finally to extinguish all his visionary dreams – Strachey significantly described as 'sanity'.

Nevertheless, though he could not follow Blake's meteoric flights, he did feel the force of their pull. 'We look,' he wrote, 'and as we gaze at the strange image and listen to the marvellous melody we are almost tempted to do likewise.' Almost, but not quite. For always his 'sanity' held him back and he translated the apprehension which assailed him whenever he contemplated such a journey about the heavens into a general condemnation of mysticism. 'Besides its unreasonableness, there is an even more serious objection to Blake's mysticism – and indeed to all mysticism: its lack of humanity. The mystic's creed – even when arrayed in the wondrous and ecstatic beauty of Blake's verse – comes upon the ordinary man, in the rigidity of its uncompromising elevation, with a shock which is terrible, and almost cruel. The sacrifices which

32. See 'The Late Miss Coleridge's Poems', *Spectator*, 100 (4 January 1908), 19.

it demands are too vast, in spite of the divinity of what it has to offer. What shall it profit a man, one is tempted to exclaim, if he gain his own soul, and lose the whole world? The mystic ideal is the highest of all; but it has no breadth.'

This view of mysticism as a strait-jacket creed donned voluntarily by inspired semi-lunatics is plausible, but entirely without real comprehension. Mysticism does not involve blindness to three-quarters of the world's objects and events, but an alteration in the focus through which one regards them. It is a product of the imagination, that blending of the emotions and the intellect which reconciles apparent opposites with a simplicity unobtainable from pure analysis or sensitive impressionism alone. Though he was attracted towards mysticism, Strachey, who had confessed himself more of an Aristotelian than a Platonist, achieved simplicity in his own writing not by this stereoscopic fusion, but by a single-minded, selective concentration which often had the effect of blotting out latent discrepancies and impoverishing the rich multi-dimensions of a story. His partly preconceived literary patterns, however cunningly arranged, do not carry somewhere within them the burgeoning seeds of tropical chaos which lie scattered about in real life. They are, in truth, *over*-simplified, for the order is largely imposed from without and not perceived to exist within the muddle and confusion of living.

Nor is inhumanity a necessary element of mysticism as Strachey fearfully suggests. The strident, ugly note in Blake, as in Beethoven, was not the result of his powerful imagination, but of his immense will. The more potent the imagination, the stronger must be the will that is needed to support it. But in those nightmare moments when doubt and terror overcome the mystic, when his imagination falters and his intuitive vision is distorted, then the volcanic power of his unimpeded will can erupt and cover his transcendentalism with a crust of militancy. It is, thus, not the power of mysticism which brings about this ruthlessness, but its impermanence, its lost battles with the will to power.

Strachey's criticism of Blake, and of men of comparable

stature, Shakespeare and Johnson, defines the limits of his own talent and points to the reason why, for all his excellence and discriminating literary sensibility, he never developed into one of the very few great creative writers himself. For Blake, as for Shakespeare and Johnson, the imaginative faculty was a means by which to transmute their deepest, most genuine response to life into the deathless anatomy of literature, to overreach the passing moment and shape the free current of their experience into indestructible, creative form. The pursuit of the imagination was for them love and truth; that of the will, lust and power. Through the imagination which yearns for union with another life, they sensed that man might apprehend a harmony which envelops, though it does not penetrate, our present existence. The will, with its passion to dominate and possess, destroyed this unity and left chaos and division.

For Strachey the imagination was something different — a magic carpet on which he set out for those impossible, dematerialized escapades away from the inhibiting confines of himself and the conventional pressures of society. In many of his essays he uses the word, and always in the same sense as when he writes of Johnson that he 'had no ear and he had no imagination'. The imagination, for him, was a symphony, every note of which found a place in his heart; and he was so weak and sensitive that it played upon him as upon an instrument. In this restricted sense, the imagination implies not *discovery*, but *effect*, measuring the purely musical quality of a work at one remove from the meaning which it happened to convey and which was itself made subject to the will. In short, he employed his own imaginative talent not so much to overhear the rhythm which underlies the discord of our lives, as to conjure forth a never-never land full of sweet, wistful harmonies which could drown such discord. Thus, in the critical writing, his imaginative power seldom penetrates to a sudden revelation of the hidden truth, but evokes, as he himself wrote in his essay on Racine, 'a beautiful atmosphere, in which what is expressed may be caught away from the associations of common life and harmoniously enshrined'. Again, in a letter which he wrote in 1909 to Virginia Stephen – showing, incidentally, how clearly he recognizes the imagination to be something quite set apart from brilliance or sheer cleverness – he writes as though it were an *inventive* rather than a creative faculty, something which, with a wave of the wand, produces a bolt-hole from the doldrums of the everyday – a wild infusion of fantasy in which one willingly suspends one's rational disbelief. 'The French seem to me a melancholy race', he wrote, '– is it because they have no imagination, so that they have no outlets when they find themselves (as all intelligent people must) *vis-à-vis* with the horrors of the world? There's a sort of dry desperation about some of them which I don't believe exists with the English – even with Swift.'

On less exacting themes Strachey's criticism is always interesting and acute, and never more so than in his essays on Beddoes and Racine which he wrote for the *New Quarterly* in the years 1907 and 1908. Perhaps his greatest quality as a critic was his capacity for appreciation, and in both these pieces he is conscious of dealing with the reverse of what had been the case with Fanny Burney – poets whose reputation in this country had never risen to the level at which they deserved to stand, so that the fallibility of other past and present literary commentators had created an opportunity for himself to make an original re-appraisal of their work, a chance of striking a novel effect with less risk of ridicule.

The only way to judge a poet, Wordsworth has said, is to love him. Certainly Strachey's love of Beddoes and of Racine was responsible for some of the finest literary criticism he ever wrote. His treatment here is far above the belletrist's mere invitation to enjoyment: it represents an attempt to define the individual quality of the work and to convey, with the exact image or similitude, the particular impression which it has made on him personally. Though Beddoes and Racine were extremely dissimilar poets, Strachey was able to detect in both some affinity with himself. Beddoes, of course, delighted in Elizabethan drama, and Strachey argues convincingly that, although born at the beginning of the nineteenth century, his proper place as a dramatist was among the Elizabethans: he was 'The Last Elizabethan'.[33]

It is easy to understand the appeal which Beddoes held for Strachey. Eccentric, mysterious, brilliant, a figure as improbable as the characters in his own dramas, this strange personality fascinated him. What little he could discover about his life – the letters displaying his humour and vitality, the suicide – whetted his appetite for more knowledge. Most beguiling of all was his companionship with Degen, a handsome young baker. 'The affair Degen is indeed mysterious,' Strachey wrote to Duncan Grant while working on the essay (11 June 1907), 'but there doesn't seem to me to be much doubt about his having been in love with him, especially as there is a German passage in one of his letters in which he says in so many words that he's a lover of boys.[34] I believe if one could get hold of the MSS one would find all sorts of wonders – love poems to Degen, perhaps, who knows? They belong to Browning's son who lives in Florence.'

So skilfully are these few biographical fragments arranged, so discerning is the criticism which runs alongside, that the effect of this essay is to re-create a living poet out of what had previously been an uneasy ghost. Strachey's apt quotations illustrate and convey the radiant intensity of that visionary world, full of unearthly pathos, of grotesque, ominous humour – like the mood engendered by the haunting symphonies of Mahler – in which Beddoes seems so much more at home than in the towns and cities of England and Germany. In such a passage as:

> I begin to hear
> Strange but sweet sounds, and the loud rocky dashing
> Of waves, where time into Eternity
> Falls over ruined walls.

33. *New Quarterly*, I (November 1907), 47–72. Collected in *Books and Characters* and in *Literary Essays* (171–94).

34. This phrase emanates from an inaccuracy of Gosse's. In one place he gives it, as Lytton reported it to Duncan Grant, as 'Liebhaber von Knaben'. But in another place he gives it, far more probably, as 'Liebhaber von Knocken' – a lover of bones. Beddoes was an anatomist as well as being absorbed by death.

there is a sure echo of those dreamland instruments that so enchanted Caliban that, on waking, he cried to dream again. The death-wish which runs through Beddoes's life is the practical, embodied expression of this cry, a reaction to the sudden, sickening descent from the supernatural to ordinary environment, from the ecstatic realms of the imagination to the coils of the enfeebled will. In his disregard for the common actualities of existence, Beddoes gave full rein to that romantic tendency which, in Strachey, was held in check by an innate caution and good sense. Both wished to awaken the drama of their times by some presentation of the bold and extraordinary contrasts so dear to their hearts; yet their finished achievements are strikingly diverse since, in spite of similar proclivities, their temperaments differed widely. Notwithstanding his admiration for the poetry of Beddoes, Strachey balances its positive accomplishments – the mastery of magnificent utterance, the power of his vast, strangely imprecise yet stimulating conceptions evoking unanalysable sensations within one, his simplicity and splendour – against the characteristic imperfections: the faulty construction, the unthinking inconsistency of the *dramatis personae*, the curious remoteness from the flesh and blood of human affairs.

The attraction of Beddoes's poetry for Strachey was partly that of psychological drama, partly mysticism. He was impelled equally by the boredom of continual safety and by the fear of solitary self-fulfilment, and he sought through literature to reconcile these two impulses, as it were, at second hand. Beddoes did not, like Blake, project that terrible blinding focus on everything; his energies were more dissipated, his poetry more uneven and diluted; and when his imagination faded he did not find sustenance in an awful, ruthless willpower, but sank into spiritless inertia – a reaction far more in keeping with the fluctuation of Strachey's own melancholic emotions. Like many imaginative persons Strachey felt at times a need to make the

> flight
> Of the poetic ecstasy
> Into the land of mystery.

But though he might respond to this dream of a transfigured universe in the poetry of Beddoes or Wordsworth, he never journeyed there himself, for his drive was not towards another world, but another personal existence in this world. In his love of literature, as in his sexual love of men, there existed some vague mystical consanguinity; but because he could not convert other people's experiences into his own, because he was after a sublime and magical analgesic rather than the revelation of a new heaven and a new earth, he could not accommodate poetic transcendentalism, despite the allure it held out for him.

Strachey's love of Racine was of an altogether different order. He could discover here no wondrous vision for the imagination to feed on, no exotic, spectacular vocabulary, no extravagant imagery, no bravura or wild fantasy to dazzle the mind and banish the cold, unfriendly regions of London from his awareness. Instead he found 'the beauties of restraint, of clarity, of refinement and of precision'. The source of his delight in these qualities lay partly in the nostalgia which they could call up in him, their formidable power of re-awakening some of the happiest and most exciting hours of childhood; and the aim of this essay[35] was to arouse in his readers something of the same exhilaration, that thrilling tide of music and greatness that had swept over him when his mother and Marie Souvestre[36] had first introduced him to Racine.

The means by which he set out to fulfil this purpose were subtle and effective.[37] How has it come about, he asks, that on this side of the Channel 'Racine is despised and Shakespeare is worshipped, on the other, Shakespeare is tolerated and Racine is adored?' In answering this question he uses as a foil to his own deeply rooted response the wide contrast that

35. *New Quarterly*, I (June 1908), 361–84, where it is called 'The Poetry of Racine'. Later collected as 'Racine' in *Books and Characters* and in *Literary Essays* (58–78).

36. Marie Souvestre, a schoolmistress and great friend of Lady Strachey's, exerted a considerable influence on both Lytton and his sister Dorothy. See *Lytton Strachey: A Biography*, pp. 54–62.

37. On 5 April 1908, while he was planning this essay, Lytton wrote to Desmond MacCarthy: 'I see that your favourite M. Lemaître is bringing

existed between a specific and typical French and English viewpoint, so that in the cross-current of *fâcheux* misunderstanding his own estimate of Racine emerges with added authority.

Throughout the essay Strachey has the full measure of Racine's genius, and although he makes an actual reference to Sarah Bernhardt, whom he had seen acting in *Phèdre* at the Royalty Theatre and elsewhere, perhaps in his most fervent passages we can overhear, too, the silent voice of Marie Souvestre, and feel within the child sitting at her feet the first great rent made in that veil which conceals the passions of men and women from the eyes of innocence:

'But to his lovers, to those who have found their way into the secret places of his art, his lines are impregnated with a peculiar beauty, and the last perfection of style. Over them, the most insignificant of his verses can throw a deep enchantment, like the faintest wavings of a magician's wand. "A-t-on vu de ma part le roi de Comagène?" How is it that words of such slight import should hold such thrilling music? Oh! they are Racine's words. And, as to his rhymes, they seem perhaps, to the true worshipper, the final crown of his art . . .

'. . . To hear the words of Phèdre spoken by the mouth of Bernhardt, to watch, in the culminating horror of crime and of remorse, of jealousy, of rage, of desire, and of despair, all the dark forces of destiny crowd down upon that great spirit, when the heavens and the earth reject her, and Hell opens, and the terrific urn of Minos thunders and crashes to the ground — that indeed is to come close to immortality, to plunge shuddering through the infinite abysses, and to look, if only for a moment, upon eternal light.'

---

out a book on Racine — do you think I might write on that? I might bring in also Mr J. C. Bailey's rotten book on French Poetry, in which he abuses the greatest poet in the world — just as you do. It wouldn't be particularly easy to carry the business off properly — but I think it *might* be done. If you could bear it, let me know — at any rate it would be more interesting — wouldn't it? — than the old rag-and-bone man Sir Henry Wotton.'

3

MARGINALIA

Between the essay-reviews which Strachey wrote for the *Independent Review* and for the *New Quarterly* there is a slight difference of tone arising from the degree of latitude he was allowed in each case. His choice of subject had been wide when writing for the *Independent Review*; he could make use of almost any book which had been published fairly recently as the basis for a long critical or biographical paper. But as a contributor to the *New Quarterly* he was even more fortunate, for the selection of theme seems to have been left entirely to himself. The bestowal of such freedom came from his friend Desmond MacCarthy, the literary editor, who greatly admired Strachey's talent and who, with a wisdom and courage rare among literary editors of periodicals, did not insist upon a cramping restriction to the topicalities of literary journalism. Consequently Strachey was at liberty to turn his attention to any subject that best suited his ability, and to compose essays neither connected with works just issuing from the press, nor confined to specific dates marking the celebration of centenaries.

It was Desmond MacCarthy too who commissioned a few anonymous book reviews from Strachey for *The Speaker* between December 1905 and October 1906. *The Speaker* had originally been founded to balance the *Spectator* after the Home Rule split in the Liberal Party. Its politics, similar to those of the *Independent Review*, were reasonably sympathetic to Strachey's outlook. Vigorously anti-imperialistic, the paper had, during the South African war, been the most emphatic organ of the pro-Boer minority in the country. Several of its regular contributors, besides Strachey, also wrote for the *Independent Review*, including Hilaire Belloc and G. K. Chesterton. In 1899 J. L. Hammond, the historian, had been appointed its editor. He began employing MacCarthy in 1903 as an occasional critic and by December 1905, when Strachey's anonymous review of John Dover Wilson's

John Lyly[38] appeared, MacCarthy had risen to a position of authority on the paper. But in November of the following year *The Speaker* was converted into *The Nation*. The new editor, H. W. Massingham, promptly dispensed with the services of MacCarthy;[39] and so Strachey's reviews, the last of which had come out the previous month, ceased altogether.

He was already by this time writing for *The Speaker*'s rival, his cousin St Loe Strachey's *Spectator*. The political policies of this paper were less to his taste and he was accorded far less freedom in his choice and treatment of subject. It was, however, at this period the most widely read of all the political weeklies, though something of a laughing-stock among the intelligentsia, and especially among the younger Stracheys who, believing the main body of its subscribers to consist of clergymen, used to apply the epithet 'Spectatorial' to its more pulpit pronouncements.

Between 1905 and 1910 Strachey contributed almost ninety long reviews to the *Spectator*, and considering that these pieces were usually the result of quick reading and hasty assimilation, their standard is remarkably high. His 'Shakespeare on Johnson'[40], for example, written in the summer of 1908, is superior to his 'The Lives of the Poets' composed two years earlier and included in both *Books and Characters* and the posthumous volume, *Literary Essays*, in the collected edition of his works. For the first time Strachey displays some real understanding of Johnson's merits as a writer, and balances his aesthetic limitations against the breadth and sanity of his outlook upon human affairs. Being moved more by humanity than by poetry, Johnson 'was not in essence a critic of literature', Strachey explains, 'but a critic of life'. And his conclusion on Johnson as a literary critic loses nothing of its humour for being comparatively just: 'It is hardly an exaggeration to say that Johnson's criticisms are such as might have

38. 'John Lyly', *The Speaker*, 13 (9 December 1905), 236.

39. Massingham later admitted that discharging MacCarthy had been one of his few mistakes as editor. See *Humanities* by Sir Desmond MacCarthy (1953), p. 16n.

40. *Spectator*, 101 (1 August 1908), 164-5. Later collected in *Spectatorial Essays* (59-66).

been made by a foreigner of great ability and immense experience who was acquainted with Shakespeare solely in a prose translation.'

Another of his best articles was 'John Milton'[41], an appreciation written in December 1908 to mark the three hundredth anniversary of Milton's birth. Though he responded to Milton's lofty and grandiose vision, the vast sublimity, the superhuman splendour of his poetry, and though he greatly admired Milton's unceasing struggle for artistic perfection in the grand style, yet Strachey was never swayed into overlooking his faults, in particular his withering lack of humour. Nor was he misled, as many critics have been, by the exterior frigidity of Milton's stern self-discipline, into supposing that he was a cold and passionless man. On the contrary, he maintained that, despite this formidable carapace, Milton was especially susceptible to women, and afraid of their terrible power over him. 'D'you know, I sometimes *hate* beauty', he once exclaimed to Sheppard (12 January 1907). 'I feel like Milton when he wrote Samson – "Yet beauty, though injurious, hath strange power." Oui, il y a des Dalilas dans ce monde que je ne pardonnerai jamais.' By means of several pertinent quotations, contrasting passages that vibrate almost unwillingly to the agitations of his heart with others emphasizing an austere, even cruel Puritan dogma, he shows us a Milton torn between his sensibility and his egotism. It is an interpretation at once percipient and convincing, by a critic who always felt that his own remote manner belied the inner strength and turmoil of his emotions.

But on the whole the quality of these reviews does not match those assembled in his collected volumes. Without the attractions of their delicately fashioned aesthetic unity, their studied brightness of phrase, or the absorbing cut and thrust of their narrative, the actual thought that these *Spectator* pieces contain is often revealed as rather commonplace. We learn, for example, that genius is not invariably popular; that great writing is frequently not recognized at once for its true worth; that to see performed on the stage some play of

41. *Spectator*, 101 (5 December 1908), 933–4.

which we have only a literary knowledge is interesting; that Shakespeare is the greatest of poets, and so on. The metaphors, most of which are culinary or architectural, are used unsparingly and, though decorative, seldom carry that original explorative quality which can catch and communicate the uniqueness of a particular book. His images are pleasing, but a little too vague and easy, so that (as words and similitudes become increasingly cheapened and abused) they have in many cases grown too quickly outworn, his recommendations at their worst seeming to resemble advertisement copy instead of positive criticism. Similarly, the analogies which he liked to draw between literature and music or painting – tragedy is a symphony, light comedy is a water-colour sketch, etc. – are facile rather than really illuminating. For to gain certain effects, Strachey tended to separate artificially the intrinsic literary elements of a great work, such as humour and tragedy, which are so essentially part of each other, and did not examine the peculiar composition in which they have been put together.

At other times, at first glance more surprisingly, Strachey is apt to sound a little pompous, as when, for instance, he explains that although literary digressions may be entertaining, they can never be instructive; or that the question of marriage is too serious a business to be treated in a light manner as Shaw does in *Getting Married*[42]. By the same token he almost always qualifies the word 'gaiety' with the epithet 'irresponsible'. But most of this earnestness may fairly be attributed to 'Spectatorial policy', and the dominating influence of St Loe. Every Tuesday morning Lytton called on St Loe at the *Spectator* offices where they discussed his next article. And very often St Loe would lay down the general lines he would like it to follow.

On the other hand Lytton does not, as in some of his other compositions, sacrifice what he believes to be true for what is over-emphatic – perhaps, in part, a consequence of writing anonymously. As a result, many of his personal opinions and feelings can be read more obviously from these

42. See 'Three New Plays', *Spectator*, 100 (13 June 1908).

Spectator reviews. For him, it appears, the past was not an illustration of the present, but a refuge from it, attracting him by virtue of its associations curiously remote from himself. So eager was he to dispel the shades of sombre Edwardian England, the ever-watching, ever-disapproving eyes of Mrs Grundy, that even the perusal of some old Elizabethan manuscripts in the illustrative appendix to one of the books he was given to review quickly evaporated the repressive gloom of his immediate surroundings. 'As one reads these dry and faded extracts, these preserved remnants of a vanished age,' he commented[43], 'the world of which they were a part seems to take shape and substance before the eye of the mind. An air of mysterious antiquity arises from them like the fumes from an alchemist's alembic; the reality of the present disappears; its place is taken by the phantasma of the past.'

One of Strachey's Bloomsbury concepts – the overwhelming value of original aesthetic unity, of 'significant form' – is almost parodied in a criticism he wrote on an exhibition of pictures at the New Gallery.[44] Noticing a painting that had inadvertently been hung the wrong way round, he describes the effect, with only partial irony, as follows: 'Two dancers seem to be flying upwards in impossible attitudes towards an impossible piece of scenery in mid-air. If the picture were turned round, the dancers would be brought back to earth and the scenery would take up its natural position at the side of the stage. But perhaps after all the change would be a mistake, for as the picture now hangs the lack of verisimilitude is almost compensated for by the curiosity of design.' This same aesthetic emphasis – where pattern is partly divorced from content and given priority over it – is reiterated through much of this literary criticism, where he often likens literature to the art of painting, as when, for example, he writes of the pastoral tradition of the Elizabethans: 'To borrow an

43. 'Shakespeare's Marriage', *Spectator*, 95 (29 July 1905), 153–4.
44. On the one or two occasions when Henry Strachey was ill, Lytton was jockeyed into doing an article on art criticism. These should not be taken too seriously as expressions of his own taste, for he usually went to the exhibitions with Duncan Grant and absorbed his views. See 'The International Society', *Spectator* 100 (18 January 1908), 97–8.

analogy from painting, Jonson's introduction of realism has destroyed the harmony of his tones.'

In addition to his rather unsystematic but wide reading, Strachey possessed a more negative virtue – the amazing lack of what E. M. Forster called 'pseudo-scholarship'. It was this honest and industrious quality, combined with good sense and a really deep love of French and English literature, that elevated his *Spectator* contributions well above the standard of other reviewers. To a large extent he reserves the full measure of his common sense for contemporary writers, indulging his auricular appreciation of fine writing more freely the further back the scene is set in the past. He is admirably sane, for example, when disavowing Professor John Churton Collins's contention that the merit of good poetry is to be weighed by its moral effects, and that the only real justification of poetry lies in its educative influence. After ridiculing the notion that one must, or could, compare the benefits of poetry with those of the birch-rod, and pointing out that, judged by such pragmatic standards, no great poetry ought to be pessimistic, he then gives expression to his own personal response to poetry: 'For it is not by its uses that poetry is to be justified or condemned. Its beauty and its goodness, like the beauty or the goodness of a human being, have a value of their own, a value which does not depend on their effects. We love poems, as we love fields and the rivers of England, and as we love our friends, not for the pleasure which they may bring us, nor even the good they may do us, but for themselves.'[45]

This literary credo, which could hardly be improved on as a concise statement of Strachey's critical beliefs, is crucial to the understanding of all his writing, and goes some way to explaining why it is that these and his other literary essays have tended to be undervalued in comparison with his purely biographical work. Unlike his biographies, his criticism is not, on the whole, polemical, but impressionistic; and although it is sometimes more imaginative, it is also apt to be rather diluted of intellectual matter. In some of these essays there is

45. 'The Value of Poetry', *Spectator*, 97 (21 July 1906), 93–5.

not enough solid meat: they represent the hors d'oeuvre, as he would say, not the main dish.

A humanist by temperament, Lytton was very far from being a 'practical critic'. If asked what use great literature could be – and forced to reply – he might have given Coleridge's answer that it increases our range of understanding of ourselves, of other people, of our world; that it has the power of humanizing human beings, that it can revitalize the mind away from narrow prejudice, and magnify our sympathetic awareness. Literature and the arts offered Strachey a surcease from pain, protecting his senses from the atrophy of tedium, and opening up a more abundant avenue of imaginative existence which might lead away from his half-life of agonized self-scrutiny. In short, the arts were 'life-enhancing', not in the sense that they promoted good citizenship, but because they increased 'the pleasure which there is in life itself'. Such are, or can be, the benefits conferred on us by other people's books. But for the genuine creative writer – in whatever field of literature – the *effects* of writing are of secondary interest. It is not what one gets out of any art that is important, but what one puts into it. In this, the truest sense, literature is a culmination of life, concentrating and releasing our past experience, and divining that current of poetry which flows beneath all the whirlpools and waterfalls of our immediate joy, perplexity, sorrow. The purpose of literature, in so far as the word is applicable, is therefore to discover the truth. Not merely the objective, 'scientific' truth, but that residuum of happiness barely noticeable in the stress and discord of living, that aspect of reality which emerges from the relationship between the writer and his material – be it his own or other men's lives or work – an inner truth, refined and made subject to the laws of reason; something personal which rises to a universal yet still individual significance. All reasonable beings love truth; but it is not primarily a functional commodity. Rather it stands like a rock amid all the swirling eddies and passing torrents of our conflicting egotisms, and, being constant itself, promises something that does not pass away.

In order to account for the relative neglect shown to Strachey's critical essays in general, one must set against them those aesthetic standards and values which he upheld, the critical precepts that have emerged ever higher in the ascendant since his death. It is a popular misconception to believe that impressionistic criticism can only flourish in an atmosphere of ethical indifference. According to Desmond MacCarthy, Strachey was often moved in his writing by moral passion, but this was always controlled so as not to disrupt the artistic unity of his compositions. 'The public thought he was a frivolous and detached ironist,' MacCarthy wrote, 'but he was much more of a moralist. Only in writing he avoided carefully, for aesthetic reasons, the portentous frown of the earnest writer.'[46] And Clive Bell too observed: 'Like all moralists he had his standards, unlike most he kept his temper and was never self-righteous.'[47] Strachey had too much humour to be accepted as a moralist in the traditional sense; he never made any book the platform from which to pontificate on all manner of biologico-social activities. But he was of course a moralist in the sense that we all are: he held strong, sincerely-felt and reasoned opinions on fundamental and controversial topics, and he believed passionately in certain qualities in human nature. In our critical jargon none of this signifies very much. What matters, and what is beyond dispute, is that he was not an *Arnoldian* moralistic critic. And in this obvious fact lies much of the cause for his neglect in this branch of writing.

Strachey died in 1932, the same year as *Scrutiny*, that organ of the new criticism, was founded.[48] Since that time the task of formulating modern critical principles has been increasingly taken over by dons and teachers of the English language, who have developed the kind of dogma propounded as early

46. See 'Lytton Strachey and the Art of Biography', in *Memories*, 31–49.
47. *Old Friends*, p. 32.
48. In a review of *Characters and Commentaries* which appeared in *Scrutiny*, Vol. II, No. 3 (December 1933), T. R. Barnes dismissed Lytton Strachey's literary criticism as nothing more than a string of epithets, and described his prose style as a tasty pastiche, a skilfully sentimental compact of snobbery and querulous inferiority feelings. '[Lytton

as 1906 by Professor John Churton Collins.[49] These men have felt strongly that in this age of unprecedented scientific progress, literature was in danger of becoming regarded as a thing of the past, a quaint relic of some defunct and antique civilization, without any place in the modern world. This danger was, for the professional and academic literary disseminator, a very real one: it threatened to affect his job, his prestige and his position in society. To avoid the risk of humiliating redundancy – in inverse proportion to the expanding

---

Strachey's] success among the "middlebrow" public was, I think, based on the fact that Strachey competently and directly, with judicious subtlety, and appropriately Freudian and free-thinking reasoning, appealed to that desire for fantasy satisfaction through "characters" or substitute lives, which is the basis of commercial fiction. His attitude flattered post-war up-to-date mechanized amoralism. ... His formula was the familiar Metro-Goldwyn-Mayer heart-throb and mirthquake one. ... Always the patina, not the form excites him. ... But more surprisingly, he has a following. Though Sitwellism is no longer *chic*, Strachey is an influence in life as well as in letters; he set a tone which still dominates certain areas of the highbrow world – e.g. that part of Bloomsbury which has a well-known annex in Cambridge. The deterioration and collapse represented by Mrs Woolf's latest phase (*Orlando, Common Reader 2nd Series, Flush*) is one of the most pernicious effects of this environment.'

49. John Churton Collins (1848–1908), who had been at Balliol College, was bitterly disappointed at having failed to secure the Merton Professorship of English at Oxford. A teacher of Greek and English literature at W. P. Scoones's coaching establishment, he soon made himself into a much-feared literary reviewer, the scourge of the late Victorians. He was also a keen amateur student of criminology, and incorporated some astringent police methods into his criticism. One of his favourite targets was Sir Edmund Gosse, then Clerk Professor of English literature at Cambridge. 'What has embittered Mr Collins against me, I cannot imagine', complained another of his victims, John Addington Symonds. '... Do you observe how a creature like Churton Collins omits in his review all real discussion of the material in books, confining himself to the one object of carping, sneering and personal insult?' Collins always strenuously denied being a spiteful or malicious critic. His literary censure, he claimed, implied no personal animosity, but was a means of upholding true scholarship and accuracy. Lytton, it appears, was generally sympathetic to Collins. After reading his *Ephemera Critica,* he wrote to Lady Strachey (2 May 1901): 'It is vigorous enough and also amusing, and I really hardly think exaggerated or unnecessarily enraged.' In 1904, Collins was appointed Professor of English at the University of Birmingham. Four years later he was drowned at Oulton Broad near Lowestoft.

authority of his scientific colleagues – he had to advertise literature as a craft with a future, with new frontiers to cross. Much dead wood from the past had to be eliminated; the study of English had to be brought up to date, given a new look – a practical function in a practical world. The benefits of literature as thought of by Coleridge and Strachey were at best too insubstantial to recapture the interest of a materially minded population. Other less romantic slogans had to be adopted and drilled into the students. With this object in mind they cultivated and improved on the original precepts of Matthew Arnold – himself, of course, a schools inspector and son of a headmaster – gearing it up to keep abreast with scientific advancement.

By these means they attempted, and still attempt, to foist literature on the community as a National Moral Health Service, essential to the proper evolution of society. Science may provide its power, but only with modern, new-look literacy can one settle the direction in which it should travel. Only thus, it was felt, could the literary educationist command the respect of the scientist. In fact, however, the dictatorial, poker-faced, rigidly exclusive dogmas which have been propounded especially under the dynamic management of Dr F. R. Leavis,[50] amounted at worst – and increasingly as time went on – to a vote of no confidence in the real afflatus of literature. Dressed up on the shelf as a revolutionary wonder-drug, providing stimulating new disciplines, it is bound eventually to lose out to the scientific range of products. And

50. In the 70th Foundation Oration at University College, London (March 1966), Lord Annan compared the influence of the Bloomsbury Group on the generation which followed the 1914–18 war with that of Dr F. R. Leavis after the 1939–45 war. The Bloomsbury Group took Voltaire and Hume as their models and never lost an adolescent delight in shocking people. They thought the artist laboured under only one obligation, the duty to express himself. Their first commandment was a respect for the integrity and happiness of other people. While they came from the upper-middle class, Dr Leavis was the son of a small Cambridge businessman, a vigorous rationalist and a republican. Most of his followers, the detractors of Bloomsbury, came from the same background as himself, but 'he [Leavis] has an eagle eye for anyone who wants to join the bandwagon and even the devout are snubbed'.

why, after all, should the so-called two cultures be combined either in collaboration or in rivalry? – you cannot harness a steam-roller and a gazelle together and look for a multiplication of horsepower. The one attempt leads only to the most flatulent banalities; and under the futile influence of the other in the form of cut-throat literary criticism, the springs of modern literature have, if anything, been weakened, its imaginative purpose degenerated and funnelled down from 'life-enhancement' into a single, monotonous paean of paranoiac self-importance.

In all this modernizing, Strachey's contribution to literary criticism has played no part at all, since it is not a branch of schoolmastering, but of the old-fashioned humanities. He is, in fact, more of a critical essayist than a critic pure and simple. Consider, for example, his views on Shakespeare. From his 'Shakespeare's Final Period' to 'Othello', an unfinished paper on which he was working at the time of his death, he produced a far greater volume of criticism on Shakespeare than on anyone else. But he was, in fact, a sounder critic of Shakespearian commentators than of Shakespeare himself, whose poetry liberated in him emotions too vast and universal to be coaxed into words and reduced to a neatly contrived essay. He is, on the other hand, adroit in using other critics' commentaries as a foil to sharpen up his own sensible opinions about Shakespeare, before launching into his sometimes rather watery impressionistic appreciation. He argues well, for instance, against Sir Sidney Lee's assertion that the sonnets, far from being the outcome of any intense emotion, were merely literary exercises addressed formally to his patron, the Earl of Southampton.[51] After quoting some instances of the emotional tone which dominates this entire series of sonnets, Strachey then proceeds to offer his own reasons for preferring William Herbert, Earl of Pembroke, as the person to whom they were written. He could feel the thrill of literary detective work, and the emotions of those who set out at length to establish the true identity of Mr W.H., yet his common sense was not to be over-persuaded,

51. 'Mr Lee on Shakespeare', *Spectator*, 97 (1 December 1906), 887–8.

and he reminds us that the 'enjoyment of Shakespeare's sonnets need not – fortunately enough! – wait on our unravelment of the mystery of "W.H." '

Mystery, however, always added a certain spice to his literary compositions. From the dozen articles which he wrote on Shakespeare for the *Spectator*, it is evident that, quite aside from the pure and miraculous melodies of Shakespeare's poetry, Lytton was attracted partly by the lack of firm biographical data surrounding the subject (which conferred upon it a touch of magic that made absolute the divorce of art from day-to-day living), and partly by the immense complexity and passionate force of Shakespeare's genius, which brought with it a sweet eclipse to Lytton's own unhappy and debilitated self-consciousness.

Most writers tend to be unreliable judges of the work of their contemporaries, which they relate too intimately with their own. Yet since even the wildest aberrations of the creative man – Tolstoy on Shakespeare, for example – are often of more interest than the reasoned and better proportioned views of less exceptional men, what Lytton had to say on the poets and playwrights of his day would in any case be worth recording. Because his love of literature was fastidiously partitioned off from the present, he was apt to evaluate the work of contemporary poets by rather settled and unadventurous standards. Rudyard Kipling was the only modern writer of verse whose genius he considered to be indisputable. All the other celebrated poets, Austin Dobson, Edmund Gosse, Herbert Trench, lacked inspiration.[52] He was excessively bored, too, on one occasion at Arnold Bennett's house, where he was mercilessly subjected to a recitation by Edith Sitwell of some passages from her versifying, which he dismissed as 'absurd stuff'. He also found the long, over-ambitious fiction of Thomas Hardy terribly tedious, and much preferred the condensation of his poetry, with its unromantic sobriety, its bitter speculation and appealing undertow of regretful recollection. As for A. E. Housman, he was delightful of course, but he had narrowed his territory and 'was content to reign

52. See 'Modern Poetry', *Spectator*, 100 (18 April 1908), 622–3.

over a tiny kingdom'. Of J. C. Squire he thought nothing, and of Robert Nichols only a little more. About the earlier poems of T. S. Eliot his feelings were more mixed: he seems to have recognized a genuine poetic quality in them, but to have felt that they were still not to his taste. W. B. Yeats's poems he defined as 'romance in process of decomposition'.[53] Despite some Celtic charm and an obvious felicity of expression, the cumulative effect of Yeats's poetry was faint and rather innocuous. Lytton's final conclusion has about it something of the annihilating logic of Dr Johnson: 'The poem is not only completely divorced from the common facts of life, but its structure is essentially unreasonable, because it depends on no causal law, and thus the effect which it produces is singularly fragmentary and vague. It is full of beauties, but they are all unrelated, and slip out of one's grasp like unstrung pearls.' Much later Lytton was to meet Yeats as a fellow guest of Lady Ottoline Morrell. A photograph of them, taken in about 1923, shows them seated next to each other in garden chairs. Yeats, looking somewhat stout and business-like, appears absorbed in his own monologue, while Lytton, all beard and spectacles, is twisted round in his chair towards the poet, and wears an expression which conveys not so much an air of rapt attention, but the strain of trying to indicate such attention. Yet perhaps the impression of the camera is misleading, and they are discussing with animation the Wildean theory, which they seem to have shared, that life does not create form, but form life; that so long as the writer possesses a style he has something significant to say. One would like also to imagine them debating, with equal enthusiasm, the bizarre and highly strung individuality of Donne, whose hatred of the commonplace, whose love poems so ingeniously worked out with dialectical quibbling, and whose devotional verses full of rhetorical eccentricity, appealed so enormously to them both.

Apart from his unsigned book reviews, Lytton also contributed to the *Spectator* over a dozen theatrical reviews above the pseudonym 'Ignotus'. This appointment as dramatic critic was a high tribute to his skill and trustworthiness

53. 'Mr Yeats's Poetry', *Spectator*, 101 (17 October 1908), 588–9.

as a Spectatorial writer. 'The *Spectator*, in all its long history, had never printed an article on the theatre', James Strachey records.[54] 'But now, on 30 November 1907, the revolutionary step was taken. Very special measures had, of course, to be provided for blanketing the shock to vicarage nerves. The articles were to be signed *"Ignotus"*, to insulate them from editorial responsibility.' At the termination of the first of these articles, St Loe Strachey appended an explanatory note which reads as follows: 'We hope to publish from time to time papers by "Ignotus" dealing with the theatre, but we desire to take the opportunity of pointing out that the critic in question expresses his personal views, and that we are not to be held editorially responsible for his judgements. As long as the opinions given make "les honnêtes gens"[55] laugh or think, and are honest opinions honestly expressed, as unquestionably they will be, we shall be content to leave our readers to determine for themselves whether "Ignotus" distributes his praise or blame successfully.' In the long-winded tone of this exposition, one can understand clearly the essential difference between the sort of freedom permitted Lytton on the *Spectator* as opposed to that, say, of the *New Quarterly*. The type of periodical which needed to broadcast the exceptional circumstances of a contributor's written opinions coinciding with his actual thoughts irrespective of editorial policy was obviously far less congenial to his temperament.

54. The *Spectator* was not quite so bereft of theatrical notices as James Strachey suggested. Although Lytton was the paper's first dramatic critic, he was not the first contributor to appraise the contemporary theatre. In a letter to *The Times Literary Supplement* (31 December 1964), Robert H. Tener from the University of Alberta, Calgary, points out that 'during Richard Holt Hutton's editorship of the literary pages (1861–97) a number of non-professional critics reviewed current performances, for, right or wrong, the *Spectator* believed, according to a sub-leader of 22 June 1867, that "every cultivated man, with a love for dramatic literature, and no fettering relations with the theatres and leading performers, will give a better conception of the merits or demerits of any actor, or actress, or any piece", than would a professional critic'. Among these amateur critics of the stage were F. W. Myers, Oliver Elton, Frederick Wedmore, Wilfrid Ward, Meredith Townsend and Hutton himself.

55. This referred to a quotation from Molière in the article.

These theatrical reviews are marked by the same qualities of reason and insistence upon an 'attachment with the common facts of life' which characterize his criticisms of contemporary poets. His case, for example, against the establishment of a National Theatre[56] – that an element of officialdom might well stifle all independent effort, and that State control could so easily lead on to a dull uniformity – is very cogently argued. But his literary appreciation, on the whole, is less acute, so that his censure is usually of more value than his praise. He admired Harley Granville-Barker both as an actor and producer, but had little that was original to write about him.[57] His strictures on Beerbohm Tree and J. M. Barrie,[58] on the other hand, are revealing. Of the imaginative delicacy and pathos which Tree sometimes displayed in the delineation of straight romantic parts, and which so greatly impressed dramatic critics such as Max Beerbohm, Desmond MacCarthy and Bernard Shaw, Strachey has nothing to say. He missed, too, those moments of imaginative sympathy when Tree's metamorphic genius, in the words of his biographer Hesketh Pearson, 'transcended the art of acting and lifted the spectator out of the world of make-believe'. But almost certainly he was unlucky on the few occasions he saw him act, for Tree was a notoriously erratic performer. In any event, he dealt only with Tree's characteristic habit of clowning, accusing him, with some justice, of preferring what was stagy to the image of life itself, and describing him as a man obsessed with his audience – 'a great dumb-show actor, a master of pantomime', whose performances held one while they lasted, but left one with 'a feeling of flatness and barrenness, a feeling almost of dejection', once the curtain had come down.[59]

56. L'Art Administratif', *Spectator*, 99 (28 December 1907), 1093–4. Later collected in *Spectatorial Essays* (213–17). See also 'The Shakespeare Memorial', *Spectator*, 100 (23 May 1908), 820–21.
57. 'Mr Granville Barber' *Spectator*, 100 (28 March 1908), 499–500. Later collected in *Spectatorial Essays* (203–7).
58. See 'Mr Beerbohm Tree', *Spectator*, 100 (1 February 1908), 185–6. Later collected in *Spectatorial Essays* (194–7). And 'Mr Barrie's New Play', *Spectator*, 101 (26 September 1908).
59. Strong support for Lytton's denigration of Beerbohm Tree comes

Lytton diagnosed Tree's failure to produce a comprehensive impression as being due to his predilection for a succession of isolated, momentary effects, uncoordinated and contributing nothing to the inner consistency of the play: and he detected a similar failing in J. M. Barrie, upon whose grossly inflated dramatic reputation he poured a much-needed cold douche. In review of *What Every Woman Knows*, he described the progress of the event-plot as a 'succession of disconnected notes leaving an effect of emptiness'. He was not so taken in by the machine-made neatness of the play as to imagine that presentment of character was anything but indistinct. Nor was his mood sweetened by Barrie's excessive sentimentality, and he came to the conclusion that 'Mr Barrie is in reality a master in the art of theatrical bluffing'.

Strachey's period of employment with the *Spectator* was of much practical benefit to him. He was obliged to study many new biographies, and crystallized during this time his own views as to how, artistically, to reconstruct a person's life. He also gained in self-confidence, and was able to condense and refine his prose style. At the end of 1905 he had, for example, written: 'The splendours of triumphant art are often so dazzling as to blind us as to the actual detail of its qualities;

___

from James Strachey who, with what seems incredible fortitude, saw all his Shakespeare productions and a great many others. 'I'm astonished that you should have anything to say in favour of Tree. He was *appalling* in every respect. You should have *seen* his production of *Antony and Cleopatra*. Not thinking it fair that Cleopatra should monopolize such a large bit at the end of the play, he rearranged it so that both of them died in the same scene. But good heavens! his way of reciting Shakespeare! How on earth can you quote that remark by Hesketh Pearson! And Christ! you should have seen the final scene in the *Tempest*, with Caliban (Sir Herbert Tree) sitting by himself on a rock in gloomy despair – the hero of the play. The only thing he was any good at was pure melodrama – *A Man's Shadow* [adapted by Robert Buchanan from the French play *Roger la Honte*, and first produced in 1889 at the Haymarket Theatre] doubling the parts of the hero and the villain – most enjoyable.' In fairness to Tree, however, it must be pointed out that neither Lytton nor James Strachey have anything to say of his best parts – as Fagin, or Svengali, or Thackeray's Colonel Newcome, as Paragot in *The Beloved Vagabond*, or even as Beethoven in a dreadful play by René Fauchois. It was in parts such as these that he impressed his critics and fellow actors.

and it is only when we have coolly examined a bad imitation that we come to comprehend the hidden values of the original.' Three years later this same idea had been compressed in the columns of the *Spectator* to: 'It is only after a study of an imitation that we begin to understand the real qualities of an original.'[60]

There are many other illustrations of such simplification and improvement. At Cambridge, one of his aphorisms had run: 'It is the highest proof of the genius of Byron that he convinced the world that he was a poet.' More just and hardly less epigrammatic is an ordinary sentence which crops up in 'Andrew Marvell'[61]: 'In English, the most notorious example of a poet without style is Byron.' Throughout his *Spectator* reviews are scattered many similarly compact sentences which, if they do not always reveal any unsuspected profundity that he did not exhibit already at Trinity, do indicate a natural tightening up of his style:

'The surest test of the eminence of a poet is the number and variety of literary dogmas which he sets at nought.'

'Nothing can be vainer than promiscuous praise.'

'It is difficult to decide which is the most remarkable thing about Napoleon – his generalship or his lack of humour.'

'The fun of a parody often lies simply in its likeness to the original.'

'A beautiful country is like a beautiful woman – none the worse for a veil.'

(Of Voltaire): 'The most consummate of artists, dancing in a vacuum on the tightrope of his own wit.'

'Laughter is the expression of a simple emotion; but a smile (no less than a tear) is an intellectual thing.'

'The basis of all true comedy is ethical.'

(Of Coleridge as a philosopher): 'He speculated too much and thought too little.'

(Of Chaucer): 'A page or two of his writings will no more contain the true significance of his work than a bucket of sea-water the strength and glory of the sea.'

Although surprisingly few of Strachey's sentences, as

60. 'Elizabethanism', *Spectator*, 100 (8 February 1908), 213–14.
61. *Spectator*, 96 (14 April 1906), 582–3.

George Carver has observed, 'are detachable as aphorisms or quotations of a wider implication', his writing, as it matured, gives increasingly the impression of an uninterrupted flow of intimacy, wit and effortless imagery. In the leisurely atmosphere of Cambridge he had been too preoccupied with the morbid abstractions of stylization, with the result that his prose sometimes becomes too languid and self-conscious. But now, when turning out hebdomadal reviews for the *Spectator*, he found that he no longer had time or space for overelaborate convolutions. The pace and immediacy which were injected into his pieces did much to liberate him from a self-imposed enslavement to extended similitude and metaphor. For the most part his images, such as the one about Chaucer, gained in effect by their greater directness. By 1910, when he was preparing to start work on his first book, *Landmarks in French Literature*, he had learnt to manipulate his prose with such enviable skill that, with the minimum amount of effort, the reader could receive at once the exact nuance of meaning that he wished to convey.

4

END AS A JOURNEYMAN

'It is many years since he wrote for us,' the *Spectator* said of Lytton Strachey on his death in 1932, 'but we remember with some pride his early literary criticisms, particularly of French literature, that appeared in the *Spectator*.' As with most obituary appreciations of the newly dead, the impression given here of Lytton's special relationship with the *Spectator* is misleading. For although St Loe Strachey was highly delighted with his cousin's contributions, their relationship was uneasy, while Lytton's own feelings as a member of the paper's staff became increasingly dissatisfied.

With the exception of 'A Russian Humorist', a paper on Dostoyevsky which was the last of his criticisms to appear in the *Spectator*, and which was later included by James Strachey in the posthumously assembled *Characters and Com-*

mentaries and *Literary Essays*, none of these *Spectator* pieces were reproduced in his volumes of collected essays. 'I've got a huge box full of *Spectator* reviews – 2 columns I wrote every week for a year and a half', Lytton wrote to Lady Ottoline Morrell on 18 March 1912. 'I've sometimes had thoughts of collecting the least offensive and trying to have them published in a volume. But I'm afraid it would mean touching them up again, which would be a great bore. I wish I had some faithful acolyte who'd do it for me.' Though it was sometimes suggested to him after the publication of *Eminent Victorians* that he ought to make such a collection, he always put it off.[62] He was well aware that a number of these essays contained, almost word for word, repetitions of metaphor and idea, hardly detectable in the continuing stream of periodical writing, but heavily accentuated, of course, when bound together in a single volume. Besides which, he sometimes used these unsigned reviews as germs for longer, more elaborately constructed essays. His 'French Poetry' (December 1907), for example, acted as the starting point for his celebrated essay 'Racine', in the *New Quarterly* six months later. Many of his other contributions dealing with French literature were to reappear at least in substance and with many delightful variations and additions in *Landmarks in French Literature*; while the gist of several others again – on the Elizabethans, on Carlyle, Macaulay, Pope and Shakespeare – can be found elsewhere. There was, to Lytton's mind, little additional prestige to be gained from reissuing in a more durable form what sometimes amounted to hardly more than an echo of his other writings. By the time he was famous enough to make this selection of essay-reviews an attractive publishing venture, he was no longer in urgent need of money, the lack of which had provided the original occasion for their composition. As for the dramatic criticisms of 'Ignotus', they would perhaps never be worth resurrecting, since, as he him-

62. In the autumn of 1964, James Strachey brought out *Spectatorial Essays*, a volume containing thirty-five of Lytton's contributions to the *Spectator*. Deliberately, this selection was not just a compilation of the best of Lytton's essay-reviews, but the most representative.

self wrote of A. B. Walkley's *Drama and Life*, 'there is no form of literature more apt to be ephemeral than the review of a theatrical performance written for the daily press'.[63]

Then there were other considerations too which weighed in his mind. The reviews he penned each weary week for the *Spectator* recalled to him not simply the drudge of repetitive literary hack work, but a whole period of his career that seemed to hold more misery than happiness and almost no prospects of personal advancement. These Spectatorial essays symbolized his failure to create a completely independent way of life, and reflected back his prolonged reliance on his family, from whom, he knew, he must break free if he were to enjoy life fully and develop his literary talent to anything like its real potential. Frustration mounted within him to an almost unbearable tension as he laboured week after week at articles that were promptly dispatched and circulated among those hundreds of eager country clergymen. The incongruity between himself and his readers was too preposterous, hardly to be endured. If only the circulation figures had *dropped* while he was taken on the reviewing staff, that at least would have been something. But no, they actually increased! What was happening to him? Possibly, though, it was fortunate that he so seldom had the opportunity for doing more than 'bringing out' an author, of realizing his strong points and enabling him to display himself at his very best. It was an arduous enough task, but one that never approached the final criticism which must discriminate accurately and comprehensively between an author's grain and chaff. After so much time spent picking out only the grain, it was not surprising that after he broke free from the *Spectator*, he should eventually write a book, *Eminent Victorians*, which laid such refreshing emphasis on the chaff in human nature.

As editor of the *Spectator*, St Loe Strachey did not actively interfere with his cousin's compositions to any significant extent, yet it was tacitly assumed by him, as by most subscribers, that the literary section of the paper should consist

63. 'Mr Walkley on the Drama', *Spectator*, 99 (16 November 1907), 776–7.

of a coordinated series of articles planned to reinforce, wherever practicable, the political opinions which were expressed in the main body of the paper. St Loe's son, the late John Strachey, told the present author that 'my father always said he [Lytton] was the one reviewer he ever had in whose work he never altered a word'. But James Strachey remembered having seen a few small editorial alterations on Lytton's typescripts. If such interventions were seldom called for, it was largely due to the form of pre-censorship that Lytton himself adopted. The situation with which he had to contend has been described by James Strachey, who for six years worked as St Loe's private secretary. 'Numbers of contributors called on him [St Loe] in the early part of each week: leader-writers (Harold Cox, the economist, John Buchan, the unknown journalist), Eric Parker, who wrote the nature article, the clergyman who wrote the weekly sermon, and, later in the week, the various reviewers. To all of these, indifferently, the same treatment was applied. St Loe was a tremendously fluent talker, producing floods of remarkable ideas and amusing anecdotes – many of which would have startled the vicarages. These he poured over the heads of his visitors at top speed, interlaced with detailed instructions about what was to be written in the leader, the sermon or the review concerned. The visitors had hardly a moment for breathing before they were whirled out of the room. But this was not all. On Thursday afternoons, silent, perhaps, for the first time in the week, St Loe sat back comfortably in a chintz-covered armchair with a pencil in his hand, and read through the galley proofs of the whole of the forthcoming issue. He altered a word here and there, he scribbled a fresh sentence in the margin, he struck out a whole paragraph and replaced it by one of his own.'[64]

These most drastic intrusions were never necessary with Lytton's reviews, yet some of St Loe's unmistakable editorial first person plurals do occasionally crop up, and his unseen influence and guiding hand is discernible in a few of these pieces – 'William Barnes', for example; and 'America in Profile', in which Lytton launches on an unconvincing eulogy

64. Preface to *Spectatorial Essays.*

of the United States; and again in 'Bacon as a Man of Letters'; and 'The Grandiloquence of Wordsworth', a typically Spectatorial title.[65] The most blatant example of St Loe Strachey's own opinions obtruding into an article retrospectively attributed to Lytton is 'The Prose Style of Men of Action', a subleader which they may in fact have written in collaboration.[66] After a chronological description of the enthralling and stately sentences of Elizabeth and of Essex, the 'stupendous power' of Cromwell, the 'charm and force' of Lincoln, 'the splendid trenchancy' of Clive, and the 'swelling and romantic utterance' of Warren Hastings, the piece concludes that men of action make better writers than men of letters. No mere scribbler, working from hearsay, could ever hope to compress into the printed page the spirit of such turbulent and splendid epochs. This lowly concept of the vocational writer in the hierarchy of worldly values was one of which St Loe was always firmly convinced. But Lytton, though he sometimes felt his own miserable inferiority to men of action – in something of the same romantic and frustrated fashion as Walter Scott – nevertheless had begun to rebel against this, and later, in 'The End of General Gordon' and elsewhere, attempted to turn the tables on them. This major change in his attitude was only completed after what he termed his 'Spiritual Revolution' in about 1911, before which, though he had no sympathy with St Loe's opinions on morals, religion or intellectual politics, he did share something of his undismayed, sentimental adulation of the Strachey family. This adulation, which again began to assert itself in his last years, was particularly potent in any matter with which his father had been personally connected, and perhaps its most direct expression is contained in a review of Colonel Sir G. J. Young-

65. 'The Poetry of William Barnes', *Spectator*, 102 (16 January 1909), 95–6. 'American in Profile', *Spectator*, 101 (25 July 1908), 132–3. 'Bacon as a Man of Letters', *Spectator*, 101 (24 October 1908), 621–2 and later collected in *Spectatorial Essays* (82–7). 'The Grandiloquence of Wordsworth', *Spectator*, 100 (9 May 1908), 746–7 and later collected in *Spectatorial Essays* (160–65).

66. Spectator, 100 (25 January 1908), 141–2.

husband's *The Story of the Guides*,[67] which shows that he was still under the spell of the history of British India – a history in which his own ancestors on both sides had played such a prominent part. For this reason, it is easy to exaggerate St Loe's influence over him as his 'secret collaborator'. In fact Lytton was never prevailed upon to write anything in which he did not believe. The pre-censorship he practised was not a perversion but a dilution of the truth; the mixture was less Lytton-and-St Loe than Lytton-and-water. And this restraint actually assisted his development as a mature writer, giving his hand an added cunning and sense of irony.

In the long run, however, the temperaments of Lytton and St Loe Strachey were bound to clash. St Loe was some twenty years older than Lytton, and his childhood at Sutton Court had been spent in what he called 'a *Spectator* atmosphere', regaled by anecdotes of Clive – 'the Patron saint of the family' – by stories of the American Civil War, and by the recapitulated exploits of countless Stracheys who had mingled with the mighty. In 1898, at the age of thirty-eight, he became the sole editor and proprietor of the *Spectator*. From this time onwards the paper was to be the central pivot of his life.

In the last quarter of the nineteenth century there had been a close tie between the Strachey family and the *Spectator*; and during St Loe's editorship this connection had been drawn even closer, so that no less than ten Stracheys were numbered among its contributors. This was a result of the particular pride which St Loe took in his heritage. He saw his paper as 'the watch dog of the nation', a means by which to strengthen the British Empire, that very bulwark of all that was finest in modern civilization. And he was equally determined that the Strachey family, which could boast of such magnificent historical associations in the past, should continue to take its place in the shaping of British political policy and cultural environment. Consequently his own strong opinions were transparently reflected in each issue of the paper. Being a man of great energy, he never allowed, we are told, 'the slightest

67. 'The Guides', *Spectator*, 101 (15 August 1908), 232. Later collected in *Spectatorial Essays* (46–52).

news item to find its way into the *Spectator* without first dominating it with his own mind and fixing upon it the special impress of his own character. As many have said, he *was* the *Spectator* for more than twenty-five years.'

This, then, was the peculiar atmosphere that St Loe had established by the time he took Lytton on to his reviewing staff, an atmosphere which united so much that Lytton, in his bid for liberty, had hoped to leave behind him. There were, however, no arguments, no outward show of irritation or hostility between the two cousins while they were working together, and perhaps the best indication of the marked if latent incompatibility between them is to be found in that final essay of *Eminent Victorians*, that account of 'The End of General Gordon', with its distinctive portrait of Sir Evelyn Baring.

Sir Evelyn Baring, or Lord Cromer as he became, had been a colleague of Lytton's father and of his uncle, Sir John Strachey, on the India Council. But by far his most intimate friend among the Stracheys was St Loe. 'I had a regard for him,' confessed St Loe, 'and for his wise, stimulating mind which touches the point of veneration.' And it is no surprise to find that in St Loe's autobiography, *The Adventure of Living*, Cromer is placed first in a chapter entitled 'Five Great Men' – all of whom, of course, were soldiers or statesmen. The extent of St Loe's veneration may be measured by the fact that, while his elder son was christened Thomas Clive, his second was named Evelyn John St Loe after Sir Evelyn Baring, who was also his godfather.[68]

For Lytton the name of Evelyn Baring came to represent that part of his inheritance which he was most determined to shed. Baring was a reviewer for the *Spectator* at about the same time as himself, and, ironically, they were bracketed together by St Loe as the two most brilliant critics in his employment.

---

68. Evelyn John St Loe Strachey (1901–64), who preferred to be known as John Strachey. He was Minister of Food and Secretary of State for War in the Labour Cabinet of 1945–51. A political economist, he was the author of several brilliant books on the theory and practice of socialism, including *The Coming Struggle for Power*.

Baring, we are told, took immense trouble to understand the *Spectator* point of view, and to submit to St Loe nothing that might prove distasteful. But since his outlook, unlike Strachey's, was already remarkably similar to his editor's, there was really little enough need for such trouble.[69] 'We wanted the same good causes to win, and we wanted to frustrate the same evil projects', wrote St Loe. 'In public affairs we agreed not only to what was injurious and to what was sound, but, which is far more important, we agreed to what was *possible*.' When Lord Cromer died in 1917, the year before *Eminent Victorians* was published, St Loe composed a long obituary notice of him, which opened with a characteristically generous and provocative challenge: 'The British people may be stupid, but they know a man when they see him. That is why for the last thirty years they have honoured Lord Cromer.'

St Loe was not to know that while he was penning this tribute to the man whose attitude was so similar to his own, his cousin was already taking up his challenge and drawing a pen-portrait of Lord Cromer that must surely rank among the coldest and most hostile in the whole gallery of his work. This portrait appeared in print the following spring, and a summary of it, fairly recording the part which Sir Evelyn Baring is given to play in 'The End of General Gordon', will, by direct implication, reveal some of those differences that Lytton and St Loe had for so long concealed under a politely non-committal front:

'When he [Sir Evelyn Baring] spoke, he felt no temptation to express everything that was in his mind. In all he did, he was cautious, measured, unimpeachably correct. It would be difficult to think of a man more completely the antithesis of Gordon. His temperament, all in monochrome, touched in with cold blues and indecisive greys, was eminently un-

69. It should be noted that, although in political opinions Cromer and St Loe Strachey were practically identical, their personalities were totally dissimilar. Cromer was a cautious, reserved, methodical man; St Loe a frantically wild character, whose chimerical schemes – the hundred-pound cottage, the National Reserve, the Referendum Bill – were proverbial. Cromer could never have fabricated such schemes, all of which, from the very start, were doomed to failure.

romantic. He had a steely colourlessness, and a steely pliability, and a steely strength.... His life's work had in it an element of paradox. It was passed entirely in the East; and the East meant very little to him; he took no interest in it. It was something to be looked after. It was also a convenient field for the talents of Sir Evelyn Baring. Yet it must not be supposed that he was cynical; perhaps he was not quite great enough for that. He looked forward to a pleasant retirement – a country place – some literary recreations.... His ambition can be stated in a single phrase; it was, to become an institution; and he achieved it. No doubt, too, he deserved it.'

Set in its true biographical context, this passage may be taken as an affirmation of the precarious new freedom that, in the war years, Lytton had finally managed to secure for himself, an independence, financial and emotional, from the dead trappings of his family. His attitude towards his family had for long been very ambivalent, and was to remain so, with several lurches one way or the other, till the end of his life. St Loe he always regarded as belonging to the other side of the family – the Sutton Court Stracheys,[70] who, to his mind, never had the true Strachey character at all. So far as religion was concerned, he frankly despised their ways and the ways of the *Spectator* – as, for example, his 'Colloquies of Senrab' shows. His political and social opinions, however, were only now shaping themselves, and turning against the Spectatorial St Loe. Like much in *Eminent Victorians,* the caricature of Evelyn Baring as a totally orthodox, passionless and insensate being, was intended to sting into anger those militaristic bigots whom he associated with the Spectatorial régime. At the same time he was still fond of St Loe, who had always been kind to him, and who had a quite special affection for his mother. Nevertheless, St Loe's public personality was Spectatorial, and Lytton must have written on Baring with the editor of the *Spectator* very much in mind. Thus, there was a complete and quite unrealistic division in his feelings. He did not wish to

70. The senior branch of the family, whose ancestral home was at Sutton Court, Somerset. For an exhaustive account of the Strachey family see Charles Richard Sanders's *The Strachey Family 1558–1932* (Duke University Press, 1953).

offend his cousin personally; yet unless he retaliated, Lytton knew that his onslaught had not been really effective. If he had written really well, St Loe could not ignore it.

And so it turned out. After some weeks of stunned silence, St Loe was moved to inform Lady Strachey that the *Spectator* felt a moral duty to attack her son's clever but unfair book. Lytton was at once relieved and concerned. 'As you say,' he wrote to his mother (5 June 1918), 'it's really surprising that there have been no attacks to speak of. I was beginning to feel rather uneasy, but I am reassured by your news of the *Spectator*. This is certainly quite as it should be. I only hope that St Loe was not personally annoyed by my remarks on Lord Cromer.'

It is, however, wellnigh impossible to be annoyed *impersonally*. St Loe was closely identified with Lord Cromer, and his annoyance provided a sure test of the strength and point of Strachey's writing. The first notice taken of this hostile study by the *Spectator* was mild enough. A letter appeared in the correspondence columns, in which Maurice Baring stated that he wished 'to correct one or two errors of fact in this delicate impressionistic portrait'. He then went on to state that he had known Lord Cromer personally, that Lord Cromer *had* taken an interest in the East, that his retirement consisted of incessant work in London, and that he had looked forward only to what he could look back on, 'tireless devotion in the service of his country'.

But this, as it happened, was no more than an overture to the main offensive. The following week St Loe himself charged in with a letter of his own, in which his efforts to be as bland and courteous as Maurice Baring are almost totally expunged by the pressure of his outraged sensibilities. Lytton Strachey, he maintained, had launched a thoroughly ridiculous and ill-informed attack upon Lord Cromer. To say that he took no interest in the East was 'the most absurd and unpardonable blunder'. And he drove home his protest in language that verges on a spluttering incoherence: 'But it is impossible to follow Mr Lytton Strachey in his farrago of conventional unconventional misapprehensions of Lord

Cromer and his attitude. Instead of Lord Cromer being a kind of embalmed Bureaucrat, he possessed one of the most alert and least hidebound and least limited intelligences that I have ever encountered.'

More was to follow, for still, even after this outburst, St Loe could not leave the matter alone. Further letters of disagreement were printed, and then, nearly two months after the actual publication date of *Eminent Victorians*, the *Spectator* gave the book a leading review – described by St Loe as 'trenchant' – which again picked up the question of 'misstatements about Lord Cromer', of whose invaluable and public-spirited work Lytton Strachey had given no suggestion. After allowing that the four essays contained in the book all exhibited a quota of literary skill, the anonymous Spectatorial reviewer went on to point out other errors, if not of fact at least of interpretation of fact, and ended up by stating that the author was 'lacking a sense of responsibility for the truth of his historical portraits'.

To all this censure Lytton himself replied nothing, and indeed never contributed another word to the *Spectator* during the remainder of his life. It was, of course, a favourite literary technique of his to make use of a subsidiary character as a foil to the principal figure in his books and essays, and in this role, as the absolute antithesis of General Gordon, he had cast Sir Evelyn Baring. But in the particular selection of Baring to fulfil this part, and in the zeal which went towards dressing him up for it, Lytton may be said to have been flaunting his freshly won independence. Certainly St Loe appears to have taken the whole affair in a highly personal way. Only a grievous and acutely felt injury could have driven him to criticize so adversely and in public a fellow Strachey. Even four years later, in 1922 when his autobiography came out, he had not forgotten the matter, and he is obviously – though now only by implication – slighting his cousin when, in the course of summarizing Lord Cromer's attributes as a writer, he comments: 'He [Lord Cromer] gave "lively characters" of the men described, without being unduly literary or rhetorical. What fascinated me about these portraits, however, was that they were like the best literature, you felt that Cromer had never let himself be betrayed into an epigram, a telling stroke, or a melodramatic shadow in order to heighten the literary effect. The document was a real State Paper, and not a piece of imitation Tacitus or Saint-Simon.'

The interest of this episode is that it shows Lytton's break with his past, Spectatorial self to have been, for all its vigour and intensity, incomplete. In *Eminent Victorians* and elsewhere he did not openly attack his own family, but his family's friends and associates. Baring became the embodiment of the *Spectator*'s public policy, while St Loe he liked to think of as being in many ways far from Spectatorial. Had it not been for the war, perhaps there would have been no attack at all. For though, in peacetime, he had felt stifled by the monstrous regiment of relatives who, like himself, were connected with the paper, he had always taken what opportunities there were for sounding an individual note. But at the outbreak of war, sanity and forbearance were thrown out of the window, and Lytton's political views and those of Lord Cromer and St Loe Strachey, which the *Spectator* lost no chance of advocating each week, were in such total opposition that it became almost impossible for either side to consider the other's point of view with detachment. The *Spectator* proclaimed that there was a fundamental debility in the German mind, and a natural supremacy in the British. It refused to apologize for or feel ashamed of the hostilities between the two countries. Rather it rejoiced in the holocaust. Though entirely of Germany's making, the fight soon took on the aspect of a 'righteous war', in which Britain was undertaking to save the civilized world by replacing German militarism with benefits indistinguishable from those bestowed upon the colonies of the British Empire.

Lytton Strachey, of course, was a conscientious objector, as was his brother James, whose position as St Loe's private secretary became increasingly awkward. Eventually, early in December 1915, James was dismissed. 'Apparently he was not altogether surprised at what happened,' Lytton wrote to Dorothy Bussy (7 December 1915), 'as St Loe has been for months past saying in the Spec. that it was the duty of all employers to dismiss young men in their employment unless they joined the army. He at last told James that he could not continue to employ him consistently with these views. He was very polite and nervous, and they parted in quite a friendly way. It seems to have been inevitable, as St Loe is a conscriptionist, and James's opinion on that subject as on all others, are diametrically the opposite of his.'

Four days later, in a letter to Lady Strachey – 'Aunt Janie' – St Loe expressed something of the same sadness and inevitability. 'In the first place let me assure you that I have no sort of doubt about James's personal courage and good heart. He behaved throughout the whole transaction as I felt sure he would, like a Strachey and a gentleman. His first thought was not to embarrass me or to make me feel that I was doing anything brutal. He told me he recognized that the position had become impossible and unbearable and that I had no other course to take. I was very sorry to part with him for I like him very much, and I feel most awfully sorry for him in the position into which he has got himself, owing I fear, alas, to his sophisticated, socialistic point of view. I am afraid he is very unhappy, and it is dreadful to see that in a person one likes and not to be able to help them [*sic*]. I suppose I am a monster, but to me the notion that it is so dreadful to take human life, or indeed any life, seems so amazingly foolish that I get quite rabid and unjust about it. It is a commonplace to say so, but I feel sure James will grow out of it ... I do hope in the first place that he will keep quiet and not go and affiche his follies. I have good hopes that he may keep quiet, because, oddly enough, when he is as it were on the other side he begins to see all their stupidities and finds he cannot go with them. Now the rock-bed of his trouble is a sort of indecision and a sort of intellectual fastidiousness which makes him unable to take any course, and also, as you know, to admire anything.'

Lytton shared exactly James's 'sophisticated, socialistic point of view', his intellectual fastidiousness, his pacifism and pessimism over the war. He too did not wish to embarrass St Loe unnecessarily, and seems to have felt no personal antipathy for him despite the wide divergence of their opinions. But for all the diffidence, the nervous good manners, the clannish regret, the dissension between them ran deep. Lytton did not keep quiet, but threw off his indecisiveness and chose to ventilate his 'follies' in his work, the clash between St Loe and James and himself helping to act as a catalyst in the production of 'The End of General Gordon'. Yet even at this moment of utmost, wartime rebellion, at heart Lytton too still remained a 'Strachey and a gentleman'.

THREE

Landmarks in French and English Literature

'Can anything be more bitter than to be doomed to a life of literature and hot-water bottles, when one's a Pirate at heart?' *Lytton Strachey to George Mallory* (1913)

'I think it's usually better to sacrifice comprehensiveness to lucidity, especially in prose. One can only hope at best to say a part of what one thinks, and so one may as well make up one's mind to choose the part that's simple.' *Lytton Strachey to George Mallory* (25 September 1911)

1

LANDMARKS IN FRENCH LITERATURE

Landmarks in French Literature was published on 12 January 1912, as No. 35 in the Home University Library. Strachey's dedication of the book to 'J.M.S.', his mother, was particularly appropriate; for it was she who had initially fostered his interest in French writing and had provided him with something of an Anglo-French education. Despite a timid disinclination to speak the language, he had grown up to be 'one of those rare Englishmen', to use H. A. L. Fisher's words, 'who knew French from the inside'. Like his mother he was a true francophil. André Maurois, in a letter to the present author, emphasizes the relevance of this special twofold understanding in Strachey's interpretation to English audiences of typically French authors. *Landmarks in French Literature*, he writes, 'is a book I greatly admired because it said so much in so few pages. No other Englishman would have been able to write about Racine and, more generally, about French poets as Strachey did. As a rule French poetry is very little known in England because French, as a language, is not accentuated and therefore the rules of English prosody do not apply to French poets. Strachey had the mysterious power, and probably the taste, that enabled him to judge Racine, as a good French critic would. Of course, he was also a very good judge in French prose and had learned quite a lot from Voltaire.'

Strachey's deep and passionate enjoyment of the best French writing pulses through every page of this book. There are passages where his personal nostalgia swells up and sweeps away the balanced critical and documentary framework in which they are set. His sense of historical realism is buried beneath a layer of sweet and undismayed prejudice. He was, for example, well aware of the terrifying atrocities committed in eighteenth-century France, but for him they were transfigured by the passing of time into a beautifully blended pattern in the rich tapestry of the era. The same process of idealization is applied to the age of Louis XIV; and, remembering some halcyon days he had spent at Versailles with Duncan Grant, he depicts the palace as a memorial and grave of what had been the embodiment of a superhuman ideal – a strange, haunting cemetery, the majesty of which could still fill his imagination and stimulate his sentimental fancy. Envisaged thus, Versailles took on for him a personal significance, symbolizing the supernal aspirations and desolations of his own loves. Though he knew well enough the squalid intrigues of those times, he preferred to treat Versailles not as the emblem of degraded snobbery, but as a splendid and spiritual *tour de force*. Across the centuries he felt the thrill of old, untold adventures:

The fact that the conception of society which made Versailles possible was narrow and unjust must not blind us to the real nobility and the real glory which it brought into being. It is true that behind and beyond the radiance of Louis and his courtiers lay the dark abyss of an impoverished France, a ruined peasantry, a whole system of intolerance, and privilege, and maladministration; yet it is none the less true that the radiance was a genuine radiance – no false and feeble glitter, but the warm, brilliant, intense illumination thrown out by the glow of a nation's life. That life, with all it meant to those who lived it, has long since vanished from the earth – preserved to us now only in the pages of its poets, or strangely shadowed forth to the traveller in the illimitable desolation of Versailles. That it has gone so utterly is no doubt, on the whole, a cause for rejoicing; but, as we look back upon it, we may still feel something of the old enchantment, and feel it, perhaps, the more keenly for its strangeness – its dissimilarity to the experiences of our own days. We shall catch glimpses of a world of pomp and brilliance, of ceremony and decoration, a small, vital passionate world which has clothed itself in ordered beauty, learnt a fine way of easy, splendid living, and come under the spell of a devotion to what is, to us, no more than the gorgeous phantom of high imaginations – the divinity of a king. When the morning sun was up and the horn was sounding down the long avenues, who would not wish, if only in fancy, to join the glittering cavalcade where the young Louis led the hunt in the days of his opening glory? Later, we might linger on the endless terrace, to watch the great monarch, with his red heels and his golden snuff-box and his towering periwig, come out among his courtiers, or in some elaborate grotto applaud a ballet by Molière. When night fell there would be dancing and music in the gallery blazing with a thousand looking-glasses, or masquerades and feasting in the gardens, with the torches throwing strange shadows among the trees trimmed into artificial figures, and gay lords and proud ladies conversing together under the stars.[1]

Landmarks in French Literature is disposed in seven chapters, each one scoring the crescendo and diminuendo of a separate epoch and literary movement. As he charts each individual landmark, pin-points it and neatly connects it with what is destined to succeed, Strachey weaves a graceful series of literary-historical contours that give the book its cohesive texture. The pattern is simple but immediately effective. In every chapter he erects a temple at which to worship; and then, after the architectural climax has been reached, introduces a figure who opposes the foregoing *Zeitgeist* and

1. Logan Pearsall Smith, who had a great admiration for Lytton's writing – especially his critical writing – used to recall this passage as being especially fine. But when in 1944 he looked it up again, his admiration wilted a little. 'What intolerable clichés!' he exclaimed to Robert Gathorne-Hardy. 'Let's rewrite the passage.' After a few minutes, however, of removing the worn-out expressions, they decided that the task was too formidable, and gave it up.

heralds the new emergent spirit of creation. By these means the link between one literary age and the next is drawn with fluency and eloquence. In the full blossoming of each flower one can detect that seed of decay, which, when transplanted under a fresh climate of thought and feeling, will burst into new, vigorous efflorescence. Of every writer he has something appreciative to say. The 'potent and melancholy voice' of Villon, which 'gave utterance in language of poignant beauty to the deepest sentiments' of the Middle Ages, gives way to the glamour of the Renaissance. 'The poems of Villon', Strachey explains, effecting a characteristically ornate transition between two chapters, 'produce the impression of some bleak, desolate landscape of snow-covered roofs and frozen streets, shut in by mists, and with a menacing shiver in the air. ... Then all at once the grey gloom lifts, and we are among the colours, the sunshine, and the bursting vitality of spring.'

To reduce and illustrate fairly the entire literature of a country within the compass of a short dissertation is a notoriously difficult undertaking. Closely following H. A. L. Fisher's preliminary advice, Strachey used J. W. Mackail's manual on *Latin Literature* as a model, his style being somewhat similar to Mackail's impressionistic prose – in those days much copied by students and, for that reason, much disparaged by academic teachers. The structure of his criticism makes no pretensions to originality, but it imposed a convenient neatness and unity of tone upon the book and conveyed the impression of constant development. The many merits which this skilful organization helps to bring out are freely displayed on almost every page. Above all else, his compression and terse, though never austere, economy of verbal description is, in many passages, quite masterly. At his best, Strachey conveys in the briefest possible space the peculiar charm of each author, the unique flavour of his work, the literary influences which he first inherited and later exerted, the teachings of the various critic-philosophers, the obsessive themes of the novelists, poets, dramatists. On the more academic side he also elucidates the particular prose style into which each successive movement infused its thoughts and emotions, the historical background from which it naturally evolved and against which it must be set, and the quality of enjoyment which its chief exponents can liberate in the sensitive twentieth-century reader. Although, inevitably, no one will find himself in exact agreement with all Strachey's canons – his contention, for example, that the pen portraits of Saint-Simon are never caricatures because 'his most malevolent exaggerations are yet so realistic that they carry conviction' is surely an unnecessary piece of special pleading – or applaud the omission of some French writers – the exclusion of Prosper Mérimée and Gérard de Nerval are certainly controversial – yet as an example of pure literary craftsmanship, *Landmarks in French Literature* could hardly be bettered.

Lingering over the writers whom he really loves, Strachey's style is at its most opulent. Though his criticism is never inept, his appreciation does occasionally become rather too fulsome. In places the writing grows overripe, loaded down with a profusion of high-sounding, ornamental adjectives and adverbs, not always very originally chosen. There are fewer obvious clichés than in the biographies, fewer calculated extravagances, and less straining after dramatic effect. Yet these characteristics are present, and tend to stand out more conspicuously in the less intimate, conversational tone of his literary criticism. The luxurious abundance of praise sometimes gets out of control, too, as when he writes of Voltaire that his 'prose is the final embodiment of the most characteristic qualities of the French genius. If all that that great nation had ever done or thought were abolished from the world, except a single sentence of Voltaire's, the essence of their achievement would have survived.' The reader profits little, also, on being informed that 'still waters run deep' or that 'it is so difficult to take the measure of a soul!'

Apart from several such blemishes, there is little really indiscriminate eulogy and no awkward exposition. The narrative contains not a single obscure sentence from beginning to end. Perhaps the most fitting tribute to the book as a work of fine aesthetic analysis came from the Cambridge critic A. Y.

Campbell, who summed up his opinion thus: 'In general style and conception it is the model of what a book in this kind of series should be; showing a sense of proportion both in its entire design and in the author's selection of what to discuss and what to discard; maintaining, on the whole, a singular freedom from prejudice; written (unlike many modern works) in excellent English; and above all absolutely clear.'

Amid so much that is near-perfect, it may seem a little un-gracious to complain at the general impact, which is sur-prisingly tame. Despite the marvellous skill of presentation, something solid is lacking in the book, something to get one's teeth into. Its leaves reflect the profuse colouring of tropical flowers no longer in their natural place of growth under the wind and rain and the hot glare of the sun, but removed and tastefully arranged as window-dressing in an over-heated exhibition room, where they are kept extant by phosphorescent lighting and artificial fertilizer. The real world is shut out; from behind the glass, the salesman gesticulates, and one receives the queer impression of being exhorted by a rhetorician without lungs. The book is supremely tidy and self-contained, and has the air of being almost embalmed. In scene after scene, the men of letters whom Strachey outlines pass before us like illuminated phantoms. They are not dead; nor are they quite alive; but something in between: they are asleep. Or perhaps it is we, the readers, who are sleeping, lulled by the seductive charm of Strachey's tranquil imagina-tion. The impression which this dreamlike panorama leaves upon the mind is of an elysium, serene and undisturbed.

In his essay upon Racine, Strachey had written: 'It is the business of a poet to break rules and to baffle expectation; and all the masterpieces in the world cannot make a pre-cedent.' *Landmarks in French Literature* is a very good but not a great book, since it achieves the difficult feat of obeying all the rules all the time. This was partly the result of following Mackail's *Latin Literature*, where he might equally have been guided by another volume brought out in the same series at the same time – Gilbert Murray's review of Greek literature. It does not possess anything like the same aesthetic balance and precision, but by its very incompleteness, by the positive assertions of dislikes and prejudices, even by its imperfections, Murray's book does in some respects gain. It is a more individual work, for the author's mind overflowed the mould in which it worked and touched life too closely to attain absolute flawlessness of form.

Strachey interpreted the development of literature through the ages as a constant struggle waged between the divergent traditions of the Classical and Romantic schools, and between the opposing forces of scepticism and mysticism. By means of this interpretation, he sought to achieve a complete synthesis within his book. But in his determination to steer a middle course, he sometimes sacrifices matter for shape. Something of this preference for 'significant form' is here and there reflected within his own criticism, as, for example, in the lengthy comparison between Racine's *Bérénice* and Shakespeare's *Antony and Cleopatra*. He admits the general superiority of *Antony and Cleopatra* – the principal characters are more interesting and more proud, and the whole catastrophe is more inevitable and complete – but at the same time he considers it inferior 'as a play'; that is to say, less distinguished by unity of tone and concentration of development. To A. Y. Campbell, who objected to this eclipsing preference for the classical structure, Strachey replied by letter (27 October 1913): 'The comparison with A & C was rather too dashing, I dare say.... What good tragedies are there in English, outside the Elizabethan drama? – I mean tragedies that are fit to act? – I can hardly think of any. The Wild Duck is a good tragedy, and is successful on the stage in England, but then of course it belongs to the Racine tradition (as far as form goes). Also it seems to support my case that the only really successful Shakespeare play is Othello – the only play of his which is almost classical in form.'

Elsewhere, though his fondness for classical writing is detectable, he is scrupulously impartial, putting one in mind of Oscar Wilde's observation that the only person who can appreciate all schools of art is an auctioneer. After generously conferring accolades of praise upon the Romantic writers, he is obliged to excel himself when turning his attention to the classicists, so that as this alternating sequence proceeds, the crescendo of applause at times grows deafening. This excess of approbation, which often does no more than roundly assert what he hopes the reaction of his reader will be to his more measured analysis, becomes increasingly exuberant when he deals with such favourites as Racine and Voltaire. He presents a superlatively good idea of the distinctive qualities of Racine's tragedy, but then weakens his argument by adducing an English parallel which, though apparently to Racine's advantage, is really quite misleading:

'Now and then, however, even in English literature, instances arise of the opposite – the Racinesque – method. In these lines of Wordsworth, for example:

> The silence that is in the starry sky,
> The sleep that is among the lonely hills –

there is no violent appeal, nothing surprising, nothing odd – only a direct and inevitable beauty; and such is the kind of effect which Racine is constantly producing.'

But Wordsworth's lines do not achieve a typical Racinesque effect; his virtues are of an altogether different quality. Indeed, the difference between the two poets is fundamental. Wordsworth was a visual writer, as the above lines show; whereas a simile or metaphor in Racine is never meant simply to be visualized – it is dramatic.

Later, when he comes to examine the novels of Victor Hugo and Balzac – to whose sonorous harmonies he seems a little unresponsive – Strachey must strain every nerve to be fair, and more than fair, so that they will not be put in the shade by the greater luminaries who have preceded them. The estimate of Victor Hugo is, in fact, far nearer the truth than were the unbalanced encomiums of Swinburne, to which it acted as a wholesome corrective. Even so, his partial dislike of Victor Hugo is evident. He is out of sympathy with his bombastic egotism and false pathos, his rodomontade and journalistic cant, his lack of humour and overplus of vanity, all of which were qualities essential to Hugo's genius. Strachey's letters reveal that he used occasionally to enjoy brief seasons of enthusiasm for Hugo at Cambridge, yet his appreciation in *Landmarks in French Literature* does not seem quite spontaneous – more a succession of carefully chosen compliments, written out of season. In the case of Balzac, he appears to suspend his powers of penetrative critical detachment, allowing himself to be swept off his feet by the sheer masculine vitality. 'The whole of France is crammed into his pages', he exclaims in rapture. Yet if this were really so, there would be only two types of person thriving in French civilization – frenzied demoniacs based on Balzac's idea of Napoleon, and village simpletons founded on Balzac's conception of Christ. By surrendering himself unconditionally to the passionate energy of Balzac's genius, Strachey lost the faculty for distinguishing between vitality and variety.

Where Strachey's comparisons grow more reckless, his language becomes correspondingly luscious and repetitive. One sees not a vision of the author fixed in the composition of his work, but a picture of Strachey himself absorbing it; and it is this echo rather than any vibrations set up by the original inspiration which chiefly communicates itself to us. On every page one is presented with an invitation to sensitive enjoyment as a fellow reader, but is given little clue as to the source and urgency of the creative process. And, since the personality of the authors whose work Strachey discusses is largely excluded from his criticism, several of the passages which express in a general way his own enjoyment of their writing are so similar that they could be exchanged without doing much violence to the sense. He delights, for instance, in the plays of Molière; and he delights equally in the fables of La Fontaine. Technically, both were masters of their art – though as writers they were, of course, quite dissimilar. Yet since Strachey admires them both, since his criticism of their workmanship is almost entirely impressionistic, since the praise he bestows on each of them is mainly conditioned by an imprecise pleasure in something perfectly executed, his writing is formalized into a kind of valueless metaphorical jargon. Of La Fontaine he writes: 'He is like one of those accomplished cooks in whose dishes, though the actual secret of their making remains a mystery, one can trace the ingredients which have gone to the concoction of the delicious whole. As one swallows the rare morsel, one can just perceive how, behind the scenes, the oil, the vinegar, the olive, the sprinkling of salt, the drop of lemon were successively added, and, at the critical moment, the simmering delicacy served up, done to a turn.' So much for La Fontaine. Previously, in a *Spectator* review of A. R. Waller's translation, *The Plays of Molière*,[2] Strachey had expressed something of the fascination and appeal which the French dramatist held for English audiences in the following words: 'To read one of his scenes is to watch some wonderful cook at work over a delicious dish – keeping it on the simmer while each savoury ingredient is dropped in: the oil, the olive, the salt – and then at the psychological moment whipping it off the fire, and setting it before you done to a turn.' In the intervening two or three years the style had grown more polished and the formula was exploited more thoroughly. Yet it remains little more than a long-winded manner of saying something which could be said – could almost be taken for granted – when considering very many of the finest creative writers.

It is only when he curtails these stereotyped metaphorical flights and mixes in some intellectual interpretation of his emotional response that the true individuality of La Fontaine and Molière emerges. 'La Fontaine's creatures', he writes, 'partake both of the nature of real animals and of human beings, and it is precisely in this dual character of theirs that their fascination lies. ... The creatures of La Fontaine's fantasy are not simple animals with the minds of human beings: they are something more complicated and amusing: they are animals with the minds which human beings would certainly have, if one could suppose them transformed into animals.' This is charming and acute comment, and probably as far as literary criticism can go without actual reference to La Fontaine himself. Strachey, however, sees him as little more than an ideal

2. *Spectator*, 99 (26 October 1907), 612–13 and later collected in *Spectatorial Essays* (121–6).

embodiment of the influence and character of the age in which he happened to live. 'In the nineteenth century', he writes, 'one can imagine him drifting among Paris cafés, pouring out his soul in a random lyric or two, and dying before his time.' Yet surely it was by his unique nature and not by contemporary influence that La Fontaine was spared from 'pouring out his soul'? It is difficult to believe that he was as malleable and feckless as Strachey makes out, for his peculiar literary gifts and pervading sense of humour were certainly quite foreign to the genius of Verlaine or Baudelaire.

In contrast to La Fontaine, Strachey sees Molière as a more universal than national figure, and his treatment is correspondingly freer. Equally unsentimental, Molière is presented as a darker, more substantial personality than La Fontaine, holding an exact balance between the egotisms of solitude and society. 'It is the more remote quality of his mind – his brooding melancholy, shot through with bitterness and doubt – that may at first sight escape the notice of the reader, and that will repay the deepest attention. His greatest works come near to tragedy.'

To achieve the aesthetic unity at which he is aiming, Strachey everywhere ties in his literary panorama with its historical background. It was the obvious method to adopt for a generic book like this, yet it has severe drawbacks. He provides us with a series of set-pieces, eloquent, dignified disquisitions, informative and well-balanced. The chapters are all admirably constructed, and interspersed with some very good critical passages. But though the words are so elegantly spun about, there is no live centre to them, since Strachey fails to relate his criticism to the lives and natures of the authors concerned. One is left to deduce from his treatment that their writing emanated from the social, cultural and political crosscurrents of the day. Amid all the talk of literary technique, of influences, effects and tendencies, the real character and impulse behind any poem or novel is lost from sight. He discusses almost every work as if it were a direct or indirect symptom of the times in which it was produced, not the fruit of certain individuals' experiences within those times; and in

139

failing to explain this, he passes over the quintessential quality of all literature.

For this weakness, the blame must partly be laid, of course, on the Home University Library. *Landmarks in French Literature* was, after all, intended as a textbook for students. Although it includes a large amount of material that was meant and felt very seriously, the volume was to some extent written as a pot-boiler. At the same time, Strachey's rather preconceived aesthetic theories were partly responsible for its limitations. Though, naturally, any work of art must by definition have form, this form should be engendered organically from within, not artificially applied like a strait-jacket. Nor need all artistic form be simple. The unblemished unity of *Landmarks in French Literature* is the result of a measured dilution of realism. The various works of literature as Strachey depicts them are not the creations of flesh-and-blood human beings, but magnificent appendages of some dressed-up props which are moved regularly across a shifting background of historical pageantry. Seen thus, they are deployed as convenient representations of the chameleon-like characteristics of the French national genius. Only now and then does some superabundant figure resist being assimilated into the overall pattern — Voltaire, for instance, to whom more pages are devoted than to anyone else. Here, as an exception to the general rule, we are given some biographical information. But Strachey is more eager to project a vivid surface-personality — 'curious', 'amazing', 'extraordinary', 'singular' — than to reconcile the diverse elements of his temperament. 'His character', Strachey writes, 'was composed of a strange amalgam of all the most contradictory elements in human nature, and it would be difficult to name a single virtue or a single vice which he did not possess. He was the most egotistical of mortals, and the most disinterested; he was graspingly avaricious, and profusely generous; he was treacherous, mischievous, frivolous, and mean, yet he was a firm friend and a true benefactor, yet he was profoundly serious and inspired by the noblest enthusiasms.'

Strachey knew well enough that if a man belongs altogether

to his own epoch, then he cannot speak with the greatest literary significance to later generations; he knew too that only the mannerisms of genius, in whatever sphere, can be inherited and passed on. But the pattern imposed, perhaps inevitably, upon this study of French literature forced him to emphasize these more ephemeral matters. Throughout the book Strachey frequently uses – and with evident relish – the word 'psychological'. Yet he employs little psychology himself, little of the expansiveness and subjective complexity of his new literary hero, Dostoyevsky. The connections which he draws between one writer and the next are more often ornamental or dramatic than really imaginative. This method of association could sometimes appear contradictory when set against the more matter-of-fact survey which he conducts. The charm of Versailles, viewed retrospectively from the distance of the eighteenth century, seems moribund, autocratic. The Age of Reason is then extolled, but only to be seen, even in its prime, as having been a dry, shrivelled-up husk, 'something thin, cold and insignificant', from the succeeding Age of Romance.

In his essay on Stendhal (January 1914)[3] Strachey wrote: 'Perhaps the best test of a man's intelligence is his capacity for making a summary.' Judged by this standard, Strachey's own intelligence is paramount. But, perhaps also, the best test of a man's imagination is his capacity for seeing connections between elements that at first sight appear to be unrelated. It is when evaluated by this standard that Strachey disappoints – a disappointment in this case largely due to the cramped and restrictive nature of the series for which he was writing. His criticism is of a kind which is constantly making the reader reflect that its author is exceedingly cultivated and skilful, but only comparatively seldom does it discover some unobvious truth. Like Sainte-Beuve, he did not set himself up as a judge but as an interpreter between the writer and his unknown public. Both were really biographical essayists rather than critics or thinkers, and, in playing all sides successively in the Classical–Romantic war, found imperfect sympathy with only

3. 'Henri Beyle', *Edinburgh Review*, 219 (January 1914), 35–52. Later collected in *Books and Characters* and *Literary Essays* (151–70).

the most extreme Romantics – such as Victor Hugo. Since they showed greater interest in personality than ideas and, though never tedious or obtuse, tended at their worst to dwindle into the gossipy, the trivial and the 'feminine', both gained something of a reputation for being rather catty old women-of-letters. But Sainte-Beuve always insisted that it was possible to understand a writer solely through knowing the man, a belief that Strachey himself put into practice only after *Landmarks in French Literature*.

Round the central unreality of this biographical void the more brilliant stars in his firmament cluster surely, serenely. *Landmarks in French Literature* teems with rewarding observations which bring us directly and easily in contact with an alert and ingenious mind. Today its distinction seems to lie less with Strachey's skill in phrasing – though this is impressive – than with his strain of perceptive and discriminating good sense. The most valuable passages are those where the intellectual content is not dwarfed into insignificance by the effusive impressionistic framework surrounding it, where the two divergent elements in his own nature hold an even balance. 'It is a measure of the quality of Strachey's little book', wrote J. G. Weightman in the 1969 edition, 'that it still remains one of the best introductions to the subject and that its emphasis, at least as regards works published up to 1850, have not on the whole been altered by subsequent discoveries or changes of taste.'

2

POLEMICS AND PROPAGANDA

The war altered fractionally the direction in which Strachey's writing had been developing, and hastened the speed of that development. By inciting as never before his anger, sorrow and contempt, it lent him a sort of Dutch courage that helped to transform the academic quietist into a subtle literary propagandist. The war also changed, if not his values, the immediate priority of those values. Friendship and aesthetic beauty might still be more important to him than political ethics, but, for the time being, the latter were more urgent.

This rearranged scale of precedence led to some apparent contradictions in his ideas, especially between those expressed in his published and private writings. He had always disliked, as we already know, the Post-Impressionism which infiltrated Bloomsbury; but he now nourished a far greater dislike for the principal calumniators of Post-Impressionism, the type of people who in peacetime had so often been spoiling for a fight, and who were now united in a lustful hymn to battle. In order to present an equally united body of opinion opposed to this heedless militarism, it was necessary, Strachey considered, to join up with people he did not readily like, and to associate himself with ideas that were not his own.

What had chiefly struck him about Post-Impressionism was its capacity for angering the opposition – mostly men and women of little intelligence who were unable to formulate their objections into coherent speech or account rationally for their inflamed sense of outrage. 'Pure pornography', 'admirably indecent' – such were some of the more appreciative comments which Strachey had overheard at the Second Post-Impressionist Exhibition. A year earlier, at the first exhibition (November 1910) organized by Roger Fry and Desmond MacCarthy at the Grafton Gallery and entitled 'Manet and the Post-Impressionists', the public reaction had been even stronger. 'The exhibition is either an extremely bad joke', wrote Wilfrid Blunt in his diary, 'or a swindle. I am inclined to think the latter, for there is no trace of humour in it.' Other visitors, however, saw it as purely humorous; and one gentleman laughed so loud that 'he had to be taken out and walked up and down in the fresh air for five minutes'. Never less than four hundred spectators turned up each day to be diverted, bemused or exasperated. As the storm of blustering abuse grew in volume so its tone became more vindictive. Respectable country gentlemen loudly reminded each other that Roger Fry's wife was in an asylum and predicted that it would not be long before he joined her. They prayed anxiously that he might be confined before too much irreparable mischief had been done to the country through subverting the morals of the young.

In the ordinary course of events Strachey never took to the extraordinarily chimerical views of Fry, who was a family friend, considerably older than most other members of the Bloomsbury Group, and in appearance even older than his age. The bushy black eyebrows, the spectacles through which he projected such magnified visual organs, his magnificent full deep bass voice, his invariable dull Jaeger suit – a homespun loosely cut jacket and shapeless trousers which gave him the aspect of a fasting friar in brown habit with a rope around his waist – all this endeared Fry to Strachey. He was that odd combination – a man of scientific mind who had a strong feeling for painting, and very sure taste in it. He had an extraordinarily open mind, and was always ready to change his opinion if he could find a *reason* for doing so, for he was a man governed by ideas. Sometimes these were very silly. He would take up a casual remark made in conversation by an intellectually inferior person, amplify it, and make it sound much more interesting than it was intended to be. Strachey sometimes felt irritated by Fry's extreme credulity that found expression through the most weighty, judicial manner. Speaking with grave deliberation, he was given to enunciating highflown aesthetic theories that amounted to little more than unpractical jokes. The most far-fetched manifestation of this bigoted naïvety was, to Strachey's mind, the Omega Workshops, whose textiles, dress fashions, precarious furniture and pottery, continued to fill him with a kind of wonderment. At the same time he appreciated that Fry was genuinely on the side of the artists. The Omega Workshops, however amateur their productions, did provide a number of impoverished painters with the security of part-time employment which could act as a sympathetic extension to their real function as artists. And, conversely, another of Fry's principal aims was to launch a fresh attack on the firmly implanted philistinism of the British towards the visual arts in general.

The British public, however, had not welcomed Fry's efforts to educate them. The overall hubbub provoked by the two Post-Impressionist Exhibitions and now by the Omega Workshops, increased Fry's natural indignation against their arrogant insensitivity; and it was this indignation, comprising a violent repugnance against sentimental morality and a determination to overcome the abject indifference traditionally shown to all art by Britain, that, above all else, attracted Strachey. Art, in his view, was a civilizing and peaceful influence. But he and Fry were strong in their hatred of social hypocrisy; they wanted to shatter this and all other loathsome aspects of what they considered to be the British way of life and remould it nearer to the pattern of enlightened French society.

In times of crisis it is necessary to oversimplify one's thoughts if they are to be heard and heard effectively. For Strachey, the feud which sprang up after the Post-Impressionist Exhibitions between the new artist and the art critics of established reputation acting as spokesmen for the public at large, came to represent a fierce and exhilarating encounter in the age-long struggle between light and darkness. He elected to see Fry impersonally, symbolically, as a lieutenant on the side of human moderation and liberality campaigning against the forces of human folly and barbarism.

And so, though the references in his private correspondence to Fry, the man, are frequently unflattering, in public he was now impelled into the combat beside Fry's banner. In the manner of Voltaire, he did not believe in what Fry was doing in the arts, but he strenuously defended his right to do it. His sense of purpose was sustained by a belief that the world's spirit of toleration had not advanced all that far since Galileo was imprisoned for blasphemously asserting that the earth went round the sun. Nobody, it was true, was going to put Dr McTaggart on the rack for writing a book which destroyed the legend of the Trinity, but, Strachey declared, 'after the late fulminations of Sir William Richmond[4] against Post-Impressionism, nobody could be very much surprised if a stake was set up tomorrow for Mr Roger Fry in the courtyard of Burlington House'. And in his opening article for J. C. Squire

4. Sir William Blake Richmond (1842–1921), Slade Professor of Fine Art at Oxford (1879–83) and a Royal Academician. He was a highly successful portrait painter, though perhaps his best-known work is the rather indifferent mosaic decorations for St Paul's Cathedral.

in the *New Statesman*[5] Strachey makes the nature of his allegiance to Fry quite explicit: 'It seems clear that the change which has come over us is not so much a change in our attitude towards persecution in general as a change in the class of subjects which raise our zeal to persecute.'

By 1914 the everlasting spirit of intolerance had been hunted out of metaphysics, had been transferred to the field of ethics, and gave signs of moving in the direction of aesthetics. It was partly because of this last transition that Strachey chose to wear odd clothing; in the absence of anything else, clothes were as good a means as any of signifying revolt. He was seldom unsuccessful, too, in deliberately stimulating stupid remarks from stupid, narrowly conventional people who, in their sartorial opinions, incoherently confused ethics with aesthetics. If a man looked out of place, wore an eccentric long red beard and black Quaker cloak, then automatically, the uniformly grey, respectable, bowler-hatted population knew what deductions to make concerning his *moral* behaviour. It stood to prejudice. 'What is known as bad taste', Strachey wrote, 'is certainly persecuted at the present day. The milder transgressions of this nature are punished by private society with extreme severity; the more serious are rigorously dealt with by the State. Again, the conventions connected with apparel fill our minds with feelings of awe and sanctity which our ancestors of the Middle Ages reserved for articles of their faith. If a man wears unusual clothes, we hate him with the hatred of a Franciscan for a Dominican in the fourteenth century. If he goes so far as not to wear black clothes at dinner, we are quite certain that he is doomed to eternal perdition; while if he actually ventures to wear no clothes when he bathes, we can stand it no longer and punish him by law.'

In another *New Statesman* article, 'Bonga-Bonga in Whitehall',[6] the idea of which, cast in the form of a dialogue between

5. 'Avons-nous changé tout cela?' *New Statesman* (6 December 1913). Collected in *Characters and Commentaries* (161–6).

6. *New Statesman* (17 January 1914), 459–60. Collected in *Characters and Commentaries* (175–80).

a certain African chief named Bonga-Bonga and a minister of the British Government, was suggested to him by Adrian Stephen and Horace Cole's escapade on board H.M.S. *Dreadnought*, Strachey again sharply ridicules the naïve but popular assumption that the Liberal Party stood for genuinely liberal principles. The satire, however, is not really successful because he is over-anxious, within the limits of a meagre two thousand words, to hit too many targets – the Government's attitude towards suffragettes, its illogical arguments in favour of corporal and capital punishment, and the notion that it encouraged Freedom of Speech or Liberty of the Press.

With the possible exception of four pieces which he wrote in 1918 for Leonard Woolf's periodical *War and Peace*, this small but detached body of his work for the *New Statesman* is unique in the number of its references to topical events. These papers also convey a tone of unusually determined self-assurance. In a critical appraisal of John Palmer's *The Comedy of Manners*,[7] he casts an amused glance over his shoulder at the apprehension which in earlier days had afflicted him over the danger of making a fool of himself as a critic. The awe-inspiring prestige of literary reputation, which had previously impressed him as being retrospectively unchanging, now strikes him as flexible; even, in part, ephemeral. He likens its rise and fall, as many have done, to the fluctuations of a stock market, with its accidental cross-currents of luck and prevailing sentiment. 'What are the subtle causes which led, quite lately, to the rise in Donne, after he had lain for two hundred years a drug on the market?' he asks at one point. 'He is still rising, and shareholders who picked him up for next to nothing – an old song, one might say – fifteen years ago, are now congratulating themselves.' Looking to the future, he recommends for those who enjoy the occasional flutter, an investment in the Restoration comedy, at that time being quoted well below par.

This attempt to promote the popularity of the Restoration playwrights was for Strachey an oblique way of enhancing the esteem and status of English men of letters among English-

7. 'The Old Comedy', *New Statesman* (6 December 1913). Collected in *Characters and Commentaries* and in *Literary Essays* (47–52).

men. Perhaps, his argument seems to have run, the English would treat their literature with greater respect were it seen to embody the easily recognized and popularly admired Anglo-Saxon virtues. At present, English literature stuck out as a mere adjunct to the country itself, some freak growth, an architectural peninsula whose most celebrated pinnacles and spires stood curiously dissociated from the firm, undulating terrain of the British mind. Admittedly there were Fielding and Scott, but what could be less British, in any accepted meaning of the word, than the intellectual subtleties of Donne and Browning, the high fantasies of Shelley and Swinburne, the precocious artistry of Keats and the peculiarly independent qualities of writers such as Sir Thomas Browne, Sterne, Lamb, and George Meredith? Yet there existed another side to the coin. In the solid, rough-and-tumble comedies of Wycherley, with their breath and bustle of common life, one was constantly being brought into contact with 'the confused and crowded atmosphere of an English inn'; and in the works of the talented but unjustly disregarded Sir John Vanbrugh one found 'the jovial, high-hearted gaiety of English outdoor life'. Even Congreve, notwithstanding his marvellous verbal felicity and the nimbleness of his wit, had his feet squarely planted upon good English earth. The quintessence of the extrovert English genius was embedded in the dramatic compositions of such men; the effect of their plays was Hogarthian; their air of 'solid British beef, thick British beer, stout British bodies, and . . . stolid British moralising' was unmistakable.

Sustaining the propaganda of this essay there lies the schoolboy's prostration before the familiar heroic figure of the man of action. If only, Strachey seems regretfully to have sighed, writers were inherently as attractive as ploughboys or soldiers, then writing might be a more exciting profession. Of course it was not so, it could never be so – yet the Restoration playwrights, with their bawdy humour, their full and native masculine vigour, were imbued with something of the same virile glamour. Unfortunately they were largely ignored, while the best-known literary oracles of the past were, in comparison, very queer fish indeed. Matthew Arnold, for instance. What spectacle could be more uninviting than this earnest inspector of schools, with his high-toned fleerings and erudite self-righteousness, when contrasted with the natural graces of the ordinary man of action? Yet, almost wantonly, Arnold prompted such damaging comparison by his repeated assertion that literature should act as a criticism of and a corollary to the one serious matter in the world – the living of an active, useful life. To be burdened in his propaganda efforts with this type of totally unprepossessing paternal figure was insupportable. If only Arnold had been on the other side! But 'unfortunately,' Strachey complained,[8] adopting one of his favourite forms of comic speculation, 'he mistook his vocation. He might, no doubt, if he had chosen, have done some excellent and lasting work upon the movements of glaciers or the fertilization of plants, or have been quite a satisfactory collector in an up-country district in India. But no; he *would* be a critic.'

In these doleful circumstances Strachey set about changing the past by means of a new type of vigorous polemic. Between the lines of his essays he put over what amounted to a lack-of-confidence trick, acting as the eloquent public relations officer for a select number of the more stimulating, attractive men of letters. Concurrently, he undermined the reputations of well-established leaders in the world of affairs, statesmen, clerics, and bureaucrats of letters, whom he depicted as being slightly crazy, and, though incidentally diverting, without a trace of redeeming humour or humanity. The author of *Landmarks in French Literature* and *Eminent Victorians* had thus cast himself in the dual role of a Dr Jekyll and Mr Hyde, a twofold part that suited his divided nature so neatly that, at his most forceful and adroit, he rose to become what he himself called Voltaire – a journalist of genius.

In deliberate contravention of the revered literary canons of Matthew Arnold, Strachey considered it best to divorce literature from day-to-day affairs, presenting the former as an alluring fantasy world, the latter as more mundane. Otherwise

8. 'A Victorian Critic', *New Statesman* (1 August 1914), 529–30. Collected in *Characters and Commentaries* and in *Literary Essays* (209–14).

there was the risk that he might succumb to temptation, begin to despise the whole business of criticism, and, like Macaulay or Leslie Stephen, make use of it mainly as a vehicle for propounding views on other matters. At the same time he wanted to stress the compensations and rewards which attached to writing – the coruscating lustre that permanently illuminated the craft of letters. In extreme cases it could light up and confer immortality on even the most eccentric or obscure relatives of the poets – Shelley's father, for example, 'an unwilling ghost caught up in everlasting glory'.[9]

The kind of posthumous reputation enjoyed by a great writer depended largely upon the temper and personality of later critics – and here lay the real trouble in the organization responsible for renovating literary façades and images. In 'Rabelais', the last of his articles to appear in the *New Statesman*,[10] Strachey places the blame squarely on the shoulders of the dons, who, in his opinion, had achieved the almost impossible task of making great writing seem dull and commonplace. They wanted literature to be distinguished by reason of its exclusiveness – *and few there be who may comprehend it.* Strachey's aims were precisely the opposite of this. He wished to purge literary criticism of all restrictive, puritan influence, and develop the widest possible appeal and popularity of literature – to throw open its many mansions to universal delight. And so, at the end of 'Rabelais', he concludes by poking fun at the methods by which dons and teachers tended to impoverish the majesty of literature and limit its multifarious attractions. 'He [Rabelais] is read by many as a great humanist and moral teacher; by many more, probably, as a teller of stories, and in particular of improper stories; others are fascinated by his language, and others by the curious problems – literary, biographical, allegorical – which his book suggests. Mr W. F. Smith, of St John's College, Cambridge, belongs to another class – and it is a larger one than

9. 'An Adolescent', *New Statesman* (31 March 1917), 613–15. Collected in *Characters and Commentaries* and in *Biographical Essays* (229–35).

10. *New Statesman* (16 February 1918), 473–4. Collected in *Characters and Commentaries* and in *Literary Essays* (31–5).

might have been expected – the class of those who read Rabelais for the sake of making notes. ... Rabelais, so extraordinary in his nature, was no less extraordinary in his posthumous fate. Of this, the mysterious Fifth Book was the earliest manifestation; the latest is Mr Smith's volume; but no doubt it will not be the last.'

Landmarks in French Literature marks the culmination of Strachey's pure literary criticism, after which his writing moved further and further towards biography. The four major essays which he produced between January 1913 and October 1915 for the *Edinburgh Review* take, each for its subject, some figure from the French literary world; and together they form a continuation of the main flow of those literary and biographical essays which first appeared in the *Independent Review* and the *New Quarterly*.

'Madame du Deffand'[11] invites favourable comparison with the essay Strachey had written a little over six years earlier on her protégée, Mademoiselle de Lespinasse. The latter glitters with all the spontaneous brilliance and enthusiasm of a born raconteur; the former has the more studied flow of a practised conversationalist. Though packed with information, the tone is polished, the pace even and unhurried. The balanced classical style and structure exert, too, a more disciplinarian control over Strachey's romantic excesses, so that the residue of histrionic and rhetorical asides, which were sprinkled through the pages of 'Mademoiselle de Lespinasse',[12] has here been dissolved into the central narrative stream. 'Madame du Deffand' is also composed of a more intricate texture – a measure of the greater detail with which it had been charted in advance. In the opening paragraph Strachey presents the historical frame within which the finished miniature of his subject will be placed. When Napoleon, he tells us, set off for his Russian campaign he ordered the proof sheets of a forth-

11. *Edinburgh Review*, 217 (January 1913), 102–3. Collected in *Books and Characters* and in *Biographical Essays* (165–86).

12. *Independent Review*, 10 (September 1906), 345–56. Collected in *Characters and Commentaries* and in *Biographical Essays* (153–64).

coming book, Madame du Deffand's correspondence with Horace Walpole, to be put in his carriage, so that he might decide what suppressions ought to be made for the published edition. Shortly afterwards the book (which had appeared in England two years previously) came out for the first time in France. 'The sensation in Paris was immense', Strachey wrote; and evoking the spell that this correspondence cast, and can still cast, over its readers, he carefully underlines his own desire to promote imaginative literature as a subject at least as worthy of public attention as the topical problems of politics.

The accent he places on the glamour and consequence of letters is reasserted in the other three essays that he contributed to the *Edinburgh Review*, and constitutes an extension to his policy of popularizing literary personalities in this country. In *Landmarks in French Literature* he had successfully applied a beauty treatment to the changing face of writing in France, pointedly stressing the high favour in which the supreme artist was held in that country. Now he set out to spread that esteem over to this side of the Channel.

At the end of his study of Madame du Deffand, as a means of indicating the emergence of a new and vital generation, Lytton had introduced the personality of Voltaire, who reappears as the leading character in two of his other Edinburgh essays. The first of these, 'Voltaire and England', has as its theme the Frenchman's direct and significant connection with English influences.[13] This note is struck at once:

'The visit of Voltaire to England marks a turning-point in the history of civilization. It was the first step in a long process of interaction – big with momentous consequences — between the French and English cultures. For centuries the combined forces of mutual ignorance and political hostility had kept the two nations apart: Voltaire planted a small seed of friendship which, in spite of a thousand hostile influences, grew and flourished mightily. The seed, no doubt, fell on good ground, and no doubt, if Voltaire had never left his native country, some chance wind would have carried it over

13. *Edinburgh Review*, 220 (October 1914), 392–411. Collected in *Books and Characters* and in *Biographical Essays* (56–79).

the narrow seas, so that history in the main would have been unaltered. But actually his was the hand which did the work.'

The metaphorical vagueness of this opening passage makes plausible and even impressive the rather mythical *entente cordiale* that forms the basis of Strachey's advocacy. Well aware that if he were to advertise French culture as being wholly superior to English he would run the risk of alienating his audience and thus, at the very outset, defeating his own purpose, he recommends a compromise between the two. This idea is never stated flatly, but is everywhere implied, and like all the best methods of persuasion, leads the reader to the very brink of a certain conclusion which, since he must actually formulate it himself, exerts a far more lasting impression on his mind.

At first we are shown Voltaire in 1726 as the pet of the aristocratic élite which then governed France, a position of distinction unknown to equivalent English writers. Then we are told the story of how he insulted the Chevalier de Rohan-Chabot, of the powerful family of the Rohans, how he was beaten up by the Chevalier's gang of lackeys, and finally, how the high-born company with whom Voltaire had always supposed himself to be so popular and intimate, 'now only displayed signs of frigid indifference. The caste-feeling had suddenly asserted itself.' The law too was eaten up with social prejudice. Although no police action was taken against Rohan, Voltaire himself was subsequently arrested on suspicion of taking duelling lessons, and conducted to the Bastille. Strachey deals at unusual length with this incident, the bitter realism of which is used to qualify his adulation of the French aristocracy, and to demonstrate that, for all their many admirable qualities, they possessed none of the fresh congeniality of English high society. The reverse side of their greater sophistication is in these episodes depicted as the hidebound, callous stupidity of a still half-barbarous nation.

After a fortnight's solitary detention, the authorities acceded to Voltaire's petition begging them to substitute exile for imprisonment, and he was released on the condition that he remained at a distance of not less than fifty leagues from

Versailles. Little is known of the two or three years he then spent in England, but Strachey sketches in the tantalizing details, and recounts his various adventures, notably the occasion when, surrounded by a hostile crowd of pedestrians, he turned their jeers of 'French dog!' into a clamour of enthusiasm 'by jumping upon a milestone, and delivering a harangue beginning – "Brave Englishmen! Am I not sufficiently unhappy in not having been born among you?" '

Despite the lack of well-authenticated information concerning Voltaire's life in England, Strachey confidently rejects as impossible the theory that he acted as a spy in the pay of Walpole, and that he eventually left the country under a cloud. On the contrary, he maintains that during the period of his exile he became highly popular and that these two or three years were extremely beneficial to his typically French genius. The most powerful stimulus that England exercised upon his vivid imagination can be seen in his *Lettres Philosophiques*, that epoch-making book which could only have been written after the more cosmopolitan and polyglot Voltaire had returned to France. It was not a work of literature, Strachey explains, but something *more substantial and important* – 'a work of propaganda and a declaration of faith'. For, like Strachey himself, Voltaire had gone through a spiritual revolution. No longer was he a mere literary butterfly, feeding on the condescension of a narrow, prejudiced, wholly French aristocracy. He was a true anglophil; 'whatever quips and follies, whatever flouts and mockeries might play upon that surface, he was to be in deadly earnest at heart. He was to live and die a fighter in the ranks of progress, a champion in the mighty struggle which he was now beginning against the powers of darkness in France.' In short, the moral of this long essay is that England had made Voltaire into a fighter in the noble cause of humanity, that same cause for which an admixture of French culture had made Strachey and Roger Fry such staunch comrades-in-arms two centuries later. After Voltaire's return, England became the fashion in France in much the same way as Strachey now wished to see France become the fashion in England. The 'whispered message of tolerance, of free enquiry, of enlightened curiosity, was carried over the land. The success of Voltaire's work was complete.' Strachey's work lay along a parallel course, and in the enriching cross-fertilization of French and English ways of life he saw the final destruction of those 'powers of darkness' which still held sway in both countries disunited.

In conclusion, after Voltaire's direct association with English influences had ceased, Strachey likes to picture him as what almost seems like a kind of nostalgic eighteenth-century André Maurois. 'For the rest of his life, indeed, he never lost his interest in England; he was never tired of reading English books, of being polite to English travellers, and of doing his best, in the intervals of more serious labours, to destroy the reputation of that deplorable English buffoon, whom, unfortunately, he himself had been so foolish as first to introduce to the attention of his countrymen.'

So the pattern of the essay is rounded off. Voltaire rejected only the timid and pompous conservatism of the English mind. His mature attitude to the world was not exclusively of either country, for he took a midway path which no insular Englishman or cynical Frenchman could ever tread. Strachey concludes his essay on a fitting military note, a rousing call to the newly allied populations on both sides of the Channel. The real fight – not with Germany but with the enemy in their midst – was in danger of being forgotten, swamped by the international conflict. The only way in which he felt that he could still be heard was to appeal to this prevailing spirit of warfare, to mobilize it to the cause of humanity, and remind people that such a cause was more, not less, urgent in times of political and military crisis. 'With what reckless audacity, what a fierce uncompromising passion he charged and fought and charged again! He had no time for the nice discriminations of an elaborate philosophy, and no desire for the careful balance of a judicial mind; his creed was simple and explicit, and it also possessed the supreme merit of brevity: "Écrasez l'infâme!" was enough for him.'

This is a stirring motto, but like most propaganda, however passionately felt, it shows only an acutely-angled vision of the truth. That Voltaire developed to maturity by virtue of his trip to England during the late 1720s is partly contradicted by Strachey himself in another of his Edinburgh essays, 'Voltaire and Frederick the Great',[14] where he makes it clear that Voltaire only became conscious of the true nature of his genius and the real work for which it was suited once he had reached the threshold of old age.

Strachey starts off this essay with a determined effort to woo the reader's sympathetic attention. In time of war it was natural, though ultimately tedious, that everyone's attention should be fixed upon the soldiers and statesmen of the day. Setting out to redress the balance of this attention, Strachey puts forward a modest yet seductive plea for the solace, and for the expediency, of reflecting upon other, less immediate matters. There might be valuable advantages to be won, he suggests, by turning one's mind away from current uncertainty to the settled tranquillity of the past. In recollecting afresh the familiar intercourse between the leading man of letters and the leading politician of the eighteenth century, and in recapturing something of a life intimately connected with several of the most agitated events in European history, one could hardly fail to find respite from present suffering, as well as some harmless entertainment, and perhaps even a little instruction also.

The ensuing account which he gives of the 'curious drama' that took place between Voltaire and Frederick the Great is certainly entertaining. The instruction which it contains is skilfully unfolded as the essay proceeds and expressly stated at the end – that in the cut and thrust of human diplomacy, Voltaire, the most celebrated writer of his day, could match and outwit Frederick the Great, the most powerful man of action, whose twentieth-century counterparts now so bemused everyone's minds. 'But their relationship was no longer that of master and pupil, courtier and king', Strachey concludes; 'it was that of two independent and equal powers. Even Frederick the Great was forced to see at last in the Patri-

14. *Edinburgh Review*, 222 (October 1915), 315–73. Collected in *Books and Characters* and in *Biographical Essays* (80–105).

arch of Ferney something more than a monkey with a genius for French versification. He actually came to respect the author of *Akakia*, and to cherish his memory. "*Je lui fais tous les matins ma prière,*" he told d'Alembert, when Voltaire had been two years in the grave: "*je lui dis, Divin Voltaire, ora pro nobis*".'

Yet it is not as equals that these two are really presented in the main body of the essay. As a literary and philosophical pupil Frederick was inept; as a courtier Voltaire was flagrantly rebellious. We are shown all Frederick's faults and all Voltaire's, but at the same time we are constantly being made aware that only Voltaire possessed the consummate genius to compensate for his shortcomings. Not for long did he remain under any delusion about the king's poetic talent; whereas Frederick all the time persisted in his mistaken belief that he could tame the Frenchman and transform him into the brightest ornament at his court. Among the blind masses of the world Frederick was the one-eyed man, whose cold gaze observed with absolute clarity all that was close at hand. He noted each defect in his rival, yet was still manifestly blind to his prevailing merits. And so, though he could measure to a nicety all the complicated components in the diplomatic game, he was limited in the perspective that Voltaire, with both his eyes open, could command. For this reason Voltaire was, by and large, a realist; whereas Frederick remained a typical cynic, callous in action, lachrymose in sentiment. Despite his natural cunning, he was baffled by Voltaire's inexplicable superiority, which neutralized so much of his cleverness and made him seem to act in a manner, for him, highly ingenuous. Thus, in Strachey's interpretation of their relationship – which some critics, notably James Pope-Hennessy, have disputed – it is evidently not the King of Prussia but his Court Chamberlain who deserved the epithet 'great'. And the instruction implicit in this story points to a moral: that it was, even in 1915, not the statesmen who saw things wholly and effactually, but the philosopher – not Lloyd George, say, but Bertrand Russell.

The subject of Strachey's fourth Edinburgh essay was,

significantly, another rebel – Stendhal.[15] 'In his blood', he wrote, analysing his dissimilarity to the Patriarch of Ferney, 'there was a virus which had never tingled the veins of Voltaire. It was the virus of modern life – that new sensibility, that new passionateness, which Rousseau had first made known to the world and which had won its way over Europe behind the thunder of Napoleon's artillery.'

In the full flood of the Romantic revival, Stendhal represented the spirit of the eighteenth century without, perhaps, some of its elegance and artificial neatness. There existed in him, as in Strachey himself, a mingling of the Classical and Romantic strains. 'In his novels this characteristic co-habitation of opposites is responsible both for what is best and what is worst.' Both had a natural flair for narrative; and at their finest, when these two usually conflicting forces pulled in unison, when their prose was at its least emphatic and most controlled, then 'the procedure is almost mathematical: a proposition is established, the inference is drawn, the next proposition follows, and so on until the demonstration is complete. Here the influence of the eighteenth century is strongly marked.'

The particular occasion of this essay was Stendhal's sudden upsurge of current popularity in France. André Gide had recently named him as the best French novelist of all time, and his literary reputation, confined until then to a small distinguished circle, had all at once begun to expand enormously. Strachey now hoped further to extend the circumference of this popularity so that it encompassed Britain. Many Englishmen, of course, had read *Le Rouge et le Noir* and *La Chartreuse de Parme*, but how few had any further knowledge of 'a man whose works are at the present moment appearing in Paris in all the pomp of an elaborate and complete edition, every scrap of whose manuscripts is being collected and deciphered with enthusiastic care, and in honour of whose genius the literary periodicals of the hour are filling entire numbers with exegesis and appreciation'!

Having thus in his first paragraph shamed the British reader

15. 'Henri Beyle', *Edinburgh Review*, op. cit.

with this accusation of unfashionable ignorance, Strachey then proceeds to pique his curiosity by establishing the unknown Stendhal as a bewitching and controversial character. First he treats us to a brief biography in which he is careful to point out that the creator of one of the most magnificent battle scenes in the whole of literature possessed only the scantiest military experience; for, as the example of Stephen Crane confirms, it is unnecessary for an imaginative writer to undergo the personal experience of warfare in order to describe it with psychological exactitude. Stendhal, in fact, was a lieutenant of dragoons for hardly more than a year during the Italian campaign, and was present at only one great battle – Bautzen.

From this introductory sketch Stendhal emerges as a highly fascinating personality, almost the ideal embodiment of the life of letters with 'his adoration of Italy and Milan, his eccentricity, his scorn of the conventions of society and the limits of nationality, his adventurous life, his devotion to literature, and, lastly, the fact that, through all the varieties of his experience – in the earliest years of his childhood, in his agitated manhood, in his calm old age – there had never been a moment when he was not in love.'

Strachey follows up this biographical résumé with an appraisal of the novels and miscellaneous writings. He notes with approval Stendhal's attempt to reach a real precision and detachment in his prose, and describes his literary style in words which apply equally well to his own writing at its most restrained. 'In fact, Beyle's method is the classical method – the method of selection, of omission, of unification. ... His pen could call up pictorial images of startling vividness, when he wished. But he very rarely did wish: it was apt to involve a tiresome insistence. In his narratives he is like a brilliant talker in a sympathetic circle ...'

It is to this sympathetic circle of friends that Strachey returns at the end of his essay. In the penultimate section we are shown Stendhal as a public figure, a born rebel, with his enlightened 'hatred for the proudest and most insidious of all authorities – the Roman Catholic Church', whose fulminations against all authoritarian forces give 'a surprising fore-taste of the fiery potion of Zarathustra', But it is as Henri Beyle, the private man, whose character seemed almost to give the lie outright to all his autocratic prophecies, that we finally take leave of him. The dramatic emphasis Strachey extracts from this dichotomy, suggests that he recognized in Stendhal's double role some parallel to his own – to that equivocal juxtaposition between the stern, revolutionary message which, in a disguised form, he wished to put over to the modern reading public, and the more amiable composition of his shy and peace-loving nature.

To Strachey the world appeared as a circus, full of gaudy colours and unnecessary cruelty, fascinating yet repellent. But he did not really want to have the animals liberated and returned to their native wilds, only transferred to the more comfortable amenities of a well-run zoo. The boredom and bestiality of life could be eliminated solely through love and the intimate pursuits of friendship. Therefore he appreciated the apparent inconsistency in Henri Beyle, whose 'wayward, capricious and eccentric' personality stood out in such vivid contrast to Stendhal's uncompromising, anarchic outlook. If men like Henri Beyle were to continue flourishing, then they would need their Stendhals to fight for them against the encroachments of the barbaric universe. Beyle's world of civilized intercourse and communion comprised the ends that vindicated all Stendhal's most bitter denunciations. So the final, nostalgic valediction is addressed to the real, inner man, the private individual, in his ideal environment. 'And in such a Paradise of Frenchmen we may leave Henri Beyle.'

FOUR

Eminent Victorians

'*Eminent Victorians* is the work of a great anarch, a revolutionary textbook on bourgeois society written in the language through which the bourgeois ear could be lulled and beguiled, the Mandarin style.' *Cyril Connolly, 'Enemies of Promise'*

'Much of the present interest in the nineteenth century is often written and spoken of as a reaction against Strachey; but I do not at all feel it so ...
'The views of history with which I grew up were almost entirely created by Victorians; and Strachey did not necessarily contradict them; he directed attention to a rather different Victorian field, and he also woke me up to the possibility of treating the Victorians themselves as interesting, problematical, extremely relevant to my own life and the general life I was born into.' *Humphry House, 'All in Due Time'*

'Brethren,
The President has asked me to propose the toast of "Eminent Victorians". I shall be delighted to do so. But I feel one difficulty: I find it very hard to decide what an eminent Victorian is. ... Definitions are curious things and I've never been able quite to understand their workings. ... There was once an eminent Victorian called Mr W. G. Ward, who used to say "When I hear men called 'judicious' I suspect them; but when I hear them called 'judicious and venerable', I know they are scoundrels". Similarly when I hear people called "Victorians", I suspect them. But when I hear them called "Eminent Victorians" I write their lives. So an Eminent Victorian might be defined, on this principle, as the sort of person whose life would be likely to be written by Lytton Strachey. And perhaps that's as near as one can get.' *Lytton Strachey, Speech to the Apostles, proposing 'Eminent Victorians'*

1

DEFINITIONS

While reviewing biographies and histories for the *Spectator,* Strachey had evolved the credo which he later aimed at putting into practice in *Eminent Victorians*. As early as 2 January 1909, he had set out those principles by which he would seek to be guided, in a review[1] of Guglielmo Ferrero's *The Greatness and Decline of Rome*, some passages of which read almost like a first extended draft of his celebrated Preface nine years later:[2]

When Livy said that he would have made Pompey win the battle of Pharsalia, if the turn of the sentence had required it, he was not talking utter nonsense, but simply expressing an important truth in a highly paradoxical way, – that the first duty of a great historian is to be an artist. The function of art in history is something much more profound than mere decoration; to regard it, as some writers persist in regarding it, as if it were the jam put around the pill of fact by cunning historians is to fall into a grievous error; a truer analogy would be to compare it to the process of fermentation which converts a raw mass of grape-juice into a subtle and splendid wine. Uninterpreted truth is as useless as buried gold; and art is the great interpreter. It alone can unify a vast multitude of facts into a significant whole, clarifying, accentuating, suppressing, and lighting up the dark places with the torch of the imagination. More than that, it can throw over the historian's materials the glamour of a personal revelation, and display before the reader great issues and catastrophes as they appear, not to his own short sight, but to the penetrating vision of the most soaring of human spirits. That is the crowning glory of the greatest history – that of Thucydides, for instance, or Tacitus, or Gibbon; it brings us into communion with an immense intelligence, and it achieves this result through the power of art. Indeed, every history worthy of the name is, in its own way, as personal as poetry, and its value ultimately

1. 'A New History of Rome', *Spectator*, 102 (2 January 1909), 20–21. Collected in *Spectatorial Essays* (13–17).

2. He had put forward the same point of view at greater length in a paper that was written in answer to 'The Science of History', J. B. Bury's inaugural lecture as Regius Professor of Modern History at Cambridge in 1902. Strachey disputed Bury's contention that history was a science, arguing that the greatest historians were invariably artists.

depends upon the force and the quality of the character behind it.

The Preface to *Eminent Victorians* is a distillation of the ideas expressed in this paragraph and elsewhere, and it raises two distinct questions: How valid is Strachey's definition of the historical biographer's task? And to what extent did his own work conform to the principles he had laid down?

For the sake of convenience, historical biography may be divided into two opposing, though not wholly incompatible, categories: the non-artistic or 'scientific', and the literary. Each is designed to communicate a rather different sort of truth, the first documentary and factual, the second personal and imaginative. Only perhaps in the lives of writers, with their cento of recorded incidents and interpretative literary criticism woven into a pattern, can these two schools of biography be harmoniously brought together. Since Strachey always chose men and women of action and affairs, he was faced with a more simple choice. His credo, figuratively expressed in several essays, is an able formulation of those canons of historical biography which govern the artistic approach. A biographer or historian, he believed, should command a certain attitude of mind, should possess a certain natural ability, and should employ a certain literary method. The attitude of mind he defined as a civilized detachment or freedom of spirit coupled with a personal point of view. The ability he diagnosed as a scholar's capacity for absorbing facts together with a novelist's or dramatist's gift for presenting them. The most effective method of communicating not the flat threadbare actuality of events, so abstract and impersonal, but the true living relationship that existed between writer and his subject, he analysed as a selection of salient and an omission of superfluous matter. This was the boiling-down process by which from rough grape-juice he distilled a potent spirit. The biographer should strive for a brevity which elucidated and simplified the impact of the past upon the sensitive retina of his mind, imbued, through the perspective of years, with an impartial vision.

It is largely because of these views that Strachey has been dismissed by some professional historians as having nothing

to contribute to their subject. His arbitrary and partly concealed method of selection, his flashy yet commonplace style
— half-fictional and wholly superficial — emanated, in their
belief, from a defective angle of approach. To the sober, pedagogic recorder of history, both his detachment and his point
of view were unacceptable. The former, by severing the umbilical cord which joins a figure of historical importance to
the background of his age, artificially disentangled him from
the religious and political climate of the day, and permitted the
biographer to apply modern standards to bygone customs and
ways of thinking. By such means were the great events of history distorted so as to resemble mere ephemeral exploits, often
unplanned and inconsequential, and embodying not the dignity
of human endeavour, the measured progress of civilization, but
the abundant farce, imbecility and blackguardism of unrefined
human nature. The latter further trivialized the study of history
by reducing major historical problems to questions of primitive
behaviour and eccentricity, to coincidence, to accident, and to
a succession of puerile brawls, childish bigotries and petty
crimes. Further, in the academic view, the literary historian
was guilty of naïvely focusing his readers' attention on the
graphic details of personality, and made no evaluation of the
social and economic forces of life, thereby demonstrating his
preference for artificial colouring and neatness over the proper
utilization of complex data. His claim that history was an art
suggested only a predilection for fantasy above authenticity,
and in practice meant that a historian should be more interested in himself and in the smoothness of his story-telling than
in his subject-matter. Finally, his credulous trust in 'psychology'
acted only as a licence for squalid or romantic speculation —
an occupation usually associated with lightweight historical
novelists of the female kind.

Such, in brief, is the burden of the orthodox historian's complaint against the innovations outlined in the
Preface to *Eminent Victorians*. In counteraction to these
criticisms, Strachey, like Goethe, believed that history yielded up more of her secrets to the heightened intuition of the
artist than to the over-diffident, over-earnest, humdrum and

humourless investigations conducted by scientific minds. With the revived form of historical biography that he inaugurated, he sought to disrupt the impression left by conventional historians, who, eager to enter the spirit of the times they were studying, mimicked the generals and statesmen of the past, condoning and making acceptable the worst excesses of history. The bloated solemnity of 'serious' historical narrative, weighed down with the pompous importance of its material, dealt onerously with events rather than sensitively with people, and devoted endless dry-as-dust disquisitions to the problems of political necessity, strategic reason and economic cause as if they constituted self-sufficient entities, divorced from the ambitions of mortal men.

In his Preface, Strachey asserts that the individual human being, as the spearhead of sensibility and the residence of consciousness, should no longer rank last in the hierarchy of human values. The business of the historian should not be wholesale and unreal, but must involve a recreation of human life in perspective, which, by putting a fine edge on our own days, tells us more about the present than the present by itself can tell us. The historian therefore should neither abstain from judgement nor should he indulge in tedious vituperation, but satirize the follies of the past; he should not depict a panoramic but a telescopic view of the ages; he should not relinquish the interpretation of all events entirely to the reader, but seek to direct him as a judge in the summing-up of a trial. Nevertheless he should, if possible, avoid drawing out one single conclusion, necessarily narrow and polemical, and rest content with a complete effect of irony, intensified in places to the point of wonderment.

'It is not his business to be complimentary', the Preface concludes; 'it is his business to lay bare the facts of the case, as he understands them. That is what I have aimed at in this book – to lay bare the facts of some cases, as I understand them, dispassionately, impartially, and without ulterior intentions. To quote the words of a Master – "*Je n'impose rien; je ne propose rien; j'expose.*" '

An altogether different stricture on Strachey's concept of

biography has come from another quarter. Harold Nicolson, in his Hogarth Lecture, *The Development of English Biography*, suggests that by adopting a point of view, the biographer inevitably imposes upon his material a personal thesis which is destructive of 'pure' biography. To illustrate this contention, he contrasts Strachey's method with that of Boswell and Lockhart, who held no thesis, but 'worked wholly on the inductive method'. Yet, for all the dissimilarity of their writing, it would appear that Strachey, quoting Voltaire, has only put forward a more streamlined technique of achieving, under different circumstances, roughly the same ends as Boswell and Lockhart, who, in Harold Nicolson's words, 'neither propounded nor implied a theory; they merely, with the requisite degree of taste and selection, furnish facts. Their facts, although extensive, were limited by the taste of their age.' The inductive method of Boswell and Lockhart was also in practice destructive of 'pure' biography. For although they paraded no ulterior intentions, they did harbour some ulterior, partly unconscious motives – as all human beings must. Boswell's personal attitude to Johnson, for instance, though not raised to a point of awareness or control where it could be crystallized into a thesis, nevertheless highlighted a particular aspect of Johnson's character, and, by insisting on the Doctor's verbal ascendancy, tended to further the impression that he was a bigoted champion of the social conventions and the established order, obscuring his genuine individuality to a degree where, so Bernard Shaw claimed, 'Johnson' became an invention of Boswell's. Lockhart's loyalty to Scott, also, was at least equal to that of Boswell to Johnson, and the love and admiration which flows uninterruptedly through his ten volumes of biography is recurrently expressed at the unjust expense of minor figures in the book.

Harold Nicolson's concept of 'pure' biography is thus idealistic, as, perhaps, too, is Strachey's theory of how to recreate artistically *and* objectively a man's life. Boswell's and Lockhart's personal feelings played like a warm, luminous glow about their subjects; Strachey's 'point of view' was a concentration of this radiance into a sharp beam of light focused from the side and back of the theatre upon the centrally staged personality. By implication Nicolson's criticism is an admonition of Strachey for not upholding his own theories. Both Boswell's and Lockhart's Lives could be said to contain a superabundance of dispensable material. Strachey, working solely from published sources, recommended paring this material down to a special pattern, the design of which was to be arranged by the biographer's particular interest in and response to his subject. By these means one might offer, instead of a whole mine of information, simply the jewels extracted from that mine. Nicolson decries a notion of biography that encouraged natural prejudice, and that sought to elaborate a preconception of character by slanting the materials subsequently consulted to fit in with an initial, ill-informed bias. The former method was genuinely artistic; the latter apocryphal – a form of higher journalism. In his Preface to *Eminent Victorians*, Strachey had propounded biography as an art; to what extent he practised biography as polemics may be seen from an examination of the four essays which follow this Preface.

2

ALLEGRO VIVACE

Eminent Victorians is Strachey's best full-length work. Though it does not maintain the uniform texture of *Landmarks in French Literature*, though it does not quite achieve the immaculate synthetic cohesion of *Queen Victoria*, though it does not perhaps conjure up the Victorian age as vividly as *Elizabeth and Essex* does the Elizabethan, yet it touches reality more closely than any of these. For the impact between Strachey and his biographical subjects was of greater urgency and took place at a more intense level of experience during the war years, and while he was still unknown, than at any other period of his career. His four eminent Victorians are rendered with the acuteness of true caricature. They are not photographs in literature, and some of the lines of character in their make-up bear only misshapen resemblance to the originals. But seen as creatures of parody and extravagance, each one constructed round a few easily recognizable and strongly developed traits, they each convey the impression of an authentically lifelike countenance.

In *Landmarks in French Literature*, Strachey had treated his writers exclusively as pioneers or reactionaries to the historical exposition of the book, and had appraised their literature, in terms of tendencies and schools. Now he claimed to be doing away with these trappings of prestige and the ephemeral whims of fashion, to be presenting individuals as interesting in their own right. 'Human beings are too important to be treated as mere symptoms of the past', he wrote in his Preface. 'They have a value which is independent of any temporal processes – which is eternal, and must be felt for its own sake.' The widespread and collective reaction to *Eminent Victorians* when it came out belies this admirably strict individualistic approach. It is possible that Strachey, not gifted with any great depth of self-knowledge and holding the opinion that art must depend on consistency, really believed that his four sitters symbolized for him nothing beyond themselves. But the distortions which he manipulated on all four of them are consistent with George Simson's view that *Eminent Victorians* represents his greatest and most prolonged onslaught upon the evangelicalism that was the defining characteristic of Victorian culture, and which, Strachey believed, had been indirectly responsible for the First World War. Once again the reader is given a dramatized conflict between the powers of light and darkness. Extolling the virtues of reason, simplicity, moderation and tolerance – qualities which he himself possessed in a high degree – he shows us how, to a greater or lesser extent, his Victorian quartet sacrificed these attributes by becoming, as Lord Annan succinctly puts it, 'the dupes of two false moral systems: ecclesiastical Christianity and the religion of success'.[3]

In order to disperse the sacrosanct myths enveloping Cardinal Manning, Florence Nightingale, Doctor Arnold and

3. Introduction to Collins Classics edition of *Eminent Victorians* (1959).

General Gordon, he was compelled to marshal a good deal of his critical attention on them as non-representational beings. Yet in all four studies, the parallel oversimplification resulting from his monochromatic biographical technique impoverishes the rich complexity of human life.

'Cardinal Manning', the longest of the four essays in *Eminent Victorians*, is also one of the most severe. The opening is skilfully handled. In a few paragraphs the silhouette of Manning's intransigent character is imperishably etched in – that of an ambitious schemer, prone to illusions of romantic grandeur, a self-deceiver whose acid inhumanity and morbid aloofness, bred of a puritan preoccupation with hell, cuts him off from his fellow beings. On the very first page, in a series of apparently searching questions, Strachey charts the course which his essay will take, and lays bare his essential preoccupation with Manning's character:

'What had happened? Had a dominating character imposed itself upon a hostile environment? Or was the Nineteenth Century, after all, not so hostile? Was there something in it, scientific and progressive as it was, which went out to welcome the representative of ancient tradition and uncompromising faith? Had it, perhaps, a place in its heart for such as Manning – a soft place, one might almost say? Or, on the other hand, was it he who had been supple and yielding? he who had won by art what he would never have won by force, and who had managed, so to speak, to be one of the leaders of the procession less through merit than through a superior faculty for gliding adroitly to the front rank? And, in any case, by what odd chances, what shifts and struggles, what combinations of circumstance and character, had this old man come to be where he was?'

J. K. Johnstone likens this passage to the outline drawn by an architect upon the turf denoting where the building shall rise. 'He [Strachey] has flourished the grand plan before us, and, with a few waves of the hand, has indicated the proportions of the structure.' The questions themselves are, of course, rhetorical; they have been carefully loaded, they all point in a certain direction and the answers to them are already implied both in the manner in which they are phrased and the order in which they are placed. 'Such questions', Strachey commented, 'are easier to ask than to answer.' And this may be because they are not genuine queries, but problems artificially posed above an already fixed solution. For the theme of 'Cardinal Manning', which delivers a foregone verdict to this inquest, is the indictment of an age which could permit an astute and ruthless opportunist, whose repressed sexual drive was sublimated into religious fanaticism, to gravitate naturally to a position of such high authority.

So as to make this indictment really convincing, Strachey felt that he needed to establish, without reservation, his view of Manning as a superstitious egotist, goaded by unlimited personal ambition, and skilled in the sophistry and dissimulation of ecclesiastical politics. His chief dramatic method of pressing home this interpretation was to contrast Manning's career with that of the saintly, lamb-like Newman. The antithesis between the two men is made complete.

'In Manning, so it appeared, the Middle Ages lived again', Strachey wrote. 'The tall gaunt figure, with the face of smiling asceticism, the robes, and the biretta, as it passed in triumph from High Mass at the Oratory to philanthropic gatherings at Exeter Hall, from Strike Committees at the Docks to Mayfair drawing-rooms where fashionable ladies knelt to the Prince of the Church, certainly bore witness to a singular condition of affairs.'

This is the tone which Strachey resourcefully employs to turn Manning's superficially impressive mask of virtue round to something slightly improbable. By the introduction of a faintly incongruous detail or two he gives it an added twist which effectively screws the whole picture up to an angle of absurdity.

The same rather incredulous note is struck in the description of Manning's peram bulations about the countryside, where he is made to reveal as preposterous a silhouette as in the performance of his earnest and energetic antics about the towns. The following passage amusingly depicts his active life as a country clergyman, its attitude of mock-sympathy exposing just one facet of character – vanity.

'His slim, athletic figure was seen everywhere – in the streets of Chichester, or on the lawns of the neighbouring rectories, or galloping over the downs in breeches and gaiters, or cutting brilliant figures on the ice. He was an excellent judge of horse-flesh, and the pair of greys which drew his hooded phaeton so swiftly through the lanes were the admiration of the county. . . . He was a good talker, a sympathetic listener, a man who understood the difficult art of preserving all the vigour of a manly character and yet never giving offence.'

Manning was fundamentally a man of action – almost a 'blood' – someone cut out for worldly success. Newman, whose prose style Strachey particularly admired, is seen as 'a child of the Romantic Revival, a creature of emotion and of memory, a dreamer whose secret spirit dwelt apart in delectable mountains, an artist whose subtle senses caught, like a shower in the sunshine, the impalpable rainbow of the immaterial world'. The Victorian era, Strachey infers, had more in common with the Middle Ages than with the Age of Romance. It was a retrogressive, barbaric epoch, that preferred the ascetic and pretentious Manning to the finer, simpler nature of Newman – which, to a large extent, it also perverted, driving him to misuse his poetic faculties in the purposeless pursuit of everlasting theological lucubrations. Newman possessed none of Manning's downright, matter-of-fact determinism, his natural grace or athletic prowess – fair virtues all. Instead, like Strachey himself, he was a quietist, of donnish and didactic temper, destined, despite great gifts, to remain for many years unaided, misunderstood, ignored.

'His delicate mind,' Strachey explained, 'with its refinements, its hesitations, its complexities – his soft, spectacled, Oxford manner, with its half-effeminate diffidence – such things were ill calculated to impress a throng of busy Cardinals and Bishops, whose days were spent amid the practical details of ecclesiastical organisation, the long-drawn involutions of papal diplomacy, and the delicious bickerings of personal intrigue.'

All biographers, however painstaking their research, however scrupulous their methods, inevitably fall into some errors of fact and of interpretation of fact. But Strachey's small deviations from the strictest documentary truth were seldom haphazard: they have a peculiar consistency which shows them more likely to have been calculated than accidental, and which partly invalidates his high-toned claim to write 'dispassionately, impartially, and without ulterior intentions'. Several pertinent facts in Manning's life are omitted and their implications ignored, while both his character and that of Newman are over-simplified in order to fit in better with Strachey's personal point of view.

As an exordium to Manning, the scheming and dogmatic papist, Strachey shows him as a young man at Oxford contemplating visions of a splendid political career that is all at once cut short by the sudden bankruptcy of his father. Still indulging his secular dreams, he enters the Colonial Office as a supernumerary clerk, but is soon persuaded to take orders by 'his Spiritual Mother', the pious Miss Bevan. She, Strachey deduces, played shrewdly on the aspiring nature of the young man by planting within him the vainglorious notion that his father's bankruptcy was an example of the mysterious way in which God moved, His chosen vessels to select. That their crucial conversation should have taken place 'one day, as they walked together in the shrubbery' adds a certain ambiguous spiciness to the story. *In the shrubbery!* The phrase is, of course, Strachey's own. In Purcell's biography of Manning, on which he relied for this scene, there is mention only of 'walks together'. The added detail, like some suggestive backstage setting, gives interpretative colour to the whole business of the conversion. It is a slight and subtle manipulation of the available evidence, but it cannot be counted as inaccuracy unless, that is, *any* paraphrase of an original source is to be judged as such.

When the offer of a Merton Fellowship seemed to depend upon the taking of orders, a full awareness dawned upon Manning that he might fulfil a more exalted destiny than that of Member of Parliament. Strachey's assumption of Manning's motives, by throwing into the shade one side of his character, makes his decision to become a priest wholly one of long-sighted expediency.

To expediency Strachey then adds callousness. In sharp contrast to Newman, 'a creature of emotion and of memory', we are shown Manning numbering his wife's premature death as among 'God's special mercies', since it fortuitously released him for service in the Roman Catholic Church. 'In after years,' he writes, 'the memory of his wife seemed to be blotted from his mind; he never spoke of her; every letter, every record, of his married life he destroyed.'

This passage has come up for some adverse comments from later critics. Baron von Hügel subsequently recorded Manning's last words, uttered in the presence of Bishop Vaughan, which partly contradict Strachey's assertion.

'This is what happened shortly before his death', Bishop Vaughan told Baron von Hügel. 'I was by his bedside; he looked round to see that we were alone; he fumbled under his pillow for something; he drew out a battered little pocket-book full of a woman's fine handwriting. He said: "For years you have been to me as a son, Herbert: I know not to whom else to leave this – I leave it to you. Into this little book my dearest wife wrote her prayers and meditations. Not a day has passed since her death on which I have not prayed from this book. All the good I may have done, all the good I may have been, I owe to her. Take precious care of it." He ceased speaking and soon afterwards unconsciousness came on.'

It seems unreasonable to criticize a man on his death-bed, but Manning's nostalgia was really little more than sentimentality, in that he preserved only that part of his dead wife which chimed in with his own far-reaching career. Strachey, in his efforts to accentuate Manning's unsympathetic nature, his abnormal coldness and emotional castration, played down this sentimentality, which would in fact have added depth to his portrait. As it is, he just over-states his case, giving us not the direction of a judicial summing-up, but a prosecutor's more exclusive slant before a jury who must be treated, like all juries, as a mixed bag of impressionable incompetents.

All the major decisions which Manning made during his career, Strachey interprets as having arisen from an over-weening desire for self-aggrandizement. He insinuates, for example, that Manning's repeated repudiations of Newman's Tract No. 90 were nothing more or less than a series of determined efforts to dissociate himself from a party which was being condemned by the authorities and passed over for ecclesiastical preferment. That he might have acted from a less unsavoury motive has been intimated by Arnold Lunn, who suggested that his 'practical genius and common sense forced him to adapt himself to the ruling spirit of the Church. He was a sound Anglican, and later a sound Roman Catholic. A sense of practical realities rather than time-serving prevents such men ploughing the lonely furrow of revolt.'

It may well be that Strachey's intuition here is sounder than Arnold Lunn's, and certainly more percipient than that of most latter-day Catholic apologists, but his theory of artistic uniformity forbade him from putting at his readers' disposal the evidence necessary for them to come to their own opinion or to reach a reasonable assessment of his, without detailed reference to the sources mentioned in the bibliography. One's initial doubts are sometimes raised, too, by his reluctance to concede that a man's motives may be mixed. One is aware that some factor is missing, and often unjustly leaps to the conclusion that certain passages have been falsified.

There are, also, some occasions when Manning would appear to have acted with more sincerity than Strachey liked to admit, since real sincerity would of course conflict with his pungent study of a relentless power-seeker flourishing in an age of humbug. He maintains, for instance, that Manning's rejections of immediate short-term success were actually shrewd political decisions attracting to them far greater if more distant advantages. Yet this view, without some additional explanation, does not always bear even cursory examination. It is impossible to detect any practical gain in Manning's refusal of the office of sub-almoner, a position which almost certainly involved the reversion of the mitre, let alone his final refusal to have his name put forward as pope, the supreme honour which would have served as a perfect apotheosis to Strachey's essay. As it is, this final act of 'self-sacrifice' gives the lie to Strachey's too straightforward portrayal of Manning. His avowed objections to election – namely, the conviction that a foreign pope might, for political reasons, disrupt the vital reconciliation of Italy with the Holy See – Strachey does not deem worth mentioning. This was too impersonal, too irrelevant to his theme. At the same time he can put forward no explicit alternative reason for this refusal which is both plausible and in line with his central argument. Manning's reasons, he hints darkly, were unspecified, vague yet sinister. 'Thus it happened', he wrote, 'that the Triple Tiara seemed to come, for a moment, within the grasp of the late Archdeacon of Chichester; and the cautious hand refrained.' Why? Of what was Manning afraid? Strachey had always claimed to illustrate rather than to explain, and he dismisses the episode in under a dozen lines as though it were not real – '*seemed* to come' – hurrying on as if anxious to deflect attention from a possible stumbling-block to his main thesis.

But it is the account of Manning's conversion to Catholicism that has stimulated the greatest controversy. Several historians, objecting to Strachey's uncompromising portrait of a proud and worldly prelate, have centred their attack upon this crucial point, and have, between them, built up a formidable-looking case. At the age of forty-three Manning was already an archdeacon. His prospects of a brilliant career in his own Church were extremely bright, especially since he could count on the support of Gladstone. Before him he could see the fate of Newman, certainly an inauspicious precedant which appeared to signify that the Church of Rome had little enough to offer its late English converts. Yet he turned his back on an easy and swift advancement and chose to become instead a middle-aged neophyte at the base of a steeper ladder where he could reckon on nothing like the same chances of success.

'Nevertheless,' Strachey wrote, 'it is difficult to feel quite sure that Manning's plunge was as hazardous as it appeared.

Certainly he was not a man who was likely to forget to look before he leaped, nor one who, if he happened to know that there was a mattress spread to receive him, would leap with less conviction. In the light of after-events, one would be glad to know what precisely passed at that mysterious interview of his with the Pope, three years before his conversion. It is at least possible that the authorities in Rome had their eye on Manning; they may well have felt that the Archdeacon of Chichester would be a great catch. What did Pio Nono say? It is easy to imagine the persuasive innocence of his Italian voice. "Ah, dear Signor Manning, why don't you come over to us? Do you suppose that we should not look after you?" '

The popular and widely accepted criticism of this passage is that Strachey has deliberately contrived a mystery where none existed and seasoned it with his own picturesque fancy. As F. A. Simpson has pointed out in a now celebrated article, Manning did not preserve a guilty silence concerning his interview with the pope on 11 May 1848, though there is only a cryptic reference to it in his contemporary diary – 'At eleven had audience at the Vatican.' Apparently, then, Strachey concocts his hypothesis round the brevity of this entry, which, he assures us, is very significant. The one other scrap of information which has come down to us about Manning's papal audience, Strachey contends earlier in his essay, only serves to make the whole episode doubly remarkable.

'Precisely what passed on that occasion never transpired; all that is known is that His Holiness expressed considerable surprise on learning from the Archdeacon that the chalice was used in the Anglican Church in the administration of Communion. "What!" he exclaimed, "is the same chalice made use of by every one?" "I remember the pain I felt," said Manning, long afterwards, "at seeing how unknown we were to the Vicar of Jesus Christ. It made me feel our isolation." '

A pope so ignorant of the chief ceremonials of the Anglican Church was hardly likely, Strachey's detractors have argued, to be more conversant with its hierarchical values, or the subjective tendencies of its members – though such political and psychological knowledge must have been essential for him to conduct the sort of seduction scene which Strachey had envisaged. This passage, they therefore claim, is of great interest as exposing Strachey's inflexible bias, not only by virtue of its implied contradiction to the 'mysterious' implications which, ten pages later, he essayed to draw out of this audience, but also by its indirect revelation that, so far from being 'all that is known' about the audience, it is not even all that Strachey himself knew. One critic has likened the effect of these two separated passages to that of a time-bomb, planted on one page and set to explode with calculated force at the beginning of the subsequent chapter. Yet the line between them is so faulty that if there is any explosion at all it is under the feet of Strachey himself rather than of Manning.

For the words of Pio Nono and of Manning have been taken from a journal which Manning later wrote up to repair the omissions of his contemporary diary, and which puts on record far more than the little that Strachey describes as 'all that is known' of this interview with the pope. As F. A. Simpson, the arch-detractor, has pointed out,[4] Strachey 'omits also to tell us that the "Journal" itself was supplemented by a further verbal account of "what passed on that occasion" dictated by Manning to his biographer Purcell; and this though that account stared him in the face on the open printed page opposite the one from which he drew upon Purcell's extract from the "Journal". The single topic which Strachey elects to mention (presumably because he regarded it as the most comic) as the one thing known about the interview was, in fact, but one of half-a-dozen or more of subjects which Manning records as having been discussed at it, even after its primary purpose had been discharged. That purpose too Manning describes and Strachey suppresses. There was nothing in the least mysterious about it. During his visit to Rome, his fellow Harrovian, Sydney Herbert, had charged Manning with the task of getting translated into Italian, at the expense of the

4. 'Methods of Biography', *Spectator*, 172 (7 January 1944), 7–8.

British Government, a pamphlet by Sir Charles Trevelyan on English activities in relief of the recent Irish famine: this translation he was to present in person to the Pope.'

Pio Nono's reading from the most important passages of this pamphlet – which Manning with typical competence had marked – in addition to the harmless exchange of civilities which followed, were fully set out in Purcell's Life of the cardinal which heads Strachey's brief bibliography, 'and on a page of that book which there is internal evidence to show must actually have lain open before his eyes'.

Much has been made of Simpson's sweeping exposé: perhaps too much.[5] 'I know nothing about this matter', wrote

5. Some brief account of F. A. Simpson's career as a historian is perhaps relevant in this context. He was born in 1883, educated at Queen's College, Oxford, and brought to Trinity College, Cambridge, by G. M. Trevelyan. 'Our best living historian', as Clive Bell called him, he is the author of two books, *The Rise of Louis Napoleon* (1909) and *Louis Napoleon and the Recovery of France* (1923) – part of an originally planned but never completed tetralogy. In a special Note to the 1960 impression of the third edition of *Louis Napoleon and the Recovery of France*, he wrote: 'When this volume was first published, unsigned condemnations of it from the same pen appeared in the two most authoritative journals in the language. And during the thirty years' silence on their part which followed, the author was given some reason to suppose that, in the interests of consistency, similar treatment would await any continuation of his work; continuation which the various consequences of disparagement so sponsored tended in any case to make difficult. In the last few years, however, their condemnation has in both journals been tardily, but most handsomely, retracted. Had this kindness come sooner, the present reissue might have been not of two volumes only, but of the four volumes originally designed. But glad though the author is to have lived long enough to receive it, he lacks strength now to rekindle a flame which he ought perhaps never to have suffered to be snuffed out.'

Commenting on the words 'given some reason to suppose', Mr Simpson told the author that some time after the original attack on his book, while he was staying with the Hammonds, Lawrence Hammond showed him a review article he had just written for *The Times Literary Supplement,* from which the editor had deleted at the last moment, in final proof, without consulting the writer, a laudatory reference to the Louis Napoleon books – treatment unique in Hammond's experience as a reviewer. From this fact Mr Simpson deduced that *The Times Literary Supplement* deliberately intended to deal with volumes 3 and 4 as they had dealt with volume 2.

Frank Swinnerton as recently as 1963. 'I take the criticism from F. A. Simpson's *Spectator* article, which, if it is correct

---

What in fact had happened was this. *Louis Napoleon and the Recovery of France* was finished in 1921 and scheduled to be published in 1922. But, being delayed at the printers' and the publishers', the book was eventually held back until the following year. In July 1922, Philip Guedalla's *The Second Empire* came out, this work not being referred to in the bibliography of Mr Simpson's volume. Such an omission may possibly have incensed Guedalla, that so-called Stracheyesque biographer (though one never personally admired by Lytton). In any event, Guedalla anonymously held up the book to ridicule in *The Times* on the morning of its publication, and followed up this attack by a slashing review in *The Times Literary Supplement* – 'simply a travesty of criticism', as Leonard Woolf later called it. Shorn in consequence of its sales and of other reviews the book survived precariously until it received the praise that was its due from Frank Swinnerton, J. L. Hammond and many other literary critics and historians. But although Simpson had already completed some portion of the succeeding two volumes, *Louis Napoleon and the Liberation of Italy* and *The Fall of Louis Napoleon*, he never recovered the momentum to finish his *magnum opus*, delay giving way to abandonment when, in 1940, the entire stock of the existing volumes was destroyed in circumstances which made immediate replacement impossible, and even eventual republication improbable.

Mr Simpson's own attack on Lytton Strachey's 'Cardinal Manning' was published in two forms during the year 1943 – first in the *Cambridge Review*, then in the *Spectator*. 'My Spectator article', he explained to the author (24 February 1966), 'was merely a condensed version, furnished at the request of its editor, of the original Cambridge one. And owing to war-time paper shortage he could only allow me just over a page of space. Hence it was far *too* condensed.' Most people, however, have only read the *Spectator* piece, which partly suppresses, for example, Mr Simpson's admiration for Lytton Strachey's prose style, and omits all mention of the particular occasion of his essay – Max Beerbohm's Rede Lecture.

In answer to the author's questions, Mr Simpson allowed that 'the most damning exposures of Purcell's inaccuracies were only published after Strachey's death, so that it was not his fault not to know about them. And Purcell himself was quite as much concerned to run Newman up – "the illustrious Oratorian" as he always called him – as to run Manning down. So there again Strachey was outpacing him. What however *was* very unworthy in him was an occasional lack of honesty in his use of an authority whose *own* lack of honesty he did not know enough about the subject to recognise.'

Mr Simpson also added that, so far as he could discover, the accuracy of *Queen Victoria* could not be faulted.

explains why, for all his brilliance and amusingness, Strachey was not admired by men able to estimate the travesty of Victorian principles and manners.' *If it is correct*. Most critics have blandly assumed that it is so – written by an English Churchman and a distinguished historian, in a convincing manner which suggests that he has rigorously checked every strand of the material used by Strachey. But most critics, unlike Frank Swinnerton, have not admitted that they 'know nothing about this matter'. In fact, if one consults the relevant chapter in Purcell's biography and applies the same strict method of checking Simpson's account as he appeared to have applied to Strachey's, one discovers that he has perhaps formulated a somewhat misleading summary himself.[6] The conclusion of his article is that Strachey, through deliberate irresponsibility, misrepresented this vital conversation in all its essential details; that he invented out of nothing its sinister undertones and motives, by tampering with the evidence supplied by Purcell. There was, he explains, nothing underhand about the interview with Pio Nono; its air of mystery was concocted by Strachey through unsub-

6. Strachey's first reference to the Papal audience of 1848 is on p. 44 of *Eminent Victorians* (1st edn), and is drawn from Purcell, pp. 389–417 (1st edn). But, according to the ecclesiastical historian Derek Jennings, Manning appears to have had *three* audiences in Rome during his stay. The first reads (Purcell, p. 389): 'April – was presented with Lady N. and G.N. to the Pope'. Purcell notes: 'In a diary so copious in its notes and comments on men and things not an allusion, strange to say, is made by the Archdeacon to his first presentation to the Pope'. The second audience would seem to have been on 8 May, referred to on p. 417 of Purcell from the notes of Manning when a Cardinal. Here a full account of the audience is given – also this is the audience to which Purcell refers in note 1 on p. 416. But there is no reference to it at all in Manning's contemporary diary (on p. 401). However, on p. 401, the entry for 11 May reads: 'At eleven had audience at the Vatican.' This presumably is the audience referred to by Strachey when he attributes to Pio Nono his persuasive innocent speech. About this audience we apparently know nothing – unless it is to be equated with that of 8 May, making allowance for the memory of an old man. But it still remains possible that, on the final 11 May meeting, Pio Nono did say something of the kind that Strachey suggests. This is certainly not rendered any less likely by F. A. Simpson's comments on the 8 May audience.

stantiated innuendo and the suppression of published information. Having absorbed Simpson's account, one is prepared for something rather commonplace in Purcell. Nothing of the kind! It was Purcell himself who suggested some mystery, who declares that no one knew for sure what happened during Manning's visit to the Vatican in 1848, who pointedly comments that 'not a line, not a word, not a syllable beyond the mere record of the fact' was entered in Manning's diary, who contends that – despite Trevelyan's rather unimportant pamphlet – we do not know for certain why Manning was granted this interview. Nor can one see in what way it would really have been to Manning's benefit had Strachey quoted or paraphrased more of Purcell's account, which displays a greater sense of high politics than of spiritual holiness. Here is what Purcell writes – and that it is closer in tone to Strachey than to Simpson is surely obvious:

'Still more unaccountable is the utter absence of any record in his Diary of its writer's private audience with Pope Pius IX. Not a line, not a word, not a syllable beyond the mere record of the fact, and that in the baldest form: "Audience to-day at the Vatican." The Pope's name even is not mentioned; Newman's name was not indicated in the Diary further than by its initial letter. Even such scant recognition was denied to Pius IX – Pius IX with whom, and only a few weeks later, he was on terms of such close and intimate friendship. To a man of Archdeacon Manning's antecedents, not to speak of his position in the "sister Church", a private meeting, still more a long conversation with the Pope of Rome, could not but be an occasion or an occurrence of exceptional interest. Was the wise and cautious archdeacon afraid that, if once committed to paper, an account of his conversation with the Pope might somehow or other reach suspicious ears, and arouse perchance against him the clamours of a too susceptible Protestantism at home? On the other hand, it is just possible that the grave and reverend Archdeacon of Chichester was disappointed with the Pope's reception, and preferred to pass over in silence what perhaps appeared to him the flippant or ignorant allusions of Pius IX to the Anglican Church. The Pope, it seems, knew a great deal about Mr Fry and the Quakers, but little or nothing about Archdeacon Manning's own creed, and even less about Anglican worship. His Holiness expressed his surprise on learning from the archdeacon that the chalice was used in the Anglican Church in the administration of Communion. "What!" exclaimed Pius IX, "is the same chalice made use of by every one?"

'Such an amazed expression of surprise; such ignorance of Anglican ritual and belief on the part of the Pope, unwitting of offence, may well have fallen like a douche of cold water on the susceptible temper of a high Anglican dignitary. Little wonder then, if such were the case, that Pius IX's name is omitted from the Diary, and the archdeacon's audience with the Pope reduced to a form so bald as almost to be obscure.'

Unwitting of offence? Strachey, who seldom weighs up his evidence in public, chose to take the pope's declared astonishment as a subtle offence, implying – almost defining – the narrow limits of Manning's Anglican prestige. If his instinct is right, then of course the objections of those critics who claim that Pius IX's genuine ignorance of Anglican ceremony indicates a similar ignorance of Anglican hierarchy – a dubious enough point anyway – automatically fall to the ground. In any event, there can be little doubt that Manning left the Vatican aware of his lowered standing as an archdeacon, and that this feeling of inferiority and isolation may well have contributed towards his later conversion – it would be peculiar if it had not done so. But where Strachey may be said to err is in his theatrical reconstruction of the unknown scene. Writing, as he always did, from books – many of them incredibly tedious – he was at pains to present his material not just briefly, but dramatically, and in this case melodramatically. The effect here is lamentable: 'It is easy to imagine the persuasive innocence of his Italian voice. . . .' The words and gestures with which Strachey supplies the pope are peculiarly stagy. Whatever happened, it is far from easy to imagine it taking place quite like this.

For Strachey, then, the story which he uncovered between the lines of Purcell's biography was childishly simple. When

Manning succumbed to the Church of Rome, he acted under the ungovernable impulse of megalomania. Any man possessing just the ordinary, healthy appetite for a little fame would have found satisfaction enough with high office in the Anglican Church. Not so Manning. Ignoring the dictates of uninspired common sense, he obeyed a deeper, intuitive call. He had, so Strachey tells us, 'scented nobler quarry. To one of his temperament, how was it possible, when once the choice was plainly put, to hesitate for a moment between the respectable dignity of an English bishop, harnessed by the secular power, with the Gorham judgment as a bit between his teeth, and the illimitable pretensions of the humblest priest of Rome?'

That Manning went over to Rome, not because of secular ambition and a preoccupation with the supernatural, but for the more 'curious' or 'singular' reason that he believed the immortality of his soul depended upon his being admitted to the one true Church, the Church of Christ, is never seriously entertained by Strachey – even as a possibility that needed to be dismissed. For theological motives and spiritual struggles of this traditional sort held no reality for him, and he reduced them to a series of comically futile gymnastics in the void. They could, however, usefully serve his aesthetic ends. He deals leniently with the Oxford Movement in order to deck his sympathetic picture of Newman with an appropriate setting; while to achieve the opposite effect, he gives a marvellously sarcastic account of the General Council of 1869 at Rome – a fitting frame for his astringent portrait of Manning.

Although these summaries are very adroit, and nowhere rely on invention, Strachey's ironic incomprehension of the instinctive appeal which all such pullulating rites and ceremonies hold for certain natures, his hilarious indifference to the obscured emotional ideals of ecclesiastical Christianity, may be said in some measure to diminish the dramatic panoply that he was so anxious to unfurl. The necessary contrast is very cleverly made, but one senses that really he considered it all six of one and half a dozen of the other. To his mind, established religion was a farrago of fantastic superstitions, mercifully susceptible to comic and picturesque presentation. Manning's religiosity – whether Anglican or Roman Catholic – was little more than a perverted form of bigotry; while poor Newman's was a naïve and grotesque mental aberration which poisoned the clear springs of his poetical genius. At best, religious belief was inspired nonsense; at worst, dangerous, seductive humbug. 'He investigates the feelings of Newman or Keble as a naturalist might the contortions of an insect,' wrote Edmund Gosse, '. . . and in their presence, if he suppresses his laughter, it is solely to prevent his missing any detail precious to his curiosity.'

One of the pivots of Strachey's thesis is Manning's behaviour on the occasion when Newman's name was mentioned with regard to a cardinalate. Being fascinated by personalities rather than ideas, Strachey represents Manning's dubious actions as emanating simply from feelings of petty jealousy over Newman's fame and potential eminence. Yet the two men were neither quite so incompatible nor so resolutely fixed in enmity as he wished to make out. The facts suggest that while Manning disliked Newman's theology and had no desire to see it sanctioned, even honoured, in Rome, he felt little animosity for Newman personally. Thus, although he did much to ensure that Newman would never attain great power in England, he spoke up for him several times in Rome, and, on one notable occasion, his warm defence successfully diverted the official censure which Newman's reply to Gladstone seemed likely to bring about. This ambivalent attitude, which eludes Strachey, puzzled Newman himself, who, prone to take everything personally, was unable to conceive that Manning could differentiate between his public influence – i.e. the theological concepts which he represented – and the effect of his personality. His bewilderment at this discrepancy is perfectly reflected in a letter he sent to Manning which Strachey quotes only as evidence of the insuperable breach between the two men. 'I can only repeat what I said when you last heard from me', Newman wrote. 'I do not know whether I am on my head or my heels when I have active relations with you. In spite of my friendly feelings, this is the judgement of my intellect.'

Despite a clerical brother-in-law's unkind observation that Manning's apparent magnificence of forehead was attributable to the fact that he had no face, he does largely resemble the rapacious eagle to which Strachey compared him. 'We might well pause in contemplation before the terrible face that confronts us in the best known photograph of Manning,' wrote John Stewart Collis,[7] 'with the senseless severity and fear and disapproval in the eyes, and the ghastly tension of the lips drawn tight as by a bit in restraint of all the natural man within.' The complementary miniature of the dove-like Newman, a bewildered victim whose innocent and ethereal spirit is crushed by the tyrannical compulsion of a scheming prelate, is a long way from the truth, and is supported mainly by excisions (sometimes concealed) in his quotations and by the running together of letters written years apart (as in the letter quoted above), all tending to make Newman appear milder and weaker than he really was. 'Anyone less like a dove than J.H.N.', commented Augustine Birrell, 'it would be hard to picture.' And Strachey himself later conceded the truth of this censure. 'Your criticism of the "eagle and dove" passage went home', he wrote to Birrell (2 June 1918). 'It is certainly melodramatic, and I should like to alter it. I think perhaps my whole treatment of Newman is over-sentimentalized – to make a foil for the other Cardinal.' Most of Newman's biographers have corroborated this view, including Sean O'Faolain, who remarked that Newman 'had a devilish temper, passions so ungovernable as to unman him, and a tongue that could clip a hedge'. Newman's own Memoranda too are full of instances of his impatience and ill-temper, and he undoubtedly was, as Manning nostalgically acknowledged after his death, 'a good hater'.

But, from the first, Strachey had a precise artistic end in view. He thought he needed a passive, sweet-tempered human sacrifice to emphasize more effectively Manning's blistering, pitiless inhumanity. At one point he writes that since Newman

7. *An Artist of Life. The Life and Work of Havelock Ellis* by John Stewart Collis (Cassell 1959) p. 92.

'rarely left the Oratory, and since Manning never visited Birmingham, the two Cardinals met only once or twice'. This is obviously based on Purcell, who wrote (vol. 2, p. 571, 1st edn): 'They never met as Cardinals except twice, once in June 1883 ... The second occasion was a return visit made at Birmingham by Cardinal Manning in 1884.' Strachey must have deliberately altered his source to make Manning appear more unbending than was in fact the case. One of the most fascinating modifications of fact, skilfully introduced at a crucial moment in the narrative lending colour to his argument that Newman was eclipsed by the propaganda of Manning's confederates, is the scene in which a tearful Newman returns incognito to Littlemore, and being accidentally recognized, refuses all offers of consolation from the sympathetic curate:

'At about this time the Curate of Littlemore had a singular experience. As he was passing by the Church he noticed an old man, very poorly dressed in an old grey coat with the collar turned up, leaning over the lych gate, in floods of tears. He was apparently in great trouble, and his hat was pulled down over his eyes, as if he wished to hide his features. For a moment, however, he turned towards the Curate, who was suddenly struck by something familiar in the face. Could it be – ? A photograph hung over the Curate's mantelpiece of the man who had made Littlemore famous by his sojourn there more than twenty years ago; he had never seen the original; but now, was it possible – ? He looked again, and he could doubt no longer. It was Dr Newman. He sprang forward, with proffers of assistance. Could he be of any use? "Oh no, no!" was the reply. "Oh no, no!" But the Curate felt that he could not turn away, and leave so eminent a character in such distress. "Was it not Dr Newman he had the honour of addressing?" he asked, with all the respect and sympathy at his command. "Was there nothing that could be done?" But the old man hardly seemed to understand what was being said to him. "Oh no, no!" he repeated, with the tears streaming down his face, "Oh no, no!" '

This scene, which is presented as the climax of Newman's

humiliation at the hands of Manning, is of especial interest for two reasons. As a piece of writing, the paragraph, for all its vividness, demonstrates clearly Strachey's inability to convey pathos. He overdoes it: Newman has to be in 'floods of tears' as well as 'in great trouble', after which the tears must again be pointed out 'streaming down his face' – a high-water mark never approached in the original account. Written without the implied nuances essential to catch and communicate that most fragile of emotions, this description is less moving than it should be and strikes one as being an apocryphal device, swamped by a chorus of loud questionings, heavy punctuation and superfluous gestures. One's suspicions that the episode is not wholly authentic are confirmed when one compares it with the source from which Strachey took it – an account written by Canon Irvine for Wilfrid Ward, who published it in his biography of Newman. From this it appears that Newman returned to Littlemore undisguised and accompanied by his Catholic friend, Father Ambrose St John. He did say 'Oh no, no!' not, as in Strachey's version of the story, in answer to the Curate's deferential inquiry as to whether he might have the honour of assisting the eminent Dr Newman, but in reply to the suggestion that he might visit a Mr Crawley. Finally he was prevailed upon to do so, 'and had a long chat with him. After that he went and saw several of the old people in the village.'

Out of this incident Strachey manufactured a fragment which appears to complete the pattern of his theme with the absolute perfection of a piece in a jigsaw puzzle. Yet, in one sense, this contrived drama goes some way to contradicting the very concept it was designed to uphold. For, realizing that a fight between an eagle and a dove makes a pretty feeble spectacle, Strachey transformed the dove into a tamer, more incompetent eagle itself. Newman was lachrymose by nature, and the tears he shed on this visit to his beloved retreat at Littlemore – his first return there after twenty-three years – were occasioned by the sight of his old home with all its sacred memories and its associations of old friends and companions, many of whom still remembered him with heartwarming vividness. So much is evident from a letter chronicling the visit that Newman wrote to Henry Wilberforce. This letter, in which Newman confesses that he had always hoped to see Littlemore again before he died, appears in Wilfrid Ward's biography directly above Canon Irvine's impressions. Strachey elected to overlook this and ascribe Newman's tears not to nostalgia – which would have been in keeping with 'a creature of emotion and of memory' – but to a sudden bitter regret over his 'wasted efforts, disappointed hopes, neglected possibilities, unappreciated powers', for so much of which Manning had been directly or indirectly responsible. But by so interpreting the 'floods of tears' as a violent, immature expression of frustration, Strachey obliquely attributes to Newman an aspiring nature hardly less keen than Manning's own.

Near the beginning of his essay, Strachey states that his interest in Manning depends mainly upon two considerations – 'the light which his career throws upon the spirit of his age, and the psychological problems suggested by his inner history'. The fact that he chose the 'eagle and dove' motif, and went, in John Raymond's words, 'bald-headed after it', shows that he was chiefly interested by Manning's inner history in so far as it illustrated certain abhorrent aspects of Victorianism, particularly that fanaticism and rigid adherence to a repressive code of behaviour which violated the amenities of civilized human intercourse. Had Strachey been really interested in Manning, not as a representative of a debased Victorian culture, but as an individual human being too important to be treated as a mere symptom of the past, his biographical motif must have been rather different. For a dramatic enough conflict lay to hand within the very character of Manning, torn all his life between an inborn fascination with the supernatural and a persistent susceptibility to worldly honour, precedence, and the society of great people. He was, as Strachey depicts him, allured by the promises of mundane glory; but he was also an honest and scrupulous man by and large, whose writings reveal little talent for self-pretence but rather a tormented awareness of the struggle between secular temptation and the fear of divine punishment that raged within him.

Even before putting pen to paper, Strachey's opinion of Manning, one feels, was irretrievably settled. 'Some of you may be shocked to hear', said Ralph Partridge in the course of a B.B.C. talk (8 October 1946), 'that Strachey had the plan of a book already formed in his head before reading up all the authorities on the subject.' But one is not shocked, since a certain preconception is detectable in the style and structure of his books. In the very first chapter of 'Cardinal Manning', for example, we are told a story of him outwitting a Harrow schoolmaster, which, by revealing the cunning and the opportunism he habitually displayed whenever his own interests were at stake, acts as an allegory of his whole character and career. Manning's dexterity of conduct was always more than equal to the task of outmanoeuvring his earnest concern for the salvation of his soul. He was throughout a tremendous egotist, but about halfway in the essay Strachey seems to become all at once aware of Manning's divided nature. His eye by then was already well focused upon a predestined end, and he deliberately discounts his own valid observations:

'In such a situation [the death of Cardinal Wiseman] the voice of self-abnegation must needs grow still and small indeed. Yet it spoke on, for it was one of the paradoxes in Manning's soul that that voice was never silent. Whatever else he was, he was not unscrupulous. Rather, his scruples deepened with his desires; and he could satisfy his most exorbitant ambitions on a profundity of self-abasement. And so now he vowed to Heaven that he would *seek* nothing – no, not by the lifting of a finger or the speaking of a word. But, if something came to him – ? He had vowed not to seek; he had not vowed not to take. Might it not be his plain duty to take? Might it not be the will of God?'

By these ingenious means did Strachey endeavour to disentangle the paradox, to unify the concept of a prelate whose 'scruples deepened with his desires' with the picture of a Machiavellian self-seeker, unfettered by any deeply sincere religious considerations. His scruples are therefore shown mainly as the mute complaints of an outwitted conscience.

Some of the features of Strachey's essay stem from Edmund Purcell's haphazard and unhistorical biography of Manning. It was Purcell's two-volume, amorphous *Life* that Strachey brilliantly synthesized into a concentrated, coherent shape. Purcell was his chief source, and indeed, as Manning's most recent biographer (1962), Vincent Alan McClelland, has pointed out, 'remained the sole source of information concerning this "Eminent Victorian" until ... the early 1920's'. For this reason it is useful briefly to compare the two works.

Purcell's *Life of Cardinal Manning* is, in short, the very antithesis of Strachey's essay. Purcell's aim was to further the importance of Manning and – not least – of himself; Strachey's was to frame an indictment of those factors within institutional religion that fostered an elevated lack of humanity. Purcell's method of achieving his aim was to give the world much of the available evidence, the unedited correspondence of the archbishop including those letters which Manning had intended to destroy; Strachey's method was to digest this evidence in private, to eliminate the random and discursive quality of Purcell's volumes, and filter off from them his personal point of view, sharpened to the needle precision of an icicle. The effect of Purcell's indiscreet panegyric was explosive, since it contained enough irrefutable disclosures to justify a verdict for the prosecution. The reader, reacting to the biographer's suppressed bias in favour of his subject, fixes his attention on the latent truth of the matter and hastens to his own most hostile conclusions. Strachey, on the other hand, endeavoured to do all his reader's work for him. The result was, in some part, opposite to the one for which he had striven so hard. After the first shattering impact, the public has come to regard his interpretation as attractive fiction founded only casually on fact – which is very far from being the case. His style, with its moments of emphatic oversimplification and romantico-psychological innuendo, has tended to liberate exaggerated misgivings over his own Voltairian prejudice. This reaction accounts for the weaker explosion produced in some quarters by his 'Cardinal Manning' than by Purcell's inartistic biography, 'packed with secret dynamite', as Professor Trevor-Roper described it, 'whose detonation, in 1896, had shattered the unnaturally smooth front of Popery in England'. Explaining the incongruous fact that some of Manning's followers actually welcomed Strachey's tirade, Trevor-Roper continues: 'Against the documentary revelations of Purcell the defenders of Manning were helpless, and it is instructive to look back at their agonised and desperate writings. Strachey, by his excessive zeal in converting unassailable facts into questionable judgements, supplied an unexpected defence. Manning's supporters could thenceforth discreetly forget the name of Purcell and complacently dismiss his revelations as being "only Lytton Strachey".'

But Strachey's heart does momentarily soften towards Manning in old age, and there is a note of genuine respect in his writing when he shows us the octogenarian cardinal addressing, with magical effect, the dock strikers at Bermondsey. In funereal prose, rich and slow, he also pays tribute to Manning's 'bold and tenacious spirit' which struggled step by step with approaching death.

The reason for this more lenient tone seems to have been twofold. First, by skilful use of quotation, he is able to indicate that now, for the first time, the lonely old man realized the futility of his worldly ambitions, the dismaying emptiness of self-regarding achievements – and he is grateful to Manning for providing him with such a fitting last scene. His imagination is touched too by another change in the cardinal, a metamorphosis which renders him far more sympathetic. 'Though his bodily strength gradually ebbed,' we are told, 'the vigour of his mind was undismayed.' Being of such a fragile physical constitution himself, Strachey responded to mental power, but was repelled by an abundance of animal energy where it was combined with physical ugliness in the young and middle-aged. It was this overplus of unattractive vitality that had helped to alienate him from Manning, and, too, from Florence Nightingale, whom he also likened to an eagle.

3

ANDANTE

Strachey's dislike of Florence Nightingale was tempered by three factors: first, her ready and percipient wit, which he complimented by borrowing without acknowledgement ('Yet her conception of God was certainly not orthodox. She felt towards Him as she might have felt towards a glorified sanitary engineer; and in some of her speculations she seems hardly to distinguish between the Deity and the Drains'); secondly, her health, which broke down, leaving her an invalid, after the ordeal at Scutari, while she was still a comparatively young woman; and thirdly, her practical efficiency, which he held in high esteem.

His general attitude towards Florence Nightingale was more divided than his view of Manning, and this gives rise to some dislocation in the thread of his second essay. She had, of course, been born into a similar stratum of life to which it had pleased God to call Strachey himself, and he sincerely admired the amazing persistency with which she fought to cut herself free from its conventional shackles, to make her own way in the world and live in independence. But he abhorred her moral and active self, which gained ascendancy over her more amiable qualities. Like Manning, she turned her back on an assured unambitious happiness, preferring the egotism of ruthless devotion to duty, and just as he had consecrated himself to celibacy within the Roman Catholic Church, so she denied her womanhood and suppressed her erotic life in a frigid indifference to human relationships. Through her choice of career, Florence Nightingale developed that side of her character which was in every respect opposed to Strachey's own. 'She would think of nothing', he complained despairingly, 'but how to satisfy that singular craving of hers to be *doing* something.'

In order to assert this barren drive for action, Strachey switches the emphasis in Sir Edward Cook's narrative, bringing out far more dramatically her morbid affection for sickness, her self-righteousness, her sexless energy. The main driving force in her life, however, may have been a little less spinsterish than he cares to admit. It was the very improbability of happiness with the kind of person considered eligible by Victorian society that fortified her zeal. She was not led on by visions of active good, so much as running away from sexual nightmares which she had no way of assuaging except through unremitting work. This would seem to be the truth delicately hinted at in the pages of Cook's biography.

As the very incarnation of nineteenth-century humanitarianism – that movement which salved the conscience of Victorian England – Florence Nightingale has been enshrined as a legendary figure, saintly and self-sacrificing – the Lady with the Lamp. By exploding for ever this romantic fable, Strachey struck directly at the popular mythology of Victorian England. *His* Florence Nightingale is a woman no less remarkable or romantic than the angelic vision of modest female virtue which he now so brilliantly disintegrated, but far less agreeable, an Amazon who embodied the paradoxical spirit of her age by becoming transfigured into the symbol of humanitarianism through the total rejection of 'the most powerful and the profoundest of all the instincts of humanity' – in other words, the sexual instinct.

As in his study of Manning, Strachey first charts the area which his essay will cover by propounding a series of rhetorical questions: 'Ah! To do her duty in that state of life unto which it had pleased God to call her! Assuredly she would not be behindhand in doing her duty; but unto what state of life *had* it pleased God to call her? That was the question. God's calls are many, and they are strange. Unto what state of life had it pleased Him to call Charlotte Corday, or Elizabeth of Hungary? What was that secret voice in her ear, if it was not a call? Why had she felt, from her earliest years, those mysterious promptings towards ... she hardly knew what, but certainly towards something very different from anything around her? Why, as a child in the nursery, when her sister had shown a healthy pleasure in tearing her dolls to pieces, had *she* shown an almost morbid one in sewing them up again? Why was she driven now to minister to the poor in their cottages, to watch by sick-beds, to put her dog's wounded paw into elaborate splints as if it was a human being? Why was her head filled with queer imaginations of the country house at Embley turned, by some enchantment, into a hospital, with herself as matron moving about among the beds? Why was even her vision of heaven itself filled with suffering patients to whom she was being useful? So she dreamed and wondered, and, taking out her diary, she poured into it the agitations of her soul. And then the bell rang, and it was time to go and dress for dinner.'

There are two chief objections to this passage. The prognosis obscures rather than clarifies the real theme of the essay, which is an examination of how a true epic story became translated by the pressures of Victorian society into a mock epic. But worse than this is Strachey's hackneyed attempt to find some dark, psychological significance in the growing child's everyday activities. In his eagerness to stress this precocious obsession, he manipulates to his own ends a number of rather trivial facts. The dog, for example, did not belong to Florence Nightingale, but to an old shepherd; it was not a pet but an outdoor working dog; Florence did not put its 'wounded paw into elaborate splints as if it was a human being', but merely assisted the local parson in the ordinary first-aid that was administered. All tiny errors, but needless. Sir Edward Cook, from whose biography Strachey's statements were taken, also wrote that 'it has been recorded that she used to nurse and bandage the dolls which her elder sister damaged'. The chief authority for this story which Strachey characteristically dramatized, appears to have been a Mrs Sarah Tooley, whose popular *Life of Florence Nightingale*, written in 1904, he very wisely does not include in his bibliography. But, less wisely, he ignored, too, Cook's explicit warning about the doubtful authenticity of tales illustrating Florence's precocious interest in nursing; and his attempt to give a modern psychological veneer to his essay was not so great a novelty as some critics were led to believe.

'It is a natural temptation of biographers', Cook had sensibly written, 'to give a formal unity to their subject by representing the child as in all things the father of the man; to date the vocation of their hero or heroine very early in life; to magnify some childish incident as prophetic of what is to come thereafter. Material is available for such treatment in the case of Florence Nightingale. ... But these things are after all but trifles. Florence Nightingale is not the only little girl who has been fond of nursing sick dolls or mending them when broken. Other children have tended wounded animals.'

There are no enormities of perverted truth in Strachey's essay, but he did consistently embroider small details to reinforce his view of Florence Nightingale as a being possessed by the overmastering mania for healing mankind. This type of treatment – which divests her of a certain sense of humour – constitutes not so much, as John A. Garraty has claimed, a violation of his oath as a biographer, but rather a naïvety in believing that his 'new' psychological approach was much less romantic than the conventional panegyric against which he was reacting.

The second chapter of 'Florence Nightingale' covers the twenty months that she spent at Scutari. Strachey's description of the inferno that raged there on her arrival, ten days after the battle of Balaclava, is excellent. He allows the dreadful facts to tell their own absorbing story without accompanying the scene with picturesque questions or theatrical dashes and dots, exclamations and semicolons. The result is that he succeeds in doing what he often found most difficult as a writer – conveying in simple terms his deeply felt emotional response to a situation. 'One feels', wrote Professor Humphry House, 'that his very finger-tips were sensitive to the practical tasks which Florence Nightingale had to do, and his nose to all the smells of Scutari; and yet the design and proportion and becoming brevity are kept.' The prose in which he describes the condition of the dying and wounded is sufficiently compelling in itself to eradicate for ever the popular image of him as a heartless, cynical and insincere pacifist, whose preoccupations were pre-eminently frivolous. The impact of these passages comes from their order and restraint, but once or twice this control falters, and he seems for a moment to recollect his readers, and to interpose them as a barrier between himself and the events he is describing. At the very end of the following paragraphs, for example, his style degenerates from the truly eloquent to the more positively loquacious, as soon as he leaves off recording his own impressions at the calamity of administrative collapse, and turns his attention to the task of striking his audience with the full horror of such chaos.

'The principal doctor was lost in the imbecilities of a senile optimism. The wretched official whose business it was to provide for the wants of the hospital was tied fast hand and foot by red tape. A few of the younger doctors struggled valiantly, but what could they do? Unprepared, disorganized, with such help only as they could find among the miserable band of convalescent soldiers drafted off to tend their sick comrades, they were faced with disease, mutilation, and death in all their most appalling forms, crowded multitudinously about them in an ever increasing mass. They were like men in a shipwreck, fighting, not for safety, but for the next moment's bare existence – to gain, by yet another frenzied effort, some brief respite from the waters of destruction.

'In these surroundings, those who had been long inured to scenes of human suffering – surgeons with a world-wide knowledge of agonies, soldiers familiar with fields of carnage, missionaries with remembrances of famine and of plague – yet found a depth of horror which they had never known before. There were moments, there were places, in the Barrack Hospital at Scutari, where the strongest hand was struck with trembling, and the boldest eye would turn away its gaze.'

By and large Strachey selects his facts with imagination, and lucidly, forcefully presents them. The occasional excrescences of his prose are matched by a number of rather far-fetched claims, all of which tend to bring out more graphically Miss Nightingale's demonic personality. He glorifies this vision of a black and rapacious eagle with hooked bill and crooked talons, and gloats over her pitiless spirit of philanthropy, her ruthless compassion. Under his pen her obstacles wax even more stupendous, her achievements more astonishing. The smaller irritations which beset her are magnified in such a way that everyone will acknowledge her to have been 'overburdened by the strain of ceaseless work, bound down by the traditions of official routine'. The hospital orderlies, for instance, who assisted her, were not, as Strachey describes them, a 'miserable band of convalescent soldiers'. A good many of them were willing and able-bodied N.C.O.s who, as Florence herself complained, were often sent back to the front after they had been given the bare modicum of hospital training. Her frenzied zeal too is stressed beyond the limits of human endurance. She did not literally, as Strachey makes out, carry out 'the whole business of purveying to the hospitals', and he rather overplays, too, the job she actually did in reclothing the army in socks, boots, shirts, trousers and dressing-gowns. He also maintained that her report, privately printed and at the time of his writing almost unobtainable, was 'to this day the leading authority on the medical administration of armies' – an exorbitant claim. In addition to all this, Strachey imbues her with a tenacity and strength of will that is little short of the miraculous: 'Her powers of resistance seemed incredible,' he wrote, 'but at last they were exhausted. She was attacked by fever, and for a moment came very near death. Yet she worked on; if she could not move, she could at least write; and write she did until her mind had left her; and after it had left her, in what seemed the delirious trance of death itself, she still wrote.' Although this account is not actually untrue, the impression which it produces is far in excess of the facts – 'two little bits of paper, perhaps not thirty words in all, were the origin of the passage', commented Rosalind Nash.

The problems which hampered Strachey in securing a complete synthesis through the steady development of a single psychological thread were more complex in 'Florence Nightingale' than in any of the other studies which make up *Eminent Victorians*. He felt a deep and awful admiration for her extraordinary achievement in ending the turmoil at Scutari, for her consummate art in circumventing the pernicious influences of departmental etiquette, and, too, her enlightenment in treating the other ranks as if they were human beings and not insentient brutes. He therefore sought to reconcile this admiration with the theme he had chosen, by so heightening her superhuman powers as to reveal the underlying seeds of inhumanity which the soil of Victorian England would later nourish into full flower. The idea was a good one, but needed all the delicacy of understatement and subtle implication if it was to come off. Unfortunately Strachey was too insistent, too hyperbolic in his handling of this theme. The result of his over-emphasis was to transform Florence Nightingale into a schizophrenic monster, a female Dr Jekyll and Mr Hyde, at one moment a saintly crusader in the cause of hygiene, at the next a satanic personality, resorting to sardonic grins, pantomime gestures and sudden fits of wild fury. Between these two Florence Nightingales, Strachey charts some latent consistency, by contrasting the prosaic, common-sense figure she cut before her assistants, with the gracious angel of mercy in which guise she appeared before the wounded soldiers. The apparent inconsistency in her character, then, is shown as being partly impressionistic, depending on the angle of vision, that of patient, opponent or helper.

Strachey's deference sprang naturally and eloquently from the point of view of the invalid, and echoed the adulation of those wounded and dying soldiers. But though honouring some aspects of her personality, he could not approve of what she later came to represent – the legendary humanitarian cut off from humankind. As with Manning, Strachey was not simply interested in his subject as an individual person, but in the interaction between her and the abhorrent age in which she lived. To stamp out the counterfeit fable of her as the sentimental Lady with the Lamp, he added to his realistic portrait another interpretation, founded on modern psychological theories:

'It was not by gentle sweetness and womanly self-abnegation that she had brought order out of chaos in the

Scutari Hospitals, that, from her own resources, she had clothed the British Army, that she had spread her dominion over the serried and reluctant powers of the official world; it was by strict method, by stern discipline, by rigid attention to detail, by ceaseless labour, by the fixed determination of an indomitable will.'

Had Strachey been content to draw attention in this way to the relentless willpower which was indispensable to her success, his portrait would in no way have been controversial. But then, obliquely, he hints at her perverted sexual compulsion which he presents as being responsible for her actions. By sacrificing her erotic love to her desire for power – especially power over men – she turned herself into a neurotic, whose frustrated sexual instincts were kept at bay only by a force which had to expend itself often on needless trivialities. Unstable and psychotic, her outward manner of quietly persuasive charm concealed a nature burning and belligerent:

'Beneath her cool and calm demeanour lurked fierce and passionate fires. As she passed through the wards in her plain dress, so quiet, so unassuming, she struck the casual observer simply as the pattern of a perfect lady; but the keener eye perceived something more than that – the serenity of high deliberation in the scope of the capacious brow, the sign of power in the dominating curve of the thin nose, and the traces of a harsh and dangerous temper – something peevish, something mocking. and yet something precise – in the small and delicate mouth. There was humour in the face; but the curious watcher might wonder whether it was humour of a very pleasant kind; might ask himself, even as he heard the laughter and marked the jokes with which she cheered the spirits of her patients, what sort of sardonic merriment this same lady might not give vent to, in the privacy of her chamber.'

These disagreeable qualities are elaborated more fully in the following chapter. As he rightly pointed out, the popular Victorian myth of Florence Nightingale – 'that gentle vision of female virtue which first took shape before the adoring eyes of the sick soldiers at Scutari' – rested on some superficial knowledge of her activities in the Crimean War, and a total ignorance of the more than fifty years of her life after it, during the greater part of which she was working to the full extent of her remarkable powers. In her own political estimation, the Crimea was a mere episode – 'scarcely more than a useful stepping-stone in her career' – an adventure which had given her knowledge and whetted her taste for power. For, as Strachey ably illustrates, her need for power – as 'for work – had developed into an obsession, arising from the repression of her womanhood. Though her health had been shattered, she was ravenous for more action. Like Manning in the grip of a more emasculated megalomania, she could pay little heed to common sense, to the voice of reason and moderation. Despite a constant expectation of death, she would not rest. A merciless addiction to work, to the exercise of political power from behind the scenes, had become her only relaxation. 'The doctors protested in vain,' Strachey wrote, echoing their fruitless expostulations, 'in vain her family lamented and entreated, in vain her friends pointed out to her the madness of such a course. Madness? Mad – possessed – perhaps she was. A demoniac frenzy had seized upon her.'

Strachey traces the path of this demoniac frenzy, kindled by her supernatural energy, to a pitch of murderous inhumanity – chiefly through her relationship with Sidney Herbert. This relationship fascinated him, as did other associations between a man and a woman – Victoria and Albert, Elizabeth and Essex, the Empress Dowager and the Emperor of China – in which the dominant partner was the woman, whose stronger, more coarse-grained nature devoured the high-born, effeminate, less tenacious male. Strachey's treatment of Sidney Herbert is quite dissimilar to his handling of Miss Nightingale. While she was utterly repugnant to him, Sidney Herbert obviously attracted him sexually, and he depicts him as attractive in order to make Florence's cool attitude to him less sympathetic. But though he approved of Sidney Herbert's moderation, his candour and aristocratic gentleness, his imagination was not fired by such altruism and lack of ambition.

1. Lytton and his sister Pippa at Rothiemurchus

2a. Goldsworthy Lowes Dickinson

2b. G. E. Moore

2c. Harry Norton

2d. Clive Bell

3a. Desmond McCarthy
3b. Bertrand Russell

4a. Members of the Shakespeare Society (sitting: far left, Lytton Strachey; far right, Leonard Woolf)

4b. Giles Lytton Strachey

5a. Vanessa Stephen (about 1902)
5b. Virginia Stephen (about 1902)

6a. Lytton teaching
Carrington to read Gibbon

6b. Lytton:
the Augustus John period

7. Roger Fry

8a. Francis Birrell, Lytton Strachey and
Saxon Sydney-Turner

8b. Sebastian Sprott, Gerald Heard, E. M. Forster
and Lytton Strachey

9. Beerbohm caricature

10. Lytton Strachey: bust portrait by Stephen Tomlin

11. Lytton Strachey: portrait by Henry Lamb

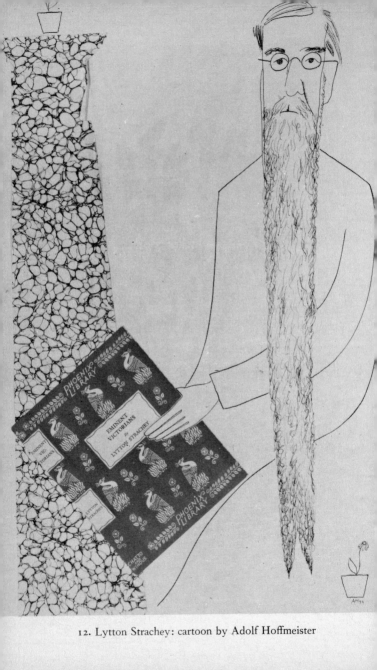

12. Lytton Strachey: cartoon by Adolf Hoffmeister

The description he gives of Sidney Herbert's personality is almost embarrassingly flat and so sentimental that one has to remind oneself that the 'great anarch' is not being ironic. Yet certainly he isn't. What has happened is that his romanticism has taken over from his more intellectual side. As with the contrast between Manning and Newman, Strachey externalizes the cleavage within his own character, so that the caustic wit and sharpness of observation – products of his mind – are replaced by something more affected when he deals with Sidney Herbert:

'He was a man upon whom the good fairies seemed to have showered, as he lay in his cradle, all their most enviable goods. Well born, handsome, rich, the master of Wilton – one of those great country-houses, clothed with the glamour of a historic past, which are the peculiar glory of England – he possessed, besides all these advantages, so charming, so lively, so gentle a disposition that no one who had once come near him could ever be his enemy. He was, in fact, a man of whom it was difficult not to say that he was a perfect English gentleman.'

In his literary criticism, Strachey had favoured culinary metaphors and similes; in his biographical essays, he made great use of zoological images and gestures. His 'Florence Nightingale' bristles with these literary animals like some weird menagerie. Lord Panmure was a bison of sorts ('the hide was the hide of a Mexican buffalo, but the spirit was the spirit of an Alderney calf'); Dr Hall was 'a rough terrier of a man'; Florence Nightingale herself, after hatching out into an eagle during early life had metamorphosed into a tigress; and Sidney Herbert was a stag, 'a comely, gallant creature springing through the forest; but the forest is a dangerous place. One has the image of those wide eyes fascinated suddenly by something feline, something strong; there is a pause; and then the tigress has her claws in the quivering haunches; and then – !'

The analogy is clear: Miss Nightingale killed Sidney Herbert. That force in her which had created order at Scutari, which was naturally intended to love and give life, had now been transformed in the swamps of Victorian England into a force that destroyed. 'It was', Strachey explained, 'her Demon that was responsible.' She lured the defenceless Sidney Herbert out into 'that tropical jungle of festooned obstructiveness, of intertwined irresponsibilities, of crouching prejudices, of abuses grown stiff and rigid with antiquity', and there he met his doom. The strain which she imposed upon him was too great. She spurred him on, deeper and deeper into that chaotic jungle until his health and spirit broke, and he no longer cared whether he lived or died. And then she suddenly sprang at him, chewed up and absorbed the last ounce of digestible matter, and spat out the remainder with disgust.

As so often when advancing an unconventional point of view, Strachey's eagerness to 'convince' led him to adopt rather questionable methods of persuasion. He suggests, for example, that Sidney Herbert was not the only man who fell victim to Florence Nightingale's relentless and unheeding zeal. Arthur Clough – 'this earnest adolescent, with the weak ankles and the solemn face, [who] lived entirely with the highest ends in view' – also succumbed, he points out with a hilarity which, like much of the humour of Belloc, considerably lessens the seriousness of the charge he is making, worn out by his meticulous tying-up of brown paper parcels.[8] For similar reasons, Strachey stresses, too, her selfish unconcern with

8. There have been a number of objections to this passage, among them one from B. A. Clough, Arthur Clough's daughter, who defended her father on the grounds that he was a conventional man. More sensibly, Lady Ritchie also demurred to this description, and in a letter to her (5 December 1918) Strachey replied: 'I think it was very good of you to write, and I am proud to think that (with reservations!) you like my book. As to reservations – perhaps I am wrong about Clough – it is difficult to be certain, but I can only say that my remarks represent my genuine opinion. I did not, of course, attempt to tell the *whole* truth about him: he was an incidental figure, and it was impossible to do more than set down what appeared to me the salient features. You say that I "dwelt on puerilities"; it was precisely the puerilities about him that seemed to me so important and so remarkable. You say he was a "sincere man, who all his life tried to do his duty". Of course; no one would dream of denying it; and if I have said anything to give a contrary impression, I must have failed in my object. But I cannot think that he was a wise man, or a man to be held up as an example to future generations. In fact, he seems to

other people's personal, non-medical affairs, citing the passionate diatribe she hurled against her ageing and faithful Aunt Mai, who had at last decided to leave her for more imperative duties with her own family.

But it is when dealing with Sidney Herbert's final illness, and his last interview with Florence Nightingale, that Strachey's methods become freer and more controversial. For in these pages he set out to show, in dramatic terms, not that she was simply driving willing horses too hard, but that she was possessed by a depraved Demon of destructive power:

'He [Sidney Herbert] was attacked by fainting-fits; and there were some days when he could only just keep himself going by gulps of brandy. ... He could no longer hope; he could no longer desire; it was useless, all useless; it was utterly impossible. He had failed. The dreadful moment came when the truth was forced upon him: he would never be able to reform the War Office. But a yet more dreadful moment lay behind; he must go to Miss Nightingale and tell her that he was a failure, a beaten man.

'. . . and, alas! when she brought herself to realise at length what was indeed the fact and what there was no helping, it was not in mercy that she turned upon her old friend. "Beaten!" she exclaimed. "Can't you see that you've simply thrown away the game? And with all the winning cards in your hands! And so noble a game! Sidney Herbert beaten! And beaten by Ben Hawes! It is a worse disgrace . . .", her full rage burst out at last, ". . . a worse disgrace than the hospitals at Scutari."

'He dragged himself away from her, dragged himself to Spa, hoping vainly for a return to health, and then, despairing, back again to England, to Wilton . . . and at Wilton he died.'

Rosalind Nash, whose mother was in Florence Nightingale's household and who was deputed by her family to

---

me to embody a whole set of weaknesses which have been hitherto either ignored or treated as virtues, and against which it was one of the main purposes of my book to make a protest.' Among the many other letters he received was one from Max Beerbohm (28 July 1918), who wrote that 'I think my favourite passage in all the book is the Clough passage'.

advise with Sir Edward Cook when he was writing his official biography, has shown[9] how Strachey contrived this theatrical last scene by ingeniously mixing two passages from Florence Nightingale's correspondence with other people. First-person drama and jigsaw symmetry are characteristically preferred by Strachey to the more indirect methods of presentation. But since all the evidence needed to stage such a scene was lacking, some gestures and décor had to be invented. There existed, for example, no documentary source to show that, in a tirade of indignant rage, Miss Nightingale openly taunted Sidney Herbert with having been beaten by Ben Hawes – 'a worse disgrace than the hospitals at Scutari'. Something like these words were written by her in a letter to Sir John McNeill: 'What strikes me in this great defeat more painfully even than the loss to the army is the triumph of the bureaucracy over the leaders – a political aristocracy who at least advocate higher principles. A Sidney Herbert beaten by a Ben Hawes is a greater humiliation really (as a matter of principles) than the disaster of Scutari.'

Although there is no record of Miss Nightingale having mentioned Scutari personally to Sidney Herbert, in a letter to Harriet Martineau she did recall that they spoke of Cavour: 'And I was too hard upon him. I told him that Cavour's death was a blow to European liberty, but that a greater blow was that Sidney Herbert should be beaten on his own ground by a bureaucracy. I told him that no man in my day had thrown away so noble a game with all the winning cards in his hands. And his angelic temper with me, at the same time that he felt what I said was true, I shall never forget. I wish people to know that what was done was done by a man struggling with death.'

From the wording of these two letters, it would seem that Strachey's intermingling of them was not unreasonable. But, in converting this correspondence into a directly witnessed incident, he leaves out all the implied compliment which lay behind Florence Nightingale's disapprobation. In Strachey's version of their last meeting, her attitude is shown as one of

9. *Nineteenth Century* (February 1928).

violent invective, the impulse of which is only contempt; and her stern encouragement is intensified into a rabid, truculent resentment – a very death-blow to Sidney Herbert. And in the death-scene itself, Strachey's fondness for visual melodrama is again vividly illustrated. Sir Edward Cook had noted that 'among his last articulate words were these: "Poor Florence! Poor Florence! Our joint work unfinished" '. Under Strachey's alchemy this is transmuted into: '. . . then, almost unconscious, his lips were seen to be moving. Those about him bent down. "Poor Florence! Poor Florence!" they just caught. ". . . Our joint work . . . unfinished . . . tried to do . . ." and they could hear no more.'

In his last two chapters, Strachey leads Florence Nightingale down a sharp decline, past her cumbersome flirtation with Platonic mysticism and into an abyss of bland and senile sentimentality. Possessing no great imagination, he tells us, she grew bored, lonely, miserable, unless perpetually diverted by external activity. Throughout most of the essay, her superabundant energy had been pitted against the correspondingly superabundant inertia and incompetence of the authorities. Their antagonism was the battery which continuously recharged her vitality. When it dwindled, and she was driven to seek inspiration in the more abstract realms of philosophy and religion, her spirit began to disintegrate. Neither a creative artist nor yet a true scientist, she remained, like most men and women of action, simply an empiricist. 'She was a capable woman,' Strachey commented to his mother while working on this essay, 'but rather disagreeable in various ways – a complete egotist, and also very full of tiresome religiosity; and I don't think very intelligent. In spite of spending all her life in medical concerns, she never seems to have got a scientific grasp of things.' In her heyday she had deeply relished the joys of power, and now, by her rigorously enforced seclusion, she preserved and amplified the Nightingale legend.

Yet Strachey, too, now that it suits his purpose, contributes to this legend. 'Lying on her sofa in the little upper room in South Street,' he wrote, 'she combined the intense vitality of a dominating woman of the world with the mysterious and romantic quality of a myth.' To underline this still dominating spirit of the invalid, he makes great play with Dr Sutherland's loyalty to her, which he represents as the attachment of a slave to his omnipotent master. Dr Sutherland, 'an indefatigable disciple', devotes all his time to her service, and is seen shivering in his shoes whenever she throws him a contemptuous glance. Strachey does not inform the reader that, so far from acting as her full-time lackey, he had his own position at the War Office, and had agreed to become her personal secretary only during such hours as he could spare from his leisure – which appear nevertheless to have been considerable. Nor, from the recollections of those who knew him personally, does he emerge as the poor, muddle-headed mouse of a man whom Strachey depicts. Undoubtedly, however, he was bullied by the cantankerous Miss Nightingale, and there were often irascible exchanges between them.

To emphasize the 'mysterious and romantic quality' of this legend, Strachey pictures Miss Nightingale, by her own admission a fanatical advocate of sun and fresh air, as lying in her 'shaded chamber', an unseen presence above, while downstairs there raged a loud hubbub of imploring dignitaries, all desperately appealing for a few moments' interview. 'Great statesmen and renowned generals were obliged to beg for audiences; admiring princesses from foreign countries found that they must see her at her own time, or not at all; and the ordinary mortal had no hope of ever getting beyond the downstairs sitting-room and Dr Sutherland.'

Though the spirit of what Strachey describes is perfectly true, his practice of collating documentary evidence and presenting it as a theatrically produced state of affairs – something that the reader can *see* – leads him into trivial errors. For again his mischievous fancy embroiders upon the data supplied in Cook's biography – his only source-book for such information – to enhance the aura of mysterious divinity. Cook described the chamber as not shaded, but full of light. Facing south, its large windows were without curtains, while all the walls were painted white. To give dramatic contrast to her solitary, awesome, even godlike image upstairs, Strachey fills the downstairs rooms with a constant influx of clamouring nobility, whereas the facts appear to have been that visitors came only by appointment and were seldom kept waiting. On the other hand, it was true that many important people were always applying unsuccessfully for such appointments, so that Strachey's reconstruction, though it exaggerates Miss Nightingale's lack of consideration, is not wholly misleading.

In his final short chapter, Strachey sums up in two sentences the antipathy he felt towards his subject. 'The benevolence and public spirit of that long life', he wrote, 'had only been equalled by its acerbity. Her virtue had dwelt in hardness, and she had poured forth her unstinted usefulness with a bitter smile upon her lips.' But in these last years, he added, her acerbity curdled into a vague and amiable sentimentalism. And then only, once 'consciousness itself grew lost in a roseate haze, and melted into nothingness', was it deemed fitting to bestow upon her a public honour, the Order of Merit. This final revivification of the ancient myth, in all its ironic inappropriateness, makes a perfect ending to Strachey's study. 'You can feel reading the book that he [Strachey] is pleased that Miss Nightingale grew fat and that her brain softened', Duff Cooper indignantly protested to Lady Diana Manners; but, he added, 'I have enjoyed it enormously.'[10]

4

SCHERZO

'I have read only Flo and Tom', Walter Raleigh wrote to Strachey early in May. '(It is you who have made me so familiar). Pass a person through your mind, with all the documents, and see what comes out. That seems to be your method. Also choose them, in the first place, because you dislike them.'

Commenting further on 'Florence Nightingale', Raleigh implies that, in contrast to the wholly ironic manner he adopted to Dr Arnold, Strachey's divided attitude is respon-

10. *The Rainbow Comes and Goes* by Diana Cooper, p. 168.

sible for the rather inconsistent effect left by his essay:

'It's no use your jeering at those who romanticised the lady with the lamp', he wrote. 'You are a far more incorrigible sinner. You're like Kipling, who sees God in a machine. I find myself wondering whether all those stout military mules who got caught in the machine were really such sinners . . .

'No one can condemn except on the basis of a creed. Your creed comes easy to me. But I don't quite follow its dealings with Flo. "By God," I keep on thinking excitedly, "Flo has got off." A judge of feminist leanings is it?

'It's queer. Of course the cruelty of a really hard-bitten good woman is asserted, in the Flo sketch, and proved. But it is justified; and it is not deeply felt. The death of S. Herbert and Clough is enjoyable. They die because Juggernaut is great; not because they are silly . . .'

Strachey's denunciation of Florence Nightingale's hardness was, it is true, partly offset by his admission that, had she been of a softer, more pliant nature, she would never have succeeded in ending the degradation at Scutari or in bringing about humane and sensible reforms at the War Office. But if there was some justification for *her* unamiable qualities, there could be practically none for those of Dr Arnold, since his reputation as an enlightened reformer, unlike hers, was very largely sham. And so while she is let off, and her legend gingered up with a fresh if rather bitter spice, he is exposed as an appalling and pretentious impostor, with scarcely any redeeming features. An extraordinary portent, the myth which swirled about his indistinct figure still lingered on in 1918, since no one read him or knew very much about him. Strachey's portrait, unrelieved by any touches of furtive admiration or tenderness, is the most caustic in his book. It is also perhaps the most amusing.

There seem to have been both personal and literary reasons for the great enmity which Strachey felt towards Arnold. The reforms which the headmaster of Rugby enforced had made him, however unintentionally, 'the founder of the worship of athletics and the worship of good form', in which philistine climate Strachey had spent some of his most miserable days.

Many of Arnold's innovations were similar enough to those of Dr Reddie,[11] Strachey's own headmaster, for him to have felt personally bound up with them. E. F. Benson, for example, who went to Marlborough, one of the new schools to feel the influence of Arnold's reforms, underwent 'the methods of tutors ... who by making their pupils chop dry faggots of wood, hoped to teach them what was the nature of the trees that once the wind made murmurous on the hillsides of Attica' – a description which would have had for Strachey a familiar ring. His response to Arnold was therefore more directly evolved from personal experience than that to his other subjects. Much of the antagonism which he felt is revealed in such an ambiguously worded sentence as: 'The Communion service he regarded as a direct and special counterpoise to that false communion and false companionship, which, as he often observed, was a great source of mischief in the school; and he bent himself down with glistening eyes, and trembling voice, and looks of paternal solicitude, in the administration of the elements.'

The study of Dr Arnold is monochromatic in a sense that none of the other essays in *Eminent Victorians* are, since Strachey does not dramatize his career by contrasting it with that of some opponent or with the implacable façade of an antiquated institution. Instead, he places Arnold alone on the stage, and makes him rush around with the inexplicable urgency of the white rabbit in *Alice in Wonderland*, a ridiculous clown of a man, full of almighty zeal and energy, towards whom he never varies his look of blank distaste.

As delineated by Strachey, Arnold shares almost all the vices of his fellow eminent Victorians, but practically none of their few compensating qualities. Like Manning, he is vain and ambitious – 'I believe that naturally I am one of the most ambitious men alive', he once wrote – and, like Manning too, the religious element in his life, which theoretically discountenanced all worldly ambition, was modified at crucial moments to a point where the natural disharmony between ambition and

11. Strachey's headmaster at Abbotsholme. See *Lytton Strachey: A Biography*, pp. 80–92.

religion nearly vanished altogether. But he owned none of Manning's picturesque majesty or stateliness, and without his tortuous sophistication, his romantic flair for success, he remained little more than a portentous functionary. His life, to an even greater degree than that of Florence Nightingale, presented a barren spectacle of continuous activity, of – to use Carlyle's words – 'unhasting, unresting diligence'. Partly owing to a resolute lack of imagination, *she* had succeeded on a vast scale; his lack of imagination limited him, despite his untiring industry, to a comparative failure, which may have accounted for that puzzled look which Strachey discerns on his blunt, honest face. Only towards the end of her life, when her tremendous powers were at last failing, did Florence Nightingale involve herself in the solitary and awful grandeur of her chamber in South Street – 'the unseen power above'. Dr Arnold, on the other hand, chose to confuse his identity with that of the Almighty when in the prime of life, ruling 'remotely, through his chosen instruments, from an inaccessible heaven'. Nor did he possess, like Gordon, any implicitly heroic or bizarre fabric in his character to atone for this mediocrity. Even his most sympathetic qualities – his love of family and his love of nature – were kept sternly in check so that they might never interfere with his overbearing awareness of the knowledge of good and evil, his grim, humourless air of authority.

Strachey's unrelenting antipathy was also prompted by the only source-book of any importance on Arnold – that pious biography by Dean Stanley, one of his favourite pupils, from whom, however, Arnold had withheld the secrets of literary composition. Unlike Purcell's *Life of Cardinal Manning*, this biography smoothed over anything of even the most faintly controversial nature and carefully excluded all personal information concerning its subject's private life, for fear of distressing Mrs Arnold and her children. In marked contrast to Cook's *Life of Florence Nightingale*, which Strachey considered to be an excellent book, Stanley's *Life and Correspondence of Dr Arnold* was narrow in outlook, designed solely to embalm the memory of a dead man. It had been written by someone with a strong personal prejudice, conscious that he had a definite case to make. Although, chiefly through its correspondence, these two volumes contained enough material for their readers, if any, to piece together a fairly clear view of Arnold, it was not, in the modern Stracheyesque sense of the term, a biography at all, but an extended obituary notice, the final item of the undertaker's lugubrious business, calling for a wreath rather than a review.

Strachey's essay attempts to reanimate Arnold by opposing the traditional attitude as expressed in Stanley's *Life* and, more popularly, in the Rugby *Iliad*, Thomas Hughes's *Tom Brown's Schooldays*. Yet his exposition of Arnold's paltriness was neither so unjust nor so revolutionary as the general reception given to the essay assumed. Over seventy years earlier, in a once celebrated review of Stanley's *Life* – which Strachey himself did not know – Dr Martineau had written of Arnold as 'respectable in scholarship, insensible to art, undistinguished in philosophy, great in action, though his sphere was not large'. Later in this review, the Arian divine had gone on to propound a point of view almost identical to Strachey's own, marking the very same passages to assist him in the critical assessment of Arnold's character. This coincidence is startling only if one accepts the view that Strachey drew a hideously disproportionate caricature, almost unrecognizable as the Arnold who was never a man of plain simplicity, but of true and lasting greatness.

But 'Dr Arnold' *is* a caricature, and most of the hostility directed against this essay, in failing to recognize this or in naming it as such solely by way of adverse comment, has been curiously misplaced.[12] In literature the caricature has as rightful

12. Because it is the most hostile of the essays in *Eminent Victorians* many critics have assumed that 'Dr Arnold' must be the most unfair. 'It is in the essay on Dr Arnold that he has most laid himself open to counter-attack', wrote R. A. Scott-James. 'It is a brilliant caricature, but it is the reverse of impartial and is only outwardly dispassionate. It is quite evident that he is at daggers drawn with his subject.' R. J. Campbell may be said to have spoken for Arnold's later biographers when, in the Preface to his book, he wrote: 'If I have not included Mr Lytton Strachey's essay on Arnold (in *Eminent Victorians*) with the above-mentioned authorities,

and legitimate a place as in the visual arts. 'The caricature's first duty is to be expressive', Strachey once wrote of Caran d'Ache. His own sketch of Arnold, which deliberately ignored a vast quantity of documentary material in Stanley's biography and which consequently draws in only the outlines of his character, is certainly that. Occasionally – as in his description of the death of Arnold – the excision and transposition of sentences from Stanley's book, made so as to achieve a more ludicrous effect, are a little unfair. He also limits rather too severely the scope of Arnold's sympathies and greatly exaggerates his deified remoteness as headmaster. But, in the main, his purpose was to demonstrate Arnold's mediocrity as an educational thinker and reformer – and this he very effectively did. According to Lionel Trilling, the fundamental untruth of Strachey's portrait is that it translated Arnold's seriousness into sedentariousness; the central truth of the portrait, Trilling maintains, is that it convincingly exposes Arnold's seriousness as earnestness. The missing humour in Arnold's attitude Strachey supplies himself from without, and it is this injection of comedy that reduces Arnold's stature, setting it in a truer perspective.

Dr Arnold is seen as a political figure, the most influential teacher of the Victorians. His target was not merely the public-school system, the cult of which had tended to stultify all upper-middle-class intelligence through three successive

---

it is because I am compelled to regard it as a caricature and not a true impression of the character and career of a truly great and good man.' Writing to Lady Diana Manners (7 and 8 July 1918), Duff Cooper complained that Strachey's sneering attitude was that of a pamphleteer rather than a historian. 'Arnold of course is a bit too much', he concluded. And in a letter to Strachey (12 August 1918) G. M. Trevelyan also objected to this essay, but mainly it seems because he had married into the family and because Matthew Arnold had said some good things about his father. But, Trevelyan added, 'I read it [*Eminent Victorians*] at one long sitting in the train across North Italy with the most intense pleasure, approval and admiration. ... You have got a real historical sense which few professional historians have and hardly any literary people who dabble in history. You have not only historical sense, as Carlyle and Belloc have – but *judgement* which they have not.'

generations, which had set hard the mood of the Victorian age and unnaturally prolonged its insidious spirit well into the twentieth century, but the whole movement of orthodox Victorian liberalism. Arnold had often declared himself to be a liberal, and with this definition Strachey had no quarrel. Taking him as a prototype, he sets out to show that nineteenth-century liberalism was not based on the principle of progress or enlightened reform, but rather on the variation of an old and debased routine.

When Arnold was appointed headmaster of Rugby in August 1828, Strachey tells us, there existed throughout the country a general feeling of dissatisfaction with the barbaric, rough-and-tumble method of schooling typified in Keate's regime at Eton – 'a system of anarchy tempered by despotism'. The time was ripe for improvements. Public opinion was strongly in favour of educational reform. Some desired a more genuinely liberal curriculum; others, among whom Dr Arnold was one, were convinced of the necessity for a higher moral tone. Though the majority of parents would undoubtedly have opposed profound changes for the better, Dr Arnold's great reputation and authority could hardly have been resisted. 'But how was he to achieve his end?' asked Strachey, framing what was really his chief indictment of Arnold. 'Was he to improve the character of his pupils by gradually spreading round them an atmosphere of cultivation and intelligence? By bringing them into close and friendly contact with civilised men, and even, perhaps, with civilised women? By introducing into the life of his school all that he could of the humane, enlightened, and progressive elements in the life of the community? On the whole, he thought not.'

The opportunity for humanistic reform was missed. Far from breaking up the moribund conception of education, devoted almost entirely to the teaching of classical philology, Arnold merely altered some aspects in the running of an already well-established monastic institution. By introducing morals and religion into the heathen climate of the public school, by discounting intellectual ability and devaluing companionship, he gave to the ancient scheme of things a new lease of life. 'He would treat the boys at Rugby as Jehovah had treated the Chosen People.' The centre of his educational system – again like Dr Reddie's – was the school chapel, from where, with high-pitched exhortations, he diligently strove to convert his pupils into brave and useful, truth-telling English and Christian gentlemen. He might have changed the principles of education through all the public schools of England; instead he just gave them a temporary face-lift which slightly altered their physiognomy, but left untouched the basic cranial structure. He might have founded a new scheme of cultural and scholastic instruction, but 'he threw the whole weight of his influence into the opposite scale, and the ancient system became more firmly established than ever'.

Strachey's analysis of the alterations which Arnold effected within the conventional public school, the ironic discrepancy between the aims that lay behind his new measures and the results they finally brought about, is essentially just and, though short, extraordinarily complete. His sketch of Arnold's character, which was of rather secondary importance to him and which he etched in only as a shadow to his public image, is rather less satisfactory. He alludes only briefly to Arnold's more engaging qualities, and because they were always held in control, minimizes their strength, assuming that they were never very potent.

Despite his high seriousness, Arnold had never gone through the process of growing up. At the age of ten he was already as great a prig as during his headmastership. His moral philosophy was evolved not as the outcome of experience, but through a fear of the deep springs of emotion which he so successfully damped down. He embraced this philosophy with a desperate passion. 'When the spring and activity of youth is altogether unsanctified by anything pure and elevated in its desires,' he once wrote, 'it becomes a spectacle that is as dizzying and almost more morally distressing than the shouts and gambols of a set of lunatics.' This pronouncement, and many others regarding the natural evil of boys – their abundance of sin combined with so little sorrow, the absence within them of any proper, manly sense of degradation or guilt – was a disavowal of what was best in Arnold's own nature. That he felt the danger of boyish evil within himself is attested to by the power of such spectacles to move him, to make him almost lose faith in his whole system of education. His wanderlust, his nostalgic sense of family, his naturalist's love of the country – all his most endearing traits – were closely linked with the childhood years he spent at Cowes. He can be seen at his most relaxed not at Rugby, but among the moors of Westmorland during the holidays, a boyish, boisterous figure rambling about with his children and momentarily permitting himself to enjoy what he fearfully described as 'an almost awful happiness'.

In Strachey's pages we seldom catch a glimpse of Arnold in these off-duty moments. The headmaster's hardness is represented not as a protective shell covering a sensitive flesh, but as a uniform texture which extended in the same coarse consistency throughout the length and breadth of his being. We are never allowed to consider whether Arnold might have compelled himself to be hard so as to suppress those intimations of 'awful happiness' which so terrified him, threatening to surge up and swamp that sense of moral evil by which he steadfastly lived. The humanity latent in his nature found expression in some of his letters and in certain aspects of his private life which are excluded from *Eminent Victorians*. The man to whom Strachey confines his attention is the Arnold who wrote to Stanley: 'My love for any place, or person, or institution, is exactly the measure of my desire to reform them.' The Arnold who does not appear in this essay possessed a concealed poetic sensibility that came to the surface in his appreciative description of Laleham, the beautiful scenery of which he happily felt no compulsion to alter, and may also be seen towards the close of his short life in that wish to rest in Grasmere churchyard, 'to lie under the yews which Wordsworth planted, and to have the Rotha with its deep and silent pools passing by'.

'Nowhere', Dr Arnold once remarked, 'is Satan's work more evidently manifest than in turning holy things to ridicule.' Such a statement well conveys his profound lack of humour, that deficiency which Strachey so pointedly succeeds in making good, to the indignation of Arnold's admirers, who saw in his irony only another example of the Devil's work against which they had been warned. But, with his muddle-headed logic, his transcendent self-confidence, his strenuous obsession with moral righteousness, Arnold readily lent himself to caricature. He asked for it. Strachey needed to invent or suppress no major facts in order to produce the preposterous impression he wanted. All he did was to direct his readers' attention towards Arnold's public career, decorating his narrative with cunningly edited extracts from his writings and recorded statements, and away from his underdeveloped but still extant sense of poetry. By this slight readjustment of emphasis Arnold is entirely dehumanized and made to appear as totally absurd.

Much has been made of the summary shortening of Arnold's legs, which serves to show the whole man as stunted. There appears to be no evidence in the sources listed at the end of Strachey's essay to support his statement that the headmaster's 'legs, perhaps, were shorter than they should have been'. In fact both Arnold and Strachey were about the same height, though the former looked shorter and the latter taller than was actually the case. But in all other respects Arnold was the antithesis of Strachey, and their physical dissimilarity (by the general laws of a logically conducted universe, it stood to reason) must have extended to their legs. Aesthetically, at any rate, this seemed inevitable. At the same time, Strachey did not believe, as has been asserted by later critics, that he had invented this detail. Although, subsequently, he could find no authority for it, he was sure, so he told Logan Pearsall Smith, that he had read the fact somewhere, or had been told it by someone.[13] This error and other

13. A contradictory story is given by Eddie Marsh in a letter to Christopher Hassall (May 1941). 'Have you read the articles on Virginia Woolf in Horizon?' he asked. 'W[illiam] Plomer annoys me by speaking of "the slightly bow-legged Rupert Brooke", which is pure invention, like Lytton Strachey's, who told me he had said that Dr Arnold's legs were too short because he thought they ought to have been.' After Vanessa Bell had read Strachey's essay, she suggested: 'Why not Mrs Humphry Ward fol-

discrepancies scrupulously investigated by the distinguished
American scholar, George Kuppler Simson, are put in their
proper perspective by another artist in biography, John Stewart Collis:[14] 'I note that even the warm admirers of Lytton
Strachey, including Max Beerbohm, are inclined to rebuke him
for his essay on Arnold as being in too much of a vein of
mockery. The assumption is that Dr Arnold should not have
been mocked. But how could any mockery be too much for
such a man? The biographer knew what he was doing, what he
was called upon to do. It is complained that he quoted things
out of context and made them look bad. "It is very startling",
said Arnold, looking round upon the boys at Rugby, "to see
so much of sin combined with so little of sorrow." How do
you make that remark look good? – and he did say it.'

5

RONDO

For two reasons 'The End of General Gordon' stands apart
from the other essays in *Eminent Victorians*. First, there was
no single, pre-eminent source-book on which Strachey could
depend, and which controlled the shape of his essay. His
other studies had been, in a sense, miniature corrective re-
writings of official biographies: with Gordon his sources were
far more diverse and more evenly matched in their importance, with the result that his theme is less over-simplified, its
treatment freer and more liberal.

'I am inclined to rate the "Gordon" as your highest

---

lowing in her uncle's or whatever it was footsteps. It wouldn't be libel-
lous to call her legs too short, would it?' And Strachey wrote to her on 10
July 1918: 'Something certainly ought to be done about Mrs Humphry
Ward. Have you by any chance seen her reminiscences, which are now
coming out in the Cornhill? Of an incredible vulgarity. Apparently she is
furious about Eminent Victorians, and wrote to Asquith – "How *could*
you praise that horrid book?" Lord Esher, also, has become my enemy.
On the other hand I am supported by Lord Knutsford!'
14. *An Artist of Life*, John Stewart Collis.

achievement, because the construction of that seems to me the most ingenious and monumental of all', Max Beerbohm later wrote to him (7 July 1920). 'I don't say the others don't equal it in the adjustment of their beginnings to their endings – or rather, in the lack of beginnings and endings, as such. The serpent swallows its own tail every time admirably. My reason for plunging for the "Gordon" is my admiration for that to-and-fro method of narration towards the end: Khartoum – Downing Street, Downing Street – Khartoum; by which device of the steady pendulum we get all the tragic irony of the whole matter.'

This wider, more flexible treatment was entirely appropriate to his subject, since it enabled Strachey fully to display the crazy illogicality of Gordon – 'that extraordinary mixture of incompatibilities – follies and sublimities', as he described it to Ottoline Morrell (20 May 1918). From a Bloomsbury point of view – the point of view of significant form – this lack of a single, unifying principle, lucidly spun out, was disappointing; and the reaction of the critics to this particular essay has been the most widely divergent of all. One B.B.C. critic, for instance, complained that Strachey had been too lenient with Gordon in failing to allude to the homosexual strain in his nature; while, more recently, Judge Gerald Sparrow censured Strachey because 'with remarkably little evidence . . . [he] advanced the view of Gordon as a homosexual'. There is, in fact, only one specific reference to homosexuality in the essay, and that relates not to Gordon, but to Rimbaud in Africa having 'forgotten the agonised embraces of Verlaine'. Yet undoubtedly Strachey did feel for Gordon a certain amused affection. Attracted, in any case, to split personalities, he was charmed and fascinated in a unique way by his subject's extravagant personality, and drawn to probe deeper into his character. The prose itself is closer in tone to that of 'Dr Arnold' in that it relies less on rather suspect scenic devices than on the compelling power of lucid and compressed exposition. 'The writing I thought more than usually unadorned,' Virginia Woolf commented (28 December 1917), 'and surely the most flawless example of the master's style in

218

its maturity.' Though unadorned, the strain is of a higher mood. The tragic but exhilarating inevitability of Gordon's fate is cleverly built up to its final climax against an undertone of half-amused, almost filial tenderness, which leaves the impression that, unlike his Victorian counterparts, Gordon was a man more sinned against than sinning.

But even if Strachey felt no persistent enmity for him, the hero of Khartoum, with his boundless energies so misdirected by irrational religious beliefs, fitted perfectly into the scheme of *Eminent Victorians*. Behind the gentle soldier of God, he sought to reveal a half-inspired, half-crazy Englishman, with his romance and his fatalism, his brandy-bottle and his Bible. This was certainly a valid aim, but in places he again falls to the temptation of over-emphasis, and by his tamperings and deletions of evidence focuses a rather unnatural attention on the general's eccentricities. The portrait of Gordon which he wished to project is described in his essay on Li Hung-Chang[15] as an 'irresponsible knight-errant whom his countrymen first laughed at and neglected, then killed and canonised – a figure straying through the perplexed industrialism of the nineteenth century like some lost "natural" from an earlier Age'. In so far as his interest in Gordon's character prevails over his itch to shock latter-day Victorian susceptibilities, Strachey's criticism is mainly percipient, poetic and ingeniously balanced. He succeeds in shadowing him forth as a nineteenth-century Don Quixote, a bemused and deluded crusader, simultaneously comic and heroic, as seen through the half-incredulous, half-admiring eyes of a cautious, common-sense Sancho Panza.

Though Strachey's attitude to Gordon may be said to have been divided, it did not lead to the type of dislocation that had marred his study of Florence Nightingale. The contradictions in his character are neatly blended into his mad quixotism and further the artistic ends of the essay. He saw Gordon as a light, gliding figure, with candid open blue eyes, by temperament unassuming, *farouche*, and like himself a mis-

15. 'A Diplomatist: Li Hung-Chang', *War and Peace* (March 1918), 249–50. Collected in *Characters and Commentaries* and in *Biographical Essays* (268–72).

ogynist, ill at ease in conventional society – 'his soul revolted against dinner-parties and stiff shirts; and the presence of ladies – especially of fashionable ladies – filled him with uneasiness'. But he significantly edits the entries in Gordon's *Journals* so as to paint him as a wild man, contemptuous not just of sophisticated parties but of all civilization. Somewhat like himself, too, Gordon was gifted with an impish talent for satirical fancies and a fondness for romantic speculation. By nature he was not really a power-seeker but an adventurer, in whom, however, the germ of extreme religiosity, spreading like an incurable disease, had stilled the workings of his conscience. Under this illness, his ambitions were inflated to fanatical proportions, so that he interpreted his actions as being ordained by an inscrutable but absolute Providence. The essential honesty and nobility of his spirit was thus fatally contaminated by a transcendental selfishness, more insidious than any ordinary desire for wealth or titles, since it was largely irrational. As 'a man of energy and action, a lover of danger and the audacities that defeat danger, a passionate creature, flowing over with the self-assertiveness of independent judgment and the arbitrary temper of command', Gordon appealed immensely to Strachey's romantic imagination. But once those religious tendencies within him developed into a dominating factor in his life, once he became a willing instrument not of God but of the extreme imperialist section of the British Government, once he began to indulge his secret passion for fame, 'for the swaying of multitudes, and for that kind of enlarged and intensified existence "where breath breathes most – even in the mouths of men" ', then his sense of humanity and truth were perverted no less surely than those of Manning, Florence Nightingale or Dr Arnold, and he saw himself, through the eyes of pride, transfigured as a god on earth.

The initial signs of this disintegration – Gordon's impulsiveness, incoherence, and whirl of contradictory policies – exerted a spell over Strachey's mind like some larger-than-life figure from the pages of Dostoyevsky. Just as he had placed himself in Manning's congregation, had looked up at Florence

Nightingale from the sick-beds at Scutari, had described Arnold's headmastership from the viewpoint of one of his pupils, so he presented an impressionistic sketch of Gordon as witnessed from the ranks. The reverence that all soldiers felt for him is echoed in Strachey's description: 'Walking at the head of his troops, with nothing but a light cane in his hand, he seemed to pass through every danger with the scatheless equanimity of a demi-God.'

But once his peculiar malady had taken a firmer hold upon him, Strachey notes, the relationship between the general and his troops underwent a grim change. A prey to violent outbursts of temper, broken by periods of conscience-stricken generosity, he treated his subordinates at Khartoum with stern contempt, while they regarded him, no longer with admiration, but abject fear.

'Gordon's fatalism swells from his personal belief into the outer circumstances of his life', commented J. K. Johnstone, 'and into the very structure of the biography. In the first great adventure of his career, he leads an army against another religious fanatic, the Chinese Tien Wang, the Celestial King. Both Gordon and Tien Wang, Strachey tells us, turned to religion after experiencing an attack of illness – so Strachey points the similarity between them.'

At Khartoum, Gordon's last adventure, he again confronts a religious fanatic, the cruel Mohammedan divine, the Mahdi. Waiting for his strangely predestined end, he watches each day the splendid hawks that swooped and wheeled about the besieged palace. 'I often wonder', he reflected, 'whether they are destined to pick my eyes, for I fear I was not the best of sons.' This thought was prophetic, and fitted perfectly into the scheme of the essay, since Strachey represents Gordon's eyes as symbolizing all that is best and most innocent in his character, not fatally obscured by the cataract of atavistic superstition. After his death, Strachey recounts, Gordon's head was brought to the Mahdi as a trophy, and 'at last the two fanatics had indeed met face to face. The Mahdi ordered the head to be fixed between the branches of a tree in the public highway, and all who passed threw stones at it. The hawks of the desert swept and circled about it – those very hawks which the blue eyes had so often watched.'

Despite the sympathy which makes it the best of these four essays, 'The End of General Gordon' raised some of the loudest clamour against the author of *Eminent Victorians*. What right had a sickly scribbler to criticize the hero of Khartoum? people indignantly asked – this Strachey, this pacifist, who had never himself experienced the thirst and heat of the tropics or even been out under the pale English sun without a parasol? Whether his portraits of a prelate, a nurse and a schoolmaster had been worth painting, it was said, was an arguable question. Possibly they were. All were highly estimable professions, no doubt, but nevertheless a little dull – not the sort of thing to fire the ordinary man's imagination. But there could be absolutely no justification for discrediting a gallant British general. Soldiering, unlike religion and education, was no laughing matter: Strachey had gone too far.

The biography does contain several inaccuracies. In addition to his tampering with Gordon's *Journals*, Strachey makes no mention of a vital telegram from Sir Evelyn Baring which crossed with a telegram from the Government. He gives the somewhat erroneous impression that Gordon was produced from obscurity overnight by a sinisterly exploited journalistic stunt conducted by W. T. Stead. And he repeats a mistake originally made in a magazine article by G. W. Smalley, who confused two communications sent by Gordon – one in the spring, the other in the autumn of 1885 – the latter, not the former, being the one that Gladstone read in the *Dundee Advertiser*.

It was not however any of these lapses that stimulated the public outcry against Strachey, but another mighty matter. People were outraged that, as Lord Elton wrote, 'a frail scholar in intellectual revolt against his social and moral environment during the fourth year of a war of which he bitterly disapproved ... contrived, in a characteristically feline and unfounded innuendo, to convey the suggestion that Gordon was a drunkard'. Critical opinion through the years has differed widely over this controversial question. Some –

among them Professor Bonamy Dobrée – have maintained that Strachey's Gordon was never intended to be a drunkard, but that like most men in hot climates he sometimes resorted to brandy and soda as a necessary stimulant. Others, including H. W. Nevinson, loudly asserted that Strachey had charged Gordon 'with the drunken habit of continually tippling brandy and soda'. And Alan Moorehead, who, with cautious reservations, was to liken Gordon to the teetotal and married Field-Marshal Lord Montgomery, saw in Strachey's version a 'pious toper ... still brave, still quixotically generous and kind, still an erratic sort of saint, but definitely a little mad'.

There are only two main passages in which Strachey alludes to Gordon's drinking habits. 'But the Holy Bible was not his only solace', he wrote in the first and most important of these. 'For now, under the parching African sun, we catch glimpses, for the first time, of Gordon's hand stretching out towards stimulants of a more material quality. For months together, we are told, he would drink nothing but pure water; and then ... water that was not so pure. In his fits of melancholy, he would shut himself up in his tent for days at a time, with a hatchet and a flag placed at the door to indicate that he was not to be disturbed for any reason whatever; until at last the cloud would lift, the signals would be removed, and the Governor would reappear, brisk and cheerful. During one of these retirements, there was a grave danger of a native attack upon the camp. Colonel Long, the chief of staff, ventured, after some hesitation, to ignore the flag and hatchet, and to enter the forbidden tent. He found Gordon seated at a table, upon which were an open Bible and an open bottle of brandy. Long explained the circumstances, but could obtain no answer beyond the abrupt words – "You are commander of the camp" – and was obliged to retire, nonplussed, to deal with the situation as best he could. On the following morning Gordon, cleanly shaven, and in the full-dress uniform of the Royal Engineers, entered Long's hut with his usual tripping step, exclaiming – "Old fellow, now don't be angry with me. I was very low last night. Let's have a good breakfast – a little b. and s. Do you feel up to it?" And, with these veering moods and dangerous restoratives, there came an intensification of the queer and violent elements in the temper of the man.'

The second offending passage describes W. T. Stead's interview with Gordon at Southampton. 'Now when he was in the mood – after a little b. and s., especially – no one was more capable than Gordon, with his facile speech and his free-and-easy manners, of furnishing good copy for a journalist; and Mr Stead made the most of his opportunity.'

Because it is very typical of the adverse criticism frequently levelled against Strachey's biographical writing as a whole, it is worth assembling the most stringent evidence that has been brought to refute Strachey's conjecture, and deciding what it amounts to. To dispose of the second insinuation first: Miss Stead, who was present at Southampton, has contradicted outright Strachey's assertion that brandy and soda was drunk during Gordon's interview for the *Pall Mall Gazette*, by an explicit statement pointing out that no refreshments were served or consumed, and that her father never drank wine or spirits. But does that statement really invalidate Strachey's paragraph? It is unlikely that Strachey actually pictured to himself the Stead family in alcoholic conviviality with Gordon; or, alternatively, that he imagined them to be silent and scandalized spectators of Gordon's immoderate drinking. The whole point of his interpretation of Gordon's character is that he was describing a *secret* drinker. Nor did he insist that Gordon *always* drank to excess. The crucial words in this passage are '– *after* a *little* b. and s., especially –'. The implication is that Gordon, all too well aware of Stead's notorious teetotalism, may have taken anticipatory measures to offset the unrelieved dryness of their interview, the effects of which Stead, with his stoutly maintained ignorance of alcohol (inherited by his daughter), failed to detect. Of course there is no documentary material to support this supposition. Strachey did not proclaim it as an absolute authenticated fact, but, knowing Gordon's habits and judging from the fluency of his performance, he thought it possible that his tongue had been loosened by a little drink. That was all.

The first paragraph, in which Strachey depicts Gordon giving way to long drinking bouts under the influence of the African climate, being skilfully sewn together from several suspect and contradictory accounts, has been more difficult for Strachey's detractors to call in question. But by elaborate investigation, Dr Bernard Allen has shown, to his own satisfaction, that Strachey's reconstruction is totally false, an amalgam founded on demonstrably unreliable statements made by Sir Richard Burton and Colonel Chaillé-Long.

The germ of this drinking story had come from Sir Richard Burton, who could not have seen Gordon more than twice during his life, and who in all probability met him only once. After Gordon's death, he wrote in the columns of the *Academy* a review of the Khartoum Journals, in the course of which he gave instances of Gordon's peculiar changes of mind in matters of policy which he liked to ascribe to Divine guidance. 'And so in minor matters; for months he would drink nothing but water, and then prefer, very decidedly, water with whisky.' According to Dr Bernard Allen, it is clear that Burton's intention in this sentence was to comment merely on a trivial point, and not to bring a charge of intemperance in what, after all, was virtually an obituary notice. And to strengthen his argument, Dr Allen points to the inconsistency between water and whisky and brandy and soda. He also reports an interview he had with Hasan Ali, Gordon's servant, who was alive in 1931, and who bore obedient witness to Gordon's abstemiousness.

Strachey then, in Dr Allen's view, seized and dextrously twisted this extract from Burton to match it with two conflicting passages from two separate volumes of memoirs by Chaillé-Long. Blandly ignoring the considerable body of data which verified Gordon's sobriety, Strachey preferred the unconvincing picture given in these two books, though he must have known that Colonel Long did not scruple to bend facts to suit his own purpose. For Long cherished some outstanding grievances against Gordon, who had never thought highly of him, and who had been responsible for his humiliating withdrawal from Equatoria in 1875. Six years later, his sense of grievance had been further inflamed by the pub-

lication of Dr Birkbeck Hill's selection from Gordon's correspondence, which contained a number of uncomplimentary
references to himself. By 1884, when Gordon was safely
sealed off in Khartoum, he was ready to settle old scores. In a
lecture delivered in Paris, he sarcastically described Gordon as
a humbug who, to further his own ends, had resorted to brib-
ery. This same year, his first book of memoirs, *The Three
Prophets*, was published. The purpose of this book, which co-
incided well with Strachey's own theme, was to show that the
religious fanaticism of Arabi Pasha, the Mahdi, and Gordon,
had made them the tools of an unscrupulous Government in
Britain. Strachey, who does not include this book in his
bibliography, nevertheless found one extract of some value:
'In the short intervals of my stay in camp, going or returning
from expeditions,' Long recorded, 'I had occasion to remark
the singular habit which Gordon had of retiring to his hut,
where he would remain, for days at a time, engaged in the
perusal and meditation of his ever-present Bible and Prayer
Book. When in this retirement, his orders were that he should
not be disturbed for any reason of service whatever; *a hatchet
and a flag* were placed at his door as a sign he was unapproach-
able.'

More than a quarter of a century later, in 1912, Long issued
another volume of memoirs, *My Life in Four Continents*,
which purported to give his travels and experiences in various
parts of the world. Now in his seventies and, according to Dr
Allen, still consumed by a spiteful hatred of Gordon, whose
posthumous fame he took as an insult to himself, the old man
decided to add fresh details to his original tale of prolonged
ascetic seclusions with Bible and Prayer Book, converting them
into bibulous orgies carried on under the mask of piety.

'A few days after my return to Lado,' he wrote, 'the camp
was attacked in force one night. I had great difficulty in re-
pelling the savage hordes, who, with lighted torches, were
endeavouring to turn us out. Gordon was in his hut and gave
no sign of coming out. It was during one of the oft-recurring
periods when he shut himself up and placed a hatchet and a
flag at the door as a sign that he was not to be disturbed, a

seclusion which lasted from three to five days. I sent an officer to warn him of our danger but receiving no reply went myself. I entered abruptly and found him seated, very calmly at a table, on which were an open Bible and a bottle of cognac and sherry. I told him of the situation, to which he made abrupt answer "You are commander of the camp". Whereupon I hastily turned and left him, but not before I had posted an officer with a half-dozen men specially charged with Gordon's safety. The savages were finally driven away by a vigorous sortie. The next day Gordon entered my tent in the full-dress uniform of the Royal Engineers, and cleanly shaven. He came forward with a quick tripping step as was his habit, and said "Old fellow, now don't be angry with me. I was very low last night. Come and dine with me. We will have a glorious dinner." '

Sherry!

The earlier (1884) version of this episode had been followed by an invitation to a brandy-and-soda breakfast, not to an evening meal at all. But that was a minor discrepancy against the fact that no other account of this time mentions a night attack by savages. There can be little doubt that Colonel Long was an erratic and unreliable witness, the factual mistakes being endorsed by his vain and phoney style of writing. But what about Dr Allen's own case for Gordon's sturdy temperance? All one can say is that the evidence of a faithful servant interrogated by an admirer of Gordon's, the mention of drinking even in a well-disposed, virtual obituary notice, and the minor inconsistencies which attest only to the tolerance of Gordon's alcoholic tastes, hardly provide very solid grounds for establishing him as a total abstainer.

The trouble, of course, is that secret drinking is not the sort of habit to be abundantly chronicled in academic sources, nor reliably substantiated by first-hand, unprejudiced witnesses. It was, however, even in fairly recent years a well-known rumour in the desert that on occasions Gordon drank immoderately. Moreover, testimonies which have subsequently come to light have tended to support Strachey rather than Dr Allen. For example, Lord Carnock is on record as having told his son, Harold Nicolson, that Gordon was definitely a drinker.

And there is one especially relevant and vivid piece of evidence contained in a letter written many years later by Joseph Reinach (formerly Gambetta's secretary). This document was discovered among the Dilke papers, and has been quoted by Roy Jenkins in his *Sir Charles Dilke*:

'*J'ai beaucoup connu Gordon*', Reinach wrote. '*J'ai fait sa connaissance en Janvier 1880 sur un bateau qui faisait le service entre Alexandrie et Naples. Nous passâmes plusieurs journées à Naples. Il me mena chez Ismail. Je le menai un soir au théâtre à San-Carlo. Il n'était pas allé au théâtre depuis vingt ans. On donnait un ballet Sardanapale, avec beaucoup de petites femmes à demi-nues. Il se scandalisa.* "And you call that civilisation!" *me dit-il et il rentra à l'hôtel. Je l'y trouvais vers une heure du matin en déshabille, lisant la Bible et ayant vidé une demi bouteille de whisky. Il buvait terriblement de brandy. Plus tard, à Paris, il venait souvent me voir le matin. Et, au bout de cinq minutes, il demandait du cognac.*[16]

'*C'était un héros, à très courte vue comme beaucoup d'héros, un mystique qui se payait de phrases, et aussi comment dirai-je? Un peu "un fumiste". Vous savez ce que nous appelons ainsi. Il s'amusait à étonner les gens. Il ne croyait pas tout ce qu'il disait. Dans les lettres de lui que j'ai conservées, il traitait volontiers Dizzie et ses amis de* Mountebanks. *Il était, lui-même,* Mountebank . . .'

On the balance of available evidence, it would seem that Gordon probably did drink. Strachey never suggested that he became a soak, a regular and fairly steady drinker. On such a scale and with such frequency, alcohol would soon have impaired his practical efficiency – and of this there was no real sign. Far more likely, since it fits in with what few facts we know and is in keeping with his neurotic temperament, was that Gordon drank to great excess occasionally, that he was a dipsomaniac, a nervous or manic-depressive drinker, who interspersed quick fits of potation with days and weeks of absolute abstemiousness.

Probably nothing like the volume of critical attention that has been aroused by this episode would have been forth-

16. Emphasis added.

coming at all had there not been throughout England in 1918 a subconscious resentment against men like Gordon, proto-types, it was felt, of those who had been largely responsible for the Great War. The charge of drunkenness was confidently exaggerated and repeated, and Gordon was described as a dip-somaniac in magazine articles and in books. 'It was almost too good to be true', wrote Esmé Wingfield-Stratford, 'that all and sundry should be conducted to Gordon's tent, that the flap should be stealthily drawn aside, and the Christian hero revealed, like Noah, blind to the world.'

In immediate reaction to the publicity provoked by this most polemical item in Strachey's biography, various indig-nant denials were published in the Press by men who had known Gordon while in the desert. But this merely added to the general enjoyment. For who now could seriously listen to men with names like Chippendale, or Watson, or Rudolf Slatin Pasha – minor eminent Victorians themselves?

In later years the pendulum of disbelief has swung too far in the opposite direction,[17] and even now, though more bal-anced critical opinions are being aired, the bias is still set too far against Strachey. Professor Hugh Trevor-Roper, for in-stance, has written that this account of Gordon in the Sudan 'retiring into his tent "for days at a time" for secret com-munion with the Bible and the bottle is the richest flourish in his brilliant picture of that strange, unpredictable, com-plicated character. . . . The real object had not been the brandy-bottle but a prayer-book. Unfortunately, "brandy-bottle" is funnier than "prayer-book"; Strachey could not resist the final touch of absurdity; and his brilliant portrait of a crackpot crusader is, by that one dangerous detail, over-done.' But this criticism is inaccurate, and misses the point. Strachey did not invent the brandy-bottle. Trevor-Roper may have read *The Three Prophets* but must have overlooked *My*

17. Anthony Nutting, Gordon's latest biographer (1966), who believes that Gordon's career was shaped by a death-wish possibly arising from the knowledge of his homosexuality, dismisses Lytton Strachey's 'charges of drunkenness' as a complete fabrication, though without examining all the evidence.

Life in Four Continents in which the open Bible and the bottle of cognac are placed on the same table. Strachey repeated the word 'open' to increase the amusement, but he did not couple the brandy-bottle with the Bible simply because it was a funny combination of words and ideas. He believed that Gordon's addiction to religiosity and to alcohol sprang from the same epileptic source. In this way he could bring out Gordon's intoxicated, muddled, transcendentalist thinking which, allied to his thirst for fame, led inevitably to his self-destruction. As an interpretation of character, it is very similar in outline to Richard Burton's sketch, and is partly endorsed by Gordon himself, who in a lucid interval at Khartoum wrote: 'Either I must believe He does all things in mercy and love, or else I disbelieve His existence, there is no half way in the matter. What holes do I not put myself into! . . . I believe ambition put me here in this ruin.'

'The End of General Gordon' is particularly rich in minor figures. 'One catches a vision of strange characters,' Strachey wrote, 'moved by mysterious impulses, interacting in queer complication, and hurrying at last – so it almost seems – like creatures in a puppet show to a predestined catastrophe. The characters, too, have a charm of their own: they are curiously English. What other nation on the face of the earth could have produced Mr Gladstone and Sir Evelyn Baring and Lord Hartington and General Gordon?'

Gladstone, Sir Evelyn Baring and Lord Hartington, as they make their appearances in this essay, testify to Strachey's marvellous skill as a vocal and impressionistic writer. Of the three, Lord Hartington possesses by far the simplest and most straightforward nature, and Strachey's description of his solid, silent personality, seemingly proof against all quickening enthusiasms, and the ponderous and comic workings of his conscience which contributed so tantalizingly to Gordon's tragedy, is masterly – full of wit and imaginative humour, parodying, in its vocabulary and construction, Hartington's own voice and mannerisms. As a portrait, it is fully equal to P. G. Wodehouse's classic Lord Emsworth. It is also a most affectionate likeness of Hartington, who occupies a role in the essay similar to that of Wiseman in 'Cardinal Manning' and Panmure in 'Florence Nightingale':

'Lord Hartington's conscience was of a piece with the rest of him ... it was a commonplace affair. Lord Hartington himself would have been disgusted by any mention of it. If he had been obliged, he would have alluded to it distantly; he would have muttered that it was a bore not to do the proper thing. He was usually bored – for one reason or another; but this particular form of boredom he found more intense than all the rest. He would take endless pains to avoid it. Of course, the whole thing was a nuisance – an obvious nuisance; and every one else must feel just as he did about it. And yet people seemed to have got it into their heads that he had some kind of special faculty in such matters – that there was some peculiar value in his judgment on a question of right and wrong. He could not understand why it was; but whenever there was a dispute about cards in a club, it was brought to *him* to settle. It was most odd. But it was true. In public affairs, no less than in private, Lord Hartington's decisions carried an extraordinary weight. The feeling of his idle friends in high society was shared by the great mass of the English people; here was a man they could trust. For indeed he was built upon a pattern which was very dear to his countrymen. It was not simply that he was honest: it was that his honesty was an English honesty – an honesty which naturally belonged to one who, so it seemed to them, was the living image of what an Englishman should be. In Lord Hartington they saw, embodied and glorified, the very qualities which were nearest to their hearts – impartiality, solidity, common sense – the qualities by which they themselves longed to be distinguished, and by which, in their happier moments, they believed they were. If ever they began to have misgivings, there, at any rate, was the example of Lord Hartington to encourage them and guide them – Lord Hartington, who was never self-seeking, who was never excited, and who had no imagination at all. Everything they knew about him fitted into the picture, adding to their admiration and respect. His fondness for field sports gave them a feeling of security; and certainly there could be no nonsense about a man who confessed to two ambitions – to become Prime Minister and to win the Derby – and who put the second above the first. They loved him for his casualness – for his inexactness – for refusing to make life a cut-and-dried business – for ramming an official dispatch of high importance into his coat-pocket, and finding it there, still unopened, at Newmarket, several days later. They loved him for his hatred of fine sentiments; they were delighted when they heard that at some function, on a florid speaker's avowing that "this was the proudest moment of his life", Lord Hartington had growled in an undertone "the proudest moment of *my* life, was when my pig won the prize at Skipton fair". Above all, they loved him for being dull. It was the greatest comfort – with Lord Hartington they could always be absolutely certain that he would never, in any circumstances, be either brilliant, or subtle, or surprising, or impassioned, or profound. As they sat, listening to his speeches, in which considerations of stolid plainness succeeded one another with complete flatness, they felt, involved and supported by the colossal tedium, that their confidence was finally assured. They looked up, and took their fill of the sturdy obvious presence. The inheritor of a splendid dukedom might almost have passed for a farm hand. Almost, but not quite. For an air, that was difficult to explain, of preponderating authority lurked in the solid figure; and the lordly breeding of the House of Cavendish was visible in the large, long, bearded, unimpressionable face.

'One other characteristic – the necessary consequence, or indeed, it might almost be said, the essential expression, of all the rest – completes the portrait: Lord Hartington was slow. He was slow in movement, slow in apprehension, slow in thought and the communication of thought, slow to decide, and slow to act.'

Lord Hartington had left on his contemporaries a single, easily recognizable impression. Gladstone, on the other hand, was a complex and controversial personality, who impressed some as being the perfect model of an upright man, and others as an utterly detestable humbug. To employ the same sort of technique that he had used so successfully on Lord Hartington was therefore impossible, and Strachey switched apparently to a more analytical method. 'What, then,' he asks after elaborately setting forth the contradictory passions of the man, 'was the truth?' But that was not the question which he sought to answer. His portrait of Gladstone is one of the finest passages in all his work; but for all its lively imagery, its vividness and subtlety, its display of controlled verbal pyrotechnics, it does nothing to reconcile the conflicting elements in Gladstone's character. Its purpose was to glorify these splendid ambiguities, to heighten the enigma with those choice rhetorical questions that indicate nothing so eloquently as his own uncertainty of mind. But he does more than this. Strachey did not intend to worry through to some analytical formula of truth; he did not wish to 'explain', but to 'illustrate'. And so, in this passage, we are meant to overhear Gladstone's own loquaciousness, 'the long, winding, intricate sentences, with their vast burden of subtle and complicated qualifications', which 'befogged the mind like clouds, and like clouds, too, dropped thunderbolts'.

'What, then, was the truth? In the physical universe there are no chimeras. But man is more various than nature; was Mr Gladstone, perhaps, a chimera of the spirit? Did his very essence lie in the confusion of incompatibles? His very essence? It eludes the hand that seems to grasp it. One is baffled, as his political opponents were baffled fifty years ago. The soft serpent coils harden into quick strength that has vanished, leaving only emptiness and perplexity behind.... Could it not then at least be said of him with certainty that his was a complex character? But here also there was a contradiction.... His very egoism was simple-minded: through all the labyrinth of his passions there ran a single thread. But the centre of the labyrinth? Ah! the thread might lead there, through those wandering mazes, at last. Only, with the last corner turned, the last step taken, the explorer might find that he was looking down into the gulf of a crater. The flame shot out on every side, scorching and brilliant; but in the midst there was a darkness.'

According to Professor Bonamy Dobrée, Strachey made no attempt to understand Gladstone and even ceased to think about him while putting together this intricate literary mosaic. 'The complicated rhythm, the bringing of the stress upon the right word, the modulated verbal sounds accumulating upon a finality of statement', all this virtuoso construction, Professor Dobrée explained, transforms the description into a poem. But this fails to make that vital distinction between the mellifluous fluting of high sentiment, that pattern of elegant variations of word-play which describes something, and the lyrical compression which suggests far more than it actually states, and in the lingering echoes of which there resides the seed of an emotional truth. As presented by Dobrée, Strachey's miniature conceals no such echoes. It is full of clever linguistic expertise, but has no living comprehension. Yet Dobrée's intended praise, in failing to catch Gladstone's voice in this passage, to overhear that complicated speech that formed the very fibre of his being, to draw the parallel between his brilliance and Strachey's vividness, his darkness and Strachey's emptiness and perplexity, unwittingly does less than justice to the writing. For Strachey did not forget Gladstone as a human being, but tried to show him as a man who, in the confusion of his conscience and his policy, was a kind of moral opportunist, not a humbug but someone greatly self-deceived.

By stressing Gladstone's equivocality and setting it in contrast to the fumbling slowness of Lord Hartington, Strachey made fast one knot in the tightrope stretching between the religious fanaticism of the Mahdi and the deliberate passivity of the British Government – that tightrope on which Gordon found himself perilously stranded at Khartoum. Then he jerked the knot still tighter by twisting round Gladstone's baffling ambiguity and Lord Hartington's ponderous honesty, the bland irreproachability of Sir Evelyn Baring, a cool diplomat, 'cautious, measured, unimpeachably correct'.

The pages of *Eminent Victorians* certainly contain a few distortions of character – those worked on Newman and, to a much smaller extent, on Dr Sutherland, have already been noted. But there are others. Clough was dispossessed of what sense of humour he owned, together with his poetic sensibility, and shown as a ludicrous, post-office puppet. Lord Acton, who makes a brief appearance in 'Cardinal Manning', emerges, not as a miniaturist almost as acute as Strachey himself, but, as John Raymond puts it, 'ineffectual, meddling, opinionated, blinkered with scholarship, a huge purblind mammoth of erudition turning his great head this way and that in a pathetic attempt to snuff out priesthood and persecution'. Some have complained that Lord Granville was made too much of a nonentity;[18] others have observed that Julius Charles Hare was not the fanatical Low Churchman of Strachey's fancy, but a scholarly Broad Church latitudinarian. The occasional references, also, to Lord Wolseley are rather misleading, conveying a barely discernible figure of pygmy proportions, hurrying pointlessly hither and thither. And Odo Russell – 'poor Mr Russell' – is portrayed as a political cipher, a fly buzzing ineffectually in Manning's spider's web of clinging diplomacy, whereas Russell's dispatches from Rome (published in 1962) reveal that he was playing a double game, and that Strachey's picture – reminiscent of Gregorovius's sketch of Manning at the time of the Council – totally discounts the power and perspicacity underlying the diplomat's suave manner.

But the most serious charge of misrepresenting a minor character concerns the portrait of Sir Evelyn Baring. 'You are hard on Cromer, and not quite convincing', Walter Raleigh observed, and several other critics have agreed with him. In

18. In a letter to Maurice Baring, Strachey explained: 'I did not intend to convey that Lord Granville was a nonentity altogether – only that he was one as a Foreign Minister, and particularly with reference to our policy in Egypt. This I believe was so – though of course it is very difficult to disentangle the obscure complications of that Cabinet. Surely it is hardly correct to say that "Mr G. did not care a button about foreign affairs". My reading of the situation is that the two real forces in the Cabinet were Mr G. and Lord Hartington, pulling in opposite directions, and that Lord Granville, as you say, "vacillated" between them and was in effect alternately the tool of one and the other. That is why I described him as a nonentity.'

their opinion, Strachey had ignored the fact that Baring was a poor boy, was given a poor education and grew up almost completely self-made, and had cast him as a typically reserved public-school man, a character for which he felt there was a dramatic need in the essay. He wanted someone in the role of the odious, well-bred public official, whose inherent inability to understand the unorthodox Gordon would give added point to this humorous tragedy. Baring, to judge from his literary style, fitted this part pretty well, but to reinforce his characterization, Strachey seldom scrupled to ascribe to him the most damaging of motives. For example, after a fanciful description of his state of mind during his discussions over the necessity for an expedition to rescue Gordon, Strachey adds: 'From the end of April till the beginning of September – during the most momentous period of the whole crisis – he was engaged in London upon a financial conference, while his place was taken in Cairo by a substitute. With a characteristically convenient unobtrusiveness, Sir Evelyn Baring had vanished from the scene.' Strachey nowhere lets on that in London Baring was far better placed than in Cairo to urge the need for preparing for an expedition. His summary condemnation of Baring on this matter draws attention to the absence in his bibliography of Bernard Holland's *Life of Spencer Compton, eighth Duke of Devonshire*, a book which showed clearly that Baring did agitate for an expedition, while Chamberlain was one of its opponents. This omission is all the more remarkable since Strachey owned this two-volume biography, and had marked several passages in it.[19] Similarly, none of Strachey's readers could have guessed that Baring in fact strongly backed Gordon's selection of Zobier as his successor in the Sudan, and that this recommendation was only upset by a majority of one at a scratch Cabinet meeting.

The controversial question of Baring's character was hotly

19. Strachey, in fact, met Bernard Holland, who on 13 June 1918 wrote to him: 'I had not the opportunity last night of telling you that I had read your E.Vs. with much pleasure and admiration. I liked best the Gordon. I suspect that you found my life of the D. of D. useful for that because it is the best documented record of those curious episodes.'

disputed in the correspondence columns of *The Times Literary Supplement* shortly after the publication of *Eminent Victorians*. Strachey's old adversary, Sir Edmund Gosse, protested that this ill-natured caricature was hardly to be recognized as the man he had subsequently known as Lord Cromer. Far from being a colourless personality, cold and unconcerned, Baring was a copious talker, his conversation being generally stimulating and often delectable. 'It combined', wrote Gosse,[20] 'warmth of feeling with vivacity of expression. Lord Cromer was accessible and responsive. He was a sober, but essentially an ardent patriot.'

Gosse also expressed himself as particularly anxious to check, before it was crystallized into accepted history, Strachey's calumnious statement that the East meant very little to Baring and that he took no interest in it. 'There was', he indignantly objected, 'nothing in which he took so much interest. It was seldom out of his mind; it furnished four-fifths of his conversation, in the course of which he never wearied of dwelling on minute points of difference between the Eastern and Western temperament. The most important of his later writings, his "Political and Literary Essays", is full of evidence of this preoccupation. "The Government of Subject Races", written in 1907, shows how deeply he meditated upon the problems of India. He knew India from 1872 to 1876, and again from 1880 to 1883; until the close of his life he was examining with peculiar care the intimate relation between religion and politics throughout Asia, and he watched with anxiety the high explosives it produced. "Took no interest in the East" – prodigious.'

In a prompt reply,[21] Strachey defended his portrait of Baring down to the last detail.[22] His letter, by its contrast, shows up

20. *The Times Literary Supplement* (27 June 1918), 301.
21. *The Times Literary Supplement* (4 July 1918), 313–14.
22. In a reply to Maurice Baring, who, besides objecting to this portrait of Lord Cromer in the columns of the *Spectator*, had sent a personal letter to Strachey, he wrote: 'My view of Lord Cromer is entirely based on the published material; and I can only say that I have tried honestly to set down the very strong impression of a personality, which it made upon my mind. *Your* view is a private one; and it seems to me that it

Gosse's rather flatulent judgement, but indicates, too, his own immature romanticism over the mystique of the East – the sort of naïve attitude he was to ridicule in his essay 'A Diplomatist: Li Hung-Chang'.[23] It was hardly surprising, he pointed out, that the impression produced by Lord Cromer on Edmund Gosse in the private intercourse of friendship, and that produced on himself 'by a detached examination of Lord Cromer's published writings and public acts should be different'. In Strachey's opinion, since it was not always a man's friends who knew him best, the test Gosse applied to Cromer's character was superficial. His responsiveness and accessibility in the drawing-room in no way proved that his

---

does not necessarily contradict mine. It makes the character more complex than I had supposed – and for this reason I am particularly grateful for your letter; it shows that in private life Lord Cromer was very far from an official or a diplomat; but I cannot see that it affects my estimate of him as a public man. You say "his main characteristic was an outspokenness and directness and bluntness of speech mounting sometimes to brutality". It is interesting to know that this was the impression he produced in private conversation; but to argue from this that he was outspoken in his official dealings is surely impossible. To take a single instance, anything less outspoken, direct and blunt than his telegrams to the Government on the question of Gordon's appointment it would be difficult to imagine. I don't think I anywhere say in my book that he had a diplomatic *training*: but, writing of him as a public character, I judged that his cast of mind was eminently diplomatic, and nothing that you say in your letter appears to me to make this judgement untenable. Perhaps I may add, in my own justification, that, since my book has come out, I have found that my view of Lord Cromer is shared by a public man of great authority and experience.

'My error as to his "keeping up" his classics I admit and regret. But I'm sorry to say that, in face of some of the chapters in *Modern Egypt* I still find it very difficult to believe that he took any true interest in the East. As to his wishing to become an "institution", at any rate you must allow that in fact he did become one. I can't understand what posts, which you say he refused, could possibly have made him "far more of an institution" than he actually was.

'... I should be very sorry indeed if anything in my book suggested that I underrated either Lord Cromer's immense ability, or the extraordinary value of his work in Egypt. But this I think, can hardly be the case.'

23. 'A Diplomatist: Li Hung-Chang', op. cit.

mind was 'not essentially secretive, cautious and diplomatic'. Garrulity on Eastern topics and how the Eastern temperament differed from the Western was not an unusual phenomenon among such men. 'We have all of us met gentlemen who "never weary" of drawing such comparisons,' he concluded, 'but their interest in the East remains problematical. To have denied that Lord Cromer took an interest in Eastern administrative questions – as Mr Gosse seemed to suggest I did – would of course have been grotesque. But Eastern administrative questions are not the East. The signs of a true interest in the East – an interest resembling even remotely a Du Perron or a Burton – are easily discernible; and so are those of the kind of temperament constitutionally incapable of possessing it. Such a matter, no doubt, must ultimately be decided by a personal judgement; and I can only say that whenever Lord Cromer touches upon the East in his writings he produces on my mind the effect of some musical authority who has a good working knowledge of counterpoint and orchestration, but whose musical outfit is unluckily incomplete in one particular – a feeling for music.'

That Strachey, unlike Gosse, would not have liked Cromer had they met, seems certain. He did not come up with this hostile interpretation simply to complete the design of his essay – though he did add certain dubious flourishes for artistic effect. When, as early as April 1907, Maynard Keynes wrote to him, 'I have been reading Cromer's Egyptian report – he seems a very intelligent man', Strachey had at once demurred. 'I'm surprised to hear that you think Baring a clever man', he replied. 'Oh! perhaps clever; but d'you only mean that? I thought you might mean great.' Yet it is ironic to note that Cromer's report on the Nile expedition in every way corroborates Lytton's own handling of that event, and that his summary of the situation, in the opinion of Professor George Kuppler Simson, 'could very well be the thesis of the whole of *Eminent Victorians*'.[24]

24. 'In a word,' Cromer had written, 'the Nile expedition was sanctioned too late, and the reason why it was sanctioned too late was that Mr Gladstone would not accept simple evidence of a plain fact, which

6
FINALE

'As you know I think your Cromer is wrong. But I like it, all the same', Walter Raleigh had written. '. . . Nothing can make your book undelightful.' Since 1918, this delight has infected a vast audience of readers. The book challenged the highest biographical standards. In his Preface, Strachey had advocated detachment as an artistic attitude of mind; a closer scrutiny reveals that his detachment was part of a literary mannerism, skilfully employed so as to bring into sharper relief his irony and power of denigration. The historian, he had written, 'will row out over that great ocean of material, and lower down into it, here and there, a little bucket, which will bring up to the light of day some characteristic specimen, from those far depths, to be examined with a careful curiosity'. *Eminent Victorians* is apparently the haul from just such a voyage of random sampling. Strachey rowed out over the deep uncharted waters of the Victorian age, Desmond MacCarthy observed, let down his buckets and drew to the surface four major samples of odd fish – and a host of smaller fry. These he transported back to the mainland to put on show in his well-highlighted aquarium. And the large public which came to the exhibition saw that a colossal, undreamed-of change had come over the assembled representatives of marine life. Robbed of their awful surroundings in the mysterious depths of the ocean, rendered harmless inside their protective tanks,

---

was patent to much less powerful intellects than his own. Posterity has yet to decide on the services which Mr Gladstone, during his long and brilliant career, rendered in other directions to the British nation, but it is improbable that the verdict of his contemporaries in respect to his conduct of the affairs of the Soudan will ever be reversed. That verdict has been distinctly unfavourable. "Les fautes de l'homme puissant", said an eminent Frenchman [Sénancour], "sont des malheurs publics". Mr Gladstone's error of judgement in delaying too long the despatch of the Nile expedition left a stain on the reputation of England which it will be beyond the power of either the impartial historian or the partial apologist to efface.'

and somehow unnaturally distended by the shallow water that encased them, the aristocratic shark, the gorgeous octopus, the ravenous pike no longer appeared the formidable creatures of a sea-legend. With their comic grimaces, their futile perambulating to and fro, their crazy retinue of dabs and polyps and squids, they presented a circus-spectacle, half-amusing, half-grotesque. Only the good-natured, uncompetitive sole, content to lie modestly in the sand, could still be seen to any real advantage. Some of the public were delighted by this ingenuity, others outraged by what they took to be wanton cruelty. And then, inevitably, there hurried along the ichthyologists with all their critical apparatus, measuring, inspecting, checking, and finding that the glass sheets of which Strachey had made his tanks were not, as he had claimed, perfectly even and clear, but contained here a subtle convex flaw, there a concave dent, blemishes which, though invisible to the naked eye, produced magnified distortions on the specimens swimming innocently behind them.

Though the reputation of *Eminent Victorians* was damaged, it was not, and never can be, fundamentally impaired. For, with its interpretative dramatic technique, it was a genuine pioneer work which has made for itself a permanent place in literary history, as the chief influence – and one that was more often beneficial than is generally admitted – in the field of serious biography this century.

Nevertheless, although Strachey's influence as a biographer has matched that of Plutarch and Boswell, *Eminent Victorians* occupies a curiously anomalous position in modern literature. For all its penetrating individuality, it lacked a certain sweep, a richness, perhaps because, in Virginia Woolf's opinion, the age was not behind him. Strachey 'has had to open our eyes before he made us see; he has had to search out and sew together a very artful manner of speech; and the effort, beautifully though it is concealed, has robbed his work of some of the force that should have gone into it, and limited his scope'. The book's most radiant virtue was its completeness, and it is this impeccable quality that has dismayed some critics who have come to see it as something of an isolated and transitional work. Its perfection, its smooth burnished façade, was an end in itself.[25] It went as far as it was possible to go in a certain direction, then stopped dead. There were no offshoots capable of scattering, in other directions, some living seeds of development. 'There is not a line in it that gives it away, that allows one to penetrate into the workshops where it was made', wrote Gerald Brenan in a letter to Strachey (10 April 1921). 'Is it possible that it came into existence without any of those fevers of hope and despair and aridity and self-disgust that other authors have to put up with? ...

'... Books, even very great ones, ought to show signs of human imperfection. Even Shakespeare does this – almost all artists have respected the fondness we have for unevenness; they have been inspired and then to compensate they have been flat; why should you almost alone abuse this good human instinct and maintain your book at a high and even level, occasionally rising a little, but never at all sinking? I prefer Joyce to you: he does not taunt me, but leads me on, points to very far horizons, and shows me a way that leads there. He promises new discoveries, new methods, new beauties – you don't promise anything. You just are. A vision, clear, complete, and yet unattainable.

'... We are going I think to have a new age in English literature; E.V. will then be on the border-line between new and old.'

25. In a letter to Stephen Hudson (8 May 1925) Edwin Muir wrote: 'In Strachey, because there is no *Sturm und Drang*, because he dislikes *Sturm und Drang* too much even to overcome it, as the artist must, there is no joy. And on this plane of judgement I may as well agree with you that Virginia Woolf is not a figure of sufficient importance to warrant a difference of opinion between us. She does not face the problem, and it may be that when I write my final essay in this series [*Transition*] I may have to put her down along with Strachey and [David] Garnett among the forces which are imposing a premature and hardening limitation on contemporary literature – fencing it off into a small perfection which is a denial of further progress.' (Published in *Encounter*, January 1966.)

FIVE

The Great Panjandrum

> one of the most pathetic
> sights however
> is to see the ghost of queen
> victoria going out every
> evening with the ghost
> of a sceptre in her hand
> to find mr lytton strachey
> and bean him it seems she beans
> him and beans him and he
> never knows it

Don Marquis, 'archy goes abroad' from archy's life of mehitabel

1

THE DEVELOPMENT OF A BIOGRAPHER

THE change in tone and literary style between *Eminent Victorians* and *Queen Victoria* gives some indication of the post-war development in Strachey's character, and shows the greater refinement he brought to his biographical method. His real originality and force are best seen in the pages of *Eminent Victorians*. In *Queen Victoria*, written at a happier period of his life, the astringent, incisive style has softened into a kindlier mood of mellow and affectionate nostalgia. The pace is gentler too, more explorative though less acute, and the basis of the construction has shifted from a quartet of one-act dramas to a single organic unit composed of a series of interconnected chapter-scenes, more akin to a subjective novel.

Strachey's literary talent was naturally less reflective than dramatic. The spectacle he had unrolled in *Eminent Victorians* was of a menagerie of curious comedian creatures, born actors all of them, impelled towards sinister conflicts and strange dooms, grappling now with one another, now with the culminating fury of forces far greater than themselves, to be swept at last to a common ruin. Their antics presented a vivid and fascinating extravaganza, but were without much significance beyond the cages in which they performed, from where, protected by stout iron bars, Strachey coldly observed them, noting all the while that their attitudinizing, their avowed purposes and ideals were but thin disguises of the one reality of their animal life – the egotistical pursuit of satisfaction. This was Strachey's philosophy of a hostile world; and the illustration of it in his brilliantly amusing sketches of four people who all shared one dominating quality – a sense of ambition, inflated beyond reason by religious superstition, which took control of personal relationships and destroyed humanity – accorded perfectly with the spasm of disgust momentarily felt throughout England for an age which had finally collapsed with the war.

In the Preface to *Eminent Victorians*, Strachey had asserted the importance of the individual; but the essays that followed exemplified only the vanity of the self-important. The text for which his book forms such a scintillating exposition is Isabella's speech in *Measure for Measure*:

> – but man, proud man!
> Dress'd in a little brief authority, –
> Most ignorant of what he's most assured,
> His glassy essence, – like an angry ape,
> Plays such fantastic tricks before high heaven
> As make the angels weep.

Strachey's treatment of this central theme corresponds well with the commentary he had written many years earlier in the Spectatorial review of Guglielmo Ferrero's history, *The Greatness and Decline of Rome*. 'The greatest names seem to lose their lustre upon his pages; he shows us the ignorance of the wise, the helplessness of the well-meaning; the rest is darkness and fate.'[1] It was not, however, after Signor Ferrero's work that he sought to fashion his biography. His chief stylistic models came from the great French biographical tradition – Fontenelle and Condorcet. But his attitude as a biographer, so he once intimated to Hesketh Pearson, was Johnsonian,

1. 'A New History of Rome', *Spectator*, 102 (2 January 1909), 20–21.

and a foretaste of his writing might be found in Johnson's *Lives of the Poets*. Among other critics, Clifford Bower-Shore and André Maurois have attempted to develop this parallel. Strachey, in his Preface, had written of 'those two fat volumes, with which it is our custom to commemorate the dead – who does not know them, with their ill-digested masses of material, their slipshod style, their tone of tedious panegyric, their lamentable lack of selection, of detachment, of design? They are as familiar as the cortège of the undertaker, and wear the same air of funereal barbarism.' Here was a definite and perhaps deliberate echo of two of Johnson's most celebrated pronouncements on the art of biography. 'Biography has often been allotted to writers who seem very little acquainted with the nature of their task, or very negligent about the performance', Johnson wrote. 'They rarely afford any other account than might be collected from public papers, but imagine themselves writing a life when they exhibit a chronological series of actions or preferments; and so little regard the manners or behaviour of their heroes, that more knowledge may be gained of a man's real character by a short conversation with one of his servants, than from a formal and studied narrative begun with his pedigree and ended with his funeral.'

And in *The Rambler*, Johnson also wrote: 'There are many who think it an act of piety to hide the faults or failings of their friends, even when they can no longer suffer by their detection; we therefore see whole ranks of characters adorned with uniform panegyric, and not to be known from one another but by extrinsic and casual circumstances ... If we owe regard to the memory of the dead, there is yet more respect to be paid to knowledge, to virtue, to truth.'

Had Strachey taken the precepts laid down by Johnson, and by himself in his Preface, to heart, then his four 'Lives' might more closely have resembled Johnson's *Life of Savage*. But he was less troubled with discriminating between what was sound and what was false in an established reputation, than in enunciating his own humanitarian and secular convictions. The superficiality of any close comparison between Johnson and Strachey has been admirably expounded by Johnson's so-called 'Stracheyesque' biographer, Hugh Kingsmill – though he tends to belittle the concern which Strachey felt for mankind and to underestimate the intended propaganda effect of his work. There existed in Johnson, Kingsmill points out, a belief in absolute virtue combined with an equally strong awareness of how far short of it even the best human beings fall:

'Whether or not he [Johnson] had it consciously in mind, he was directed in everything he wrote by the saying of Jesus: "None is good, save one, that is God" ', explained Kingsmill. 'Strachey, on the other hand, an epicurean sceptic who remarks in one of his essays that the religious motive has quietly dropped out of the modern world, wrote from the standpoint that no one at all is good, and that man's only rational occupation is to observe from a distance the contention of conflicting egotisms. To Strachey all mythologies were equally absurd, whether they embodied the transient illusions of a particular epoch or welled up out of the depths of the soul to illumine the mystery of life. Looking at men from the outside, he interpreted their actions rationally, like Swift in *Gulliver's Travels*, and therefore found no reason in them. To Johnson popular mythology was a distortion of Christian mythology, which contained for him the sole revelation of ultimate reality; it was an attempt to attribute perfection to imperfect beings, and so a means to retarding man's progress towards the divine. The difference in attitude between Johnson and Strachey was therefore fundamental; for Johnson felt with his whole being that life cannot be interpreted as a self-contained experience and that the relation of the individual to God underlies and conditions his relations to man. To mark a man's faults and failings was, for Johnson, to indicate where he had diverged from his true relation to God; for Strachey it was an agreeable intellectual pastime, which flattered his sense of superiority both to his subject and to the illusion-ridden mob.'[2]

Though Johnson's prose, loosened by years of con-

2. *The Progress of a Biographer* by Hugh Kingsmill (Methuen 1949), pp. 6–7.

versation, gradually grew more flexible, his basic attitude, compounded of a mixture of sympathy and severity, did not change. Strachey's biographical approach was evolved at a different level, and, since it constituted only indirectly an expression of his personal relation to life – being chiefly employed as a literary device to heighten the devastating effect of his irony – it soon shifted to accommodate a new literary position. There are fewer Johnsonian overtones in *Queen Victoria*: Strachey's later peacetime point of view could not be conveyed by the majestic Corinthian order of Johnson's style. For Johnson, with his distrust of the fictitious, was not an artist in the same sense as *Queen Victoria*, with its mandarin style so exactly suited to anecdote, is a work of art. Prior to 1918, there was perhaps no conscious art of biography in the language: there were biographer-artists, but no artist-biographers. Johnson believed that the value of a story depended upon its being true – 'A story is a picture either of an individual, or of human nature in general; if it be false it is a picture of nothing.' To Strachey, biographies were less rigorous and austere instruments of truth-telling than nicely proportioned entertainments, vehicles for the dissemination of certain aspects of the truth. To assist with this milder approach to his subject, which laid more stress on amusement than on propaganda, he adopted a more novel-like narrative, very un-Johnsonian.

In *Queen Victoria*, Strachey came nearer to portraying a hero and heroine, and the artistic means by which he chose to represent them were of a quite different order. All pretence at a strictly impersonal attitude is now abandoned, and a more subjective spirit of romance is invoked. Strachey livens up his amiable portraits with just a hint of entertaining malice. His heroes were far from perfect, he is constantly reminding us. They had their full share of faults. Everything apparently conspires to a fair distribution of disqualifications. Yet the skill, of course, lies in apportioning the favoured characters with only the more diverting and endearing frailties, so that the untrained reader is led to believe, even against some of the evidence, that he has discovered for himself that Victoria was really quite a sweet little lady, and that the grossly underrated Albert possessed a considerable talent.

Strachey's gallery of villains, saddled with the more unappealing vices, were selected from among those whose robust constitutions, harnessed to an overriding lust for power, served to distinguish them clearly from himself. His heroes, now, were ordinary, homely, unexceptional people – 'the quiet little great', as Wyndham Lewis scathingly described them. 'At the head of that dazzling *élite* is usually some whimsical, half-apologetic, but very much sheltered and coddled projection of himself.' This, in the opinion of Wyndham Lewis, was the unobtrusive revolution that Strachey attempted to set in motion: the accepted heroes were villains, and the quietists heroes. But his actual influence which, as 'high priest of Gossip', extended beyond biography to political journalism, was one of partisanship. Between the 'good' and the 'bad' there was a great artistic gulf fixed. The former were to be enhaloed with an aura of charming sentimentalism; the latter subjected to a cool, clinical appraisal.

By seeking the man behind the nineteenth-century myth, Strachey had, in 1918, dealt a death-blow to the antiquated legend of the Victorian Age. But the substantive which Walter Raleigh had so eagerly awaited in no way matched up to the original adjective. For with the publication of *Queen Victoria*, Strachey inaugurated a new but no less legendary view of the queen – a whimsical, teasing, half-admiring, half-mocking view that found in Victoria a quaintly impressive symbol of a quaintly impressive age.

Nevertheless, *Queen Victoria* has claims to be considered a more mature work than *Eminent Victorians*. To a very large extent, Strachey relinquished his air of bland superiority; and the methods he used to convey a mellow and enfolding atmosphere were less arbitrary than those he had previously employed in uncovering a hidden core of diabolism. The scholarship is more thorough; the tone more finely controlled; and the writing no less lucid. His irony is lowered so that it flows like a sub-current flavouring the whole biography, and giving it its distinctive poise and harmony. In this sense, his prose style is more subtle than in his earlier book, the extreme quietness and depth of both the irony and wit being absorbed as a necessary part of the narrative. 'You've discovered a new style which gives the essential and all pervading absurdity of most human and all official life without losing anything of its pathos', Roger Fry wrote to him (18 April 1921). 'You're so kind and so unsparing. It seems to me more nearly a true perspective than anyone's yet found.'

The greater technical problems involved in *Queen Victoria* are also triumphantly overcome. Harold Nicolson has enumerated these difficulties and pointed to the craft and assiduity which Strachey needed to master them with such fluency.[3] 'The mass of his material was overwhelming. He was faced with eighty-one solid years, and each one of those years was crowded with intricate and important events directly relevant to his subject. He was faced with innumerable secondary characters, most of whom were so interesting in themselves as to distract attention from the central figure. He was faced with vast national movements, with vital developments in imperial, foreign, and domestic policy, with far-reaching changes in the industrial and social condition of England, with intricate modifications in the constitution, with obscure shapings in the national temperament, with all those hidden forces which within those eighty years completely altered the structure of the civilised world. To compress all these within three hundred pages; to mould this vast material into a synthetic form; to convey not merely unity of impression but a convincing sense of scientific reality; to maintain throughout an attitude of detachment; to preserve the exquisite poise and balance of sustained and gentle irony, and to secure these objects with no apparent effort; to produce a book in which there is no trace of artificiality or strain – this, in all certainty, is an achievement which required the very highest gifts of intellect and imagination.' And so, because the foundations of research had been so diligently prepared, the fact and fantasy so consistently interwoven and finely shaped, the valid historical interpretation merged with smooth plausibility into a

3. *The Development of English Biography*, pp. 148–50.

more fictional form of characterization, Strachey was able legitimately to persuade his readers that a book which gives the impression of a consummately written romantic novel was, in reality a serious and soundly evidenced work of history.

Another reason why, in the opinion of some critics, *Queen Victoria* carries greater conviction than *Eminent Victorians*, is that the narrative appears to have been more scrupulously put together. With the greater choice of material at his disposal, there was no need for Strachey to search after peculiar significance in trivial episodes, to manipulate quotations or to present as accredited truth some evidence which had only dubious foundation in fact. Several apocryphal anecdotes and sayings are repudiated in footnotes; and when, for example, he recounts how Albert refused to open his door to Victoria so long as she demanded entrance as Queen of England, only consenting to admit her as his wife, Strachey, though not wishing to omit the story, describes it fairly and openly as 'ill-authenticated and perhaps mythical, yet summing up, as such stories often do, the central facts of the case'. At the same time, partly perhaps because of this greater scrupulousness, *Queen Victoria* remains a much less witty and irreverent book than *Eminent Victorians*.

It would have been almost impossible for Strachey to provide greater amusement at the expense of the Victorians, and the same crisp felicity of phrase is not to be found in the pages of *Queen Victoria*. In the first part of the biography, it is true, there are a few isolated flashes of his scintillating wit. His description of Baron Stockmar – 'Dyspeptic by constitution, melancholic by temperament, he could yet be lively on occasion, and was known as a wit in Coburg' – certainly has a Johnsonian ring to it. The miniature too of King William is very vivid – 'a bursting, bubbling old gentleman, with quarter-deck gestures, round rolling eyes, and a head like a pineapple'. But in the main, such sallies as there are do not have the same rapier-like thrust as those in *Eminent Victorians*. When we read that the Baroness Lehzen 'had habits which betrayed her origin. Her passion for caraway seeds, for instance, was uncontrollable'; or when we learn of Albert that 'His Royal

Highness's technical acquaintance with the processes of fresco-painting was incomplete', we are diverted, but realize that Strachey's irony has lost some of its cutting edge through being directed towards rather trivial targets. The arrow no longer has a poison head to it, only a rubber sucker to mark the place of impact. This change reminds us, too, how easily, in the spectrum of emotional attitudes, scepticism shades off into awe, since it is always haunting that perplexing borderline between the two.

As R. A. Scott-James observed, 'having grown up at twenty he [Strachey] had allowed something of the extremities of youth to master him at thirty-eight'. One feature of this alleged Immaturity Regained in *Eminent Victorians* was his obvious delight in the absurd names held by august divines, scholars and officials – Dowbiggin, Philpots, Wegg-Prosser, Gell, Burbridge, Walrond and Simpkinson. 'To allow such names to fall into the hands of Lytton Strachey', commented Guy Boas, 'was to present an urchin with a water-pistol.' His satire, without the bitterness of Swift's, was largely a form of incredulously inverted romanticism. In *Queen Victoria*, this romanticism is no longer inverted, and is used not to sharpen his mockery – either deliberately through satirizing pretensions and hypocrisies or else, more indirectly, by exposing the drama of existence as a transitory process made real to us only through habit – but to make it more playful, more charming and innocuous. His intense preoccupation with religion, the irrational duties and dogmas of which, he believed, induced a blindness to real moral values, had fired his imagination. But this sharp, intermittent beam of reality faded into an agreeable roseate glow, not unattractive but less revealing, when he substituted for his quartet of superstitious egotists, a single secular egocentric. *Eminent Victorians*, for all its overselection and over-simplification, has something of the clean taste of truth; while the taste left by *Queen Victoria*, despite several superior literary ingredients, is more cloying. For in one book Strachey had ruthlessly laid bare the complacent credulity of the nineteenth century; and in the other he merely enshrined it with faint dispraise.

2

VICTORIA AND ALBERT

The characters in *Queen Victoria* arrange themselves into three sharply defined categories: there is the heroine and the hero; there is a procession of minor, mostly flamboyant figures; and there are several off-stage, unsubstantial beings who appear to control from their shadowy recesses the central machinations of the plot.

Towards Victoria herself, Strachey's feeling imperceptibly alters as his story unfolds. The playful irony, the mixture of affection, amusement and respect with which he regards her in the days of her youth, passes, after the death of Albert, into a tender and more sentimental eulogy. In 'Mr Creevey', the essay published in 1919[4] he had written: 'Clio is one of the most glorious of the Muses; but, as everyone knows, she (like her sister Melpomene) suffers from a sad defect: she is apt to be pompous. With her buskins, her robes, and her airs of importance she is at times, indeed, almost intolerable. But fortunately the Fates have provided a corrective. They have decreed that in her stately advances she should be accompanied by certain apish, impish creatures, who run round her tittering, pulling long noses, threatening to trip the good lady up, and even sometimes whisking to one side the corner of her drapery, and revealing her undergarments in a most indecorous manner.' While writing the first part of *Queen Victoria*, Strachey saw his function as to reveal the littleness underlying great events and to remind his readers that the unlikely pageant of history was itself once everyday life. But as he proceeded, his attitude shifted slightly. The extent of this change may be gauged by comparing his early description of Victoria's coronation with his much later account of an official visit made to England by Napoleon III and the Empress Eugénie. In describing the first occasion, Strachey

---

4. *New Republic* (7 June 1919), 178–81; *Athenaeum* (13 June 1919), 453–5; *Living Age*, 302 (19 July 1919), 158–62. Collected in *Books and Characters* and in *Biographical Essays* (236–42).

accompanies Clio, with appropriate gestures, as the young queen goes through her formal gyrations and the surrounding ceremonial works itself out, 'like some machine of gigantic complexity which was a little out of order'. The second passage is set in an entirely different key, and fuses together the historical and fabulous elements, being coated with a rather mawkish adulation, unmixed with irony, which he latterly reserves for the secondary characters such as Gilbert Scott.

There are, in fact, two Victorias whom Strachey elects to portray, the first of whom engages his intellectual attention, and the second to whom he responds emotionally. There is, of course, no reason to prevent one admiring some good qualities in a person whom one otherwise adversely criticizes. But it is perhaps a sign of his own split nature that these two simplified images seldom coincide. The result is that his Victoria loses something of the richness, the variety and irregularity of live portraiture – that organic complexity which an integrated portrait might have held.

In the closing two chapters of the book, this double image of Strachey's gives rise to a curious paradox. The final thirty pages contain a full inventory of Victoria's shortcomings – her imperialism, her religious obscurantism, her social reactionariness, her censorship of Greville, her nasty insistence on etiquette, her absence both of aesthetic taste and of any but the most unsubtle form of humour, her domineering character, above all her complacency, pride, egotism, her lack of sensitivity and of imagination. It is a formidable compilation; one made entertaining by anecdotes, well documented by reference notes, and apparently unanswerable. How, then, can it be that most readers have taken away from these last chapters a warm and sympathetic impression of the queen? How was it that G. M. Trevelyan could proclaim that Lytton Strachey had come to curse and stayed to bless Victoria – an opinion that is certainly untrue as describing Strachey's biographical intention or conscious attitude?

There would seem to be several factors that, taken together, might account for this anomaly. At no point in *Queen Victoria* is Strachey's disparagement of the queen so stringent as that of non-regal figures in *Eminent Victorians* or, for that matter, of the other non-regal figures in his Victoria biography, this being partly due to the fact that his subject was the grandmother of the reigning sovereign. Strachey goes out of his way to emphasize the reverence in which she was held by those closest to her and by the country as a whole. Her popularity was of a legendary kind. In many ways she did not merit such devotion. She was out of step with her epoch and she was sometimes insufferable to her family. Yet the extraordinary loyalty persisted, so that every limitation of character that Strachey points to only serves to increase our – and possible his own – wonder at the spell of her personality. In this way is the force of his criticisms deflected and even turned to her advantage.

Strachey's tone, too, is largely responsible for his readers' reaction to these pages. He is more amused than censorious. Many of Victoria's failings are presented in a fundamentally sympathetic light. Her middle-class morals, for example, were really, we are led to believe, a distorted development of her very genuine family affection. Her passion for John Brown is, of course, laughable; but it does not take away from her intrinsic power, and it contributes to her humanity and to that most loved of English qualities – eccentricity. Her collecting instinct, which is described in terms of an obsessional neurosis, is seen to have its root in the fear of death, so that again our hearts are touched. Even her indefensible insistence upon changing the form of the verdict in cases of insanity is partly excused as being due to her memory of Albert's feelings on this subject.

The English, it is said, will warm to anyone, even a genius, providing he lives long enough. The most interesting thing about Victoria, however, is that, most emphatically, she was not a genius, not a great woman, not even in any way exceptional. What fascinated Strachey – and what is revealed by his skilled juxtaposition of incongruous facts – was her total mediocrity taken in conjunction with her grossly artificial position as Queen of England. That someone so commonplace should be elevated to the status of divinity aroused his sense

254

of the dramatic and the absurd. At the same time, by appealing to the megalomania latent in all of us, such a theme gave him an almost certain best-seller. 'Just like ourselves', middle-aged ladies from the circulating libraries could reflect with satisfaction after glancing through Strachey's flattering portrait of an essentially ordinary subject.

Yet it was not merely the accident of longevity that ameliorated Strachey's tone. It was the old queen's *lack of power*: 'Her desire to impose her will,' he wrote, 'vehement as it was, and unlimited by any principle, was yet checked by a certain shrewdness. She might oppose her Ministers with extraordinary violence; she might remain utterly impervious to arguments and supplications; the pertinacity of her resolution might seem to be unconquerable; but, at the very last moment of all, her obstinacy would give way. . . . By instinct she understood when the facts were too much for her, and to them she invariably yielded. After all, what else could she do?'

In the end therefore it is Victoria's sincerity and truthfulness that triumph. Strachey frames his picture of her old age with the abiding love of her people, and it is this love for a mother-figure that he most vividly evokes for his readers, a love which, rightly or wrongly, they felt that he too shared. He writes of her 'gentle benignity', her 'unforgettable charm', her 'impressiveness', of her writings which 'touched the heart of the public', and of 'those remarkable messages to the nation which, from time to time, she published in the newspapers' and in which 'her people found her very close to them indeed. They felt instinctively Victoria's irresistible sincerity, and they responded. And in truth it was an endearing trait.'

So it is not in the vivid impulse of her youth, nor even in the full flower of her womanhood, but as an ageing and laborious widow, a grandiose matriarch, cloistered from the vulgar intrusions of the world, that Victoria grew serene, and that her life, in Strachey's words, became 'lighted with a golden glory'. The young creature whom he depicts, with her 'ingenious clarity, her sincerity, her simplicity, her quick affections and pious resolutions', and the adoring wife overcome by love of her husband, though both charming enough, are evidently less endearing to him than the little old lady with her white hair and plain mourning clothes.

Certainly the peculiar spell that Victoria came to exert over Strachey's readers sprang from the traits of protective motherhood which she extended not just over her own large family, but all her subjects. 'The Queen was hailed at once as the mother of her people', he wrote in his penultimate chapter, 'and as the embodied symbol of their imperial greatness; and she responded to the double sentiment with all the ardour of her spirit. England and the people of England, she knew it, she felt it, were, in some wonderful and yet quite simple manner, *hers*. Exultation, affection, gratitude, a profound sense of obligation, and unbounded pride – such were her emotions, and, colouring and intensifying the rest, there was something else. At last, after so long, happiness – fragmentary, perhaps, and charged with gravity, but true and unmistakable none the less – had returned to her.'

Victoria's deepest happiness came, of course, from her marriage to Albert, which forms the central panel in the framework of Strachey's biography. Albert is introduced early on in the story, when he visits England with his brother Ernest. 'The Princes', Strachey observed, 'shared her ecstasies and her italics between them; but it is clear enough where her secret preference lay. "Particularly Albert"! She was just seventeen; and deep was the impression left upon that budding organism by the young man's charm and goodness and accomplishments, and his large blue eyes and beautiful nose, and his sweet mouth and fine teeth.'

The first impression, however, was not deep. Victoria's emotions, though intense, were seldom very profound. Albert out of sight was Albert out of mind. As queen, she soon, as Strachey shows, fell under the influence of Lord Melbourne, viewing her uncle, King Leopold's, suggestion that Albert might make her a very suitable husband with the greatest repugnance. And when the time of Albert's next visit drew near, she confided to Melbourne that she 'had no great wish to see Albert, as the whole subject was an odious one'. Yet it was only when she did see him again, danced and talked with him that she was swept off her feet by a violent sexual infatuation that had been remotely fired on their previous meeting. In what R. A. Scott-James has called 'Ouida-esque language', Strachey describes the romantic upheaval that exploded within Victoria on again encountering Albert, and the proposal which followed a few days afterwards. But, characteristically, he does not bring to the surface her extraordinary self-absorption and lack of sensitivity in failing to appreciate that Albert's feelings were totally out of keeping with her own. A woman who could not sense this, could sense very little at all about other people.

'Albert arrived; and the whole structure of her existence crumbled into nothingness like a house of cards. He was beautiful – she gasped – she knew no more. Then, in a flash, a thousand mysteries were revealed to her; the past, the present, rushed upon her with a new significance; the delusions of years were abolished, and an extraordinary, an irresistible certitude leapt into being in the light of those blue eyes, the smile of that lovely mouth. The succeeding hours passed in a rapture. . . . She received him alone, and "after a few minutes I said to him that I thought he must be aware *why* I wished them to come here – and that it would make me *too happy* if he would consent to what I wished (to marry me)". Then "we embraced each other, and he was *so* kind, *so* affectionate". She said that she was quite unworthy of him, while he murmured that he would be very happy "Das Leben mit dir zu zubringen". They parted, and she felt "the happiest of human beings".'

Strachey tended to confer even on Victoria's more disagreeable traits the aura of a childlike simplicity; but his analysis of Albert's character does pierce some way below the surface, and, in portraying a man partially akin to himself, he reveals something of his own loneliness. Although, in the eyes of the queen, the prince was a mirror of manly beauty, Strachey explains, his constitution was not a strong one, and 'owing either to his peculiar upbringing or to a more fundamental idiosyncrasy he had a marked distaste for the opposite sex'. The prospect of his marriage to the adoring

Victoria filled him with the deepest depression. But through the submissive sense of duty that had been instilled into him as a youth, he steadfastly buried his natural inclinations, the faint stirrings of personal ambition. Strachey told Hesketh Pearson that he had intended to suggest that Albert was homosexual – an interpretation of the Prince Consort's disposition likely to endorse the view that children of the British monarch are, by tradition, of virgin birth. This must be taken, however, as the key to several passages which Strachey devotes to Albert and which stress his foreign temperament, his sadness and isolation.

'A shy young foreigner, awkward in ladies' company, unexpansive and self-opinionated, it was improbable that, in any circumstances, he would have been a society success. ... His features were regular, no doubt, but there was something smooth and smug about them; he was tall, but he was clumsily put together, and he walked with a slight slouch. Really, they thought, this youth was more like some kind of foreign tenor. ... From the support and the solace of true companionship he was utterly cut off.'

Contrasting Albert's feelings for Victoria with her absolute and unconcealed devotion to him, Strachey wrote: 'He was not in love with her. Affection, gratitude, the natural reactions to the unqualified devotion of a lively young cousin who was also a queen – such feelings possessed him, but the ardours of reciprocal passion were not his. Though he found that he liked Victoria very much, what immediately interested him in his curious position was less her than himself.'

Like Strachey, Albert is seen as having the power of provoking in another an idolatry that in no way corresponds to his own innermost needs. Unlike Strachey, of course, he could not turn elsewhere for true companionship. This, then, was his 'curious position' to which Strachey returns in a later paragraph. 'The husband was not so happy as the wife', he wrote. 'In spite of the great improvement in his situation, in spite of a growing family and the adoration of Victoria, Albert was still a stranger in a strange land, and the serenity of spiritual satisfaction was denied him. It was something, no doubt, to

258

have dominated his immediate environment; but it was not enough; and, besides, in the very completeness of his success, there was a bitterness. Victoria idolised him; but it was understanding that he craved for, not idolatry; and how much did Victoria, filled to the brim though she was with him, understand him? How much does the bucket understand the well? He was lonely. He went to his organ and improvised with learned modulations until the sounds, swelling and subsiding through elaborate cadences, brought some solace to his heart. ... Thus did he amuse himself; but there was one distraction in which he did not indulge. He never flirted – no, not with the prettiest ladies of the Court. ... Throughout their married life no rival female charms ever gave cause to Victoria for one moment's pang of jealousy.'

Summing up the Prince Consort's career at the end of his short life, Strachey again cautiously approaches the same theme, barely concealing, in a commotion of vague verbal ambiguity, his real meaning. Albert, he tells us, was sick at heart: 'For in spite of everything he had never reached to happiness. His work, for which at last he came to crave with an almost morbid appetite, was a solace and not a cure; the dragon of his dissatisfaction devoured with dark relish that ever-growing tribute of laborious days and nights; but it was hungry still. The causes of his melancholy were hidden, mysterious, unanalysable perhaps – too deeply rooted in the innermost recesses of his temperament for the eye of reason to apprehend. ... There was something that he wanted and that he could never get. What was it? Some absolute, some ineffable sympathy? Some extraordinary, some sublime success? Possibly, it was a mixture of both. To dominate and be understood! To conquer, by the same triumphant influence, the submission and the appreciation of men – that would be worth while indeed! ...

'But ... Albert remained as foreign as before; and as the years passed his dejection deepened.'

Unlike Strachey, Albert was never to find a favourable niche in life. The father of a large family who did not care for women; a full-time politician who was naturally indifferent to politics; the patron of the sciences and arts who was neither a scientist nor an artist – the impulse behind all these pursuits was of a vicarious or therapeutic kind. Strachey responded very sympathetically to the lonelinesss of his exile, and to the sincerity and warmth of his nature. He does not mock, as he might have done in *Eminent Victorians*, when the dejected prince accepts his engagement to Victoria as a test of his faith in the mysterious designs of God. Indeed, he holds back from bringing out the religiosity latent in Albert's sense of duty, and poignantly revealed in some of his letters – 'I am quite sure', he wrote after his engagement in a letter which Lytton does not quote, 'that Heaven has not given me into evil hands.' Nor does Strachey deride the painstaking but often trivial reforms which Albert effected within the royal household. His portrait of the Prince Consort is moving, but incomplete, in that it fails to present the callousness that was the reverse side to his integrity. With adroitness and feeling, he shows us Albert's indifference to women as being the chief cause of his own unhappiness, but does not indicate how this misogynist bias could operate with inhumane intolerance upon others. On one occasion, for example, when Ernest, his brother from whom he had been inseparable before his marriage to Victoria, had a discreditable love-affair, Albert wrote him a violent, uncompromising letter – not mentioned by Strachey – in which he said that though he would never curse him or take away the love he owed him as a brother, he would leave him to perish in immorality.

Similarly, so as not to take away from the pathos of Albert's life, Strachey conceals that streak of arrogance and stupidity in the prince's nature which he sometimes failed to control – 'No tailor in England can make a coat', he once announced; and to a distinguished clergyman he remarked that in England 'there is nothing to do but turn rogue or marry'. The prince's brother, in his memoirs, declared: 'Of mankind in general he [Albert] is contemptuous.' His attitude towards his own family, which Strachey hardly touches upon, was extremely interesting and not irrelevant. Sexually and intellectually bored with his wife, he seemed closer to the

Princess Royal, his daughter, until she married Prince Frederick of Prussia, and left England to live in Germany. His grief at her departure was sharp, and it seems probable that her place as the closest woman in his life would have been taken by Princess Alice, had he lived longer – she never left his side during his last illness. But his attitude towards Bertie was inexcusable. He once confessed to Clarendon, rather indiscreetly, that the aggressive disciplinarian treatment of his eldest son which he and the queen meted out was a mistake. The disagreeable task of punishment, he added, always fell on him, and he had hesitated to resist this severity for fear of thwarting Victoria. Nevertheless, it is difficult to escape the conclusion that he vented on the Prince of Wales all his own disappointments and frustrations, having no other outlet for his long pent-up emotions. There was an element of cruelty in Albert's make-up. He needed an antagonist to spur him to his best efforts, and Victoria bored him with her tireless veneration. To some extent, Strachey exaggerated Albert's misery in the early days of their marriage. He was not unhappy then. Victoria's hero-worship of him – like Carrington's for Strachey himself[5] – enveloped him very comfortably, and though it did not penetrate his being to any great depth, it does seem to have ministered pleasantly enough to his well-being.

The peculiar fascination which this relationship between Victoria and Albert exerted over Strachey is clearly disclosed when he asks, 'was he the wife and she the husband?' and answers his own question: 'It almost seemed so.' For outward appearances belied the inner truth. Their marriage had begun as a struggle of angry wills. 'Victoria,' Strachey explains, 'no more than Albert, was in the habit of playing second fiddle. Her arbitrary temper flashed out. Her vitality, her obstinacy, her overweening sense of her own position, might well have beaten down before them his superiorities and his rights. But she fought at a disadvantage; she was, in very truth, no longer her own mistress; a profound preoccupation dominated her, seizing upon her inmost purposes for its own extraordinary

5. Dora Carrington, the painter, who lived with Strachey over the last fifteen years of their lives.

ends. She was madly in love.' And so, Strachey wryly tells us, 'Time and the pressure of inevitable circumstances were for him; every day his predominance grew more assured – and every night.' The picture which Strachey now draws for us is of the queen's total capitulation before Albert – and beneath him. 'Victoria,' he writes, 'overcome by a new, an unimagined revelation, had surrendered her whole soul to her husband.' And a little later: 'Victoria fell more and more absolutely under his intellectual predominance', until, 'with all the zeal of a convert', she 'upheld now the standard of moral purity with an inflexibility surpassing, if that were possible, Albert's own'. In all things, like some topsy-turvy Duke of Plaza-toro, she followed from well in advance. When he felt disappointment, she exceeded him in mortification. When he seemed contented, she was ecstatic. He was, as she herself once wrote, 'my beloved lord and master'.

The development, skilfully traced by Strachey through his narrative, though true, does not perhaps constitute the whole truth. The account which Albert himself gave to the Duke of Wellington of his role as husband puts a very different emphasis on his relationship with Victoria. He considered it his duty, he said, to 'sink his *own individual* existence in that of his wife ... – assume no separate responsibility before the public, but make his position entirely a part of hers – fill up every gap which, as a woman, she would naturally leave in the exercise of her regal functions – continually and anxiously watch every part of the public business, in order to be able to advise and assist her at any moment in any of the multifarious and difficult questions or duties brought before her, sometimes international, sometimes political, or social, or personal'.

So much for the Prince Consort's absolute predominance. From resembling a foreign tenor, he had changed during the course of his marriage, as Strachey observes, into an idealized butler. For a double process was at work. His victory over the queen's prepotent will was largely superficial and void. She had, it is true, changed; but changeability was the very essence of her shallow being, since she possessed no special ambiance of her own, merely reflecting the light of those closest to her. Albert, on the other hand, by adapting himself body and soul to the part of the Prince Consort, had sacrificed almost everything that was original in his character, to become a cold caricature of a worthy man, a figure of bleached perfection, bowed down by domesticity, loneliness, misunderstanding and overwork.

What really pricked Strachey's curiosity was not so much Albert's apparent predominance as the underlying ascendancy of Victoria. Her superabundant energies suffocated the very breath out of him. It was hardly surprising that, lacking her inert tenacity, he should confess to setting no great store by his prolonged existence. 'I do not cling to life', he once admitted to Victoria, '. . . I am sure, if I had a severe illness, I should give up at once, I should not struggle for life.' And so it proved to be.

Only when Strachey comes to see Victoria through the eyes of the declining Prince Consort does the sentimental haze enveloping her suddenly lift, and we are made to feel a positive repugnance. Albert's constitution was 'ill-adapted to meet a serious strain. He was easily upset; he constantly suffered from minor ailments. His appearance in itself was enough to indicate the infirmity of his physical powers. . . . Beside Victoria, he presented a painful contrast. She, too, was stout, but it was with the plumpness of a vigorous matron; and an eager vitality was everywhere visible – in her energetic bearing, her protruding, inquiring glances, her small, fat, capable and commanding hands. If only, by some sympathetic magic she could have conveyed into that portly, flabby figure, that desiccated and discouraged brain, a measure of the stamina and the self-assurance which were so pre-eminently hers!'

Although, owing to the subsequent publication of various papers, a few of Strachey's pages – such as the scene in which Bismarck is made to overawe the queen – have been proved to rest on false surmise, his portrait of Victoria has remained vividly in the public imagination, greatly influencing later biographies. But for those who do not share his habit of extolling her severe limitations as charming aspects of a quaint and whimsical personality, the clue to Victoria's character lies in her incredible unawareness of her husband's baleful submission to the mysterious fate that had decreed their marriage. She needed a man to whose father-like authority she could respond with constant love – a love preserved by constant challenge. To all else she was blind. It was enough for her that she was happy with Albert. That she represented for him the rigorous subordination in a virtuous life of the desire for personal happiness to the arid claims of duty never consciously occurred to her. 'Very few', she wrote, 'can say with me that their husband at the end of twenty-one years is *not* only full of the friendship, kindness and affection which a truly happy marriage brings with it, but the same tender love of the *very first days of our marriage.*' This statement, in such striking contrast to the deepening gloom of Albert's last years, Strachey does not quote. Nor does he quote the single sentence in which, after Albert's death, Victoria came nearest to realizing that her husband's sombre calm had not concealed an exquisite felicity equal to her own. 'His great soul', she wrote, 'is *now only* enjoying that of which it *was* worthy.'

3

THE PRIME MINISTERS

Strachey devoted more than two thirds of his biography to Victoria's life before the death of Albert, leaving the remaining third to cover the latter half of her career. The primary reason for this, it has been said, was the smaller quantity of available information. 'The first forty-two years of the Queen's life are illuminated by a great and varied quantity of authentic information', Strachey himself wrote. 'With Albert's death a veil descends. Only occasionally, at fitful and disconnected intervals, does it lift for a moment or two; a few main outlines, a few remarkable details may be discerned; the rest is all conjecture and ambiguity. Thus, though the Queen survived her great bereavement for almost as many years as she had lived before it, the chronicle of those years can bear no proportion to the tale of her earlier life. We must be content in our ignorance with a brief and summary relation.' According to Raymond Mortimer, the final volumes of Victoria's correspondence, which G. B. Buckle brought out between 1928 and 1932, altered Strachey's view of these later years: she was more robust, less gentle and droll than he had envisaged. But, in any case, he did not wish to expand the last four chapters of his book. The earlier chapters describe the long process by which the character of the queen was formed; once that character had crystallized, her actual life was of less significance to him. To enlarge this final section would have disrupted the biographical pattern. For there seems little doubt that Strachey really welcomed the darkness which descended over the last forty years of the queen's reign as aiding his artistic purpose, which was to re-create his subject's intimate personality, her hidden or unconscious life. It was this aim that, throughout the biography, guided his choice of material. The absence of detailed information about Victoria's widowhood legitimately opened the way to a more subjective interpretation of her temperament. Strachey regarded – as did Victoria – the death of Albert as the central turning-point in her history. 'She herself', he wrote, 'felt that her true life had ceased with her husband's, and that the remainder of her days upon earth was of a twilight nature – an epilogue to a drama that was done. Nor is it possible that her biographer should escape a similar expression.'

Critics who have complained that *Queen Victoria* omits too much of the nineteenth-century political scene have possibly failed to appreciate that the unity which Strachey brought to his book was achieved mainly by the process of seeing people and events through the eyes of Victoria herself. Though shrewd, she had little wisdom or imagination and none of the political genius of Elizabeth, with whom she has often been thoughtlessly compared. Her politics were more of the eighteenth century, and her interest in them was of a purely personal nature. She suspected political zeal and was repelled by political enthusiasm, her object being to maintain the vested interests of her family clan, at whatever expense to the British taxpayer. After Albert's death, she behaved like a widow who has been left in charge of a large estate, and means to exact the respect due to her from her less important neighbours. Her prime ministers she treated in the manner of family solicitors, whose duty it was to remain always vigilant in seeking out profitable investments for her spare moneys.

In these circumstances, it was inevitable that the professional historian should consider Strachey's treatment of nineteenth-century politics to have been inadequate. Only in order to estimate the developments which the Constitution underwent during Victoria's reign does he step aside from the main narrative of his story and allow some historical commentary. And here, by maintaining that the power of the Crown increased from 1840 until Albert's death, then steadily declined until, in 1901, it 'was weaker than at any other time in English history', he seemed to several constitutional historians to have misunderstood the significance of the Reform Bill.

Strachey's portraits of individual politicians are deliberately uneven, since they are coloured almost completely by Victoria's own personal feelings towards each one of them. It was not their politics which impressed her, but their personalities. Strachey affects to see underlying her formal and official dealings with her prime ministers a more individual relationship, and he uses these minor political characters in such a way as to contribute directly to our knowledge of the queen's inner life, and of one aspect of this inner life especially – her strong, subconscious sexuality. This he does subtly, through suggestive metaphor and innuendo.

Lost in the large shadow of her mother's domination, Victoria's early years were likened by Strachey to those of a novice in a convent. The Duchess of Kent never for a single day relaxed the pressure of her maternal vigilance. Her educational concepts were those of Dr Arnold, and she saw to it that her daughter was drilled, with unyielding conformity, in the antique, endless duties of a Christian queen. The whole household at Kensington was geared to the task of eradicating the minutest traces of ordinary human nature in the grown girl. An antiseptic odour of sanctity enshrouded her, protecting her from the contaminations of the outside world and from the disturbing presence of the male sex. The justifiable horror which Strachey felt at this unnatural process of incubating a human soul – a horror that may possibly have gained something from his own incarceration within Lancaster Gate[6] – is very pronounced in the chapter which he devotes to Victoria's childhood: 'The child grew into the girl, the girl into the young woman; but still she slept in her mother's bedroom; still she had no place allowed her where she might sit or work by herself. An extraordinary watchfulness surrounded her every step ... It was her misfortune that the mental atmosphere which surrounded her during these years of adolescence was almost entirely feminine ... Henceforward female duty, female elegance, female enthusiasm, hemmed her completely in; and her spirit, amid the enclosing folds, was hardly reached by those two great influences, without which no growing life can truly prosper – humour and imagination.'

Schooled in the absolute virtues of simplicity, propriety and devotion, she had received a training from which nothing had been omitted that might help to ensure that she ascended the Throne with the purest intentions, the most just desires. Yet, as Strachey more than once hints, the female domination to which she was subjected as a girl may itself have given rise to an unforeseen reaction, namely, her eager dependence and susceptibility in adult life to the influence of men – 'perhaps, after all, to the discerning eye, the purity would not be absolute. The careful searcher might detect, in the virgin soil, the first faint traces of an unexpected vein.' Her unwearying love of dancing, her extreme attraction towards handsome young men in uniform, were not the qualities one looked for in a convent nun. 'The "illustrious Princess" might perhaps, after all, have something within her which squared ill with the easy

6. Strachey lived at 69 Lancaster Gate from the age of four to twenty-eight. For his own account of its effect on him see *Lytton Strachey by Himself*, pp. 16–28.

vision of a well-conducted heroine in an edifying story-book.'
For all the care taken over her upbringing, for all the anxious,
unceasing watchfulness that presided over her cloistered
childhood and adolescence 'there was something deep within
her which responded immediately and vehemently to natures
that offered a romantic contrast with her own'.

This was the fundamental spring, bubbling incessantly
below the hard, regal exterior of Victoria's personality, which
Strachey sought to explore in describing her relations with a
succession of politicians and other minor figures in the book.
The romantic contrast between the queen, with her youth, her
earnestness, and her endearing simplicity, and the absent-
minded, sceptical, flippant old Lord Melbourne, her first prime
minister, was certainly striking. Strachey obviously warmed to
Melbourne, and he indulges his fondness beyond the strict
artistic limits that controlled his other subsidiary portraits.
We see Lord M. not only through the fascinated eyes of Victoria, but also with the admiring retrospective gaze of a biographer. The result is the most full and satisfying minor
impressionistic study in the book. He does not seek to 'explain' Melbourne, but to exhibit him vividly before the
reader. Consequently, Melbourne shares with so many of his
other pen-portraits that standard Stracheyesque quality of
being 'inexplicable'. Like most romantics, Strachey loved a
mystery, and he uses all his knowledge of character to add a
delicious confusion of colour to the accumulating incon-
gruities he observes on the perimeter of his subjects' personalities, presenting them as supreme enigmas, ambiguous
and contradictory, baffling all analysis. He possessed a won-
derfully sharp eye for the externals of a personality, the gestures, tricks of speech, eccentric mannerisms, but he could
seldom apprehend that directing principle, or complex of
principles, that reconciles the apparently conflicting elements
on the surface of any character. Without this clue, he is
mystified. He throws up his hands in an elegant gesture of
surrender, as if in the hope that the rhetorical grace of his
movement will camouflage the fact that, theoretically, it is an
admission of defeat.

Charles Greville once described Melbourne as 'a man with a capacity for loving without having anything in the world to love'. Victoria was enchanted by his sympathetic presence, his sophistication, his captivating masculine charm. He soon became an integral part of her existence, and his undirected capacity for loving suddenly focused upon the young queen. In his description of Melbourne's response to Victoria's infatuation, Strachey picks out words and images which suggest the latent sexuality of their attachment: 'And so, cherished by the favour of a sovereign and warmed by the adoration of a girl, the autumn rose, in those autumn months of 1839, came to a wondrous blooming. The petals expanded, beautifully, for the last time. For the last time in this unlooked-for, this incongruous, this almost incredible intercourse, the old epicure tasted the exquisiteness of romance.'

Robert Peel, on the other hand, possessed none of Melbourne's sophisticated sex-appeal. Reserved by nature, he was easily embarrassed, particularly before women, in front of whom his manner would grow unpleasantly stiff and pompous. And so, since he made little positive impression on Victoria, he occupies little space in her biography.

After her marriage, Victoria – whose simple pleasures, Strachey tells us, were mostly physical – lost her 'bold and discontented' look, and her platonic infatuation for Lord Melbourne faded gently away. Completely obsessed by her husband, her response to any man was decided by his opinion alone. Her heart even softened towards the maladroit Peel; while the jaunty and volatile Palmerston, by whom she might otherwise have been attracted, repelled her during these years of her marriage precisely because he was the very antithesis of the Prince Consort, representing all that was most hostile to him in the spirit of England. Strachey, however, does briefly introduce the gaudy, gipsyish figure of Tsar Nicolas I of Russia into his narrative, in order to illustrate that, although contentedly married, Victoria was still naturally appreciative of any strikingly handsome man.

After Albert's death this power of appreciation gradually blossomed forth again. In her own estimation, as Strachey makes clear, she was guided at all times by one principle – her deceased husband's approval. Yet whenever her strong sexual instinct was brought into play, Albert's hypothetical sanction seemed to have been taken for granted. The Prince Consort preferred Gladstone to Disraeli, yet because Gladstone, with 'his ceremonious phrases, his low bows, his punctilious correctitudes', behaved towards her not as if she were a human being but a cold embodiment of venerable traditions, addressing her, so the story goes, more like a public meeting than a woman, she could never warm to him as a man. Disraeli's personality, so romantic and oriental, was in every respect the opposite of Gladstone's. Performing like some actor in his own exotic melodrama, and with himself as applauding audience, his flattery, his charm, his bewitching strain of charlatanism intoxicated the ageing queen. By treating her first and foremost as a woman and not as a symbol, he gave her back her self-confidence. Strachey passes swiftly over Gladstone as over Peel, and for similar reasons. But his portrait of Disraeli is almost as detailed as his Melbourne, though rather less satisfactory since, over him, he could not really see eye to eye with Victoria. His metaphorical description of their relationship and of the swelling elation Disraeli aroused in her, deliberately makes use of imagery that recalls Victoria's friendship with Melbourne so many years before. 'After the long gloom of her bereavement, after the chill of the Gladstonian discipline, she expanded to the rays of Disraeli's devotion like a flower in the sun.'

To experience the sense of physical security for which she longed, Victoria needed to become filially dependent upon some man. But the extraordinary liberties which she permitted the Highland gillie, John Brown, would certainly never have been approved by Albert. That she obscurely sensed his mute protest from beyond the grave is suggested by the odd emotional spiritualism which she concocted – 'the gruff, kind, hairy Scotsman was, she felt, in some mysterious way, a legacy from the dead. She came to believe at last – or so it appeared – that the spirit of Albert was nearer when Brown was near.' Yet the truth of the matter was perhaps more mundane. The shade of Albert was receding in her mind. She never totally forgot him, but, as was natural, his loss became less terrible, her awareness of his overriding tastes and opinions more intermittent. Significantly, Munshi Abdul Karim, her Indian attendant who took the place of Brown after his death, was invested with no transcendental ties with the deceased Prince Consort.

Strachey constructed his *Queen Victoria* as a series of self-contained but inter-related chapter-essays. The chapters are neatly parcelled up round the principal men in Victoria's life, and sometimes by-pass the strict chronological sequence of historical events in a manner that can be misleading. The characters surrounding the queen appear and disappear as if they had no existence before or after the few paragraphs or pages where they are mentioned. In Chapter 4, 'Marriage', for example, we are shown Albert's ascent from a nonentity to a man of importance not only in his home life but in his position with the Government and the people of the country. We watch him gradually breaking down the antagonism and gaining the respect of the man in the street, and winning, too, the confidence of the ministers of state. Opposition dies away, and in the final section of this chapter his triumph is crowned by the Great Exhibition of 1851. But in the next chapter we learn with some surprise that Palmerston was Albert's bitterest opponent, and that since 1846 he had been foreign minister, continuing in this office until November 1851. During these years there had been a constant struggle between the two of them. But it is only now, in Chapter 5, that we discover, for the first time, this major obstacle in the political advancement of Albert, which is the subject-matter of Chapter 4. This technique of parcelling chapters is most disconcerting in 'Mr Gladstone and Lord Beaconsfield'. Both these men, well past middle age, who had for many years played important political roles, are only now introduced at this late stage into the story. The one intimation given to us that Disraeli was an eminent parliamentarian even in the time of the Prince Consort is that the prince once declared that he 'had not one single element of a gentleman in his composition'. Gladstone,

Strachey tells us, 'had been the disciple of her revered Peel, and had won the approval of Albert'. By showing Victoria succumbing to the outrageous flatteries of Disraeli and regarding Gladstone with distrust and dislike, Strachey intended to illustrate how the queen's strong and unconscious sexuality overpowered her avowed determination to be governed by the doctrines and opinions of her late husband. What Strachey omits – and it is an omission which stems mainly from the structure of his biography – is that Disraeli in fact won Albert's qualified approval during his brief time of ministerial office before the Prince Consort's death, by his wholehearted support of Albert's crusade to strengthen England's military defences. Albert, who had a distinct strain of effeminacy in his character, had also sometimes taken a hesitating pleasure in conversing with the Leader of the Opposition, finding that Disraeli was more cultivated and better read in English history than any other British statesman, and that his deferential attitude to the Throne was irreproachable.

4

UNSEEN POWERS

The third type of character in *Queen Victoria,* that collection of sinister and dimly-seen supers who lurk histrionically behind the scenes of power, contributes less to the reader's knowledge of facts than to the pervasive atmosphere and artistic design of the book. These mysterious, immaterial beings – the Duchess of Kent, Lehzen, Leopold and Stockmar – are little more than stage props supporting the star performers in the cast. Strachey had devised them as the cog-wheels which made up the mechanical tricks of his trade, and any resemblance between them and actual human beings was coincidental. To some extent these artificial entities, and the parts they play, are products of his romantic and cynical conception of political intrigue and the struggle for power behind the scenes. But Strachey also uses them to great aesthetic effect. As latent supremacy passes from one to the other, so the kaleidoscope of the biography subtly shifts from one pattern to another.

The Duchess of Kent is seen as the first to exercise her hidden authority. 'Great forces and fierce antagonisms', Strachey wrote, 'seemed to be moving, obscurely, about the royal cradle.' As Victoria grows up, a battle for her allegiance develops between the child's mother and her governess, Baroness Lehzen. And it is Lehzen who finally emerges triumphant. Strachey describes her victory in highly charged, dramatic style. 'The pastor's daughter observed the ruin of her enemies. Discreet and victorious, she remained in possession of the field. More closely than ever did she cleave to the side of her mistress, her pupil, and her friend; and in the recesses of the palace her mysterious figure was at once invisible and omnipresent.'

During these first few years of her reign, Victoria is dominated by Lehzen, whom Strachey depicts as the real mistress of the royal household, responsible for the freezing etiquette that was permanently in control there. 'Over the whole of Victoria's private life the Baroness reigned supreme,' he informs us, 'and she had not the slightest intention of allowing that supremacy to be diminished by one iota. Since the accession, her power had greatly increased. Besides the undefined and enormous influence which she exercised through her management of the Queen's private correspondence, she was now the superintendent of the royal establishment and controlled the important office of Privy Purse.'

In international affairs it is Leopold, Victoria's uncle, who attempts to gain ascendancy over the young queen. For a while it looks as if he might be successful, but eventually his creeping policies are overcome by Victoria's unyielding front. It is, however, Leopold's 'confidential agent', Baron Stockmar – a sort of Professor Moriarty controlling the destiny of kingdoms from his invisible lair – who at length carries all before him. If Victoria is Lehzen's pupil, Albert is the genie whom Stockmar calls out of his bottle to enact his every wish. After Albert and Victoria's marriage a kind of Punch and Judy show starts up, Stockmar and Lehzen violently activating the marionettes upon the stage until Punch-Albert-Stockmar is acclaimed the winner. Lehzen 'lost ground perceptibly', Strachey recorded. The prince, Stockmar's mouthpiece, is at first cautious. Then he waves a wand and the full annihilating power of his magic is at once omnipotent. 'He spoke, and Lehzen vanished for ever.'

And so the kaleidoscope shifts again. 'The tide of circumstance was flowing now with irresistible fullness towards a very different consummation.' It is hardly an exaggeration to say that, in Strachey's version, the queen and the Prince Consort were allowed to possess free will only within those limits ordained by the all-prescient baron. He is the good fairy of the pantomime, working with all the tireless energy of disinterested devotion, cautious and wise, never acting under the spur of personal ambition; while the royal couple are but two mandarin figures, nodding their heads in assent or shaking them in denial as their master pleases.

Strachey's reconstruction of Lehzen's great influence over the queen was founded pre-eminently on romantic conjecture. His analysis of Stockmar's character and the description he gives of the powerful role the baron played in politics is adapted very largely from the mythical version which Stockmar himself perpetuated in the self-hypnotic throes of senile optimism. The passage in which Strachey conjures forth the supernal baron is far-fetched in the extreme. 'The satisfaction of his essential being lay in obscurity, in invisibility – in passing, unobserved, through a hidden entrance, into the very central chamber of power, and in sitting there, quietly, pulling the subtle strings that set the wheels of the whole world in motion.' His trap-door exits and entrances to and from these high places, Strachey later assures us, were of the utmost political significance – so much so that, despite the most cunning discretion, a vague rumour of his power percolated through to the general public. 'Stockmar's pupil had assuredly gone far and learnt well. Stockmar's pupil! – precisely; the public, painfully aware of Albert's predominance, had grown, too, uneasily conscious that Victoria's master had a master of his own. Deep in the darkness the Baron loomed.

Another foreigner! Decidedly, there were elements in the situation which went far to justify the popular alarm. A foreign Baron controlled a foreign Prince, and the foreign Prince controlled the Crown of England. And the Crown itself was creeping forward ominously; and when, from under its shadow, the Baron and the Prince had frowned, a great Minister, beloved of the people, had fallen. Where was all this to end?'

In order to establish Stockmar from the very start as the Invisible Man who exercised so prodigious a hold over the prince, the queen and the whole of English politics, Strachey instances his peremptory dealings with Melbourne. For with the extinction of Lord M. as an influence over the queen – which Stockmar is made to engineer – came the final emergence of his pupil, Albert. 'Stockmar, who had returned to England, watched the departure of Lord Melbourne with satisfaction', Strachey wrote. 'If all went well, the Prince should now wield a supreme political influence over Victoria. But would all go well? ... He [Melbourne] continued to write to the Queen as before; and two more violent bombardments from the Baron were needed before he was brought to reason. Then, gradually, his letters grew less and less frequent, with fewer and fewer references to public concerns; at last, they were entirely innocuous. The Baron smiled; Lord M. had accepted the inevitable.'

So far from Albert having been a creation of Stockmar's, this Stockmar was an invention of Strachey's. His misconception of the baron's position – like part of his account of the queen's character in old age – follows the popular beliefs held at the time by the uninformed man in the street. The records, however, go some way to proving precisely the opposite of what Strachey attempted to foist on his readers as the hidden truth. Albert turned to Stockmar not for political guidance but for personal reasons – he felt more at home conversing with another foreigner. Melbourne too seems to have taken little heed of the baron or his bombardments. When the political content of Lord M.'s letters to the queen eventually became less abundant, it had not been due to Stockmar's intervention, but to the new trust which Albert and Victoria had by then learnt to repose in Peel and the Tory Government. 'Stockmar's son,' E. F. Benson has sensibly pointed out in his own biography of Victoria, 'who compiled his Memoirs, seems to have been conscious of this, and very judiciously omits all mention of this signal defeat. The Queen and the Prince were very fond of the Baron, he had come to England with Uncle Leopold before either of them was born; Melbourne, Peel, Aberdeen and Palmerston in turn had the firmest belief in his integrity, and they liked a talk with the shrewd caustic old man, and he enjoyed it too; and then he went to his room and put down all the good advice he had given them. Sometimes they had agreed with him and then all was well; sometimes they thought otherwise, and then Stockmar recorded what a sad mess they had made through not listening to him. Whenever, as happened more than once, he interfered in political matters, we find that, as here, his schemings were singularly fruitless. The public misjudged him: his constant intimacy with the Prince led to the belief that he was a sinister foreign adviser, potent and mysterious, whereas he was an honest dyspeptic old gentleman, useful to him in many ways, with the harmless foible of thinking that he directed and controlled his old pupil. This conviction remained with him, and in 1855, shortly before he left England for good, he wrote of Albert and the Queen: "They have passed the point at which leading is required." But evidence that he had ever led them in their political dealings with the government is entirely lacking, and Albert had long ago assumed the position for which Melbourne himself had always considered him so admirably fit.'

The end of Strachey's Stockmar is heralded by the death of Albert. Deprived of his medium, his ventriloquist's dummy, the baron is suddenly made redundant. He is a magician without his magic wand. Having no further comic function to perform in the biography, he feels the full force of this disaster. 'The Prince was his creation. ... The Baron, by his fireside at Coburg, suddenly saw the tremendous fabric of his creation crash down into sheer and irremediable ruin. Albert was gone, and he had lived in vain. Even his blackest hypo-

chondria had never envisioned quite so miserable a catastrophe. Victoria wrote to him, visited him, tried to console
him by declaring with passionate conviction that she would
carry on her husband's work. He smiled a sad smile and
looked into the fire. Then he murmured that he was going
where Albert was – that he would not be long. He shrank into
himself. His children clustered round him and did their best to
comfort him, but it was useless: the Baron's heart was
broken. He lingered for eighteen months, and then, with his
pupil, explored the shadow and the dust.'

Then, for the last time, the kaleidoscopic pattern alters.
Victoria, her being no longer animated to new life by the
master puppet-maker from behind the stage, can only go
through all over again her old familiar tricks. Her friendship
with Disraeli is a distorted mummery of her earlier love for
Melbourne; her antagonism to Gladstone recalls her coldness
towards Peel. With sedate majesty she enters into her second
childhood.

The direction under which Baron Stockmar acts in *Queen
Victoria* illustrates both the peculiar distinction and limitation of Strachey's book, as a perfect example of his biographical methods. Technically it is a dazzling *tour de force*.
Despite a little tinsel in the extraneous ornament of its
chapters, its excellence resides chiefly in the skilfully constructed architectural design. As a craftsman in biography,
Strachey was second to none. 'He it was who first saw the
possibilities of this new medium', wrote Lord David Cecil. 'He
it was who evolved the technical equipment for its expression.
We may extend his building, but we must always construct
on his foundations. He was the man who established the form.'

What shortcomings there are reside in the comparatively
small amount of mental and emotional nourishment to be
absorbed from his writing. In life, Strachey was habitually
self-conscious with strangers and in matters of intense passion.
Because he always bore his public in mind as a writer, this
reserve of manner fastened on to his style, strangling the free
communication of feeling, drowning pathos in reverberating

rhetoric. His emotions tended to turn inwards, curdle, and show fitfully in half-embarrassed spurts of sentimentality. The characters in his biographies are, perhaps more often than not, vividly painted pieces of cardboard, moved by a marvellous machinery of strings and pulleys within sharply defined margins, to give the illusion of life. Though memorable for this colour and dramatic décor, they are imbued with little real animation of their own, and leave the impression, for all the contrivances which have gone into their making, of being rather flat. Where he does feel a bond of direct personal sympathy – as with Albert – his inclination to exaggerate and dramatize can sometimes oversimplify – for the sake of immediate entertainment – a really original interpretation of character.

The last, finely shaped paragraph in *Queen Victoria*, too well-known to be quoted, where Strachey makes the dying queen call up the shadows of her past, has been compared with James Joyce's stream of consciousness. For almost a decade this finale set a fashion for biographers, who, if anxious to please their publishers, would indulge themselves in a last-minute orgy of plagiaristic retrospection[7] – a habit which Strachey himself wittily ridiculed in *Elizabeth and Essex*, in the last passage of which he makes Robert Cecil gaze prophetically into the future. Now that this fashion has long worked itself out, the real literary value of Strachey's evocation may be more accurately measured. We now have the eye-witness account given by the Duke of Argyll, who watched the queen sinking like a three-decker ship, now rallying, now failing, and who heard the last coherent word she spoke – 'Bertie'. Strachey's imaginative peroration suffers by contrast with this account because it contains no suppressed humour and none of the pathos suggested by the ut-

---

7. But the most extraordinary piece of plagiarism is provided by Edith Sitwell's *Victoria of England*, in which, as Geoffrey Grigson rightly observed (*The Times Literary Supplement*, 11 February 1965, p. 107), the author looked up Strachey's quotations and merely extended them, modifying Strachey's accompanying comments, or sometimes paraphrasing them word for word, substituting a synonym for each in succession.

terance of that single name, with all the regret it implied and all she could no longer say. In the biography, the formal and gently scaled diminuendo of ordered imagery is softened by a tenderness that transforms this last scene into a charming, fairy-tale ending. Strachey, as producer and director, stands over the ebbing queen, receives, interprets her final thoughts and sensations, and confers on her his absolute blessing.

But the pathos of Victoria's death is everywhere mitigated by a feeling of admiration for Strachey's splendid artifice. Who, reading of Falstaff's death, thinks of William Shakespeare? And who, finishing *Queen Victoria,* does not think of Lytton Strachey and his biographical technique?

5

THE QUINTESSENCE OF STRACHEYISM

On both sides of the Atlantic, *Queen Victoria* was an instantaneous success, and has remained ever since Strachey's most popular work. Described by some as the quintessence of Stracheyism, and acclaimed by many as a classic, the book quickly established itself as a best-seller – four thousand copies of the first English edition of five thousand were sold within twenty-four hours – was awarded the James Tait Black Memorial Prize in 1922, and adapted by Walter Pritchard Eaton for the stage. Most readers recognized that the biography represented a mainly flattering tribute to Victoria, and Strachey was deluged with letters of congratulation from prime ministers, colonels and clergymen. In academic circles the word went round that he had fallen in love with the queen. *The Times Literary Supplement* was loud in its thanksgiving, and a great sigh of relief went up from the universities – Sir Edmund Gosse much affected, Professor G. M. Trevelyan totally overcome, and all the dons astonished and delighted.[8]

Although Strachey was gratified by the large sales, he felt rather apprehensive over this fanfare of critical acclaim. It was

8. On 6 May 1921 Trevelyan wrote to Lytton: 'Dear Strachey, I expect

all very well for Max Beerbohm to declare that he was the wittiest writer of the age,[9] but when he read reviews in the papers, written by second-rate critics whom he had long disparaged, stating that the dawning age had here bequeathed to posterity a model biography, his reactions were more mixed. To Hesketh Pearson, who asked him how it felt to be the author of a best-seller, he replied that it left him unmoved – 'indeed the success of my work is beginning to make me question its merit. Can a popular author be a good one?' Whenever he heard people say his treatment of the queen had been mature and discreet, he interpreted it as meaning that the book was tedious and flat. 'At any rate I feel that I ought to do something particularly outrageous for my next book,' he wrote to his brother James (April 1921), 'in order to retrieve my reputation. It's alarming to be welcomed with open arms by Gosse, Jack Squire and the Times – though I suppose it's paying also.'

Even loftier honours seemed to be within his reach when he was suddenly summoned to Buckingham Palace for an audience, so he understood, with the king. As he waited to be ushered into the royal presence, the door silently opened, Lord Stamfordham entered carrying an open copy of *Queen*

---

you are tired of hearing how good Queen V is. But I would like to say it to you. Much as I liked your last book, I think it beats it a lot. Did you ever meditate a book about Voltaire? "It would be such a nice change", as they say. Yours ever, G. M. Trevelyan.'

9. 'Have you read Lytton Strachey's *Queen Victoria*? That I *am* a Stoic is proved by my having no jealousy of him at all, though his mind and his prose are so like mine and so exactly like what I should have loved mine to be. For sheer divine beauty of prose, and for clairvoyance of mind in dealing with past personages, and for wit, and for much else, nobody comes within a hundred miles of him. I was rather amazed and horrified that you did not seem to have quite realized what manner of book *Eminent Victorians* was. Pray tell me that you have been respectably bowled over by this other book.' (Max Beerbohm to Reggie Turner, 20 June 1921.) In a letter to another friend Max wrote: 'No! I am not nearly so witty as Chesterton for one. But certainly I have not prostituted and cheapened my wit as he has. How about Lytton Strachey? There's the wittiest mind of the age – and the virtue of it guarded even more strictly and puritanically than I have guarded the virtue of mine.'

Victoria, in a quiet voice corrected its author on one minor point of *fact,* and departed as noiselessly as he had come in. Strachey was then free, he ascertained, to leave the Palace and return home.[10]

Some readers – a small minority – were disappointed. 'We're looking forward with the greatest excitement to the arrival of Queen Victoria', James had written to his mother (9 March 1921). 'I wonder whether Lytton's read it to you yet, and whether it's very shocking. Will the whole family be involved in disgrace?' Other admirers too of *Eminent Victorians* must have expected that, in his subsequent portrait of the queen who had given her name to such a prudish and barbaric

10. There are various versions of this story, the one above being told by Strachey himself to William Gerhardie, from whom the author heard it (see also *Resurrection* by William Gerhardie). In a letter to her brother Noel, Carrington wrote: 'The King accepted a copy. But his sec Lord Stanfordham wrote to Lytton "that his Majesty having read his book, there were a few points he would like to discuss would L.S. please call at Buckingham Palace at his earliest convenience". Lytton very wisely rang up to say he was just leaving for Italy. Evidently Lord S wasn't accustomed to SUCH treatment, for he was rather snooTY Still Lytton mainTained, which was true that he was just off, and dashed down the receiver and ended the conversation.'

Strachey too referred to this episode in his correspondence with Mary Hutchinson (1 May 1921): 'Just back from Buckingham Palace and an hour's interview with Lord Stamfordham. His Majesty did not come up through a trap-door in the middle of it – as I'd rather expected he would. The poor old thing (a respectable maiden lady) was very amicable, though at moments pettish. The point of his remarks was very difficult to catch, but I rather gathered that the elder Princesses had insisted on "something being done", and that this was all they could think of. The world grows steadily more and more fantastic, I find . . .'

The response to *Queen Victoria* at Buckingham Palace seems to have been unequal. Miss Frances Stevenson (later Countess Lloyd George) notes in her diary (11 April 1921): 'Went down to Trent over Sunday after hectic week of unfruitful negotiations over coal strike. P[rince] of Wales came on Sunday with Mr Dudley Ward. We spoke of Strachey's life of Queen Victoria, which had just been published and the Prince said: "That must be the book the King was talking about this morning. He was very angry and got quite vehement over it". P of W had not seen the book, so we showed it to him and presently he was discovered in roars of laughter over the description of the Queen and John Brown.' See *The Decline and Fall of Lloyd George* by Lord Beaverbrook (1963), pp. 49–50.

epoch, with its outrageous fogs, its antimacassars and bed-bugs, Strachey would 'display his qualities of cold detachment, of sardonic scrutiny, and of a wit which had the sharpness, as well as the brightness, of a keenly polished dagger'. But, as Ivor Brown wrote, 'instead of being caustic he was genial; instead of writing in a mood of urbane detachment, he became, though still of course urbane, engaged and even affectionate. His book, with its closeness and cordiality of approach to its subject, surprised by the warmth of its tone. ... So the cool and unsparing portrayer of Victorian notables was no longer the aloof scrutineer. Following the queen herself down the decades, he found himself at last engaged in a sentimental journey.'[11]

Queen Victoria was dedicated to Virginia Woolf, who told Strachey that she considered it magnificent, 'an incredible gem, and a masterpiece of prose', even better on the whole than *Eminent Victorians*. After a party given to celebrate its publication and to congratulate Strachey, she confessed privately in her diary to a deepening jealousy of his success. Envy had so choked her appreciation of the book that she found herself unable to admit having finished it, and both she and Leonard later told Gerald Brenan that they considered it unreadable. Though he did not care for Strachey's flat spongy style, which gave him the sensation, he said, of treading on linoleum, Brenan very reasonably objected to this prejudiced opinion. But both Virginia and Leonard continued to pronounce decisively against the biography, while qualifying their verdict by speaking of Strachey's great subtlety of mind, his discrimination as a critic, and their personal attachment to him as friends. It was this personal consideration that prompted Virginia Woolf to send Strachey a letter on 17 April which was generous in its evidently unfelt praise. 'I've seldom enjoyed anything more,' she told him. 'I suppose the chief marvel is the way you spin the story perfectly straightforwardly, never a line slack, and yet contrive those wonderful little portraits, one after another, each exactly in its place, illuminating, without interruption or fuss or for a moment

11. Introduction to Collins Classics edition of *Queen Victoria* (1958).

stopping, it seems, to go on talking simply. The effect is not merely satiric by any means. You seem to have reduced it to the last possible ounce, and yet to have kept all the meat and bone and guts. The great moments seem to me really moving. And the Queen herself comes out somehow surprising, solid and angular, and touching, though not exactly sympathetic. Amazing woman! My only criticism (and I'm not sure of its truth) is that occasionally I think one is a little conscious of being entertained. It's a little too luxurious reading – I mean, one is willing perhaps to take more pains than you allow.'

In spite of Virginia's observations to Gerald Brenan, such an appreciation does not read insincerely. Over ten years later, when Strachey was dead, when she was famous as a novelist and there was no more cause for envy, she composed a long essay on 'The Art of Biography'[12] in which she warmly commended *Queen Victoria* as 'a triumphant success', adding that it 'is a life which, very possibly, will do for the old Queen what Boswell did for the old dictionary maker. In time to come Lytton Strachey's Queen Victoria will be Queen Victoria, just as Boswell's Johnson is now Dr Johnson. The other versions will fade and disappear. It was a prodigious feat . . .'

Another critic who at first condemned the book and later recanted was Arthur Quiller-Couch. The essay[13] in which he indicts Strachey for being 'smart and amusing' and contends that 'the book aims at showing up Albert the Good to ridicule' has often been quoted by critics who could not have known that several years later Quiller-Couch entirely reversed his opinion. 'When I first read the book,' he wrote to Strachey (15 September 1925), 'old and perhaps "impossible" loyalty raised certain bristles in me, and I spoke rather sharply about it in a lecture at Cambridge. Later on Dover Wilson staying here [The Haven, Fowey, Cornwall] with me, read my lecture, borrowed the book and read it in his bedroom, and

12. 'The Art of Biography' was included in Virginia Woolf's posthumous volume *The Death of the Moth and Other Essays* (1942), and in Volume 4 of her *Collected Essays* (1967).

13. Quiller-Couch's essay appears in his *Studies in Literature, Second Series* (1927).

informed me next morning that I had made a fool of myself. What is worse he convinced me.'

When, in 1926, Quiller-Couch brought out his *Oxford Book of English Prose,* he included extracts from *Queen Victoria.* This led to a strong criticism of Strachey's prose style by Herbert Read. In an unsigned Front Article[14] in *The Times Literary Supplement* (4 March 1926) reviewing the anthology, he declared that there were in the creative act of writing two elements – the visual image and the emotions associated with this image. 'The image is there, stark, visible and real; to find the right words, the only right words, to body forth that image, becomes in the writer an actual passion. The image evokes the words; or if it fails, if to the visual memory there comes no corresponding emotive or expressive memory, then there is no art. A good writer must then be silent; and only the bad writer will accept the approximate expression – the first expression that comes into his head, which is usually a stale expression, for it is ever so much easier to remember phrases than to evoke words. These memorable phrases press invitingly round the would-be writer; they are the current coin and counters of verbal intercourse; and to refuse them, and to deal only in freshly minted coin, is possible only to a few autocrats. But these are the rulers of literature, the creators of style; and they should find a place in an anthology of best prose.'

To exemplify his argument, Read then analyses the differences between two selected pieces of prose – the final paragraph from *Queen Victoria* and a passage from Joyce not included in the anthology.[15] Lytton Strachey's writing is not

14. Reprinted in *A Coat of Many Colours* by Herbert Read (1945).
15. The Joyce passage which Read uses runs as follows: 'The grainy sand had gone from under his feet. His boots trod again a damp crackling mast, razor-shells, squeaking pebbles, that on the unnumbered pebbles beats, wood sieved by the shipworm, lost Armada. Unwholesome sandflats waited to suck his treading shoes, breathing upward savage breath. He coasted them, walking warily. A porterbottle stood up, stogged to its waist. in the cakey sand dough. A sentinel: isle of dreadful thirst. Broken hoops on the shore; at the land a maze of dark cunning nets; further away chalk-scrawled backdoors and on the higher beach a drying line with two crucified shirts.'

altogether bad – it is not sufficiently bad to avert the reader's thoughts. Indeed, it has all the conditions of fine prose – wit, elegance, readability – but few of its essential qualities. When one compares it with the Joyce passage, one is immediately aware of a great difference – not the difference between two kinds of goodness, but between one quality and its opposite. Lytton Strachey's prose 'causes us less surprise: we are scarcely conscious of the kind of prose we are reading – apart from a certain ironic affectation; but we are, as a matter of fact, reading a prose densely packed with images and analogies, none of which we actually visualize. "Approaching end", "astonished grief", "grief sweeping over the country", "monstrous reversal", "the course of nature", "to take place", "vast majority", "an indissoluble part", "the scheme of things", "a scarcely possible thought", "divested of all thinking", "to glide into oblivion", "the secret chambers", "fading mind", "the shadows of the past", "to float before (her mind)", "the vanished visions", "through the cloud of years", – here in eighteen lines are eighteen images or analogies, not one of which is original, not one of which is freshly felt or sincerely evoked, and consequently not one of which evokes in the mind of the reader the definite image it actually portends. Now examine the second passage: there is not a single phrase which does not evoke – which does not force the mind to evoke – the image it expresses. Art, after all, is a question of effect; and does anyone give a second thought to the death of Queen Victoria as our author has described it? But merely to read of Stephen Dedalus walking on the beach is to have come into contact with the vibrating reflex of an actual experience.'

This is a powerful but not unanswerable censure of Strachey's prose style. Read makes no allowances for the valid use of the stereotype, colloquial phrase; he evaluates the quality of imaginative writing too arbitrarily and exclusively by its visual impact; he contrasts two passages which are not properly comparable; and he does not explain that, because the artistic effect of Strachey's style is cumulative, one of a gradually induced mood in which images are conjured up in the mind as if under a shallow hypnosis, one may not legitimately extract a single passage from its true context and expect it to perform adequately its original function. No biography could be written in such a condensed style as Joyce's *Ulysses*, for although *Ulysses* is obviously a work of genius, it is surely the most tedious one ever written, for the very reason that it contains no narrative passages, no comments or analyses, so that the reader's mind is continually dazzled, and wearied, by these assaults on it of visual and olfactory imagery. Joyce was quite incapable of handling a general expository style, or of even writing a good letter. He wrote English as some African writer of the Dark Ages might have written Latin, and his relation to English prose literature is not unlike that of St Jerome's Vulgate to Cicero's prose. Read's criticism shows little understanding of the historical development of literature or of the appropriateness of certain styles for certain purposes. Strachey, however, on reading this criticism for himself, let the paper fall to the ground, sorrowfully telling his friend George Rylands[16] that its strictures against himself as a 'would-be writer' were entirely justified, every one of them.

This capitulation shows very well Strachey's reaction to the success of his books. Though this success sat very well on him, his modesty and humility went almost too far. He was an easier companion, a less potent and original writer. He was also more easily approachable, and when an unknown admirer, Hesketh Pearson, wrote to him that April to express his gratitude and delight in *Queen Victoria* – 'not merely a Life of Victoria that happens to be a work of art, but a work of art that happens to be a Life of Victoria' – Strachey replied: 'You overwhelm me!' However, he added, 'I keep my head', and he reassured his correspondent: 'But seriously you are very kind and I like your letter very much.' The following month he wrote again to invite Pearson to lunch at the Café Royal, going on to say that he would recognize him without difficulty: 'I am rather tall, with spectacles and a reddish beard.'

16. George Rylands, nicknamed 'Dadie', a Fellow of King's College, Cambridge.

At first glance, Pearson noticed, the most striking thing about him was an intense and restless nervousness, which gave him a bashful manner, not without grace, but emphasized by his thin wrists, his long, tremulous hands, tapering fingers and high-pitched quavering voice. Since his beard was not only red, but also long and square, there was, as he had promised, no difficulty over recognition. 'We shook hands, or rather I shook his hand and he winced. If I had glanced at it first I would not have shaken it with such vigour', records Pearson. Altogether, his first impression was of some hirsute god, a dry edition of Father Neptune. 'Placid, wide-open eyes, perhaps a trifle owlish, stared at me through glasses that intensified their detached yet critical expression; and the beard gave a solemnity to the whole face, which was crowned by dark hair austerely brushed flat across the head with a side parting.' But this god-like aspect, mute and awe-inspiring, was shattered as soon as Strachey uttered his first sentence in a 'high-pitched tinny voice, which on certain notes cracked and became like a squeak'.

The general roar of conversation in the grill room where they lunched was so loud that Pearson had the utmost difficulty in hearing what his host was saying, though again and again he raised his voice to its shrillest notes in response to Pearson's repeated 'What?' Because of this obstruction, Strachey soon appeared to grow discouraged and fell silent, while Pearson found himself monopolizing the talk solely in order to save his companion the annoyance of cracking his top chords. If Strachey had been hoping to encounter a pretty young lad with tastes sympathetic to his own, he was quickly disillusioned.[17] At one point in their lunch, Pearson leant right across the table and, cupping his hands, shouted out a scandalous story concerning Frank Harris in the Café Royal, which

17. After the publication of *Eminent Victorians* in 1918, Strachey had invited Lord David Cecil to lunch with him at the Café Royal, and with rather similar results. Cecil, then a schoolboy at Eton, had written a eulogistic review of *Eminent Victorians* in a school magazine. 'I hope you like Lord David C', Strachey later wrote to Ottoline Morrell (26 October 1921). 'I thought him really very nice, but so young, so young … he made *me* feel positively in my *second* childhood!'

he hoped might amuse Strachey, but which considerably startled the fastidious old Bloomsbury gossip. 'He stroked his beard,' Pearson remembered, 'looked clean through me, and smiled with a sort of frightened frigidity.'

Strachey spoke with the greatest admiration of Gibbon and Sterne, but was less wholehearted in his approval when questioned by Pearson about contemporary writers. Most of Bernard Shaw's plays, he said, were already out of date, though Shaw himself remained a great joker. Of H. G. Wells he remarked: 'I stopped thinking about him when he became a thinker.' G. K. Chesterton was interesting only when he was not being Belloc; and as for Belloc himself, he dismissed him absolutely.

The conversation then switched to the Irish War of Liberation, which was then being waged. But Strachey did not expand. 'I prefer to discuss things about which I do not feel too strongly', he explained. 'One must never confuse a people with its politicians. I love the English for all the qualities they have in common with Falstaff, not for the qualities they have in common with Cromwell.'

Questioned about his own work, he thought that he might write a play next. *Queen Victoria* had taken three years, and had exhausted him. But he had several ideas for the indefinite future – a life of Charles Darwin, a History of the World in a single, neat, easily portable volume, or a biography, perhaps, of Queen Elizabeth.

SIX

Elizabeth and Strachey

'The natural pleasure of reading it is enormous. You seem, on
the whole, to imagine yourself as Elizabeth, but I see from
the pictures that it is Essex whom you have got up as yourself. But I expect you have managed to get the best of both
worlds.' *Maynard Keynes to Lytton Strachey* (3 December
1928)

'Isn't it possible that without experience certain minds can
build up these edifices out of their sensibilities and their
dramatic power. There *is* something (as they say) "hothouse"
about the quality of his [Richardson's] sensuality – as if he
had not really fully known what enjoyment was. But, in any
case, the dramatic process remains inexplicable. Perhaps it is
really the distinguishing faculty of Man – the creature who
can imagine someone else.' *Lytton Strachey to Dorothy Bussy*
(3 January 1930)

1

STYLE AND ANALYSIS

Elizabeth and Essex has been called Strachey's only work of
fiction. In form, in planning, and partly in its illustrations, it
bears an interesting resemblance to Virginia Woolf's *Orlando*
(the experiences of whose hero with the same queen are those
of Essex himself); but the structure of this tragic history is
nearer to that of a five-act play than a novel. The long meditations attributed to the main characters have their origin in
the monologues of Elizabethan drama, where the protagonist
often occupies the stage alone, delivering in rhetorical poetry
the passions and perplexities that divide his soul. The use,
too, throughout this narrative, of omens to Essex's final disaster – such as the tempest which his expedition against Ferrol
encounters – are Senecan theatrical devices of the sort to
which Shakespeare was particularly addicted.

Wherever possible, Strachey treats his readers as direct onlookers. He avoids all formulated interpretation of action, and even his purely informative passages are cast in visual terms. So far as is practical, he transforms every source – letters, diaries and documentary eyewitness accounts – into pictorial illustration. 'Howard was Lord Admiral, but Essex was an Earl; which was the higher? When a joint letter to the Queen was brought for their signature, Essex, snatching a pen, got in his name at the top, so that Howard was obliged to follow with his underneath. But he bided his time – until his rival's back was turned; then, with a pen-knife, he cut out the offending signature; and in that strange condition the missive reached Elizabeth.' In another instance, he brings in word for word a letter from Essex to Elizabeth in such a way that the reader is given the impression that he is actually watching Essex writing, since Strachey interrupts the text several times: 'as he wrote, he grew warmer'; and 'now he could hold himself in no longer'; and again 'the whole heat of his indignation was flaring out'.

The great visual scenes which Strachey unfolds are neatly framed by theatrical entrances and exits. He writes at times as if he is giving stage directions to a group of actors. In the scene, for example, where Elizabeth makes her speech to an assembly called by the Speaker of the House of Commons, he uses her exact words and at the same time provides us with instructions as to how they should effectively be spoken: 'There was a pause; and then the high voice rang out'; and 'She stopped, and told them to stand up, as she had more to say to them'; and 'Pausing again for a moment, she continued in a deeper tone'. In conclusion, at the end of Chapter XVI, he writes: 'She straightened herself with a final effort; her eyes glared; there was a sound of trumpets; and, turning from them in her sweeping draperies – erect and terrible – she walked out.' There are many other passages, too, where he gives his characters this stage director's advice which takes the place of ordinary biographical description. When Essex has just been appointed Lord Deputy of Ireland at a Council meeting, Strachey handles the exit in a single sentence: 'With long elated strides and flashing glances he [Essex] left the room in triumph; and so – with shuffling gait and looks of mild urbanity – did Robert Cecil.' Exeunt, and the curtain falls.

Elizabeth and Essex is Strachey's *Antony and Cleopatra*. 'There is only one thing which could have blinded a man in Antony's position so completely as we now know he actually was blinded,' he had written in one of his *Spectator* reviews (2 January 1909), 'and that thing is passion.' Passion is the over-riding theme of *Elizabeth and Essex*. Essex was a typical Court favourite, and in Strachey's pages his sensual temperament and genius for friendship are brought out in a manner that helps to emphasize his similarity to Antony. Like Antony he leaves and returns to his Queen; and like Antony he dies a violent death. Elizabeth is no Cleopatra; but each in her own way was 'a lass unparallel'd' – the Queen of England's infinite variations of temper forming an obvious dramatic equivalent to the 'infinite variety' of the Queen of Egypt. In Sir Robert Cecil, the master-mind of the piece, who performs a function in the biography analogous to that of Baron Stockmar in *Queen Victoria,* there is a close approximation to the calculating Octavius. Shakespeare closes *Antony and Cleopatra* with the triumph of Octavius; Strachey, in the carefully weighed passage with which *Elizabeth and Essex* ends, employs another device borrowed from the Elizabethan stage, picturing Cecil brooding over the destiny of England and the future of his own house. With some qualifications, the comparison may be extended. Essex's loyal friends, Sir Christopher Blount, Henry Cuffe, Lord Southampton and Sir Charles Travers, who shared his shattered fortunes, may be likened to Shakespeare's Eros and Scarus. But Strachey is tempted to simplify his characters so as to transpose them into more striking phenomena. Hence, Francis Bacon is painted a blacker villain than Eno-barbus, and Sir Walter Raleigh an infinitely more sinister and capable being than Lepidus.

Elizabeth and Essex was largely a calculated biographical experiment, incorporating much autobiographical interest. Unlike *Queen Victoria,* the story is not compactly arranged around the main regal figure, but carried along in a looser episodic form. The difference in construction, narration and mood between this book and his earlier ones underlines the full flexibility of Strachey's style. It has been said that his writing is indebted to, among many others, La Bruyère, Anatole France, Gibbon, Saint-Beuve, Saint-Simon, Walter Pater and Voltaire. But although his prose was certainly a composite affair, it was also highly personal. Very characteristic, in all his biographies, is his use of indirect speech which serves to recount the facts as seen from the viewpoint of the characters themselves, which enables him to interpret the secret thoughts of these characters, and to impersonate their tricks of speech. There are many examples of this technique in *Elizabeth and Essex*. 'The Attorney-Generalship fell vacant, and Essex immediately declared that Francis Bacon must have the post', he writes at one point. Then, slipping into Essex's own reflections, he proceeds directly on: 'He was young and had not yet risen far in his profession – but what of that? He deserved something even greater; the Queen might appoint whom she would, and, if Essex had any influence, the right man, for once, should be given preferment.'

In these soliloquies, Strachey withdraws completely and conceals himself behind his characters, who present their own, often one-sided view of a situation or verdict on another person. A good instance of this occurs in the passage where Elizabeth – thinking back over her whole relationship with Essex – deliberates about his pardon. Strachey passes from an introductory statement of fact to the 'stream of consciousness' without any verbal conjunction (elsewhere, to make the connection outwardly visible, he often uses a dash or colon); but in the word 'actually' we at once begin to hear the indignant tone of the Queen's inner voice.

'The animosity which for so long had been fluctuating within her now flared up in triumph and rushed out upon the author of her agony and her disgrace. He had betrayed her in every possible way – mentally, emotionally, materially – as a Queen and as a woman – before the world and in the sweetest privacies of the heart. And he had actually imagined that he could elude the doom that waited on such iniquity – had dreamed of standing up against her – had mistaken the hesitations of her strength for the weaknesses of a subservient character. He would have a sad awakening! He would find that she was indeed the daughter of a father who had known how to rule a kingdom and how to punish the perfidy of those he had loved the most. Yes, indeed . . .'

With its marvellous dash, its changes of pace and colour, its chorus of rhetorical questions, its quickly mixed metaphors and dying falls, the narrative throws out a fine sheen of excitement, of hurtling activity. The punctuated rhythm of the shorter sentences, cleverly disposed among his more elaborate constructions, tightens up very effectively the tension wherever the event-plot quickens. Yet for all these skilful and entertaining literary devices, the impact of the writing is frequently pale and thin. It is all speed and ease and slotted-in arrangements; the texture is too shiny, too impoverished of more tough and solid matter. Strachey insists upon the importance of passion with all the urgency of a man who has never experienced it full-bloodedly in life, and whose loss naturally communicates itself, with debilitating effects, to his own prose. He uncurls his phosphorescent day-dreams about a no-man's-land that floats between two actual worlds, one dead, one powerless to be born. It was as though, with a shiver of delight, he imagined that he had lived in Elizabethan England himself, or rather that his ghost even now flitted to and fro among these gorgeous characters. He was more than half in love with all of them, and could never quite shake the gossamer of this fantasy out of his mind. Consequently the atmosphere he evokes is strangely impalpable rather than passionate. For it is in the sound and complexion as well as in the stated opinions of a writer's work that one must look for a true revelation of his temperament. Balzac, whose vitality and physical potency, though set in a filial groove, have never seriously been doubted, preached a monastic chastity as an essential part of the creative work to which he devoted himself, and offset his robust nature with themes of severe and obsessive idealism. But the earthy and profane sweep of his

Comédie Humaine is as unmistakable as is the giddy, blood-less hysteria that underlies all the hints and exaggerations of Strachey's pages. 'Incapable of creation in life or in literature,' T. R. Barnes cruelly commented in *Scrutiny*, 'his [Strachey's] writings were a substitute for both.' The implication of these words is, of course, unjust. Strachey was never impotent. But whenever his sexual desires approached boiling-point, they began to change from a more solid corporeal substance into something metaphysical, a vapour, a mist. It is this immaterial quality that one can detect, like the smell of an ether, about his style.

Probably the most noticeable feature of Strachey's prose style is his regular employment of the stereotyped phrase. Many critics have carped unduly at this aspect of his writing, for the most obvious combination of words is not necessarily the hallmark of inferior prose or second-hand thinking. By making use of a very simple vocabulary and humdrum, colloquial epithets, Strachey was sometimes able to summon forth a feeling of personal intimacy that could never have been beguiled by more recondite methods. 'Platitudes', he once wrote,[1] 'are, after all, the current coin of artists, critics and philosophers; without them all commerce of the mind would come to a standstill; and a great debt is owing to those who, like Macaulay, have the faculty of minting fresh and clean platitudes in inexhaustible abundance.' Neither Strachey nor Macaulay were perhaps deeply original thinkers. But they shared one compensating gift – the power of expressing more ordinary thoughts in the most striking manner, so that there are few paradoxes so brilliant or pleasing as their vivid commonplaces.

'To be brief', wrote George Santayana, 'is almost a condition of being inspired.' In Strachey's tightly drawn pages, the neat conversational clichés fit perfectly, like old gems made new and luminous by their improved setting. But in his weakest and most flamboyant strain, overloaded with picturesque adjectives and adverbs, he seems to be unsuccessfully trying to avoid the banal. This failure may in part be the penalty he paid

1. 'Macaulay's Marginalia', *Spectator*, 99 (16 November 1907), 743. Collected in *Spectatorial Essays* (171–3).

for trying to reproduce in English the chaste and abstract vocabulary of the French. But if style ultimately reveals the man, then the flat and simulated passion of these more high-flown, ambitious passages only shows how oddly his desire outran his performance.

In his Rede Lecture, Max Beerbohm has drawn particular attention to the great pliability of Strachey's style, which harmonized so well with every variation of his theme. Each character was accorded a special rhythm and refrain. In *Queen Victoria* this technique had shifted subtly so as to bring the reader into the very presence of a succession of widely disparate premiers. 'Note the mellow and leisurely beauty of the cadences', Beerbohm wrote, 'in which he writes of Lord Melbourne – "the autumn rose", as he called him. Note the sharp brisk straightforward buoyancy of the writing whenever Lord Palmerston appears; and the elaborate Oriental richness of manner when Mr Disraeli is on the scene.' A more personal change of manner took place when Strachey left the Mother Empress for the Virgin Queen. Her heterogeneous nature called for altogether different treatment – a new construction, of course, and a new combination of tones. The comedy becomes less farcical, the story is flavoured less strongly with his characteristic light and lambent mockery. The gentle aura of sentimentalism splits sharply into two patches of light – the one brilliant, golden, romantic; the other rancid, yellow, and perverted. 'We are aware', wrote Edmund Wilson in what was mainly a very favourable article on Strachey's writings, 'for the first time disagreeably of the high-voiced old Bloomsbury gossip gloating over the scandals of the past as he ferreted them out in his library. Strachey's curious catty malice, his enjoyment of the discomfiture of his characters is most unpleasantly in evidence in *Elizabeth and Essex*.'[2]

2. Edmund Wilson definitely preferred Strachey's Victorian essays and biographies. 'Lytton Strachey's chief mission, of course, was to take down once and for all the pretentions of the Victorian Age to moral superiority,' he declared (21 September 1932). '. . . *Elizabeth and Essex* seems to me the least satisfactory of Strachey's books. His art, so tight and so calculated, so much influenced by the French, was ill-suited to the Elizabethan Age. . . . His study of Queen Elizabeth in the light of modern psychology

Both biographies were love stories, but love stories of a very different order. In his treatment of Victoria's strong sexuality, Strachey had been decorously unobtrusive. In dealing with Elizabeth's sexual make-up, he adopted a far more salacious and erotic tone, full of suggestive allusion and innuendo. In the opinion of one reverend gentleman – who belongs to a body of men especially well-suited to nosing out such matters – he also showed himself in this last biography 'preoccupied with the sexual organs to a degree that seems almost pathological'. This is a great exaggeration. But undoubtedly there is some libidinous imagery in *Elizabeth and Essex*, and several dark passages that contain sly and vibrant

---

brings her character into sharper focus, but the effect of it is slightly disgusting; it marks so definitely the final surrender of Elizabethan to Bloomsbury England. . . . Certainly one of the best English writers of his period, he makes us feel sharply the contrast between Shakespeare's England and his. Shakespeare is expansive and untidy and close to the spoken language. Lytton Strachey, whose first-published work was a history of French literature, is so far from being any of these things that one of his chief feats consists in having managed to achieve in English some of the effects of the French.' In Edmund Wilson's opinion, the real force and audacity of Lytton Strachey's work are therefore seen best earlier in his career. 'The harshness of *Eminent Victorians* without Strachey's wide learning and bitter feeling, the intimate method of *Queen Victoria* without his insight into character, had the effect of cheapening history, something Strachey never did – for, though he was venomous about the Victorians, he did not make them any the less formidable. He had none of the modern vice of cockiness; he maintained a rare attitude of humility, of astonishment and admiration, before the unpredictable spectacle of life, which he was always finding "amazing" and "incredible". But neither the Americans nor the English have ever, since *Eminent Victorians* appeared, been able to feel quite the same about the legends that had dominated their pasts. Something had been punctured for good.'

Elsewhere, Edmund Wilson credits Strachey with making biography in England 'a form of literary art' (2 January 1924), compares his work very favourably with that of Harold Nicolson and Philip Guedalla, who both tried to copy and tended to misapply his methods (June 1925), describes *Portraits in Miniature* as 'one of Strachey's real triumphs', and praises very highly his Leslie Stephen Lecture (16 September 1925): 'One is persuaded that Mr Strachey has made out the strongest possible case for Pope and has appreciated certain aspects of his genius as they have never yet perhaps been appreciated.'

animal overtones. When endeavouring, for example, to probe the mystery of Elizabeth's virginity, Strachey wrote:

'Though, at the centre of her being, desire had turned to repulsion, it had not vanished altogether; on the contrary, the compensating forces of nature had redoubled its vigour elsewhere. Though the precious citadel itself was never to be violated, there were surrounding territories, there were outworks and bastions over which exciting battles might be fought, and which might even, at moments, be allowed to fall into the bold hands of an assailant.'

In the process of showing how the profound psychological disturbances of Elizabeth's childhood had made normal sexual intercourse impossible for her, Strachey invented on the queen's behalf an early traumatic experience carrying the most precocious and sinister implications. 'Manhood', he wrote, ' – the fascinating, detestable entity, which had first come upon her concealed in yellow magnificence in her father's lap – manhood was overthrown at last, and in the person of that traitor it should be rooted out. Literally, perhaps . . . she knew well enough the punishment for high treason.'

The punishment for treason included castration – a barbarity that terrified and obsessed Strachey. Later on in the book, while evoking the soft, insidious atmosphere of Ireland at the time of Essex's expedition against Tyrone, he again hints at this awful, absorbing topic. 'What state of society was this,' he asked, 'where chiefs jostled with gypsies, where ragged women lay all day long laughing in the hedgerows, where ragged men gambled away among each other their very rags, their very forelocks, their very . . . parts more precious still, where wizards flew on whirlwinds, and rats were rhymed into dissolution?'

If fetishism is to be explained in terms of a fear of castration, then it is not perhaps surprising that Strachey, whose erotic attention was partly directed towards the ears, should have experienced this fear. There are almost as many references to the mutilation of ears as to castration itself. At the end of Chapter V, for instance, he tells the story of Mr Booth, one of Anthony Bacon's dependants, 'who, poor man, had suddenly found himself condemned by the Court of Chancery to a heavy fine, to imprisonment, and to have his ears cut off'. This brutal tale is intended, ostensibly, to illustrate the fearful caprice and cruelty of the happy-go-lucky world of Elizabethan England. After two pages given over to recounting the sordid, ridiculous intrigue that was carried on around this sentence, Strachey concludes: 'Then there is darkness; in low things as in high the ambiguous age remains true to its character; and, while we search in vain to solve the mystery of great men's souls and the strange desires of Princes, the fate of Mr Booth's ears also remains for ever concealed from us.'

It is difficult to see what this story really adds to the vivid picture of Elizabethanism – its canting inconsistency, its savagery, its alluring mystification – that Strachey etches in so racily during the course of his second chapter – one passage of which brings together both castration and the cutting off of ears, and castigates religion as the ultimate kill-joy:

'Who can reconstruct those iron-nerved beings who passed with rapture from some divine madrigal sung to a lute by a bewitching boy in a tavern to the spectacle of mauled dogs tearing a bear to pieces? Iron-nerved? Perhaps; yet the flaunting man of fashion, whose codpiece proclaimed an astonishing virility, was he not also, with his flowing hair and his jewelled ears, effeminate? And the curious society which loved such fantasies and delicacies – how readily would it turn and rend a random victim with hideous cruelty! A change of fortune – a spy's word – and those same ears might be sliced off, to the laughter of the crowd, in the pillory; or, if ambition or religion made a darker embroilment, a more ghastly mutilation – amid a welter of moral platitudes fit only for the nursery and dying confessions in marvellous English – might diversify a traitor's end.'

This preoccupation with sexual themes and deviations is decked out with certain Freudian overtones. Significantly, Strachey dedicated his book to James and Alix Strachey, who were by this time pupils of Freud and who were to produce the standard English translation of all Freud's works. Despite his wartime tuition, Strachey did not read German at all proficiently, and until well into the 1920s Freud's writings were available in English only in extremely indifferent – and even incorrect – translations. Strachey had read a very few of these, and to begin with, was mainly sceptical as to their value. None of his character sketches in *Eminent Victorians* were influenced in the slightest by Freud, and nor was the portrait of Queen Victoria. The great psychological influence on his earlier work had been Dostoyevsky – who, of course, reveals a lot of the same material as Freud, and whom Freud himself regarded as the greatest of all novelists.

But ever since 1922, when James had published his translation of Freud's *Group Psychology and the Analysis of the Ego*, this position had altered considerably. By 1926, Strachey had learnt a good deal about psychoanalysis and psychology from talks with James and Alix. And he accepted pretty completely the interpretation that they – and especially Alix – gave him, in some detail, as to what seemed the probable underlying attitude of Elizabeth to the execution of Essex. His account of this in the later part of the book (as well as in some earlier passages preparing for it) is purely psychoanalytic. He is obviously riding a Freudian thesis, and riding it hard, as the references to sexuality – the reverend gentleman indignantly notes that the narrative contains at least eleven direct or indirect allusions to the sexual organs – attest. Freud's discovery that unconscious processes, among them infant sexuality and the adult operations of the sex instinct, permeate all human thought and action, was especially appealing to Strachey. He was attracted to a way of thought that seemed to encourage freedom from superstitious restraints in human relationships and to confirm his own fervently maintained ideals. Even though he was at first sceptical of their truth, Freud's brilliant probings into human nature gave immediate support to his general moral unorthodoxy. 'It also provided him with a scientific method whereby he could rationally cope with certain previously ignored facts of life', commented Professor Martin Kallich, ' – and so, sharpening his mind, made more acute his psychological insight.'

The use to which Strachey put his psychoanalytical knowledge was partly technical. He was able more freely to exploit his own twofold nature, from which, unconsciously, arose the literary emphasis he placed on ambiguity and dualism; and he was able to savour the enigma of Elizabeth's personality with several unsqueamish reflections. Like himself, Elizabeth commanded no great powers of self-analysis. She found it impossible to predict her own impulses or to explain the peculiar motives that lay behind her decisions. Throughout the biography, Strachey stresses this element of fluctuating uncertainty which counts for so much in directing hither and thither the tragic course of the story. But he relies on Freudian principles to suggest that, in the primitive depths of her and Essex's unconscious, their tragedy was inevitable; that, given the facts of their backgrounds, it was preordained. In bringing out this contrast between the different levels of consciousness, Strachey produces a composite pattern that is once again on Shakespearian lines:

> There's a divinity that shapes our ends,
> Rough-hew them how we will.

Strachey harboured in his nature a streak of almost superstitious fatalism, which forms part of the texture of his writing. This new employment of Freudian theses was partly a method of connecting up a general pattern of predestination at the expense of isolated character analysis, something systematic rather than intuitive. For example, he subtly implements Freud's theories concerning father–daughter relationships when, in describing Elizabeth's feelings on sending Essex to his death, he imagines, rising within her being, the spirit of her father, who had had his own wives executed:

'Yes, indeed, she felt her father's spirit within her; and an extraordinary passion moved the obscure profundities of her being, as she condemned her lover to her mother's death. In all that had happened there was a dark inevitability, a ghastly satisfaction; her father's destiny, by some intimate dispensation, was repeated in hers; it was supremely fitting that Robert Devereux should follow Anne Boleyn to the block.

Her father! ... but in a still remoter depth there were still stranger stirrings. There was a difference as well as a likeness; after all, she was no man, but a woman; and was this, perhaps, not a repetition but a revenge? After all the long years of her life-time, and in this appalling consummation, was it her murdered mother who had finally emerged? The wheel had come full circle.'

The real deteriorating force at work in *Elizabeth and Essex* would appear to have been Strachey's own physical weakness, mental and emotional weariness. Signs of this enfeeblement are freely discernible in these pages. There are, of course, passages which eloquently show off his verbal artistry – the description, for instance, of Elizabeth's vacillating disposition, which he likened to a ship: 'Such was her nature – to float, when it was calm, in a sea of indecisions, and, when the wind rose, to tack hectically from side to side.' And there are a few ironical flashes, such as the portrait he paints of King Philip, the spider of the Escorial 'spinning cobwebs out of dreams', who is troubled on his death-bed by one thought: 'Had he been remiss in the burning of heretics? He had burnt many, no doubt; but he might have burnt more.' Around these oases stretch flat and sandy deserts of dry words, colourless transitions, weak puns. 'On the whole, it seemed certain that with a little good management the prosecution would be able to blacken the conduct and character of the prisoners in a way which would carry conviction – in every sense of the word.' 'The state of affairs in Ireland was not quite so bad as it might have been.' 'They [the Spanish ambassadors] had come into contact with those forces in the Queen's mind which proved, incidentally, fatal to themselves, and brought her, in the end, her enormous triumph.' Such sentences as these lack the incisiveness and bite of the Strachey who wrote *Eminent Victorians*.

Critics have put forward two main reasons for the comparative failure of *Elizabeth and Essex* as measured against *Queen Victoria*. Strachey's temperament was, they have suggested, too wildly incompatible with the Elizabethan Age; and, because of the overall lack of information relating to this age, he was forced to adopt an inadequate biographical technique. Such opinions cannot be accepted without qualification. Perhaps significantly, it has always been literary critics and not historical commentators who have pointed to the alleged dearth of material. About Victoria all was known; about Elizabeth very little. And so, Virginia Woolf deduced, everything seemed to lend itself to a fresh artistic combination which gave the biographer freedom to invent, yet guided his invention with the signposts of some fact. 'Nevertheless,' she continued, 'the combination proved unworkable; fact and fiction refused to mix. Elizabeth never became real in the sense that Queen Victoria had been real, yet she never became fictitious in the sense that Cleopatra or Falstaff is fictitious. The reason would seem to be that very little was known – he was urged to invent; yet something was known – his invention was checked.' J. K. Johnstone, who also found something weightless and incomplete in Strachey's biography, attributes this lack of substance, like Virginia Woolf, to the paucity of historical data: 'The main cause of Strachey's difficulties in *Elizabeth and Essex* is a lack of intimate information', he wrote. 'He is unable to take us into the minds of his characters as often as he does in *Queen Victoria*; and when he does reveal their inner lives, the revelation is not always convincing ... Bacon's character is revealed to posterity more fully, thanks especially to his essays and his letters, than the character of any other of the Elizabethans with whom Strachey is concerned, and the letter in which he warned Essex may still be read, and is quoted from by Strachey. There can be little doubt that *Elizabeth and Essex* would have been more successful if Strachey had had more material of this sort at his disposal.'

In striking contrast to this statement, G. B. Harrison, in the Commentary which appears at the end of his *Robert Devereux, Earl of Essex,* has written: 'A complete bibliography of materials for the life of Essex would include every major source for the last twenty years of the reign of Elizabeth. There is so much material that between 1591 and 1601 it is possible to trace Essex's whereabouts almost for every day of his life.' In the book itself, Harrison gives the texts of numerous letters sent by Elizabeth and Cecil to Essex, and Essex's letters to the queen and her secretary.

A great many historians and biographers have written on Elizabeth, and the number and variety of anecdotes, of scandals involving personal relationships between the queen and her subjects which appear in their books would seem to suggest that the period was especially well documented. The Elizabethans were great correspondents, and the lives of both Elizabeth and Essex are remarkably fully, if not always intimately, recorded in the letters that passed between them. But although there was no great lack of original material in the Public Record Office, the Manuscript Department of the British Museum, and the stores of the Bodleian and other archives, Strachey confined his research entirely to published sources. An examination of his bibliography shows, too, that he has omitted at least five of the most important source-books for the life of Essex. The need, then, was perhaps less for invention than for imagination. From the start he had envisaged *Elizabeth and Essex* as a work of creative drama, not of historical exploration. Essex himself was a character of no great historical significance – he finds no place, for example, in G. M. Trevelyan's *History of England*. Moreover, Strachey did not have to cover a life span of over eighty years, crowded with complex political incident, as he had done in *Queen Victoria*. Instead, he limited himself to a period, comparatively placid, of about one sixth of that time. Essex's close association with the queen had lasted only a fairly short span of her long reign, and most of the issues of great historical moment preceded his brief rise to power. He was nineteen when first he began to assume a position of prominence, and just thirty-four at the time of his execution. During those fifteen years, he was away from England on a number of occasions and over the final twelve months of his life saw Elizabeth only once – or possibly twice – since he was first occupied with his ill-fated Irish command, and subsequently in disgrace. There was, too, a monotonous repetition in their highly-charged emotional relationship – a short period of unnatural affinity; a quarrel (generally arising from some rash or incompetent action on the part of Essex); a separation, during which Essex would sulk and the queen rage; then a reconciliation accompanied by new and greater favours. At each spin of the wheel, the violence of their discord grew more intense, their alienation more bitter, and their reconciliation harder to achieve. Using this classic pattern of mounting tragedy, Strachey felt he could break free from the restricting conditions of orthodox biography, and by a deft orchestration of this theme, produce a more histrionic and sumptuous work of dramatic literature.

The film of nebulous vacancy, of dream-like soundlessness that both Virginia Woolf and J. K. Johnstone discovered in *Elizabeth and Essex* arose not so much from any hindrances inherent in the art of biography, or from any absolute lack of day-to-day documentary information, but more from the peculiar quality of Strachey's temperament and his romantic attitude towards the sixteenth century. It was by no means true, as has sometimes been suggested, that he was largely ignorant of Elizabethan history. 'Underneath the sceptic and scholar', wrote Cyril Connolly, 'flamed a passionate Elizabethan.' Yet he was still largely out of his element in those remote, half-barbarous times. The Elizabethans, as no one can help feeling, found their inspiration in the pulse and glow of reckless living; while it seems equally clear that Strachey found his simply in the Elizabethans. Decked out in scarlet and gold brocade, these imponderable, airy phantoms peopled a distant fantasy world, lit up by exotic paradox and enigma, into whose outlandish and intemperate realms he might elope, away from his own so shy and vaporous personality. The Utopian contrast of these days gave him a wonderful inebriated release from the coils of his mordant self-obsession, an illusory flight into that chimerical, intoxicated, extramundane land that never seems quite real to the sober reader. For Strachey preferred to feel that the spirit of Elizabethanism belonged not to the actual world at all. 'In fact,' he declared in one of his *Spectator* reviews,[3] 'the

3. 'Elizabethan Drama', *Spectator*, 100 (20 June 1908), 975–6.

Elizabethans when they were most themselves turned their backs upon realism, and rushed towards the extraordinary, the disordered, and the sublime, so that if one wished to sum up their most essential qualities in a single word, "extravagant" would probably come nearest to the truth. Their extravagance was of course the extravagance of greatness; it was based on strength and knowledge and it was controlled by the high necessities of art.'

Yet because the realism of the epoch could never be totally expunged, the dream might in an instant swivel into nightmare. It was this mingling of allurement and revulsion, of palpitating horror and sentiment that made up the cataleptic fascination Elizabethanism held for Strachey.

As a work of passion and drama, *Elizabeth and Essex* has the agreeable period texture of finely twilled fustian: as an historical reconstruction, it is often stagy and unreal. Strachey skims lightly over those aspects of Elizabeth which make her unacceptable as the heroine of a great and tragic love-affair, and, so far as is possible, rejects any direct interpretation of sixteenth-century England that does not convey the impression of a varied landscape, flooded with the last blaze of evening light. It is a personal evocation of a never-never land, thrilling and unfathomable; a deliberate construction, by theatrical processes, of the inexplicable quality that formed, in his opinion, the essence of the finest art. 'With very few exceptions', he wrote, '– possibly with the single exception of Shakespeare – the creatures in it meet us without intimacy; they are exterior visions, which we know, but do not truly understand.' Strachey exploits this recognizable lack of understanding until it becomes part of the very fabric of the book. But it is because his characters are simply exterior visions that we are moved so little by their misfortunes, do not grieve at their deaths. They are no more to us than monumental silhouettes, the shadows of substantial beings who never appear. At best we may picture them as the figures in a game of chess, knights, bishops, pawns and the all-powerful queen, ivory pieces whose carved beauty we may admire, whose movements will engage our interest, but for whom we can feel nothing personal. Nor can we become very emotionally caught up by the game itself, for it is not being carried on between two ordinary mortals, but vast and unrealizable super-beings:

> 'Tis all a Chequer board of Nights and Days
> Where Destiny with Man for Pieces plays:
> Hither and thither moves, and mates, and slays,
> And one by one back in the Closet lays.

2
ESSEX AND ELIZABETH

By choosing *Elizabeth and Essex* as the subject for his book, Strachey may vainly have hoped to escape the appalling exhaustion that had beset him after *Queen Victoria*. His research was not so thorough, and he needed to delve into far fewer books of reference. In any case, there were artistic as well as practical advantages offered by such a theme. Everyone knew the legend of old Gloriana. But then, need he accept this legend without subtle reservations, without some amplifications appropriate to that most enigmatic of epochs? With his brand new psychoanalysis to give him confidence, was he not entitled – was he not, perhaps, even compelled – to inquire into that peculiar absorption which bound together the bold, exquisitely boyish courtier and that old and extraordinary regal creature? What could the secret of their incongruous association be? From what exotic, bitter-sweet essence had their weird, disturbing passion been so cunningly distilled? Such questions, with their cloak of inscrutable mystery, were tantalizing. Yet where it was injudicious to assert, was it not still possible to suggest? Where one was unable to define, might one not, by some unexpected juxtaposition of opposing syllables, catch a reverberating echo of those remote, vital times, so oddly melodious?

So, in parody, may Strachey have reflected to himself. Yet there existed other, deeper causes, more instructive and of greater psychological significance, to account for the compelling attraction he felt towards the handsome Essex, the baffling Elizabeth, and their tempestuous affair – causes which, running between the lines of his narrative, evince an extraordinary sense of tension and design.

The first two chapters act as Argument and Prologue to the main story. In less than seven thousand words of rich, romantic prose, Strachey parades the extravagant excitement and inconsistency of the age, his baroque, metaphor-studded sentences sounding like a fanfare of trumpets to set the mood and background of his tale. He also offers a brief sketch of Essex and a longer, more involved analysis of the queen, tracing their separate lives up to the early summer of 1587, when the tragedy of their dual history may be said to have begun.

It was Essex's 'double nature' – that standard Stracheyesque quality – which partly led Strachey to identify his own personality with that of the glamorous courtier. As depicted in this book, the more latent side of the earl's temperament – that of the pale and sorrowful scholar, incapable of great thought or action, shivering in the agonies of ague, lying in darkness upon his bed and dreaming of happiness only in his obscurity from convivial society, from the loves and hates of ordinary people – bore a good enough resemblance to the conditions of Strachey's own student days. But Essex's more flamboyant qualities – reflected best, perhaps, in the early, breathless evocation of a 'handsome, charming youth, with his open manner, his boyish spirits, his words and looks of adoration, and his tall figure, and his exquisite hands, and the auburn hair on his head, that bent so gently downwards' – infatuated Strachey, and proclaimed a vision of himself as he often imagined he would like to have appeared before the world, the type of man he found irresistible – his own self, romantically idealized. In the contemplation of this physical transformation from sickly recluse to dashing man of action, Strachey seems himself to have experienced a kindred lifting of the spirit, and he clearly attributes some of his own feelings to Elizabeth, giving his biography an unusual emotional synthesis.

The short description of Essex which Strachey introduces

into his opening chapter contains one particular passage that touches on this alluring duality: 'The youth loved hunting and all the sports of manhood; but he loved reading too. He could write correctly in Latin and beautifully in English; he might have been a scholar, had he not been so spirited a nobleman. As he grew up this double nature seemed to be reflected in his physical complexion. The blood flowed through his veins in vigorous vitality; he ran and tilted with the sprightliest; and then suddenly health would ebb away from him, and the pale boy would lie for hours in his chamber, obscurely melancholy, with a Virgil in his hand.'

This picture of Essex at Trinity catches both the social and sexual appeal of the young man. Strachey was immediately anxious, however, to dispel the notion that, by choosing this young earl as his hero, he was simply displaying an esoteric prejudice. Essex's career, he maintained, illustrated an important social change brought about by the English Reformation. On the first page of his biography he tells us that in Essex, the outgoing social system – 'the spirit of the ancient feudalism' – flamed up for the last time. The old dispensation had met its inevitable doom when the Duke of Norfolk was beheaded. 'Yet', Strachey argues, 'the spirit of the ancient feudalism was not quite exhausted. Once more, before the reign was over, it flamed up, embodied in a single individual – Robert Devereux, Earl of Essex. The flame was glorious – radiant with the colours of antique knighthood and the flashing gallantries of the past; but no substance fed it; flaring wildly, it tossed to and fro in the wind; it was suddenly put out.'

Historically, this image has little enough meaning; its purpose was brilliantly ornamental. Strachey may have wished to blind his audience to his personal attitude towards Essex which would at least have been considered trivial, and to deepen and enlarge the temper of a Court squabble by making it symbolize the overthrow of one world by another. Along with the falling of Essex's head, we are invited to hear the fall of thousands of hearts and hopes for a lost way of life.

If Essex, the protagonist, was to represent the old doomed way of life, then Elizabeth, it followed, must embody the new.

The crafty old queen, though bewitched by the earl's mercurial and seductive chivalry, nevertheless places her reliance on the new dry-eyed servants of absolutism, the Bacons and Cecils, in conflict with whom Essex is fated for destruction. The queen is, naturally enough, 'the supreme phenomenon of Elizabethanism'. But Elizabethanism, he eloquently explains, is a vague and equivocal cargo. 'It is, above all, the contradictions of the age that baffle our imagination and perplex our intelligence', he states. And in a full paragraph containing eight rhetorical questions, he shows how 'the inconsistency of the Elizabethans exceeds the limits permitted to man'.

It follows that if Elizabeth is to symbolize the spirit of such an unaccountable age, she herself must be supremely, astonishingly, unaccountable. 'Under the serried complexities of her raiment', Strachey writes, '– the huge hoop, the stiff ruff, the swollen sleeves, the powdered pearls, the spreading, gilded gauzes – the form of the woman vanished, and men saw instead an image – magnificent, portentous, self-created – an image of regality, which yet, by a miracle, was actually alive. Posterity has suffered by a similar deceit of vision. The great Queen of its imagination, the lion-hearted heroine, who flung back the insolence of Spain and crushed the tyranny of Rome with splendid unhesitating gestures, no more resembles the Queen of fact than the clothed Elizabeth the naked one. But, after all, posterity is privileged. Let us draw nearer; we shall do no wrong now to that Majesty, if we look below the robes.'

The implication of this passage is that a rarer satisfaction is to be found in tracing the ambiguous convolutions of reality than in reposing upon the comfortable simplifications of romance. But the impressionistic language with which he lingeringly describes the queen's outward apparel indicates that, despite his zest for the guidance of that interior psychoanalysis which he will shortly introduce, he was still at heart concerned with the theatrical fitness of things.

The long analysis which he then devotes to Elizabeth is full of percipient observations. He notes, for example, that she was flatly unromantic except about her own charms. 'Her clear-sightedness, so tremendous in her dealings with outward circumstances, stopped short when she turned her eyes within. There her vision grew artificial and confused.' Her political habit of vacillation – which is exalted into a genius for the policy of delay – was composed, he suggests, partly out of a deliberate means for gaining time and so prolonging peace, partly from an innate predisposition to hedge. This passion for postponement revealed both masculine and feminine traits inextricably fused together. After briefly describing the horrible circumstances in which her childhood and puberty were passed, Strachey then goes on to explain that the result of these early years upon the mature woman had been seriously to warp her sexual organization. Of a severely neurotic temperament, it was only her immense and brittle vitality that carried her through to her seventieth year, since she was never of a robust constitution, but fed ravenously off her will and nerves. This second chapter bristles with many arresting images. But they are never wholly coordinated so as to present a balanced study of character. Every time Strachey's diagnosis threatens to unravel the enigma of the queen's personality, he seems to pull himself up short, since, for aesthetic purposes, the queen must remain regally enigmatic, the emblem of her magnificently shrouded age.

His preference, too, for a psychological explanation of Elizabeth's motives, especially of her virginity, though extremely acute, is sometimes indulged at the expense of some pertinent biographical and historical facts. 'The crude story of a physical malformation', he wrote, 'may well have had its origin in a subtler, and yet no less vital, fact. In such matters the mind is as potent as the body. A deeply seated repugnance to the crucial act of intercourse may produce, when the possibility of it approaches, a condition of hysterical convulsion, accompanied, in certain cases, by intense pain. Everything points to the conclusion that such – the result of the profound psychological disturbances of her childhood – was the state of Elizabeth.'[4] That the horrors she suffered as a child could have caused her neurotic condition seems extremely probable. Yet other memories too, of which Strachey no-

4. From a letter written by Lytton's sister-in-law, Alix Strachey, it

where takes account, may also have contributed to her fear of marriage and her aversion from sexual intercourse. Jane Seymour, the mother of Elizabeth's small half-brother, to whom she was greatly attached, had died in childbirth, as had Catherine Parr – then the wife of Thomas Seymour – with whom Elizabeth lived after her father's death. Death in childbirth was by no means uncommon in the sixteenth century. One of Alençon's confidential London agents once wrote to him: 'She [Elizabeth] wants nothing in the world so much as you; there is no one in the world she would rather have near her if only, *il se pouvait faire sans enfants.*' In spite of what the doctors had said, '*il semble que par la disposition de son corps elle a peur de mourir.*'

From this it seems at least possible that Elizabeth nursed a very natural, if extreme, fear of the dangers of childbirth. Strachey, intent upon furnishing a more intricate explanation for her virginity and ennobling her unhappy appetites with similitudes from Greek mythology, overlooked this simpler reason. By relying so heavily on a system of psychoanalytical theory to interpret Elizabeth's character, he produces, from the aesthetic point of view, a rather too insubstantial picture for so realistic and terrestrial a nature.

It is the purely descriptive passages which succeed best in this second chapter. Strachey portrays Elizabeth as a forceful, baroque personality, a larger-than-life being of resplendent courage. It may be that he deliberately withheld from attributing to her an abnormal but conscious apprehension of death, associated in particular with childbirth, because this might have disturbed the impact of such an otherwise superhuman figure. 'Deep in the recesses of her being,' he tells us, 'a terrific courage possessed her.' Elsewhere he alludes to her 'personal fearlessness', and declares that 'considerations of her own personal safety were of no weight with her'. Her courage was certainly spectacular – but was it so vastly un-

seems likely that he believed Elizabeth to have suffered from vaginism (or vaginismus), a contraction of the vaginal muscle rendering intercourse painful or even impossible. It is usually a neurotic symptom, due to anxiety, but can sometimes be due to physical causes.

qualified as Strachey makes out? She did not fear anyone or anything she could see or understand. But the terrible dreams that harrowed her nights testify to a terror of the unknown. The almost insane ferocity too, which she showed to anyone who, directly or indirectly, threatened her life or wounded her vanity suggests – as does her reluctance to set a regal precedent by executing Mary, Queen of Scots – that her early experiences had bred into her not just a repugnance for sexual intercourse, but also a dread of old age and of extinction.

Preoccupied with Elizabeth's sexual maladjustment, anxious to inject an extra zest into his love-story, Strachey spotlighted the thwarted, passional side of her being without ever indicating how a more predominant, hereditary strain had overshadowed her sensuality. The daughter of Henry VIII and Anne Boleyn, she inherited not only a strong susceptibility to the opposite sex, but also a still stronger lust for power. Her high-arched nose, prominent cheek bones, firm mouth and watchful eyes all call attention to this prevailing bent handed down from her father, and greatly stimulated by the long sequence of dangers through which she passed between the ages of fourteen and twenty-five. Of all Strachey's subjects, Elizabeth was perhaps the most ruthlessly ambitious. Yet she is not treated to the summary justice previously meted out to his eminent Victorians, since his relationship to the Virgin Queen was of an altogether more fantastic character. At first sight no two figures could be more dissimilar than the rather masculine Elizabeth and her effeminate biographer. But seen through the perspective of *Elizabeth and Essex*, their lives appear to run along parallel lines – sharing something of the same resilient tenacity, fluctuating nervous constitution, and personality bewildering even to their closest associates – until they meet at vanishing-point in their feelings for Essex. From the intellectual standpoint, both looked on him with an amused, sometimes infuriated scepticism; but both were powerless to resist for long the hypnotic spell he cast about him.

Having in his two preliminary chapters painted a resplendent décor, Strachey then proceeds to plot the intersection of his two momentous lives in a style that is generally lean, sparse and fast-moving. For the most part Essex is rather an unanimated figure, but in one passage Strachey does adumbrate an excellent subject for his tragedy that he never quite succeeded in developing: 'The motives of the most ordinary mortal are never easy to disentangle, and Essex was far from ordinary. His mind was made up of extremes, and his temper was devoid of balance. He rushed from opposite to opposite; he allowed the strangest contradictories to take root together, and grow up side by side, in his heart. He loved and hated – he was a devoted servant and an angry rebel – all at once. For an impartial eye, it is impossible to trace in his conduct a determined intention of any kind. He was swept hither and thither by the gusts of his passions and the accidents of circumstance. He entertained treasonable thoughts, and at last treasonable projects; but fitfully, with intervals of romantic fidelity and noble remorse.'

As a man of action, Essex may have lain outside the range of Strachey's knowledge, and, by projecting his own romantic dreams into the figure of this tragic hero, he made the portrait original but not wholly convincing. Essex was a born opportunist whose charm would have lost its potency had it been controlled by the prudence necessary to make the most of it. Though occasionally paying lip-service to the virtue of prudence, Strachey glories in Essex's most absurd and reckless feats of audacity. He recreates the earl's personality largely from his elevated epistolary flourishes. 'Never were his words more gorgeous and his rhythms more moving,' he writes of one of Essex's short letters to the queen, 'never were the notes of anguish, remonstrance, and devotion so romantically blended together.' Rather in the manner of Oscar Wilde, Strachey wanted to believe that a beautiful and ornate style must reflect physical good looks. Despite evidence to the contrary, he pictured Essex as magnificently handsome, rejecting the portrait of him at Trinity because it made him appear too cerebral. 'It is certainly very fine,' he told Charles Prentice after having gone down to inspect the portrait (3 August 1928), 'but I had not remembered how extremely intellectual the face was.' Eventually, he chose from Woburn Abbey a more idealized likeness which, in Keynes's view, bore some resemblance to Strachey himself.

Strachey also repeats the somewhat dubious legend of Essex's tremendous popularity throughout the country, without giving any of the stories that might perhaps have accounted for it. At the end, when Essex marches upon the City, the citizens' supposed devotion to him vanishes so swiftly that 'not a creature joined him', a catastrophe which Strachey represents as the triumph of patriotic loyalty to the queen over the more personal hero-worship for Essex. Again, Strachey fails to reveal that Essex was inordinately susceptible to mockery, and that he destroyed Dr Lopez not out of misguided chauvinism, but from motives of trivial revenge, since Lopez had made him appear ridiculous before the queen and others at court.[5] The explanation which he offers for Essex's merciless hounding of Lopez is one of his least plausible theories put forward to uphold the ardent and capricious chivalry of this young cavalier. Dr Lopez was palpably innocent, and his terrible fate shocked and fascinated Strachey. One could understand professional politicians and intellectuals such as the Bacons, Burghley or Sir Robert Cecil cynically failing to recognize the rights of truth and justice, but never Essex. 'Generous, strong, in the flush of manhood, is it possible that he failed to realise that what he was doing was, to say the least of it, unfair?' Strachey asked. 'Years afterwards, when Spain was no longer a bugbear, his animosity against Dr Lopez seemed only to be explicable on the ground of some violent personal grudge. But in truth no such explanation was necessary. The Earl's mind was above personalities; but it was not above the excitement of political rivalry, the cruel con-

5. The truth of the Lopez affair seems to have been that, very foolishly, Lopez chose to double-cross Essex. He would receive information from foreign parts which he first gave to the queen and Burghley, and subsequently to Essex. When Essex came bursting into the palace with his information, he would be laughed at for bringing stale news. Moreover, if Bishop Goodman is to be believed, Lopez gossiped about Essex's private infirmities; and (so Goodman hints) let it be known that Essex was suffering from V.D.

ventions of human justice, and the nobility of patriotism.'

In one of his *Spectator* reviews, Strachey wrote: 'Tragedy cannot flourish without a little barbarism at its roots.' There is plenty of barbarism in *Elizabeth and Essex* – the burning of heretics by King Philip of Spain; the hideous hanging, castrating, drawing and quartering of Dr Lopez, and a number of vivid and terrible death scenes: Essex stretching out his scarlet-sleeved arms as the signal for his own execution; Elizabeth lying speechless on a cushioned floor, four days and four nights, with a finger in her mouth; Philip waiting in his gloomy mausoleum of a palace to be welcomed into heaven by the Trinity. These scenes of magnificent anguish and ghastly mutilation are described with many strokes of telling detail and act as a contributory means to a general artistic end – that of making our flesh creep. By such methods did Strachey hope to bring alive again that golden blend of idealism and savagery that was the nucleus of the English Renaissance. In this hope he has succeeded far better than most of the well-thought-of Elizabethan scholars such as J. E. Neale or Milton Waldman, from whose books one might infer that to have one's ears or hands chopped off under the reign of Elizabeth I would have hurt very much less than in the reign of Elizabeth II. The special virtue of Strachey's book is that he had a peculiar and uncanny insight into the atmosphere of the sixteenth century, highly personal and fantastic, combined with a special literary gift for delineating an era through its most representative personalities.

Against the violent and brutal mood of this age, Strachey sets the comparative humanity, the sensitivity, of his two mighty principals. Of Essex, he wrote with truth that 'there was no settled malignancy in his nature'. After leading the successful assault on Cadiz, Strachey tells us, Essex's 'humanity had put a speedy end to the excesses that were usual on such occasions. Priests and churches were spared; and three thousand nuns were transported to the mainland with the utmost politeness.' Yet Strachey steers away from the fact that Essex's humanity was a highly temperamental affair, depending entirely upon his uppermost feelings at the time. At

Cadiz he had unquestionably been merciful to the enemy in the afterglow of his personal triumph. Much later, in Ireland, when his campaign against Tyrone was going badly and he felt miserable and unwell, he behaved – as Strachey fails to mention – with excessive brutality to his own soldiers, cashiering and imprisoning all the officers of a detachment of some hundreds of men which had shown cowardice in the field, executing a lieutenant, and having every tenth man in the rank and file put to death.

Strachey is equally charitable to Elizabeth in furthering the questionable theory of her unusual benevolence. 'Undoubtedly there was a touch of the sinister about her', he conceded. 'One saw it in the movements of her extraordinarily long hands. But it was a touch and no more – just enough to remind one that there was Italian blood in her veins – the blood of the subtle and cruel Visconti. ... On the whole, though she was infinitely subtle, she was not cruel; she was almost humane for her times; and her occasional bursts of savagery were the results of fear or temper.' As an apologia, this seems a little disingenuous. A study of Anglo-Saxon history does not lead to the conclusion that the British have lagged very far behind the Italians in the practices of barbarity. Nor do most inhumane people indulge in acts of cruelty except as the result of fear or temper. Elizabeth's venom and resentment stemmed from her neurotic condition, in particular her fear of death and her overblown vanity, and they were often directed against relatively innocuous people. It was in one of these bursts of unwarranted cruelty that she ordered Stubbs's right hand and that of his publisher to be cut off because of a pamphlet which, although in itself an expression of loyalty, offended her *amour propre*. Public opinion in this instance was decidedly against her, though she herself deplored the fact that the law would not permit the hanging of them both. Neither can she be exonerated from all blame for the execution of hundreds of the poorer folk who took part in the Northern Rebellion. Although urged by her ministers to approve this act, she must have been fully aware of the injustice in which she acquiesced by allowing the wealthy leaders of the Rebellion to ransom their lives to her exchequer, while their destitute followers were being butchered. Moreover, in signing the death-warrant of Dr Lopez, her physician-in-chief and old acquaintance, she was impelled not even by fear or temper, but mainly by a passing wish to gratify Essex's immoderate self-conceit. She herself was never properly convinced of the Doctor's guilt, yet her supposed humanity did not deter her from sanctioning the full rigours of the law. Strachey, however, concludes his chapter on the Lopez episode on a mild and whimsical note: 'Elizabeth was merciful to the Doctor's widow. She allowed her to keep the goods and chattels of the deceased, forfeited by his attainder – with one exception. She took possession of King Philip's ring. She slipped it – who knows with what ironical commiseration? – on to her finger; and there it stayed till her death.'

Strachey shows us that Elizabeth's infatuation for Essex arose, against her better judgement, from an insatiable craving for the devotion of young men, while he, though not immune to the very real aura of personal magnetism with which Elizabeth was able to invest herself, was impelled forward mainly by the dazzling prospects of power, prestige and the financial benefits accruing from such a relationship. This relationship is presented as being very similar in its underlying pattern to all the others in Strachey's writing. In every case the predominant partner is the woman, whose terrific overplus of vitality crushes the gilded butterfly male. Essex, Strachey recounts, 'was a man, with a man's power of insight and determination; he could lead if she would follow; but Fate had reversed the roles, and the natural master was a servant. Sometimes, perhaps, he could impose his will upon her – but after what an expenditure of energy, what a prolonged assertion of masculinity! A woman and a man! Yes, indeed, it was all too obvious! Why was he where he was? Why had he any influence whatever? It was not only obvious, it was ludicrous, it was disgusting: he satisfied the peculiar cravings of a virgin of sixty-three.'

In unfolding what, in places, almost amounts to an imaginary love-affair with himself, Strachey failed to explore and clarify the emotional changes that developed in Elizabeth's attitude to the young earl. Each was flattered, as Strachey brings out, during the early years of their friendship, by the other's attentions. Her preposterous vanity was gratified; his search for high renown was given direction. But while Elizabeth's affection for Essex deepened with time, the turbulent though platonic affair which she carried on with him never came so near to shaking her virginal resolution as had her previous liaison with his stepfather, Robert Dudley, Earl of Leicester. The reason for this, of course, may have lain partly with her greater age, partly with the more complex emotions which the warm and headstrong nature of the young man aroused in her. Her lust for flattery was voracious. At the age of sixty, with a red wig and a few blackened teeth, she could still relish Walter Raleigh picturing her with 'the gentle wind blowing her fair hair about her pure cheeks, like a nymph; sometimes sitting in the shade like a goddess; sometimes singing like an angel; sometimes playing like Orpheus'. Yet her shrewd sense of reality was never altogether extinguished. The highflown flattery of her court favourites was, she always knew, a tribute to her immense personality and power, not her charm. She was thus drawn to Essex partly because his insolence made her feel a woman, however much she resented it as a queen. When, on one occasion, she refused a request he made of her to appoint Sir George Carew as Lord Deputy of Ireland, he turned his back on her, and she boxed his ears. In fury he put his hand to his sword, but the Earl of Nottingham came between them, and he rushed from the room vowing that he would not have endured such an outrage even in front of Henry VIII. Strachey narrates this incident in full, but he omits Elizabeth's significant last remark: 'He would do well', she cried, 'to content himself with displeasing her on all occasions and despising her person so insolently, but he should beware of touching her sceptre.'

As a woman, Elizabeth's fondness for Essex generally overcame the mistrust she felt for him as a queen, and which she extended wholeheartedly to his adherents, of whom she disapproved both as a ruler and a woman, suspecting them as the potential agents of Essex's wild though unfocused ambitions, and disliking them as the personal friends of the man she loved. As for Essex himself, she treated him like a small boy who was habitually associating with the wrong company. Her affection for him was composed out of a mixture of maternal feeling and starved desire, the former predominating. These sentiments had less in common with the infatuation of an elderly mistress for her young lover – which Strachey describes – and more, as G. B. Harrison has observed, with 'the jealous love of a widow towards her only son'. In his presence she seems to have experienced some consolation for the terrible loneliness of her position as Queen of England. 'Towards her ministers or servants', Harrison continued, 'she felt annoyance or approval. Essex roused in her passion, of admiration which might rise into ecstasy or of anger which might swell into hate. Moreover beneath the ceremonies and trappings of royalty she was a very lonely childless woman whom no one loved for her own sake: perhaps Robin might.'

Ever since her girlhood, Elizabeth had been fond of children, and there is ample evidence to suggest that she felt her own childless condition keenly. At the birth of James she is said to have exclaimed: 'The Queen of Scots is lighter of a fair son and I am but barren stock.' Unable to conceal from herself all that she had sacrificed to the desire for political power and the need for safety, she would erupt into insane fury whenever one of her maids-of-honour became pregnant. With men she was less violent, on the whole, than with women. But her obsessive resentment of others marrying was notorious. Pembroke and Southampton were both imprisoned; Catherine Gregg and the Earl of Hertford were sent to the Tower; and Walter Raleigh and Bess Throgmorton were similarly dealt with, though in their case Elizabeth could not plead the excuse that their offspring would stand in the line of succession. It is hardly surprising that Leicester and Essex should have smarted under her fury, since she regarded their marriages as acts of personal infidelity to herself.

It is not uncommon for a man or woman whose deepest

drive has been for power, to establish a dominant parental relationship with the opposite sex. Elizabeth enjoyed thwarting Essex in order to provoke highly emotional scenes that led to even more highly charged reconciliations, more dangerous each time, and more delicious. Tossing him about on a violent sea of passion, she would play with him like a cat with a mouse, enjoying having her own sensations tickled by Essex's beauty, while his impetuosity and contrariness added spice to the contact. She abused him for trivialities, but tolerated his more foolish actions as an indulgent mother would the sweet follies of a pampered child. Alternately caressing and chastising him, she employed a kind of primitive Pavlovian system to unhinge Essex's already unstable character, and was herself the principal architect of his final disgrace. Responsive to his charm, she held no high opinion of his capabilities or achievements. While she was with him she could not deny his wishes for long, but would experience a contemptuous reaction against her own weakness once he had departed. In long vitriolic letters she visited on him her displeasure with herself. And in this alternating response, one can see the warring of those two great forces in her nature, with her desire for power gradually displacing her need for love. During the last rebellion, her uncharacteristic behaviour shows the growing supremacy of her will over her imagination. She was calm and undisturbed amid the rising clamour which went up from Essex House, unable to acknowledge any acute danger emanating from the incompetent, boyish earl. It is even possible that Essex would not have paid for treason with his life, as Strachey points out, had it not been reported to Elizabeth that, in one of his outbursts, he had cried that the queen was an old woman, as crooked in mind as in carcass. This insult helped to harden her resolve when, in signing his death-warrant, she killed for ever her own sensual emotionalism, the dying convulsions of which fretted the surface of her being in a fit of hysterical laughter.

The mother-and-son relationship which stares out at us from the pages of *Elizabeth and Essex* was one which naturally interested Strachey, but which he did not sufficiently investigate. In one passage only does he appear to recognize this aspect of their love-affair. Describing the disciplinary tribunal that Elizabeth personally devised to punish Essex for his failure in Ireland, he wrote: 'There should be a fine show, and the miscreant should be lectured, very severely lectured, made to apologise, frightened a little, and then – let off. So she arranged it, and everyone fell in with her plans. Never was the cool paternalism of the Tudors so curiously displayed. Essex was a naughty boy, who had misbehaved, been sent to his room, and fed on bread and water; and now he was to be brought downstairs, and, after a good wigging, told he was not to be flogged after all.'

3

THE SERPENT, THE PYGMY AND THE FOX

Behind the two principal actors, the lesser characters are arranged so that they become engrafted into the main design of Strachey's Elizabethan tapestry. Some of these subsidiary figures stand out in the limelight; others are set in the shade. Among the latter, perhaps the most surprising is Robert Dudley, Earl of Leicester. Although Elizabeth's love-affair with Leicester lasted right up until his death, Strachey treats their relationship laconically and, presumably to make Essex a unique phenomenon in Elizabeth's life, subordinated his stepfather to a comparatively trifling role.

Of the other subordinates on Strachey's canvas, the most important are Francis Bacon, the serpent; Sir Robert Cecil, the pygmy; and Sir Walter Raleigh, the fox.

Bacon, the bad man of the tragedy, is brilliantly depicted. Strachey seemed to possess a specially penetrating insight into the workings of his mind. For though of a far more aggressive and amoral nature than himself, Bacon shared with Strachey some of the same tastes, proclivities and turns of mind. As an essayist, Bacon reigned as supreme master of the sententious style, which the great French writers had made their own. His aphorisms were worthy of La Rochefoucauld.

His prose combined the use of resplendent colouring with a remarkable concentration of thought. But the very qualities that enabled him to write the most sublime prose brought about his own spiritual ruin. 'His imagination, with all its magnificence, was insufficient,' Strachey explained; 'it could not see into the heart of things. And among the rest his own heart was hidden from him. His psychological acuteness, fatally external, never revealed to him the nature of his own desires.'

Bacon's part in the condemnation of Essex, though regrettable, was amazingly clever. The pamphlet which he prepared to justify the execution of his former patron evokes this comment from Strachey: 'This result was achieved with the greatest skill and neatness; certain passages in the confessions were silently suppressed; but the manipulations of the evidence were reduced to a minimum and there was only one actually false statement of fact. . . . Yet such a beautiful economy – could it have arisen unbeknownst? Who can tell? The serpent glides off with his secret.'[6]

6. 'No wonder Mr Strachey admires such handiwork,' commented the literary historian, G. B. Harrison, 'for these are his own methods.' Although Harrison imperfectly understood Strachey's attitude to Bacon, it is true that in his *Elizabeth and Essex*, by dovetailing fragments of letters and conversations, Strachey did practise a number of silent suppressions of the truth. For example, he represents Elizabeth's last speech to Parliament as far shorter and more striking than it actually was, by leaving out whole passages without indication, and by transposing the rhythms of what he does quote. The scene, as he depicts it, closes to the sound of trumpets, and the queen makes her exit with the words: 'And, though you have had and may have many mightier and wiser princes sitting in this seat, yet you never had nor shall have any love you better.' Elizabeth's own words were 'any that will be more careful and loving', after which she went on speaking for a further minute or so and finally gave directions that the whole delegation might come forward and kiss her hand. On scientific rather than aesthetic grounds, critics have also objected to Strachey's pretence of knowing what his characters were secretly thinking or feeling in certain situations – a notorious instance of this trait being his elaborate presentation of Elizabeth's state of mind just before the death of Essex.

Perhaps the most telling and significant indictment of Lytton Strachey as a serious historian on the evidence of this book, was contained in

Strachey points to a central division in Bacon's character – a hiatus between his sensitivity and ruthlessness. Describing the part he played in the preliminary examination of Essex, Strachey wrote: 'He had no hesitations or doubts. Other minds might have been confused in such a circumstance; but he could discriminate with perfect clarity between the claims of the Earl and the claims of the Law. Private friendship and private benefits were one thing; the public duty of taking the part required of him by the State in bringing to justice a dangerous criminal was another.' With all his array of fine intellect, his underlying instinct – that melting-pot of primitive emotions and undeveloped thought – was faulty. Both as a literary artist and a politician this was his flaw, his fatal limitation. Strachey illustrates this very well. Bacon, like the Prince Consort, was no enigma to him. But to accentuate the treachery of his

Professor G. B. Harrison's review in the *Spectator* (24 November 1928), entitled 'Elizabeth and Her Court'. This article, while it acknowledged the skill and vitality of Strachey's portrait of the queen, criticized his manipulations of historical data, which it referred to as 'privileges denied to the pedestrian scholar'. The piece, however, should be read with some caution, especially with regard to its remarks on Francis Bacon and on the appropriateness of the manner in which the narrative ends. For the published review was not, in fact, quite what Harrison wrote. The literary editor at that time, Celia Simpson (who later became the second wife of John Strachey, the politican and writer), finding the article less eulogistic than she desired, rewrote the first and last paragraphs herself – the latter originally being a parody of the final paragraph in *Elizabeth and Essex*: 'The Master biographer wrote on ... the enhancing of a great reputation.'

'I only discovered the changes when they sent me a proof which I had hastily to tinker in the office', Professor Harrison told the author (6 January 1967). '... I was only a beginner at that time, and since this was my first invitation to review for the *Spectator*, I was too timid to make a proper protest.' Celia Simpson had evidently objected to the view, expressed with true academic sarcasm, that Lytton Strachey did not care enough for historical facts, an attitude 'disturbing to the creeping critic – the pedant – who cares for such things'. When Professor Harrison protested that Strachey's scholarship was deficient she retorted: 'Scholars exist to provide material for people like Strachey!'

Professor Harrison also confirmed that his own *Robert Devereux, Earl of Essex* 'was partly intended to answer *Elizabeth and Essex*, which was a fine scenario but not history'.

villain – the matchless observer with the callous 'viper-gaze' –
he blew up his portrait to Machiavellian giant-proportions.
Having picked up a remark from Harvey that Bacon had 'a
delicate, lively hazel eye, like the eye of a viper', he quite
simply made him into a viper. The most serious misjudgement
that this process involved was the deprivation from Bacon of
one idea he held very fast – loyalty to the Crown. Essex's
rebellion horrified him as a monstrous breach in nature. He
had tried his best to keep Essex straight. The letter he wrote
after the Cadiz expedition contained the most brilliant diagnosis of Essex's position, but one that Essex himself never
heeded. In a sense, therefore, it was Essex who deserted his
wise counsellor rather than the other way round. Strachey
also suggests, at another point, that Bacon was always unfeeling, whereas he appears to have been extremely sensitive,
even if unable to deploy this sensitivity into his outward
manner or his style. He overplays, too, the predominance in
his make-up of a prohibitively inhumane intellect, so as to
contribute to the general atmosphere of predestination: 'The
miserable end – it needs must colour our vision of the character and the life. But the end was implicit in the beginning – a
necessary consequence of qualities that were innate.' And to
strengthen the drama of this fatalistic mood he alludes, quite
misleadingly, to the story of Bacon on Highgate Hill stuffing a
dead fowl with snow, representing him not as a scientist ex-
perimenting with the technique of refrigeration, but as a King
Lear – 'an old man, disgraced, shattered, alone'.

In the course of a *Spectator* review, 'Bacon as a Man of
Letters',[7] Strachey had written of him as being neither
spiritual, like Pascal, nor fundamentally an artist, like Keats.
He was more of a political sociologist, whose 'deepest
interests were fixed upon the workings and welfare of human
society'. The reptile that, to weird musical rhythms, slips and
slithers across the stage of *Elizabeth and Essex* would scarcely
be recognized in this Spectatorial figure. In a crucial passage
of the book, which sets out Strachey's interpretation of

7. *Spectator*, 101 (24 October 1908), 621–2. Collected in *Spectatorial
Essays* (82–7).

Bacon's character as a man of action, and shows us the dramatic purpose which he is to serve, Strachey wrote:

'He was no striped frieze; he was shot silk. The detachment of speculation, the intensity of personal pride, the uneasiness of nervous sensibility, the urgency of ambition, the opulence of superb taste – these qualities, blending, twisting, flashing together, gave to his secret spirit the subtle and glittering superficies of a serpent. A serpent, indeed, might well have been his chosen emblem – the wise, sinuous, dangerous creature, offspring of mystery and the beautiful earth. The music sounds, and the great snake rises, and spreads its hood, and leans and hearkens, swaying in ecstasy; ... His mind might move with joy among altitudes and theories, but the variegated savour of temporal existence was no less dear to him – the splendours of high living – the intricacies of Court intrigue – the exquisiteness of pages – the lights reflected from small pieces of coloured glass. Like all the greatest spirits of the age, he was instinctively and profoundly an artist. ... Intellect, not feeling, was the material out of which his gorgeous and pregnant sentences were made. Intellect! It was the common factor in all the variations of his spirit; it was the backbone of the wonderful snake.'

The Bacon of *Elizabeth and Essex* is determined to prove a rascal. The result is that as an agent in the movement of the drama he is superb, and his character is fastened together with an absorbing richness and complexity. But as a malefactor he is overcoloured, and transposed from life into the caricature of bad, conventional melodrama. 'It is the *Lion and the Snake*,'[8] Wyndham Lewis commented in a letter to Charles Prentice (27 November 1928), 'Essex as the embodiment of simple-minded chivalry and poor Bacon as the "Machiavel"! What a villain! One is almost inclined to believe after reading

8. W. K. Rose, in a footnote to his edition of *The Letters of Wyndham Lewis* (1963), p. 185, n. 6, comments: 'L[ewis] refers to his own *The Lion and the Fox* (London, 1927), in which he sees Othello as the simple-hearted, noble lion and Iago as the wily, vulgar "Machiavel".' For six years (1926–32) Lewis's publishers were Chatto & Windus, and he dealt, as did Strachey, with C. H. Prentice (d. 1949) who gave both writers his most responsive and unstinting support.

S[trachey]'s book, that he wrote Shakespeare's plays and did all the other things he is accused of.'

With his cousin, Robert Cecil, in mind, Bacon had once generalized: 'Deformed persons are commonly even with nature, for as nature hath done ill by them so they do by nature being for the most part void of natural affection and so they have their revenge on nature. Deformity stirreth in them and especially to watch and observe the weakness of others that they might have somewhat to repay. So that, upon the matter in a great wit deformity is an advantage in rising.'

Strachey presents Cecil's malformation less as a spur to his ascendancy than as the clue to a riddle. He can detect no inner spark within the man to account for his exemplary, expeditious toil: 'He sat at his table writing; and his presence was sweet and grave', Strachey wrote. 'There was an urbanity upon his features, some kind of explanatory gentleness, which, when he spoke, was given life and meaning by his exquisite elocution. He was all mild reasonableness – or so it appeared, until he left his chair, stood up, and unexpectedly revealed the stunted discomfort of deformity. Then another impression came upon one – the uneasiness produced by an enigma: what could the combination of that beautifully explicit countenance with that shameful, crooked posture really betoken? He returned to the table . . . While he laboured, his inner spirit waited and watched. A discerning eye might have detected melancholy and resignation in that patient face. The spectacle of the world's ineptitude and brutality made him, not cynical – he was not aloof enough for that – but sad – was he not a creature of the world himself? He could do so little, so very little, to mend matters; . . . At a moment of crisis, a faint, a hardly perceptible impulsion might be given. It would be nothing but a touch, unbetrayed by the flutter of an eyelid, as one sat at table, not from one's hand, which would continue writing, but from one's foot. One might hardly be aware of its existence oneself, and yet was it not, after all, by such minute, invisible movements that the world was governed for its good, and great men came into their own?'

This is an outline of the puzzling silhouette Robert Cecil

casts across the pages of *Elizabeth and Essex* – a shadowy Master Mind, not entirely disembodied but attached to a hump; an Invisible Man suspended in an almost eternal state of purposeful inanimation; an assiduous quill-pusher bent double over his orderly accumulation of papers, and directing the momentous affairs of the nation with fractional gesticulations of his feet. Like the reticent and resourceful Baron Stockmar, Cecil is made to achieve the maximum political consequences with the very minimum of behind-the-scenes action. But whereas Stockmar had in reality been a political cipher, Cecil was a major influence, and it is all the more disappointing that he should have been cast for this historical masquerade in such a darkly theatrical part.

There can be no doubt that, as Strachey tells us, Cecil's administrative aptitude and knowledge of the work he was called upon to perform as secretary was unrivalled. In early youth he had been coached for the job by the ablest man in England, his father Lord Burghley. Yet there was a marked dissimilarity between father and son which Strachey does not bring out. While both were masters of political intrigue, there was always an element of altruistic greatness in Burghley's actions, which were prompted by some consideration of what he felt was best for Elizabeth and for England. The same tempered spirit of detachment had not been granted to his son. As the years advanced, so this lonely, shrunken being withdrew ever more remotely from his fellow men. His retirement, with which Strachey makes great play, does not seem to have derived from any inscrutable motive. From boyhood Cecil had been morbidly self-conscious of his grotesque deformity, and after Burghley's death he grew, under his impassive manner, increasingly bitter and isolated. His driving-force became a personal grudge against humanity, and his actions appear to have been for the most part governed by the dual considerations of self-advancement and self-preservation.

Yet Cecil never seemed to harbour any particular malevolence towards Essex, in spite of what the young earl had said and written about him to the queen. His attitude was guided either by a determination not to leave himself vulnerable to a man who, up to the very last hour, might still be re-elevated to the royal favour, or by his understanding of what Essex meant and would always mean, wherever his impulsive nature led him, to the queen. It is even possible that he may have partly succumbed to the illimitable charm which Essex was able to exercise over his contemporaries.

A very real responsibility rested on Cecil at the time of Essex's rebellion, and Strachey credits him with a superhuman intelligence in dealing with this crisis. 'Essex could decide upon nothing; still wildly wavering, it is conceivable that, even now, he would have indefinitely postponed both projects and relapsed into his accustomed state of hectic impotence if something had not happened to propel him into action.

'That something bears all the marks of the gentle genius of Cecil. With unerring instinct the Secretary saw that the moment had now arrived at which it would be well to bring matters to an issue; and accordingly he did so. It was the faintest possible touch. On the morning of Saturday, February 7th, a messenger arrived from the Queen at Essex House, requiring the Earl to attend the Council. That was enough. To the conspirators it seemed obvious that this was an attempt to seize upon the Earl, and that, unless they acted immediately, all would be lost. Essex refused to move; he sent back a message that he was too ill to leave his bed; his friends crowded about him; and it was determined that the morrow should see the end of the Secretary's reign.'

Perhaps it was because he was asked to appear before the Council at the Lord Treasurer's house that Essex's apprehensions were so violently agitated. In fact, the Lord Treasurer was himself ill, and for this reason only was it proposed that the Council should assemble there. The summons was couched in moderate and reasonable words, merely requesting that Essex should state his grievances so that the Council might investigate them. There is no evidence to support Strachey's inference that this manoeuvre was arranged by Cecil alone. Following previous biographers, whose number includes Robert Cecil's direct descendant Algernon Cecil, Strachey presumes that the secretary was absolute master of the situation from start to finish. Yet the actual precautions he took were minimal. The guard was doubled at Whitehall, and the Lord Mayor was warned of the danger. Trained bands had been collected together, but they were not brought to London. Obviously Cecil was not of the same opinion as Strachey as to Essex's great popularity. Had the earl been the people's hero, these precautionary measures could never have proved effective against a rebel army marching on the court. And if he had simply had the sense to rush the palace instead of that futile march into the City, he might well have won.

Strachey's Cecil is that most familiar of all his stock characters – a brilliant enigma. But Robert Cecil, the little man who diminished the scope of his undoubted talent by the meanness of his spirit, was surely of a more human origin. Nowhere, perhaps, is the unpleasant aspect of his personality more obviously exhibited than in his double-dealings with Walter Raleigh – which even seem to have caused himself some qualms of conscience. Cecil's undermining of Raleigh falls outside the main course of Strachey's prose drama, but he refers briefly to Cecil's fear, some time after Essex's execution, that 'the dashing incompetence of Essex would be replaced by Raleigh's sinister force' – though he then goes on to show that Cecil was by far the more sinister individual, while Raleigh remained 'utterly unsuspecting'.

Walter Raleigh, so versatile and contradictory a man that Fuller did not know whether he should be catalogued as a statesman, seaman, learned writer or what you will, presented Strachey with a figure who could be placed with equal authenticity at almost any part of his canvas. He seems to have appreciated that Raleigh was the antithesis of Essex in temperament, and since the latter symbolized 'the spirit of the ancient feudalism', the former is represented as 'the ominous prophet of Imperialism'. But Raleigh's character is never developed in *Elizabeth and Essex*. Strachey employs him in a purely decorative capacity, shrouding his personality from all clear view, possibly from the fear that, if given a more prominent part, he might steal the show from Essex. More handsome than his rival, well-born, a cool and courageous fighter, a student and fine poet, he combined more personal advantages than any other man at court. Possessing an imaginative relish for intrigue, though of too naïve a mind to manage his intrigues very successfully, he was unable to liberate that warmth of feeling in others that Essex could call forth at will. He paraded his consummate brilliance in a manner that actively provoked hostility. Proud and arrogant he certainly was, as indeed were most men attracted to the court, but there was more, perhaps, of the open air adventurer in him than the power-seeker. Strachey, however, confines himself almost exclusively to this minor aspect of his personality. In the struggle for ascendancy behind the throne, Raleigh is depicted as Essex's principal rival, a lurking, ever-potential threat. In Chapter III he is introduced as 'a dangerous and magnificent man'. And in the following chapters there are constant references to him designed to build up in the reader's mind the vision of a dark and sinister force, menacing the career of Essex.

'Raleigh celebrated the occasion [his reinstatement in Elizabeth's favour] by having made for him a suit of silver armour; and so once more, superb and glittering, the dangerous man stood in the royal ante-chamber at Whitehall.'

'But more dangerous still was the odious Raleigh. Everyone knew that that man's ambitions had no scruples, that he respected no law, either human or divine.'

In portraying Raleigh in this manner, as the implacable enemy of Essex, Strachey was not advancing an objective historical judgement, but echoing Essex's own unbalanced opinion. 'What booteth it to swear the fox?' Essex had cried during his trial. Strachey does not quote this. But it is as a fox that Raleigh prowls about the scenery, a fine embellishment that agreeably tightens the suspense of the story, but resembles only slightly the extraordinary man who was his original.

4

MINORITY REPORT

Never had one of Strachey's books got off to such a mercurial start. How mixed the notices were in Britain – and how well it sold! Already the advance subscription sales topped twelve thousand, in addition to a further hundred of the special signed edition at four guineas, and a second impression of an extra ten thousand copies had to be hastily prepared before publication. 'It's being very successful,' Strachey wrote with amazed jubilation to Topsy Lucas (30 November 1928), 'and I gather from Prentice that the only difficulty is to get enough paper and binding material for the multitudes of editions that will have to be printed. However a good many copies will have to be sold to keep pace with my growing extravagance. Aubusson carpets. for instance – I am plunging wildly in that direction – egged on, of course, by Carrington.' By the first week in January, this pre-publication total had been doubled, and over thirty thousand copies were sold within four months.

In America, where seventy thousand copies were distributed in the first three weeks of December, the book made publishing history.[9] Even the critics here were eulogistic. Strachey

9. The manuscript of *Elizabeth and Essex* was in the hands of Harcourt Brace & Co. in May 1928, but, since it had been arranged that there should be a limited edition with the Crosby Gaige imprint as well as the trade edition, the making proceeded slowly, and, when it was found that trade dummies could not be ready for the summer visits of the travellers, the publishers boldly wiped the announcement completely off their autumn catalogue and set 1 December as their publishing date, the travellers making a special trip in November with orders for this one book. The risk was considerable, as the season might go bad, or the booksellers might already have overbought other titles and be disinclined to add any other large item to their purchased stock. As the autumn advanced, it was decided to make separate plates for the trade edition, and this was done under Donald Brace's direction at the plant of Quinn and Boden. An edition of 30,000 was printed, and an advance of 15,000 was in hand when shipments began. The first review which added a strong impulse to the sales was in the *New York Times* of 2 December.

would lie in bed during the mornings and read the extraordinary comments and appreciations his publisher had forwarded to him – 'Essex as 16th Century Lounge Lizard' was one of the headlines. 'It's really rather amazing!' he exclaimed in a letter to Roger Senhouse (14 December 1928). 'The reviews they enclose are hectic. Certainly the Americans have their uses.' Much of this transatlantic furore had been whipped up during the autumn by the serialization of extracts in the *Ladies' Home Journal*, for which he was paid the then record price of thirty thousand dollars (between six and seven thousand pounds). 'The version they print of *Elizabeth and Essex* is extraordinarily mutilated', Strachey had complained to Charles Prentice (21 September 1928). 'I suppose some abbreviation had to be made, but the result is frightful – rather like an execution for High Treason.' Nevertheless it was this tasteless hors d'oeuvre that had so colossally stimulated the sales. On New Year's Day, William Harcourt, the president of Strachey's American publishing firm, wrote to congratulate him on his 'wild success'. A week later he was writing again: the demand flowed on unchecked and the situation had become 'unprecedented'. 'For three weeks', Harcourt added, 'your book was being manufactured *night and day*.' Ninety thousand copies had now been printed – 'but doubtless they'll be gone in a minute or two'.

The publishers were on edge to see what the first re-orders would be. They did not have long to wait. When the telegrams began to pour in, no moment was lost in putting another edition on the press. In the first week after publication 17,000 copies had been added to the original 15,000, most of these on re-orders by telegraph. In the next six working days 25,000 more copies were sent out, and up to Christmas Day a total of 70,000 copies had been shipped. Not once had the book been reported out of stock. Two big presses and one small one were used, and with every revolution of these three presses one complete book was printed. When, on the week-end of 8 December, it was realized that the 15,000 in hand would shortly be wiped out, these presses and the bindery ran day and night from Saturday to Monday. Following the first edition of 30,000, editions of 10,000, 22,000, 10,000 and 15,000 were in rapid succession sent through the machines. And still the demand went on into the new year. This was a record for the quick production and distribution of a big non-fiction book – a quarter of a million dollars' worth of one biography sold in three weeks.

Strachey's contract had been based on his agreement for *Queen Victoria*, and on 1 May, six months after publication day, he received his first cheque from his two publishers, amounting, after his advance on royalties had been deducted, to some ten thousand pounds. 'I have made incredibly huge sums out of E & E', he told Dorothy Bussy (February 1929), '– chiefly owing to America where the sales have been unparallelled – but unfortunately my extravagance has kept pace with them, so that I am very low at the moment, almost in tears, with anticipations of complete ruin hovering over my head.'

Elizabeth and Essex was not what the public had generally expected, but they found it grand entertainment. In France, Italy, Germany and Sweden translations were soon being brought out, and also in Spain, where the translation rights fetched just fifteen pounds – 'a deplorable result of the Armada'. In Germany, the playwright Ferdinand Bruckner made a stage version of the book which was adapted for the English stage by Ashley Dukes. In America, a film was later made of the book.[10] In England, Henry Ayliff attempted another stage adaptation and the poet Louis MacNiece a radio version. Later still, the text of the book contributed substantially to the libretto which William Plomer wrote for Benjamin Britten's opera *Gloriana*. The idea for this was Britten's. 'He had a special liking for *Elizabeth and Essex*,' William Plomer told the author, 'and a strong interest in the character and fate of Essex, and had for some time seen the story as a possible theme for an opera. . . . Like Britten, I was impressed on re-reading the book, by its dramatic qualities, its vividness, and Strachey's sense of character and situation.'

But despite all the excitement it aroused, and the incredible number of impressions and editions it rapidly went through, *Elizabeth and Essex* was never to establish itself as the classic that *Queen Victoria* had become or to exert anything like the same revolutionary effect as *Eminent Victorians*. Reviewing the Malone Society's reprint of *King Lear* in the *Spectator*,[11]

10. The American film was planned and to some extent paid for in advance but, in the manner of films, never completed.
11. 'King Lear', *Spectator*, 100, op. cit.

Strachey had once observed that 'the greatest works of art appear to demand, like Kings in a procession, a train of noble forerunners to prepare the way; and genius only reaches its highest manifestation when it has, so to speak, a ready-made mould to flow into'. Strachey's fresh and brilliant Victorian biographies constructed an entirely new mould, and have secured a permanent place in literary history, owing largely to the new tradition that they founded. But *Elizabeth and Essex* founded no such tradition. It was an original but abortive experiment, leading up a cul-de-sac where the procession quickly came to a standstill.

Many critics have objected to the guesswork on which so much of the narrative seemed to be based. They carped at its questionable taste, its spicy modernity and the resonant, semi-flamboyant style – the phrases turning in upon themselves – which, though it might be said to harmonize with the Elizabethan pageant it described, had been indulged to the detriment of Strachey's quick and sardonic genius. Compared with *Queen Victoria* it was, as George Dangerfield put it, 'an exquisite failure'.[12]

Upon professional historians the book would appear to have had little influence. J. E. Neale, whose *Queen Elizabeth* (1934) is considered a standard modern biography, makes no mention of it, and ascribes to the behaviour of the queen one massive parliamentary motive. The fall of Essex had not been due to the temperamental reprisal of an insulted woman, but was a measure taken by Elizabeth to quench the political ambition of a subject. But if Strachey's Freudian theories won little support from academic scholars, his book has received some surprising, little-known tributes from among them. Conyers Read in his book *The Tudors* concedes that 'there are some brilliant glimpses of her [Elizabeth] and her court' in *Elizabeth and Essex*. J. B. Black, whose *The Reign of Elizabeth 1558–1603* is included in the Oxford History of England series, calls Lytton's work a 'penetrating and suggestive study'. And A. L. Rowse declared that the book was a fine evocation of the sixteenth-century scene. 'He [Strachey] had a

12. *Saturday Review of Literature,* 18 (23 July 1938), 17.

penetrating sense of motive; in my own opinion, he succeeded in unravelling the extraordinarily complex web of
Elizabeth's feelings about Essex, to a degree that was not even
clear to herself, certainly not to Essex, and perhaps only to
Cecil. His sympathy all through with the point of view of
Cecil, in that brilliant and insufficiently appreciated book, is
evident.'

Among literary critics there have also been several remarkably interesting and distinguished exceptions to the majority
verdict. E. M. Forster, for example, while admitting that the
book did contain inaccuracies, pronounced it to be 'in other
ways his greatest work'.[13] Desmond MacCarthy believed it to be
undervalued because the intellectual readers had judged the
book by wholly inappropriate standards – they 'wanted him
to do the same thing over and over again, they wanted to go
on enjoying his irony playing round historical figures, hitherto beyond the reach of irreverence and above suspicion'.[14]
Norman Douglas wrote to say it was 'so artful and sound and
pleasing. I don't know how it could have been better done.
Ripe! The cumulative touches are most effective.' And Logan
Pearsall Smith, in a letter to Strachey, described the book as
'masterly', though in another letter to Mrs Berenson he
wrote: 'Lytton must look to his laurels – his Queen Elizabeth,
the judicious feel, won't add to his reputation – it is to my
mind melodrama rather than history, and he has made no use
of his real gift – his exquisite sense, like that of Voltaire or
Gibbon, of human absurdity, of the unbelievable grotesque-
ness of men's actions and beliefs on this planet. It is a rare and
shining gift and should not be laid under a bushel.'

For many weeks following the publication, Strachey was
submerged by readers' letters – warm congratulations,
queries, advice and stiff correctitudes. 'I am deluged by E & E
correspondence,' he complained to Dadie Rylands (29 November 1928), 'it's perfectly fearful, and I foresee will continue
for weeks. Quite futile.' Of all these letters, two – both prais-
ing *Elizabeth and Essex* as his greatest accomplishment and

13. *Listener*, 43 (17 July 1943) 97–8.
14. op. cit.

testifying, one to its historical, the other to its psychological authenticity – are still of particular value. The first of these came from G. M. Trevelyan (25 November 1928):

Dear Strachey,

I have just finished Elizabeth. We have not waited 7 years in vain, and your long hesitations over a subject have been rewarded by a success as great as crowned Elizabeth's long hesitations in her happier years. She is much subtler and a much greater subject than Victoria and one more completely suited to your genius. The idea of telling the tale of her and of her age not by full biography but by this particular episode was most happy.

It is much your greatest work. And its success bears out my theory as against your own – or what used to be your view. You used to tell me that your strength was satire and satire alone, so you must choose people whom you did not much like in order to satirize them. I thought the argument bad then, and now the time gives proof of it. Your best book has been written about people to whom you are spiritually akin – far more akin than to the Victorians. And it is not a piece of satire but a piece of life.

Yours ever truly
G. M. Trevelyan[15]

A month later, Strachey received a congratulatory letter from Sigmund Freud, written from Vienna on Christmas Day. He had sent Freud a complimentary copy of his book, and in the course of a long courteous reply, transcribed in his odd, almost totally illegible Gothic hand, Freud answered:

I am acquainted with all your earlier publications, and have read them with great enjoyment.[16] But the enjoyment was essentially an aesthetic one. This time you have moved me deeply, for you yourself have reached greater depths. You are aware of what other historians

15. Noël Annan writes that 'Trevelyan loathed Strachey and his works, and his appreciative comments were insincere civilities written from a variety of motives.' What is interesting about his letters to Strachey is that, possibly from unconscious motives, he singles out for special praise the book generally accepted to have been Strachey's least successful, and downgrades the distinctive irony and wit on which Strachey's reputation largely rested.

16. In a letter to his brother James (15 February 1922), Lytton wrote: 'I was delighted to hear of the Doctor's [Freud's] approval of Eminent Victorians, and I agree with his preference of it to Q.V.'

so easily overlook – that it is impossible to understand the past with certainty, because we cannot divine men's motives and the essence of their minds and so cannot interpret their actions. Our psychological analysis does not suffice even with those who are near us in space and time, unless we can make them the object of years of the closest investigation, and even then it breaks down before the incompleteness of our knowledge and the clumsiness of our synthesis. So that with regard to the people of past times we are in the same position as with dreams to which we have been given no associations – and only a layman could expect us to interpret such dreams as those. As a historian, then, you show that you are steeped in the spirit of psycho-analysis. And, with reservations such as these, you have approached one of the most remarkable figures in your country's history, you have known how to trace back her character to the impressions of her childhood, you have touched upon her most hidden motives with equal boldness and discretion, and it is very possible that you have succeeded in making a correct reconstruction of what actually occurred.

SEVEN

Books, Characters and Commentaries

1

THE MONKEY AND THE GOOSE

AFTER Strachey's fame and prestige had been enlarged by *Queen Victoria*, he was frequently approached by publishers asking him to perform various commissions. These, unless they were to help some friend, he very rarely accepted. Thus, although he did contribute an Introduction[1] to George Rylands's anthology *Words and Poetry* (1928), he refused to provide Introductions to Paul Valéry's *Le Serpent*, to C. K. Scott Moncrieff's translation of Proust's *A la Recherche du Temps Perdu*, and, at the invitation of Richard Aldington, to a new translation of *La Vie Privée du Maréchal, Duc de Richelieu*. He also turned down the suggestion that, for the fee of a thousand pounds, he should reduce the six-volume Monypenny and Buckle *Life of Disraeli* to a two-volume edition.

One proposal, however, which did appeal to him came from his old Cambridge acquaintance, John Dover Wilson, who since 1921 had been at work on the now celebrated *New Shakespeare*. His co-editor, Arthur Quiller-Couch, had been forced to resign his post early on owing to ill-health, and in 1928 Dover Wilson received the consent of the Cambridge University Press to invite Strachey to write the introductions to these volumes. 'He seemed quite attracted by the proposition,' Professor Dover Wilson told the author, 'and came, complete with the famous red beard which I had not yet seen, to discuss the matter over a cup of tea with me at King's

1. Reprinted in *Characters and Commentaries* and in *Literary Essays* (16–19).

College in the Strand where I was then Professor of Education.' After their conversation and a talk with S. C. Roberts, Strachey accepted this offer, on the stipulation that the Cambridge University Press should allow Chatto and Windus to reprint his contributions. But this the publishers refused to do, and the agreement had to be called off.

His old university, Liverpool, had also been sounding him out as to whether he would like to succeed Oliver Elton in the Chair of English Literature there. Again he declined. He had not been happy at Liverpool; he seldom got on well with dons; and he had always been careful to avoid the fate of those great scholars of the eighteenth century who 'sat bent nearly double, surrounded by four circles of folios, living to edit Hesychius and confound Dr Hody, and dying at last with a stomach full of sand'.[2] His voice, too, still presented a handicap and virtually debarred him from taking up any appointment that involved public lecturing. When in 1928 J. R. Ackerley had invited him up to Savoy Hill to record for sound radio a number of his essays, it had failed him altogether. 'I was filled with such feelings of guilt and remorse over my behaviour in the broadcasting', he wrote apologizing to Ackerley after the disastrous audition, 'that I lapsed into what I fear was churlish silence. Forgive me.'

The possible failure of his voice worried him also in connection with one of the few offers he did accept over these years. This was an invitation from the vice-chancellor of Cambridge, A. C. Seward, to deliver the Leslie Stephen Lecture in June 1925. He had at once consented; then, as his qualms grew, he wrote again asking whether, to amplify his thin falsetto, he might make use of a loudspeaker. The vice-chancellor's reply was discouraging. 'We have no loudspeaker and from what I have heard of the use of the instrument in London I feel rather shy of suggesting an installation of one here.' Strachey's doubts now redoubled alarmingly. Would anyone be able to hear him? Towards the end of May, he developed a

2. 'The Sad Story of Dr Colbatch', *Nation and Athenaeum*, 96 (22 December 1923), 459–60; *New Republic*, 37 (26 December 1923), 115–16, Collected in *Portraits in Miniature* and in *Biographical Essays* (28–33).

sore throat, diagnosed by his doctor as being tonsillitis, and by James Strachey as a mere hysteria formation aimed at his lecture. But his aim, if it were the latter, had been over-eager, for by early June he had completely recovered, and there was no alternative but to go through with the ordeal.

When the day arrived, Strachey delivered his lecture with great character and attack, displaying not the least sign of nervousness. He knew exactly what he wanted to say, and how to say it. For the choice of subject and the actual composition of the lecture were comparatively easy matters. He had selected Alexander Pope.[3] His deep and lasting admiration for the poetry of Pope dated from his earliest Cambridge days. Often in the years since then he had thought of writing about him, and in fact had treated him briefly in several of his essays. The fullest and most comprehensive statement of his attitude to Pope the man was set forth in a Spectatorial review (20 November 1909)[4] of George Paston's Mr Pope: His Life and Times. From this article it appears that Strachey considered Pope's notoriously perverted temper and crooked habit of mind to be simply manifestations of that sickly condition which had twisted his body and made one long disease of his whole life. 'He was', Strachey explained, 'in modern parlance, a névrosé. Abnormally sensitive to stimuli, his frail organization responded frantically to the slightest outward touch. If you looked at him he would spit poison, and he would wind himself into an endless meshwork of intrigues and suspicions if you did not. But it was not only in malignity and contortions that Pope's sensitiveness showed itself; throughout his life he gave proof of a tenderness which was something more than a merely selfish susceptibility, and of a power of affection as unmistakable as his power of hate. In spite of hysterical bickerings and downright quarrels, his relations with the Blounts were animated by a sincere and generous friendship; with all his egoism and vanity, he never lost his profound admiration for the only one of his con-

3. Originally published in 1925, the lecture was reprinted in *Characters and Commentaries* and in *Literary Essays* (79–93).
4. Collected in *Spectatorial Essays* (147–52).

temporaries who was as great a writer as himself – Swift; and his devotion to his mother forms one of the most touching episodes in the whole history of letters.'

Strachey saw Pope's career as the battleground for discordant emotions, the intensity of which was the intensity of disease. Here was territory well known to him. There was much of Pope in Strachey's style and point of view. The first care in their writing was for sound. Bathos, with its sudden comic descent from the sublime to the absurd, was a favourite device they had in common. A certain discrepancy, too, between mind and emotion shows itself in the juxtaposition of studiously compressed passages making use of the shortest, plainest words, and ornamental passages in the rococo fashion. Strachey's comments upon the artificial simplicity of Pope's early Pastorals call to mind the sort of literary criticism that in recent times has been applied to his own prose style: 'Everything is obvious. The diction is a mass of *clichés*; the epithets are the most commonplace possible; the herds low, the brooks murmur, the flocks pant and remove, the retreats are green, and the flowers blush. The rhythm is that of a rocking-horse; and the sentiment is mere sugar.'

Coleridge has observed that the personal satires of Pope lack the judicial tone so effectively assumed by Dryden. Strachey, on the other hand, preferred Pope to Dryden because, he tells us, the great genius of the latter 'with all his strength and all his brilliance, lacked one quality without which no mastery of the couplet could be complete – the elegance of perfect finish'. This preference for Pope's finer technical merit betrays something of that feminine taste which Strachey shared with his subject. To his way of thinking, Dryden's verse exhibited a comparatively mundane turn of mind. Yet *The Dunciad*, modelled on Dryden's *Mac Flecknoe*, altogether lacks the largeness and geniality of that satire. Dryden's invective has little of the refined delicacy of Pope's and practically none of its malice. He sweeps forward with the undiscriminating fury of an avalanche, while the feline and meticulous Pope hits unerringly at the same sensitive spot again and again.

Both in his early Spectatorial essay and in the Leslie Stephen Lecture, Strachey expresses astonishment at the miraculous manner in which Pope had fitted the language of passion into the smooth, ordered, conventional eighteenth-century couplet. Here, he reasoned, lay absolute proof of the poet's supreme genius. How had he achieved the apparently impossible? His dextrous handling of words and rhythms increasingly absorbed Strachey — 'those fine shades', as he had enviously described them, 'and delicate gradations of sound and expression of which the secret is only known to the true artist'. This was the secret, the mysterious process of blending unstinted passion with cool detachment into a perfect literary form, that, sixteen years later, drew him back to the subject of Pope.

In his five-thousand-word address, Strachey made no effort to rewrite Pope's biography, to provide a critical conspectus of his poetry or to sum up the full nature of his genius. Brief, emphatic, teeming with vivacious imagery and scintillating comment, the lecture was designed primarily to be heard rather than read. Its main theme involved an examination of Pope's very unheroic malignity and of the heroic couplet in which he gave that malignity its undying expression. Although, therefore, the lecture was more detailed and scholarly, it had little of the breadth or balance of his earlier review, ignoring, as it did, that split in Pope's nature, which is frequently reflected in those extraordinary antitheses of his couplets.

Strachey did not primarily concern himself with the disorders of the poet, but with the exquisite structural order of his poetry. It is true that, in the opening part of the lecture, he does introduce Pope to his audience as perhaps the most representative of all eighteenth-century writers; but the picture is still essentially a literary one. Consequently, in this pen-and-ink world, he experiences no discomfort, only an appreciative delight at the agonies of Pope's victims; and he communicates no human feeling for the morbidly sensitive poet always throwing stones at others from within his own glass house. 'To us,' he declared, 'after two centuries, the agonies suffered by the victims of Pope's naughtiness are a matter of indifference; the fate of Pope's own soul leaves us cold.' Similarly his picture of the eighteenth century as the most civilized that our history has known, is a literary as opposed to a general evocation. By emphasizing this particular aspect of the age, he can bring out more clearly Pope's gratifying ascendancy over the upper classes – a supreme example of the high respect literature then commanded. The immense success of Pope's translation of Homer, he writes, 'was a sign of the times. Homer's reputation was enormous: was he not the father of poetry? The literary snobbery of the age was profoundly impressed by that. Yes, it was snobbery, no doubt; but surely it was a noble snobbery which put Homer so very high in the table of precedence – probably immediately after the Archbishop of Canterbury.' Quite so. Yet the eighteenth century was not solely the era of the sophisticated Walpole and the genteel Chesterfield, but also of Jonathan Wild and Jack Sheppard and, before the magisterial work of Fielding, a reign of cut-throat terror by night throughout London. Outside the polite world of the upper classes, England was a wild and uncivilized land.

In his Spectatorial review, Strachey had been careful to point out that Pope possessed 'a power of affection as unmistakable as his power of hate'. His Leslie Stephen Lecture deals only with Pope's malicious side. There is more than one probable explanation for this. Although Pope did on occasions express his tenderness and affection in verse – the lovely lines to Gay, 'The Epistle of Sappho to Phaon', and his 'Universal Prayer' are all fine examples – his feelings, as Strachey rightly observed in 'English Letter Writers', 'were far more easily roused into expression by dislike than by affection. Scorn, hatred, malice, rage – these were the emotions which, with Pope, boiled over almost naturally into fervent language; it is through its mastery of all the shades of these emotions that his verse has gained its immortality.' And so, since his lecture is not really concerned with Pope as a love or metaphysical poet, Strachey conveys the impression that he was a monster of malignity, and ignores to the point of contradiction that amiable side of his temperament underlined by Johnson's statement that 'in the duties of friendship he [Pope] was zealous and constant; those who loved him once, continued their kindness'. In earlier years, when he felt more closely akin to Pope in his bitterness and sickly sensitivity, Strachey had been anxious to provide a sympathetic interpretation of this malice, to uncover the frustrated generosity and love which it often concealed. But now that he was happier and better in health, he does not identify himself with Pope so readily. He is more of a spectator relishing, and urging others to relish, the rapier thrusts so excellently driven home, and interspersing his cries of appreciation with a more learned discourse on the art of fencing.

By depicting Pope as a fiendish monkey, he created for himself something of an artificial problem. 'What does seem strange', he admits, 'is that Pope's contemporaries should have borne with him as they did.' His victims included some of the most powerful and elevated people in the land. In France, the fate which Voltaire had suffered on far less provocation illustrated that 'such a portent as Pope would never have been tolerated on the other side of the Channel. The monkey would have been whipped into silence and good manners in double quick time.' Strachey's explanation – that Pope relied on his legal and physical vulnerability to escape prosecution – contributes ingeniously to the conception both of an unscrupulous monster-poet and of an enlightened eighteenth century. Yet it was more often his manner than the meat of what he wrote that earned him respect. In his *Essay on Man*, the comfortable philosophy of which was borrowed from Leibnitz, he exalts himself into the chair of wisdom in order to tell us all much that is common knowledge, and much that was unknown even to himself. His satires were so patently cruel that, to some extent, they defeated their own aims. Their very infamy may have served to shield the libeller, for there is little evidence to show that anyone thought less of a man for having come under Pope's lash. 'The Great', as the aristocracy were called, would seem to have spared him less from sportsmanlike or liberal eighteenth-century principles than from a sense of their unassailable superiority.

Moreover, many of them must have appreciated that Pope's attacks were, in some sense, a form of back-handed compliment to themselves. His scorn of 'the Great', Johnson sagely remarked, 'is repeated too often to be real; no man thinks much of that which he despises'.

It is almost certainly true, however, as Strachey points out, that Lady Mary Wortley Montagu and Lord Hervey, by publishing a lampoon in retaliation against Pope in which they emulated his style and substance, betrayed not the contempt that they so boldly asserted, but a profound admiration of his powers. Yet surely, too, it is an exaggeration to claim that *all* Hervey's imitations were 'quite ineffective', 'inept and suicidal'. When, for instance, Pope had written:

> Yes, I am proud, and must be proud to see
> Those not afraid of God afraid of me . . .

Hervey had scored an undoubted point in his reply:

> . . . the great honour of that boast is such,
> That hornets and mad dogs may boast as much.

The second part of his lecture Strachey devoted to pure literary criticism. After repudiating the strictures levelled against Pope by the Victorian critics – Matthew Arnold and Macaulay – he conducts a skilful analysis of Pope's metrical technique, rapidly tracing the birth and evolution of the heroic couplet, from its accidental practice by the Elizabethans up to its apotheosis at the hands of Pope, where it constitutes, so he maintains – in answer to the well-known objection of Arnold – Pope's 'poetic criticism of life'. This idea, which had first occurred to him many years back on a visit to Saltsjöbaden in 1909,[5] is faultlessly argued and expounded. We see how, for instance, a learned accumulation of certain accents and quantities will produce a smooth impression of polish and lucidity; or how a regular alternation of accented and unaccented syllables can give an effect, so well-ordered and scrupulously exact, of wonderful solidity and force.

To complement this analytical inquiry into the machinery of Pope's verse, Strachey then adds a brief section of im-

5. See *Lytton Strachey: A Biography*, p. 423.

pressionistic criticism, which is intended to convey more directly the passionate spirit of his poetry. Surprisingly, perhaps, this is rather less faultless. So as to illustrate that Pope could write with sensuous beauty as well as biting wit, he quotes the line

> Die of a rose in aromatic pain.

'If that is not sensuously beautiful,' he asks, 'what is?' But though the line might be called elegant, or witty, or even perfect in its peculiar manner, it is surely not a good example of *sensuous* beauty. Again, to show that Pope could call up a vision of nature as vibrant as Wordsworth, he unfortunately *misquotes* a famous couplet from *The Dunciad*. Then, in order to demonstrate that Pope could 'compose with his eye on the object' he instances those celebrated lines on the spider from the *Essay on Man*:

> The spider's touch, how exquisitely fine!
> Feels at each thread, and lives along the line.

But since these two lines were stolen almost without alteration from Sir John Davies, they could be advanced with equal weight as evidence in support of the very opposite of Strachey's contention.

For Strachey, the qualities of art – now as in his undergraduate days – were as mysterious as those of the magic ring in the Arabian romances which, in the twinkling of an eye, made beautiful everything it touched. 'The secret springs of art', he had written in a Spectatorial essay on Spenser,[6] 'cannot be sounded with a footrule.' But this, to some extent, is what he had set out to do in his lecture. The mystery, therefore, remained inviolate; and it is almost with exaltation that he finally confesses the secret which first drew him to the poetry of Pope to be as tantalizing as ever. The magical, unexplained fascination lived on. 'The essence of all art is the accomplishment of the impossible,' he declared. 'This cannot be done, we say; and it *is* done. What has happened? A magician has waved his wand . . .

'It is true: Pope *seems* to be actually screaming; but let us

6. 'The Age of Spenser', *Spectator*, 98 (23 March 1907), 457–8.

not mistake. It is only an appearance; actually, Pope is not screaming at all; for these are strange impossible screams, unknown to the world of fact – screams endowed with immortality. What has happened then? Pope has waved his wand. He has turned his screams into poetry, with the enchantment of the heroic couplet.'

Strachey's *Pope* was published in June 1925, sold well, and attracted an unusually wide press coverage for a Leslie Stephen Lecture. Although these reviews were highly favourable, the paper was generally considered to be provocative, and has since more than once been strongly attacked. There seem to be two main reasons for this hostility: a failure to understand the fairly narrow literary theme to which Strachey had tried – admittedly not with complete success – to confine himself; and secondly, despite the publication of *Queen Victoria*, a misconception that anything coming from his pen must be heartless and debunking. For both these reasons the main flow of adverse criticism has been directed only against Strachey's oversimplified view of Pope as a man, not as a poet. Professor George Sherburn incorporated the most extreme case against him in the pedagogic Introduction to his *Selections from Alexander Pope* (1929). Describing Strachey as 'the man who brilliantly ruined the art of biography', he goes on to dispute every opinion advanced in the first part of the lecture. Pope was no peevish or venomous invalid, but a man whose mind war warped into its satiristic mould by the grotesque abnormalities of the eighteenth century. The malignity displayed in some of his verse was thus not innate, as Strachey assumed, but the natural consequence of his reaction to the times. By portraying Pope as a fiendish monkey, Strachey had identified himself with that confederacy of dunces, Pope's victims, who alone of his contemporaries held such a view. Perhaps the less attractive qualities that Strachey attributed to him were in fact more attributable to the satirists of the twentieth century, since 'a satirist who hunts living game is not necessarily less sportsmanlike than one who attacks the dead'.

Slightly more tenable is the rebuke uttered by Sir Edmund Gosse, who complained that Strachey had misled his listeners as to Pope's real personality and had ignored his leading characteristic as a writer – 'loyalty to the dignity of literature'. He was appalled to learn, Gosse continued, that when Strachey spoke of Pope as a fiendish monkey ladling out spoonfuls of boiling oil from an upstairs window upon the passers-by whom the wretch felt he had a grudge against, his Cambridge audience had been delighted, breaking out into laughter. 'If it had been my privilege to be present,' sombrely recorded Gosse, 'I must have buried my face in my hands.'

Gosse's censure of Strachey, inflated into a long article in the *Sunday Times* entitled 'Pope and Mr Lytton Strachey', and later reproduced in a volume of essays, *Leaves and Fruit*, dedicated 'to Lytton Strachey with Affectionate Admiration', is interesting as a last chapter in the vexed relationship between the two biographers, the influence of whose work is closely allied in so many tomes of literary history. Neither really liked the other. Gosse, for his part, concealed his dislike under an array of fine mannerisms designed, quite probably, to promote 'the dignity of literature'. Strachey was less circumspect. On one occasion when something by Gosse was published with his name fatally mis-spelt as 'Edmund Goose', he immediately seized upon it and from then on would refer to him as 'Goose Gosse'. Each, in his dealings with the other, set up something of a double standard between, in Gosse's case, a public and a personal level of communication, and in Strachey's, between his personal attitude and his private reflections. At almost all times a polite façade was kept up between them. When Gosse asked Strachey whether he was an Edwardian, he at once replied: 'I am an Edmundian.' But whereas Gosse reserved his most truculent incivilities for letters to the Press, Strachey discharged his discourtesies into his private correspondence. In his essay on Beddoes, for example, he had referred without comment to Gosse's small edition of Beddoes's letters and credited him with throwing 'additional light upon one important circumstance'. But in a letter to one of his sisters (30 July 1907), he had written: 'I am writing an article on Beddoes for the Quarterly ... Of course the wretched Gosse had managed to trail his slug's mind over the poor man, and has left a slimy track. I shudder to think what Beddoes would have said if he'd foreseen who his editor was to be.' And when Gosse's classic auto-biography, *Father and Son*, was published Strachey observed (January 1908): 'Modern books don't seem to come to much. Mr Gosse's, though, was amusing. ... I'm sure you'd like *it*, though not *him* – he comes out of it rather worse than usual.'

Strachey certainly did not consider Gosse to be a revo-lutionary spirit in the field of biography. Though influenced by French literature, his writing lacked, for all its suavity and ironic poise, true sensibility. No one as pompous as Gosse had any right to be so slapdash and inaccurate.[7] He was, to Strachey's mind, a prolific journeyman of letters, not un-talented, but too close in temper to the hidebound Victorian way of thinking.

Gosse, on the other hand, distrusted Strachey for precisely opposite reasons – the lengths to which he exploited his anti-Victorian bias. The criticism which he wrote of *Eminent Victorians*, incorporated into his essay 'The Agony of the Victorian Age', shows that his real objection was to that streak of raciness which ran through Strachey's work, his undignified cinematographic devices and air of decadence which appealed, in his view, to tastes rooted in cheapness and superficial thinking. He acknowledged Strachey to be clever, and allowed that he possessed gifts of a very unusual order. But he held that Strachey had *misused* these gifts. He abhorred what he termed his 'errors in discretion'. The irritating glibness which was sometimes present in his four deterrent portraits, his atti-tude of hovering superiority, his lack of both sympathy and conventional insight, his intermittent mood of venomous contempt, all these had led him to pass pages that were not simply unjust, but which exhibited the very worst of all liter-ary vices – *impoliteness*.

Their exchange of letters in *The Times Literary Supplement* on the character of Lord Cromer had perfectly reflected their

7. 'The Gosse book is full of interest', Strachey wrote to Max Beer-bohm (15 April 1931). 'I observe that at one point he characteristically gives Swinburne a widow. Luckily Churton Collins is dead.'

opposing personalities and literary modes. But Gosse had found the author of *Queen Victoria* far closer to his way of thinking. This book, he insisted, was 'a riper, a more finely balanced, a more reasonable study than its predecessors'. He was particularly gratified that Strachey now paid him the compliment, admittedly unintentional, of quoting a number of times from the brief and cautious monograph of the queen contributed anonymously by him to *The Quarterly Review* of April 1901.

Although Strachey's remarks about Gosse in conversation with his friends were almost always derogatory, several of the alterations which he made to the essays appearing in *Books and Characters* were designed to show Gosse in a fractionally less distasteful light. Strachey had sent Gosse a complimentary copy of this volume, but Gosse did not review it. Instead he answered Strachey in a friendly, conciliatory letter thanking him for his kindness and courtesy, and congratulating him on a very lively and pertinent collection. Now safely in his seventies, Gosse added that Strachey was 'the best writer under fifty'.

With his criticism of the Leslie Stephen Lecture, Gosse defined more precisely still his dual attitude towards Strachey. As a biographer, he felt him to be continually in danger of indulging in uncomplimentary and vulgar bad taste; as a literary critic, preferably limiting himself to questions of syntax and philology, he was excellent.

'Also it is said you are getting up a subscription to give Edmund Gosse gold sleevelinks on his 100th birthday', Virginia Woolf mischievously wrote to Strachey in January 1926. But two years later, in only his eightieth year, Gosse died, and his powerful position as leading critic on the *Sunday Times* was taken over by Strachey's old friend and ally, Desmond MacCarthy.

2

PORTRAITS IN MINIATURE

By 1931, Strachey had reached a much-envied yet not altogether enviable stage in his career. It was almost impossible for him to increase his reputation, and extremely difficult for him to maintain it. There are two stages in the career of every successful author which may be labelled crucial. The one occurs when his work has been so long before the public that reviewers have grown tired of pointing out its merits, while inferior imitators – of whom Strachey had very many – have made them sick of his methods; and the other, when he first emerges from being the idol of a small group to become the property of the big common world.

In Strachey's case, these two stages had followed close upon one another. Nothing so cools the ardour of early admirers as hearing their applause amplified by others. When *Elizabeth and Essex* appeared, not a few of his most fervid devotees declared themselves disappointed. It was after this book, which contained some of the most original pages he had ever written, that, for the first time, the question was seriously debated as to whether, after all, he was a first-rate writer. A Renaissance subject had not stimulated his gift for ironic description, for diminishing the stature of his heroes. And there was another reason why this exciting and, in places, beautiful biography was not, in 1931, well looked upon by the critics. It had sold. In thousands, in tens and hundreds of thousands, it had sold. The time was therefore ripe for a steep critical recoil from Strachey's work. But his next book, a collection of eighteen essays, partly forestalled this response. For one thing, it seemed too slight a volume on which to launch such a major reaction. It was his least important and most amusing book. So, though there was a rather sour taste in some of the notices, antagonistic reviewers were content to tell their readers of the limited appeal of Strachey's subjects – a gathering of forgotten eccentrics, most of them, about whom these brief sketches could only serve as footnotes to history.

The vignettes which made up *Portraits in Miniature* had begun coming out in the *Nation and Athenaeum* during the autumn of 1923. On 22 February 1927 Strachey wrote to Charles Prentice: 'I find that I have now written ten of the short biographical studies which I have been contributing to the "Nation" for the last few years. Whitworth at one time suggested publishing them, and it now occurs to me that if I added two more this might be done ... The quality of the whole seems to me satisfactory; and as to the quantity, it is possible that a small volume of such things makes a better authentic whole – less monotonous and emphatic – than a big one.' But Prentice feared that a book of this kind might then interfere with the sales of *Elizabeth and Essex*, which he expected to bring out at Christmas. Then, several months after the biography had been published, Prentice suggested that he might bring out a little booklet entitled *Six English Historians*. Strachey, however, considered this a 'horrid' idea, and eventually a compromise was reached in the form of a volume containing in its first section the twelve biographical papers originally suggested by Strachey in 1927, followed by a separate section devoted to the six historians, and collectively entitled *Portraits in Miniature and Other Essays*.[8]

From the end of November, Strachey was 'plunged into the literary business' of preparing this book. Unlike *Books and Characters*, these essays needed few emendations, and his chief business seems to have been, with the aid of *Roget's Thesaurus*, weeding out the 'deliciousnesses' and 'indefatigables' that were peppered over the pages, and inserting various fancy blooms in their place. By the end of January he had finished these corrections, and two months later received the proofs 'which looked rather nice'. It was only a very small work, he warned Roger Senhouse (20 March 1931). 'I think of writing a book moulded on Malinovsky,[9] called "the Sexual Life of the English", it would be a remarkable work, but no doubt would have to be published in New Guinea. In the meantime "Portraits in Miniature" is progressing in its tamer

8. Earlier titles which Strachey considered include *Little Lives* and *Six Historians, and Other Essays*. To Dadie Rylands he wrote (26 November 1930): 'I have at last decided to bring out a book of Collected Monstrosities in the spring – and have to write some to collect. At the best it will be a tiny wisp of an affair. "Jewels five words long" might be a good title – culled from your favourite poet.'

9. Bronislaw Malinovsky (1884–1942), the Anglo-Polish anthropologist, whose *The Sexual Life of Savages in North-Western Melanesia* had just been published.

fashion. I've corrected the proofs, and now only have to settle which is the least repellent of the specimen covers for binding.'

Portraits in Miniature and Other Essays was published that May simultaneously in two editions – a limited one of two hundred and sixty copies (of which two hundred and fifty were for sale) signed by Strachey and costing two guineas; and an ordinary one priced at six shillings, of which eight thousand copies were sold in Britain within the first eight weeks. The volume was dedicated, 'with gratitude and admiration', to Max Beerbohm, and, as always, the dedication was exactly appropriate. Strachey's miniatures were painted with a precise delicacy and lightness of touch that is nicely comparable to Max's subtle and ironic art. Max himself was delighted by this compliment. 'I feel immensely proud that you should dedicate a book to me', he replied with characteristic over-modesty (21 March 1931) to Strachey's letter asking for his permission. 'Much older though I am than you, my admiration for your prose, since first I knew it, has had the fresh wild hot quality that belongs rather to a very young man's feeling for the work of a great congenial veteran. I have always felt, and shall always feel, such a duffer and fumbler in comparison with you. But I shall be better able to disguise this feeling when my eye shall have seen my name in your book.'

As an epigraph to this collection, Strachey quoted Horace:

> *Est brevitate opus, ut currat sententia, neu se*
> *Impediat verbis lassas onerantibus aures.*

The eighteen studies which follow are all constructed with the terseness and control that Horace declared necessary for effective satire. The miniature essay is one of the most difficult of literary techniques. The usual compromise between form and matter is either to leave it empty or to chatter for two thousand words or so about a series of haphazard points, and then stop. But for Strachey, this was the perfect vehicle for his talent. With the greatest tact and craft he compresses within each cameo a serried mass of biographical facts that merge into an immaculate unity of design. Though the pace apparently remains unhurried, almost leisurely at times, the manner is invariably crisp, the effect of each story, in its few brilliant pages, taut and absorbing. He uses two principal methods of construction. Either, as in the first piece, 'Sir John Harington',[10] he telescopes into ten minutes' reading the whole biography of his subject; or – as in 'The President de Brosses'[11] – he takes as his *motif* a dramatic quarrel and groups round this everything else of significance. The focus is always upon small matters, but within the narrow limits prescribed by this form, his treatment, despite its surface impression of ease and simplicity, manages to suggest far more than it actually states.

These miniature essays present the most natural expression of one side of Strachey's personality. Like A. E. Housman, he 'is content to reign over a tiny kingdom',[12] behind whose frontiers he can display his most characteristic mannerisms. Peculiarity is one of the themes that he constantly exploits. He accentuates the amusing, the extraordinary and the trifling. He makes use of eccentric situations and grotesque physical circumstances in a way that achieves striking effects but sometimes lacks the creative intensity that really penetrates through the habits and appearances of men to the human truth within.

The first section of *Portraits in Miniature* contains a dozen papers on obscure pedants, antiquaries, scientists, sectaries, biographers and other oddities. Strachey delights in bringing out the weird contrasts and paradoxes thrown up by the careers of such men, and eagerly welcomes any departure from conformity. In particular he excels in academic satire. His accounts of 'The Life, Illness, and Death of Dr North'[13] and

10. *Nation and Athenaeum*, 34 (17 November 1923), 271–2; *New Republic*, 37 (28 November 1923), 12–13. Reprinted in *Portraits in Miniature* and later collected in *Biographical Essays* (1–5).

11. *New Statesman and Nation* (11, 18 April 1931), 250–51, 281–2; *New Republic*, 66 (22 April 1931), 267–70. Reprinted in *Portraits in Miniature* and collected in *Biographical Essays* (112–21).

12. 'Modern Poetry', *Spectator*, 100 (18 April 1908), 622–3.

13. *Nation and Athenaeum*, 40 (19 February 1927), 694–5; *New Re-*

'The Sad Story of Dr Colbatch'[14] are small masterpieces of historical burlesque. With much literary malice, there was no spite or malevolence in his art. It is the comic spirit that is triumphant. He stares at the human farce with unblinking amazement, and crystallizes his astonished observations in short, pungent sentences that are all the more effective for their tranquil understatement. Sometimes he finds no need for comment of his own at all, as for example, when he quotes Dr North's remark: 'Of all the Beasts of the Field, God Almighty thought Woman the fittest Companion for Man.'

In very many of these essays there is a tone of real geniality. The very excess and remoteness of his subjects' abnormality robs Strachey of his anti-religious zeal. Poor Lodowick Muggleton, that tiny prophetic solipsist, crazy rather than eccentric, an incomprehensible priest without craft or congregation, he sees not as a frenzied oppressor of mankind but a victim of the world's strains and tribulations, badgered by the small persecutions of authority, condemned to the pillory at the age of sixty-eight when 'he was badly mauled, for it so happened that the crowd was hostile and pelted the old man with stones'. And at the end, his narrative is suffused with tenderness, and he can find words of ironic praise for the diminishing band of Muggleton's followers. His capital letters draw attention to a real if amused charity of spirit. 'Two hundred and fifty Muggletonians followed him to the grave, and their faith has been handed down, unimpaired through the generations, from that day to this. Still, in the very spot where their founder was born, the chosen few meet together to celebrate the two festivals of their religion – the Great Holiday, on the anniversary of the delivery of the Word to Reeve, and the Little Holiday, on the day of Muggleton's final release from prison.

---

public, 50 (9 March 1927), 67–9. Reprinted in *Portraits in Miniature* and collected in *Biographical Essays* (17–22).

14. *Nation and Athenaeum,* 34 (22 December 1923), 459–60; *New Republic*, 37 (26 December 1923), 115–16. Reprinted in *Portraits in Miniature* and collected in *Biographical Essays* (28–33).

> I do believe in God alone,
> Likewise in Reeve and Muggleton.

So they have sung for more than two hundred years. . . . It is an exclusive faith, certainly; and yet, somehow or other, it disarms criticism. Even though one may not be of the elect oneself, one cannot but wish it well; one would be sorry if the time ever came when there were no more Muggletonians. Besides, one is happy to learn that with the passage of years they have grown more gentle. Their terrible offensive weapon – which, in early days, they wielded so frequently – has fallen into desuetude: no longer do they pass sentence of eternal damnation. The dreaded doom was pronounced for the last time on a Swedenborgian, with great effect, in the middle of the nineteenth century.'[15]

At first sight these miscellaneous papers, on all sorts of unusual people, seem to possess no particular adhesive unity. One is entertained so much by the stories and squabbles that it is only afterwards that one becomes aware of a thread which runs through all of them – a line tracing, from the Elizabethan to the Victorian age, the evolution of modern society. The career of Sir John Harington reflects perfectly the alternating whimsicality and danger mixed with impropriety that characterized Elizabethan times. That of Muggleton exhibits the unparalleled self-assertiveness which the human mind attained about the year 1650, when the disintegration of religious authority reached its culminating point. 'If one were asked to choose a date for the beginning of the modern world', Strachey wrote,[16] 'probably July 15, 1662, would be best to fix upon. For on that day the Royal Society was founded, and the place of Science in civilization became a definite and recognized thing.' The lives of John Aubrey and Dr North are both advanced to bear out this contention. Dr North, a

15. *Nation and Athenaeum*, 35 (26 July 1924), 534–5; *New Republic*, 39 (30 July 1924), 265–7. Reprinted in *Portraits in Miniature* and collected in *Biographical Essays* (6–10).

16. 'John Aubrey', *Nation and Athenaeum*, 33 (15 September 1923), 741–2; *New Republic*, 36 (10 October 1923) 176–8. Reprinted in *Portraits in Miniature* and collected in *Biographical Essays* (11–16).

member of the old dispensation, whose ideas were rapidly becoming obsolete, is depicted as an almost pathologically inadequate Master of Trinity. Aubrey, on the other hand, is represented as belonging partly to the old world, partly to the new. 'His insatiable passion for singular odds and ends had a meaning in it,' Strachey explains; 'he was groping towards a scientific ordering of phenomena; but the twilight of his age was too confusing, and he could rarely distinguish between a fact and a fantasy. He was clever enough to understand the Newtonian system, but he was not clever enough to understand that a horoscope was an absurdity; and so, in his crowded curiosity-shop of a brain, astronomy and astrology both found a place, and were given equal values.'

Unwinding this central thread, Strachey next reconstructs the argument that flared up between Congreve and Jeremy Collier[17] and which he presents as being symptomatic of an age in which the mysterious requirements of dogmatic theology obscured all discussion of ethics and aesthetics. By introducing Macaulay's later version of this affair, Strachey also touches upon certain changes in attitude and style brought about by the Industrial Revolution. In 'Madame de Sévigné's Cousin'[18] we are shown the first signs of putrefaction, the *rigor mortis* of the great epoch of Louis XIV; while 'The Sad Story of Dr Colbatch' illustrates very well the preposterous academic life carried on during the early years of the eighteenth century, 'agitated, violent and full of extremes. Everything about it was on the grand scale. Erudition was gigantic, controversies were frenzied, careers were punctuated by brutal triumphs, wild temerities, and dreadful mortifications.'

In the following essay, 'The Président de Brosses', Strachey takes us across to eighteenth-century France. The theme of this study is a quarrel about firewood. First, in a few charming sentences, Strachey reminds us of a 'sometimes forgotten

17. 'Congreve, Collier, and Macaulay', *Nation and Athenaeum*, 34 (13 October 1923), 56–8; *New Republic*, 36 (21 November 1923), 335–6. Reprinted in *Portraits in Miniature* and collected in *Literary Essays* (53–7).

18. *Nation and Athenaeum* (4 October 1924), 14–15; *New Republic*, 40 (8 October 1924), 141–2. Reprinted in *Portraits in Miniature* and collected in *Biographical Essays* (23–7).

feature of the world as it used to be before the age of trains and telephones'. In those days there were provincial capitals, 'centres of local civilization'. The Président de Brosses was the great man of Dijon, the capital of Burgundy. Brosses' ambition, we are told, was to become a member of the French Academy, one of 'the forty immortals'. After Voltaire had settled at Ferney, he bought from the Président the neighbouring estate of Tournay. But he was not pleased with his bargain, since the cut firewood on it had already been sold to a peasant called Charlot Baudy. Voltaire, a shivery old mortal by this time, used a good deal of fuel, but he was outraged when a bill for 281 francs for wood from off his own estate was presented to him by Baudy. A prolonged and absurd argument broke out, in the telling of which we get to hear about the character of the Président, and come to understand how Voltaire's virulent vindictiveness, and the ferocious energy he flung into this trivial episode, implied a microscopic concentration upon everything connected with himself, and a feverish sense of its utmost importance. We also learn, almost incidentally, something of the relations of the provincial way of life to the central life of France in the mid-eighteenth century.

In each miniature, Strachey transforms his sitter into one of those characters in comedy who is there neither to instruct us nor to exalt us, but simply to amuse. But he also blends each character with some sympathetically glimpsed aspect of the age in which he lived. 'The Abbé Morellet',[19] for instance, is an essay designed to elucidate the meaning of Talleyrand's remark that only those who had lived in France before the Revolution had really experienced *la douceur de vivre*. Mary Berry, the friend of Horace Walpole and Thackeray, provides a curious transition-scene bridging the eighteenth century and the Victorian age. And the story of 'Madame de Lieven',[20] the

19. *Nation and Athenaeum*, 34 (26 January 1924), 602–3; *New Republic*, 37 (13 February 1924), 265–7. Reprinted in *Portraits in Miniature* and collected in *Biographical Essays* (133–8).

20. *Saturday Review of Literature*, 7 (18 April 1931), 748–9; *Life and Letters*, 6 (April 1931), 247–58. Reprinted in *Portraits in Miniature* and collected in *Biographical Essays* (219–28).

last of the Portraits in Miniature, symbolizes for Strachey the final capitulation under Victoria of the magnificent aristocratic qualities that he had so greatly admired in their full bloom in the sixteenth century. He begins: 'Aristocrats (no doubt) still exist; but they are shorn beings, for whom the wind is not tempered – powerless, out of place, and slightly ridiculous. For about a hundred years it has been so ... Madame de Lieven was one of the supreme examples of the final period. Her manners were of the genuinely terrific kind. Surrounded by them, isolated as with an antiseptic spray, she swept on triumphantly, to survive untouched – so it seemed – amid an atmosphere alive with the microbes of bourgeois disintegration. So it seemed – for in fact something strange eventually happened.' This strange something was a liaison with Monsieur Guizot, the living epitome of all that was most middle-class. 'The crash came on June 24, 1837', wrote Strachey, ' – the date is significant: it was four days after the accession of Queen Victoria.' Yet after the death of the prince, her husband, Madame de Lieven did not marry Guizot. 'Was this the last resistance of the aristocrat?' Strachey asks. 'Or was it perhaps, in reality, the final proof that Madame de Lieven was an aristocrat no longer?'

Preferring his specimens dried and pinned, Strachey approached no nearer to the contemporary world. Since the 1830s the aristocracy had been virtually dead, the last barricade swept away. For this, and for other reasons, *Portraits in Miniature* is the obverse of *Eminent Victorians* – a work of elegant sentiment rather than virulent propaganda. The men he examines are mostly very far from being thought of as eminent. Inhabitants of a dwindling civilization, their prestige and influence had disappeared with them, not lingering on to vex the twentieth century. Their butterfly careers illustrate the waywardness of the human spirit, the frustrated offshoots and cul-de-sacs of ambition. And since their reputations have lapsed, their faiths decayed, their arguments been buried in the dust, they may be treated with a disinterested amusement, an irony that is lenient, not vindictive. Like some of the minor characters in *Eminent Victorians* – Newman and Sidney Herbert

– like Albert or even Essex, the men appear to be more fragile beings than the women in the book: they seem crazier, more vulnerable. Mainly they are eccentric little gentlemen, with a tendency to gossip, and some esoteric talent distorted by a variety of social and biological disturbances. It was their queerness that fascinated Strachey, and we seldom see them so vividly as when, in the course of their mincing gait, they trip over the train of some great lady.

As in all his books, it is the conflict between the power-loving masculine side and the submissive feminine side of his characters that exercises Strachey's imagination most strongly. Usually it is the men who are most submissive and effeminate. The women belong to that special matriarchal type, virile and substantial, that held him in such awe: Mary Berry, for example, whose fate was the very reverse of Madame du Deffand's, the emotional tragedy coming at the beginning of a long life instead of at the end. 'And yet, in the structure of their minds, the two were curiously similar', Strachey noted. 'Both were remarkable for reason and good sense, for a certain intellectual probity, for a disillusioned view of things, and for great strength of will. Between these two stern women, the figure of Horace Walpole makes a strange appearance – a creature all vanity, elegance, in-sinuation, and finesse – by far the most feminine of the three.'

It was the *stamina*, the tremendous frustrated potency of these women, that Strachey enshrined. Like their prototype, Lady Strachey, they all lived to a great age – Lady Hester Stanhope and Madame de Lieven, the two youngest, died at sixty-four; Queen Elizabeth and Madame du Deffand at seventy or more; Queen Victoria at eighty-two; Mary Berry at eighty-nine; Florence Nightingale at ninety. Of these, only Flor-ence Nightingale survived into the Edwardian age, and her terrific energies alone broke out of the social and diplomatic spheres traditionally assigned to women. She was the eagle, and the rest were swans. For in the days before 1850, the great world was still a small and immaculate place, and women were debarred from major roles in life. There was nothing that

Mary Berry could not bring about in her drawing-room, Strachey tells us,[21] but 'her masculine mind exercised itself over higher things ... Had she been a man, she would not have shone as a writer, but as a political thinker or an administrator; and a man she should have been; with her massive, practical intelligence, she was born too early to be a successful woman. She felt this bitterly. Conscious of high powers, she declaimed against the miserable estate of women, which prevented her from using them. She might have been a towering leader, in thought or action; as it was, she was insignificant. So she said – "insignificant!" – repeating the word over and over again. "And nobody," she added, "ever suffered insignificance more unwillingly than myself".'

It was a similar story with Madame de Lieven, who, as an ambassadress, 'was endowed with social talents of the highest order', whose passion was for high diplomacy, who had a finger in every political pie, but whose actual influence, as Strachey demonstrates, was negligible. She might be 'the terror of the embassies', yet the force of her personality was magnificently irrelevant to serious embassy affairs. Her influence was confined to society. And it is principally as society hostesses that Strachey venerates this prepotent breed of women, within their *salons* brilliantly enhancing and intensifying the charm of life. They were the sort of imperious super-females whom he had searched for in vain in his own age; for compared with them, Lady Desborough and the Duchess of Marlborough, Lady Astor and Lady Cunard, poor dear old Ottoline and all the rest of that sorry crew were only pale imitations, 'shorn beings, for whom the wind is not tempered – powerless, out of place, and slightly ridiculous'.

In his paper on John Aubrey, Strachey had declared: 'A biography should either be as long as Boswell's or as short as Aubrey's. The method of enormous and elaborate accretion which produced the *Life of Johnson* is excellent, no doubt; but, failing that, let us have no half-measures; let us have the

21. 'Mary Berry', *Nation and Athenaeum*, 36 (21 March 1925), 856–8; *New Republic*, 42 (1 April 1925), 152–4. Reprinted in *Portraits in Miniature* and collected in *Biographical Essays* (204–10).

pure essentials – a vivid image, on a page or two, without explanations, transitions, commentaries, or padding.' Strachey's miniatures are themselves almost of Aubreyan length and split-second focus. He did in a polished form what Aubrey had done sketchily, giving the essential lines of a life, a character in a few swift pictures and penetrating phrases. But, as works of art, the historians, which make up the last third of the book, are less perfect, for it was impossible to deal adequately with these great and complex men by employing such a small-scale technique. His tendency to presume that the most absurd statements a man utters are the most revealing, is excellent for a preposterous oddity like Muggleton, but it is less suitable for a Macaulay. He has space to exhibit only one facet of each historian – the detachment of Hume, the balance of Gibbon, the philistinism of Macaulay, the morality of Carlyle, the provincial protestantism of his disciple Froude, and, finally, the ever-dry, patient, sober scholarship of Mandell Creighton. The effect of this one-dimensional treatment is, in some instances, to caricature and, unwittingly, to distort the true likeness of his subjects.

Strachey's special aptitude for judging historians by their peculiarities and literary style, though interesting, is sometimes too restrictive. As if in acknowledgement of this, he adds some of the commentary and explanation specifically excluded by him from among the pure essentials of the Aubreyan technique, which he then attempts to offset by an exaggerated lightness of touch. The five-hundred-word satirical account he gives in 'Froude'[22] of the quarrel between Professor Freeman and Mr Horace Round is as amusing as any of the other agitated academic disputes in the first section of the book. It harmonizes well with the mood and tone of these earlier pieces; but it is a disproportionate digression in a miniature essay on the historian, and, strictly speaking, an aesthetic blemish.

22. Originally published under the title 'One of the Victorians', *Life and Letters*, 5 (December 1930), 431–8; *Saturday Review of Literature*, 7 (6 December 1930) 418–19. Reprinted as 'Froude' in *Portraits in Miniature* and collected in *Biographical Essays* (257–63).

'Mr Horace Round, a "burrower into wormholes" living in Brighton, suddenly emerged from the parchments among which he spent his life deliciously gnawing at the pedigrees of the proudest families in England, and in a series of articles fell upon Freeman with astonishing force ... The effect of these articles on Freeman was alarming; his blood boiled, but he positively made no reply. For years the attacks continued, and for years the professor was dumb. Fulminating rejoinders rushed into his brain, only to be whisked away again – they were not quite fulminating enough. The most devastating article of all was written, was set up in proof, but was not yet published ... Freeman was aghast at this last impertinence; but still he nursed his wrath. Like King Lear, he would do such things – what they were yet he knew not – but they should be the terrors of the earth. At last, silent and purple, he gathered his female attendants about him, and left England for an infuriated holiday. There was an ominous pause; and then the fell news reached Brighton. The professor had gone pop in Spain.'

No other passage in the whole of *Portraits in Miniature* so stirred the feelings of the reviewers. Strachey, it was considered, this time had really gone too far. The culminating sentence of this dreadful description of Freeman's death was heartless – it was worse: it was *bad taste*. Strachey himself could hardly have felt more pleased by this outraged response. Recently he had come to fear that he might be fossilizing from the original lively saboteur of *Eminent Victorians* into a respectable literary institution. Even the latest attacks on his works had treated him almost as an established classic. One reviewer had already suggested that he should be awarded the Nobel Prize for Literature. Soon, if he did not take precautions, he would solidify into a well-loved, grand old man of letters. To avoid this fate, he particularly wanted to offend the successors of men like Freeman, his modern counterparts among the academic historians of the 1930s. And here he seems to have been reasonably successful. Shortly after 'Froude' appeared in *Life and Letters*, he wrote off happily to Roger Senhouse (17 December 1930): 'Virginia had just met Lord Esher who had told her that *he* had just met George Trevelyan, who was foaming at the mouth with rage. – "Really! I should never have believed that a writer of L.S.'s standing would use an expression like that – went pop!" So some effect has been produced, which is something.'

These six essays on English historians enable Strachey to expound his doctrine that history, like biography, should be an art. With their literary rather than historical emphasis, the essays are particularly original for the relationship they suggest between Strachey himself and his subjects. With Hume,[23] whom he greatly admired, he shared both inferior health and an inner restlessness of spirit – disruptive influences which were regulated in such a way that they never damaged the clarity and elegance of the writing. But by claiming for Hume the historical detachment that he liked to assume himself, as a literary manner, he muddled the philosopher with the historian. So far from being 'absolutely free from temporal considerations', Hume's history, as Desmond MacCarthy has pointed out, is an easy, lucid and entirely Tory pamphlet.

Strachey's style, in any case, had more in common with that of Gibbon. For both of them, physically ill-equipped to command a life of action, style became a form of power. But, as with Hume, Strachey overplays a single aspect of Gibbon's attitude – in this case, an imperturbable balance – to the point of biographical inaccuracy. Blandly he presents us with an *insouciant* Gibbon who totally neglected his fatal disease, whereas the truth appears to be that he lived in terror of it. Strachey himself seems to echo this doubtful *insouciance*. Obviously feeling the medical diagnosis to be inappropriate for a light magazine essay, he is unspecific as to the nature of the disease, merely drawing our attention to the ano-pubic region of the body – 'a protuberance in the lower part of his person'.[24]

23. 'Hume', *Nation and Athenaeum*, 42 (7 January 1928), 536–8. Reprinted in *Portraits in Miniature* and collected in *Biographical Essays* (43–9).

24. 'Gibbon', *Nation and Athenaeum*, 42 (14 January 1928), 565–7. Reprinted in *Portraits in Miniature* and collected in *Biographical Essays* (139–46).

Strachey's sketch of Froude's life reads like the biography of Queen Victoria in miniature, especially in his unconscious search for a father-substitute to satisfy his craving for authority. There was much in Froude's career to stir Strachey's sympathy. There existed some parallel in their ill, overgrown, miserable schooldays and their subsequent need for a simplifying parental relationship. There was some affinity, too, in their writing. Strachey's exposition of Elizabeth's political policy in *Elizabeth and Essex* had closely resembled Froude's own conclusion. His opinion of Froude was more complex than that of the other historians, and makes for a finely proportioned evaluation of his work. He notes the use of narrative drama sometimes raised into melodrama, of a romantic strain, and the bias which gives a spice to his prose, 'a cheap spice – bought, one feels, at the Co-operative Stores'. And in his concluding estimate of Froude's work he writes: 'A certain narrowness of thought and feeling: that may be forgiven, if it is expressed in a style of sufficient mastery. Froude was an able, a brilliant writer, copious and vivid, with a picturesque imagination and a fine command of narrative . . . the extraordinary succession of events assumes, as it flows through his pages, the thrilling lineaments of a great story, upon whose issue the most *blasé* reader is forced to hang entranced. Yet the supreme quality of style seems to be lacking . . . Perhaps, after all, it is the intellect and the emotion that are at fault here too; perhaps when one is hoping for genius, it is only talent – only immense talent – that one finds.'

What Strachey found it hard to forgive was Froude's adoption of Carlyle as a second father. His naïve and submissive acceptance of the crude Puritan dogmas propounded by that keeper of the Victorian conscience encouraged his worst qualities for a historian – insensitivity, distortion and an over-emphasis upon the momentousness of human action. Towards Hume and Gibbon, Strachey had extended an unmixed sympathy, relishing the similarity he discovered between himself and them. Towards Carlyle and Macaulay, whose likeness to himself was less gratifying, he was correspondingly less sympathetic. For this reason, he was at pains, when dealing with the first pair, to stress one primary quality that distinguished his own style; while, with the latter two, he brings out characteristics – moral dogma and philistinism – that were clearly absent from his own writing.

As the embodiment of biblical Victorian fervour, whose egotism marred his poetic genius, Carlyle exasperated Strachey, and his inspired bravura sentence on 'that most peculiar age'[25] – the star passage of Georgian condemnation of the Victorian jungle – is uncharacteristic of the rest of this volume, belonging more fittingly to *Eminent Victorians*. Abandoning his customary tone of persiflage for the rhetoric of satire, he scales up a crescendo of righteous irony. It was, he tells us, 'an age of barbarism and prudery, of nobility and cheapness, of satisfaction and desperation; an age in which everything was discovered and nothing known; an age in which all the outlines were tremendous and all the details sordid; when gas-jets struggled feebly through the circumambient fog, when the hour of dinner might be at any moment between two and six, when the doses of rhubarb were periodic and gigantic, when pet dogs threw themselves out of upper storey windows, when cooks reeled drunk in areas, when one sat for hours with one's feet in dirty straw dragged along the street by horses, when an antimacassar was on every chair, and the baths were minute tin circles, and the beds were full of bugs and disasters.'

The philistinism of Macaulay is made more ruthless to Strachey by his apparent inability to experience love. The barrenness of Macaulay's prose style conveys only too well the absence in his make-up of any intense physical emotion, just as the loss of identity implicit in Strachey's love-affairs makes itself felt in the thinness, the lack of tangible expansive warmth in his more romantic passages. 'And it is noticeable', Strachey points out,[26] 'how far more effective he [Macaulay] is

25. 'Carlyle', *Nation and Athenaeum*, 42 (28 January 1928), 646–8. Reprinted in *Portraits in Miniature* and collected in *Biographical Essays* (249–56).

26. 'Macaulay', *Nation and Athenaeum*, 42 (21 January 1928), 596–7. Reprinted in *Portraits in Miniature* and collected in *Literary Essays* (195–201).

in his treatment of those whom he dislikes than of those whom he admires ... Macaulay's inability to make his hero live – his refusal to make any attempt to illuminate the mysteries of that most obscure and singular character – epitomises all that is weakest in his work.' How well Strachey understood the mechanism of Macaulay's writing, for it involved a technique substantially similar to his own. Both of them excelled at vivid characterization and story-telling. 'History', Strachey wrote, 'is primarily a narrative, and in power of narration no one has ever surpassed Macaulay. In that he is a genius. When it comes to telling a story, his faults disappear or change into virtues. Narrowness becomes clarity, and crudity turns into force. The rhetoric of the style, from being the ornament of platitude, becomes the servant of excitement. Every word is valuable: there is no hesitation, no confusion, and no waste ... Unsatisfying characters, superficial descriptions, jejune reflections, are seen to be no longer of importance in themselves – they are merely stages in the development of the narrative. They are part of the pattern – the enthralling, ever-shifting pattern of the perfect kaleidoscope.'

As the most obscure and pedagogic of these 'Six English Historians', Mandell Creighton,[27] the last of them, might have been better placed in the first section of the book, alongside 'The Sad Story of Dr Colbatch' and 'The Life, Illness, and Death of Dr North'. In the manner of these earlier miniatures, Strachey uses Creighton's personality and career to illustrate some peculiar social facet of the times – in this case the dual Anglican tradition of scholarship and administrative energy, of which Creighton was the last exponent of a long line stretching from Whitgift to Jowett. He respected Creighton's gift for the clear exposition of complicated political transactions and the intricate movements of thought with which they were connected, and also his refusal to be stampeded by popular contemporary sentiment. But he could not warm to him. A supremely conventional man and an anaemic per-

27. 'Mandell Creighton', New York *Herald Tribune Books* (28 May 1929); *Life and Letters*, 2 (June 1929). Reprinted in *Portraits in Miniature* and collected in *Biographical Essays* (273–80) under the title 'Creighton'.

sonality, Creighton was without humour, and his writing without romance. Yet, as Strachey knew well, there are no greater figures of fun than people lacking in humour. The unamazed moderation with which Creighton dissected the worst atrocities of the Inquisition was laughably incongruous. And then, what an antiquated figure he cut, this Bishop of London, with his glinting gold spectacles, his dapper episcopal gaiters, his grizzled beard and bald forehead, gravely examining the novels of Mrs Humphry Ward and setting the teacups tinkling in Fulham with his academic paradoxes. Everything human and endearing within him had been suppressed. He was an abstract entity. Dryness was his chief quality as a historian, dryness and sobriety. Yet, in the conduct of his incombustible life, there was one faint spark of that preposterous eighteenth-century world of learning so well represented by that other reverend scholar, Dr Colbatch. Strachey hints at this resemblance between the two men by employing in his studies of them an identical technique, repeating at the very end of his monograph the previous topmost note of ridicule, the most absurd single utterance, now made more absurd still for being re-quoted out of context, shrill, insistent, bewildered – 'Arrogat, my Lord!' and 'Where's my black bag?'

Strachey was a master of beginnings and endings. *Portraits in Miniature* enabled him to exploit to the full his skill in the description of death-beds. Never did an author arrange so anxiously for the demise of his characters, or see to it that their last moments should be so typical. Where the original living portrait has been slightly distorted, then, for consistency, slight nuances have to be added to these death-bed scenes. Gibbon, for example: 'Life seemed as charming as usual', Strachey wrote. 'Next morning, getting out of bed for a necessary moment, "Je suis plus adroit," he said with his odd smile to his French valet. Back in bed again, he muttered something more, a little incoherently, lay back among the pillows, dozed, half-woke, dozed again, and became unconscious – for ever.' Lord Sheffield's statement, on which Strachey based this description, is: 'At about half past eight, he got out of bed, and got into bed again without assistance, better than usual.' The small differences – the addition of an 'odd smile', the omission of the words 'better than usual,' serve to suggest a man still philosophically happy, well-coordinated, self-sufficient. His end is an orderly, peaceful descent into unconsciousness. We are not told that he was frightened of being left alone, that after returning to his bed he twice implored his servant to stay with him, for such details disturbed the impression of impervious sang-froid. The dying man is a form of aesthetic decoration. Yet Strachey is far from unfeeling, and he describes the last days of Hume – which in many essentials would closely resemble his own slow death – in words that carry a restrained expression of the pathos of human destiny: 'In 1776, when Hume was sixty-five, an internal complaint, to which he had long been subject, completely undermined his health, and recovery became impossible. For many months he knew he was dying, but his mode of life remained unaltered, and, while he gradually grew weaker, his cheerfulness continued unabated. With ease, with gaiety, with the simplicity of perfect taste, he gently welcomed the inevitable. This wonderful equanimity lasted till the very end.'

After the publication of *Portraits in Miniature* during the last summer of his life, Strachey began 'a thing on Othello' which, he told Roger Senhouse, was 'fiendishly difficult to do, as it's all solid argument – and is perhaps rather mad; but I shall try to finish it'. 'Othello', which was never finished but appeared in its uncompleted form in the posthumous volume, *Characters and Commentaries*,[28] was planned as the first of a series of essays upon some of Shakespeare's plays. Perhaps because of his failing strength, it is a sadly disappointing piece of work, inferior by far to his 'Shakespeare's Final Period'. After many years he had returned from biography to literary criticism as a refuge from illness and the disillusion of love, with the result that there is little sense of human reality in this

28. *Characters and Commentaries* (308–15). Reprinted in *Literary Essays* (24–30).

essay. It is literary criticism written to an inanimate formula, an inorganic thing, which suffers from the method of coming to premature aesthetic conclusions, and arguing in odds and ends afterwards, often ingeniously, to fit in with them.

The 'solid argument' of 'Othello' has at its centre the concept of dramatic necessity. Shakespeare, as we know, went for his plot to the seventh story in the third decade of Cinthio's *Hecatommithi*. But was it not possible, Strachey asks, that he also deliberately submitted himself to the Greek theatrical influence? Cinthio's story was bleak and colourless; the salient features of *Othello* were its passion and strong characterization. The reason for this difference, Strachey suggests, may have been due to Shakespeare having studied Sophocles. Ignoring the fiery and intensely personal love-poem which runs through this play, its power released by a deep longing for some ideal unflawed beauty, and confining himself absolutely to its constructive principles, Strachey then draws a parallel between the basic scheme of *Othello* and that of *Oedipus Tyrannus*. The dramatic requirements of Oedipus' situation were, he explains, naturally not identical with those needed for the different plan of Shakespeare's tragedy. But he makes his comparison by noting how the incidental similarity and contrast between the two principal characters, Oedipus and Othello, stem automatically from the theatrical demands of each play. From this hypothesis, Strachey proceeds to follow his examination backwards in finer detail, conducting a postmortem on the dead carcass of the plays at the expense of the still-living spirit. That critical literature has not lost much through this dehydrated paper remaining unfinished, may be judged from such flashes as: 'At one of the supreme moments of Othello's tragedy ... Shakespeare puts into his mouth the astonishing lines about the Propontic and the Euxine. What manner of man is this? We need no telling: it is the mariner, whose mind, in the stress of an emotional crisis, goes naturally to the sea.'

In his comments both upon Othello and Iago, Strachey treats the play as a theme on which Shakespeare worked from the outside. He shows no sense of the emotional necessity which at that moment in Shakespeare's life made him attempt an imaginative solution to the conflict between his belief in virtue and his experience of human nature, and he makes use of Shakespeare's drama of jealousy and passion to distract himself from the lassitude and vain expectations of his own love-life. But why *Othello?* At first sight the choice of such a play seems entirely inappropriate. Yet Strachey's instinct and knowledge of Shakespeare were not at fault. Recently, in a more invigorated mood, he had wanted to write an essay on *King Lear.* Now he rejected that supreme masterpiece of agonizing reality for a tragedy that, although a triumph of dramatic technique, is peopled not by human beings, but by creations of stagecraft, untouched by the fresh winds of heaven and unaffected by the common things of earth. Since Strachey wanted to forget the presence of actual people, he buried himself in the world of these magnificent phantoms, whose energy was simply that of their master-manipulator. Like some of his own biographical portraits, these men were too over-simplified for reality: Othello is too noble, Iago too evil.

Iago, especially, has been the great stumbling-block of literary critics, and it is when examining Iago's character that the inadequacy of Strachey's methods is most obvious. In Cinthio's story, he reminds us, Iago was governed by a very real and powerful motive in that he, as well as Othello, loved Desdemona. Why then did Shakespeare discard this plausible motive and reduce the impulse behind Iago's treachery merely to the love of evil for its own sake? The answer, Strachey claims, lay once again in the play's dramatic requirements. To depict two characters in love with the same woman would have thrown out the artistic balance of the piece. Shakespeare, therefore, must have readjusted the regulation plot for one reason alone – to complete the structural effect of his story:

'Othello is to be deluded into believing that Desdemona is faithless; he is to kill her; and then he is to discover that his belief was false. This is the situation, the horror of which is to be intensified in every possible way: the tragedy must be enormous and unrelieved. But there is one eventuality which might, in some degree at any rate, mitigate the atrocity of the story. If Iago had been led to cause this disaster by his love for Desdemona, in that very fact would lie some sort of comfort, the tragedy would have been brought about by a motive not only comprehensible but in a sense sympathetic; the hero's passion and the villain's would be the same. Let it be granted, then, that the completeness of the tragedy would suffer if its origin lay in Iago's love for Desdemona; therefore let that motive be excluded from Iago's mind. The question immediately presents itself – in that case, for what reason are we to suppose that Iago acted as he did? The whole story depends upon his plot, which forms the machinery of the action; yet, if the Desdemona impulsion is eliminated, what motive for his plot can there be? Shakespeare supplied the answer to this question with one of the very greatest strokes of his genius. By an overwhelming effort of creation he summoned out of the darkness a psychological portent that was exactly fitted to the requirements of the tragic situation with which he was dealing, and endowed it with reality. He determined that Iago should have no motive at all ... This triumphant invention of the motivelessness of Iago has been dwelt upon by innumerable commentators; but none, so far as I know, has pointed out the purpose of it, and the dramatic necessity which gave it birth ...'

From one of Strachey's letters to Dadie Rylands, it appears that not long before embarking on this paper, he had been studying Professor G. Wilson Knight's recently published *The Wheel of Fire*, the first volume of that tetralogy which would, with the blessing of T. S. Eliot, inaugurate a new school of Shakespearian study. There is no evidence to show that this work had specifically influenced what he wrote. But, following Wilson Knight's general principles of Shakespeare interpretation, he avoids any attempt to criticize, that is to detect or point out faults, but assuming the works of Shakespeare to be of a transcendent order, he deduces that *Othello* must be perfect. Under this idealistic gaze, apparent blemishes melt away, and necessity takes their place. For Wilson Knight, it was the necessity of poetic vision; for Strachey, it is the aesthetic necessity of dramatic form. His essay is therefore in the nature of a reconstruction rather than a criticism, and follows the general tradition of Coleridge, who speaks of Iago's 'motiveless malignity', and elsewhere confesses that where he and Shakespeare are out of sympathy, it is he himself who must be in the wrong.

The disadvantages of the pure deductive approach – that it tends to substitute the play for actual life and reduce the poetry to a question of linguistics, sound and design, a question of style divorced from our personal emotions and experiences – can perhaps best be demonstrated by comparing the above passage from Strachey's essay with an equivalent passage from Hugh Kingsmill's *The Return of William Shakespeare,* a work of highly individual judgement which had come out in 1929, but which Strachey does not seem to have read. '*Othello*', Kingsmill explains, 'expresses the struggle between two opposing forces in Shakespeare himself, not, like *Lear*, the conflict between the complete man and the nature of things. Neither of the two principal characters, therefore, is a whole human being. Othello is almost exclusively passion seeking an ideal satisfaction, Iago almost exclusively the intellect disintegrating passion by exposing its roots in sensuality. ... As for Iago, I cannot see him at all. You will remember that, at the end, Othello looks at Iago's feet to see if he is hoofed like a devil; a touch which, in the equally passionate atmosphere of *Lear*, would seem unnatural if directed against Edmund.'

Within this criticism, the tragedy of Othello reflects, not just a matchless exercise in play-making, but, in a simplified and over-idealized form, the tragedy of a Shakespeare who was attempting to isolate and destroy his perception of evil with which virtue and beauty are entangled on earth, and to re-establish virtue and beauty in immaculate perfection as realizable within human experience. That Iago was not the enemy of this ideal, but some defect inherent in life itself, could only become clearer to Shakespeare after he had revenged himself on Iago and expitated his remorse in Othello – a development which has taken place in the ensuing *King Lear* and *Macbeth*.

The symbolic value which Kingsmill attaches to Othello and Iago saves one from forcing some kind of actual plausibility into Iago's motives, or from concocting some ingenious schematic reason to account for his abysmal spirit of evil. At the same time, it resolves the discrepancy between Othello, the sober, elderly general, and the Othello who strikes Desdemona in front of the Venetian envoy, Lodovico. While Othello embodies Shakespeare's generous, reawakened idealism, the function of Iago, like that of Philip Francis in Strachey's dissertation on Warren Hastings, is to force the unqualified idealist 'to see life from the opposite standpoint, which explains every action in terms of lust or self-interest; and he so far succeeds that, while the agony of Othello is not the mere rage of sensual jealousy, neither is it to be characterised as simply, in Coleridge's phrase, "the solemn agony" of a disillusioned idealist, but as the medley of both these passions which Shakespeare himself experienced.'

By constantly bringing his sense of the man Shakespeare before our view, Kingsmill – like Johnson in his Preface and Notes, like Hazlitt, Walter Raleigh, Peter Quennell and a few others – is able to show us the extraordinary generic quality of his mind. This intuitive, personal angle of criticism, though sometimes blurred by self-identification and emotional prejudice, can make us understand Shakespeare's vivid power of communication with all other minds, in ages past and present. He is like us, and he is like others too, having within himself the roots of every faculty and feeling. But Strachey's 'Othello' neglects this quality; it lies outside the scope of his examination. He presents *Othello* as a flawless dramatic pattern created, not by a man like us, but by some automaton, some tragedy-computer which has been fed with the ingredients of a simple plot and a vast store of knowledge relating to the machinery of the Greek Theatre. And that is all.

The Death of Milo

Great Milo, mightiest boxer, bound
   Homewards to Croto through the hills,
Superb and careless, young & crowned,
   Untouched the most of mortal ills,

Scenting the freedom of the morn,
   Singing the song of last night's feast,
Half swung along the path, half borne
   Forward by spirit half released

From cold impediments of flesh,
   Was sudden stopped; before his face
Wavered a green & golden mesh,
   A sunny veil of leafy lace,

Which wavering yielded not; an oak
   Across the path held out an arm.
Milo threw off his bear-skin cloak,
   And with the upstart thought no harm

To try a bout of naked strength.
   He seized the branch in his huge hands,
And passionate tugged; until at length
   His bursting muscles rent the bands

Of the toughened fibre, and the bough
   With echoing thunder-crack was reft
From the stem. In laughing triumph now
   Thrust Milo both hands in the cleft

Twixt branch & trunk, to tear in twain
   The rugged body of the tree.
With all his force he strove; in vain;
   No further budged the bough, and he,

Letting an instant his fierce grasp
   Relax, felt sudden his hands clenched
Tight in the hard & wooden clasp
   Of the cleft. One blow of terror blenched

The lips of Milo; then a bull
   Furious in agony of fear
He roared aloud & sought to pull
   In jerks his arms away; to tear

To freedom from his prisoned hands
   With severed wrists, in one wild stroke.
In vain; nor blows, nor hot demands,
   Nor tears, could move the silent oak.

And all day through did Milo strive
   In frenzy of a white despair
To drag him from the tree, contrive
   By some new twist, now here, now there,

To squeeze his anguished hands away.
   In vain; the oak-tree held him fast.
And with the ending of the day,
   The man o'erwearied sank at last

To semi-sleep, upon his sight
   Staring one vast dark rock, which grew
Ever more dark, more vast, till night
   Involved all in enormous blue.

Half hanging from tremendous arms,
   And half a-foot on dangled toes,
The hugeness of his naked charms,
   The weary splendour of his pose,

Were one with all the slumberous earth.
   His great breast heaved and fell; the thews
Rolled hard about his sinewy girth;
   Slackened his mighty legs hung loose;

Deep twixt his shoulders iron-knit
   Were caverned neck and ears; and bare
Upon each mountainous shoulder-pit
   Stood out its little tuft of hair.

Thus through the long dark of the night
   He loomed. The heavy brush of wings
Passed; and the gleam of eyes alight
   With agate-fire of cat-like things

Peered out upon his blindness. Hours
   Vanished: he moved not. Then at length
His inward body stirred. Deep powers
   Of nature, and the unconquered strength

Of youthful nerve & youthful heart
   Miraculous moved; he woke, and knew
Premonitory heaves; apart
   Were pushed his buttock's lips, and through

The opening gut came forth the dung.
   Slow as a child of anxious birth
It voyaged, so close to Death; then hung
   One trembling moment, and to earth

Thudded. On Milo's sodden sense
   The sound mysteriously tolled
The funeral of a vast suspense.
   And, as in kiss of giant mould

Once more his billowy buttocks pressed,
   Saw all at once his member drowsed
Wake too, and from its cherished nest
   Upflutter like a bird aroused.

Then happy from its loosened springs
   His yellow water ran amain,
As after roaring thunder sings
   The treble freedom of the rain.

And Milo felt his hanging cock
   Delicious as an udder drawn,
Seeing in the hollow of the rock
   The glimmer of the ghastly dawn.

24 August 1902

There is a helpful Chronological Check List of Lytton Strachey's books and published essays at the end of Professor C. R. Sanders's *Lytton Strachey: His Mind and Art* (1957). Most of the information on which the present work is based has been taken from unpublished material, the sources of which are indicated in the text. The following miscellaneous and special studies, however, have proved useful.

Allen, B. M.: *General Gordon*. London: Duckworth, 1935.
   Gordon and the Sudan, London: Macmillan, 1931.
Altick, Richard A.: *Lives and Letters*. New York: Knopf, 1965.
Annan, Noël: *Leslie Stephen: his thought and character in relation to his times*. London: MacGibbon & Kee, 1951.
Beaton, Cecil: *The Wandering Years*. London: Weidenfeld & Nicolson, 1962.
Beaverbrook, Lord: *The Decline and Fall of Lloyd George*. London: Collins, 1963.
Beddington-Behrens, Sir Edward: *Look Back – Look Forward*. London: Macmillan, 1963.
Beerbohm, Max: *Lytton Strachey* (The Rede Lecture). Cambridge University Press, 1943.
   Letters to Reggie Turner, edited by Rupert Hart-Davis. London: Hart-Davis, 1964.
Bell, Clive: *Euphrosyne* (anonymously edited). Cambridge: Elijah Johnson, 1905.
   Old Friends: Personal Recollections. London: Chatto & Windus, 1956.
Bell, Julian: *Essays, Poems and Letters*, edited by Quentin Bell (with contributions by J. M. Keynes, David Garnett, Charles Mauron, C. Day Lewis and E. M. Forester). London: Hogarth Press, 1938.
Bell, Quentin: *Bloomsbury*. London: Weidenfeld & Nicolson, 1968.
Bennett, Arnold: *Journals*, vol. 2, *1911–1921* vol. 3, *1921–1928*, edited by Newman Flower. London: Cassell, 1932, 1933.
Benson, E. F.: *As We Are*. London: Longmans, 1932.

Birrell, Augustine: *More Obiter Dicta*. London: Heinemann, 1924.

Bloomfield, Paul: *Uncommon People: A Study of England's Elite*. London: Hamish Hamilton, 1955.

Boas, Guy: *Lytton Strachey* (an English Association Pamphlet). London: 1935.

Bolitho, Hector: *My Restless Years*. London: Max Parrish, 1962.

Bower-Shore, Clifford: *Lytton Strachey: An Essay*. London: Fenland Press, 1933.

Bradford, Gamaliel: *The Journey of Gamaliel Bradford, 1918–1931*, edited by Van Wyck Brooks. Boston, Mass.: Houghton Mifflin, 1933.

The Letters of Gamaliel Bradford, 1918–1931, edited by Van Wyck Brooks. Boston, Mass.: Houghton Mifflin, 1934.

Brenan, Gerald: *South from Granada*. London: Hamish Hamilton, 1959.

A Life of One's Own. London: Hamish Hamilton, 1962.

Britt, Albert: *The Great Biographers*. New York: McGraw-Hill, 1936.

Brookfield, Frances M.: *The Cambridge 'Apostles'*. London: Pitman, 1906.

Campbell, Roy: *Light on a Dark Horse: An Autobiography 1901–1935*. London: Hollis & Carter, 1951.

Campos, Christopher: *The View of France from Arnold to Bloomsbury*. Oxford University Press, 1965.

Cannan, Gilbert: *Mendel: A Story of Youth*. London: T. Fisher Unwin, 1916.

Carrington, Dora: *Carrington: Letters and Extracts from her Diaries*. Chosen and with an introduction by David Garnett. London: Jonathan Cape, 1970.

Carver, George: *Alms for Oblivion*. Milwaukee: Bruce Publications, 1916.

Cecchi, Emilio: *Scrittori Inglesi e Americani*, revised edition. Milan: Mondadori, 1947.

Cecil, Lord David: *Mox*. London: Constable, 1964.

Clemens, Cyril: *Lytton Strachey* (International Mark Twain Society, Biographical Series, No. 11). Webster Groves, Mo., 1942.

Clifford, James L. (ed.): *Biography as an Art: Selected Criticism, 1560–1960*. Oxford University Press, 1962.

Connolly, Cyril: *Enemies of Promise*, revised edition. London: Routledge & Kegan Paul, 1949.

Cooper, Lady Diana: *The Rainbow Comes and Goes*. London: Hart-Davis, 1958.

Dalton, Hugh: *Call Back Yesterday: Memoirs 1887–1931.* London: Muller, 1953.

Devas, Nicolette: *Two Flamboyant Fathers.* London: Collins, 1966.

Dobrée, Bonamy: 'Lytton Strachey', in *Post Victorians* edited by W. R. Inge. London: Nicholson & Watson, 1933.

Du Bos, Charles: *Approximations.* Deuxième Série. Paris: Editions G. Crès et Cie, 1927.

Dyson, A. E.: *The Crazy Fabric.* London: Macmillan, 1965.

Edel, Leon: *Literary Biography,* revised edition. London: Hart-Davis, 1959.

Elton, Lord: *General Gordon.* London: Collins, 1954.

Epstein, Jacob: *Let there be Sculpture.* London: Michael Joseph, 1940.

Forster, E. M.: *Goldsworthy Lowes Dickinson.* London: Edward Arnold, 1934.

Abinger Harvest. London: Edward Arnold, 1936.

Two Cheers for Democracy. London: Edward Arnold, 1951.

Fry, Roger: *Duncan Grant.* London: Leonard & Virginia Woolf, 1930.

Garnett, David: *The Flowers of the Forest.* London: Chatto & Windus, 1955.

The Familiar Faces. London: Chatto & Windus, 1962.

Garraty, John A.: *The Nature of Biography.* London: Cape, 1957.

Gerhardie, William: *Memoirs of a Polyglot.* London: Duckworth, 1931.

Resurrection. London: Cassell, 1935.

Gertler, Mark: *Selected Letters,* edited by Noel Carrington, and with an Introduction by Quentin Bell. London: Hart-Davis, 1965.

Glenavy, Beatrice: *Today We Will Only Gossip.* London: Constable, 1964.

Goldring, Douglas: *The Nineteen Twenties.* London: Nicholson & Watson, 1945.

Gordon, George: *The Lives of Authors.* London: Chatto & Windus, 1950.

Gosse, Sir Edmund: *Some Diversions of a Man of Letters.* London: Heinemann, 1919.

More Books on the Table. London: Heinemann, 1923.

Leaves and Fruit. London: Heinemann, 1927.

Grant, Patrick: *The Good Old Days.* London: Thames & Hudson, 1956.

Graves, Robert: *Goodbye to All That.* London: Cape, 1929.

Guiguet, Jean: *Virginia Woolf* (translated by Jean Stewart). London: Hogarth Press, 1965.

Hamnett, Nina: *Laughing Torso*. London: Constable, 1932.

Harrod, Roy: *The Life of John Maynard Keynes*. London: Macmillan, 1951.

Hassall, Christopher: *Rupert Brooke: A Biography*. London: Faber, 1964.

Holroyd, Michael: *Lytton Strachey: A Biography*. Harmondsworth: Penguin Books, 1971.

House, Humphry: *All in Due Time*. London: Hart-Davis, 1955.

Huxley, Aldous: *Crome Yellow*. London: Chatto & Windus, 1921.
On the Margin. London: Chatto & Windus, 1923.

Iyengar, K. R. Srinivasa: *Lytton Strachey: A Critical Study*. London: Chatto & Windus, 1939.

John, Augustus: *Chiaroscuro: Fragments of Autobiography*. London: Cape, 1952.

Johnson, Edgar: *One Mighty Torrent*. New York: Stackpole Sons, 1937.

Johnstone, J. K.: *The Bloomsbury Group*. London: Secker & Warburg, 1954.

Kallich, Martin: *The Psychological Milieu of Lytton Strachey*. New Haven, Conn.: Yale University Press, 1961.

Kendall, Paul Murray: *The Art of Biography*. London: Allen & Unwin, 1965.

Keynes, John Maynard: *Essays in Biography*. London: Macmillan, 1933.
Two Memoirs, with an Introduction by David Garnett. London: Hart-Davis, 1949.

Kingsmill, Hugh: *The Table of Truth*. London: Jarrolds, 1932.
The Progress of a Biographer. London: Methuen, 1949.

Köntges, Günther: *Die Sprache in der Biographie Lytton Stracheys*. Marburg: Hermann Bauer, 1938.

Lawrence, D. H.: 'None of That', in vol. 3 of *The Complete Short Stories* (Phoenix Edition). London: Heinemann, 1955.
Women in Love. London: Martin Secker, 1920.
Selected Letters, edited by Aldous Huxley. London: Heinemann, 1932.
Collected Letters, 2 vols., edited by Harry T. Moore. London: Heinemann, 1962.

Lea, F. A.: *The Life of John Middleton Murry*. London: Methuen, 1959.

Lehmann, John: *The Whispering Gallery*. London: Longmans, 1955.
I am My Brother. London: Longmans, 1960.

Leslie, Seymour: *The Jerome Connexion*. London: John Murray, 1964.

Lewis, Percy Wyndham: *The Apes of God*. London: Nash & Grayson, 1930.
Self-Condemned. London: Methuen, 1954.

Lunn, Sir Arnold: *Roman Converts*. London: Chapman & Hall, 1924.

MacCarthy, Sir Desmond: *Memories*. London: MacGibbon & Kee, 1953.

Mais, S. P. B.: *Some Modern Authors*. London: Grant Richards, 1923.

Martin, Kingsley: *Father Figures: A Volume of Autobiography*. London: Hutchinson, 1966.

Marwick, Arthur: *Clifford Allen: The Open Conspirator*. Edinburgh: Oliver & Boyd, 1964.

Maurois, André: *Aspects of Biography*. Cambridge University Press, 1929.
Poets and Prophets. London: Cassell, 1936.

Mirsky, Prince D.S.: *The Intelligentsia of Great Britain*. London: Gollancz, 1935.

Moore, G. E.: *Principia Ethica*. Cambridge University Press, 1903.
Ethics. London: Williams & Norgate, 1911.

Moore, Harry T.: *The Intelligent Heart: The Story of D. H. Lawrence*. London: Heinemann, 1955.

Morrell, Lady Ottoline: *Ottoline: The Early Memoirs of Lady Ottoline Morrell 1873–1915*; edited and with an introduction by Robert Gathorne Hardy. London: Faber, 1963.

Mortimer, Raymond: *Channel Packet*. London: Hogarth Press, 1948.
Duncan Grant. Harmondsworth: Penguin, 1948.

Muir, Edwin: *Transition*. London: Hogarth Press, 1926.

Nathan, Monique: *Virginia Woolf* (translated by Herma Briffault). New York: Grove Press, 1961.

Nehls, Edward: *D. H. Lawrence: A Composite Biography*, 3 vols. Madison, Wis.: University of Wisconsin Press, 1957–9.

Nicolson, Sir Harold: *Tennyson*. London: Constable, 1923.
Some People. London: Constable, 1927.
The Development of English Biography. London: Hogarth Press, 1933.

'Olivia' (pseudonym of Dorothy Bussy): *Olivia*. London: Hogarth Press, 1949.

Oman, Charles: *On the Writing of History*. London: Methuen, 1939.

Pearson, Hesketh: *Modern Men and Mummers*. London: Allen & Unwin, 1921.

Ventilations. Philadelphia, Pa.: Lippincott, 1930.

Thinking it Over. London: Hamish Hamilton, 1938.

'About Biography' (The Tredegar Memorial Lecture, 1955); included in *Essays by Divers Hands, Being the Transactions of the Royal Society of Literature*, vol. xxix, 1958.

Pippett, Aileen: *The Moth and the Star: A Biography of Virginia Woolf*. Boston, Mass.: Little, Brown, 1955.

Plomer, William: *At Home*. London: Cape, 1958.

Quennell, Peter: *The Singular Preference*. London: Collins, 1952.

The Sign of the Fish. London: Collins, 1960.

Quiller-Couch, Sir Arthur: *Studies in Literature*. Second Series. Cambridge University Press, 1927.

Raleigh, Sir Walter: *Letters 1879–1922*, edited by Lady Raleigh. London: Methuen, 1926.

Rantavaara, Irma: *Virginia Woolf and Bloomsbury*. Helsinki: Annales Academiae Scientiarum Fennicae, Series B, tom. 82, 1, 1953.

Raymond, John: *England's on the Anvil*. London: Collins, 1958.

Reddie, Cecil: *Abbotsholme 1889–1899*, or, *Ten Years' Work in an Education Laboratory*. London: G. Allen, 1900.

Robertson, David. *George Mallory*. London: Faber, 1969.

Robertson, Graham: *Letters from Graham Robertson*, edited by Kerrison Preston. London: Hamish Hamilton, 1953.

Roosevelt, Eleanor: *This is My Story*. London: Hutchinson, 1937.

Rothenstein, John: *Modern English Painters*, 2 vols. London: Eyre & Spottiswoode, 1952, 1956.

Summer's Lease. London: Hamish Hamilton, 1965.

Rothenstein, William: *Men and Memories*, 2 vols. London: Faber, 1931, 1932.

Russell, Bertrand: *Portraits from Memory*. London: Allen & Unwin, 1956.

The Autobiography of Bertrand Russell 1872–1913. London: Allen & Unwin, 1967.

Rutherston, Albert: *Contemporary British Artists: Henry Lamb*. London: Benn, 1924.

Sanders, Charles Richard: *The Strachey Family 1558–1932*, Durham, N. Carolina: Duke University Press, 1953.

Lytton Strachey: His Mind and Art. New Haven, Conn.: Yale University Press, 1957.

Sassoon, Siegfried: *Siegfried's Journey*. London: Faber, 1945.

Scott-James, R. A.: *Lytton Strachey* (Writers and their Work, No. 65). London: Longmans, 1955.

Sherburn, George: *Selections from Alexander Pope* New York: Thomas Nelson & Sons, 1929.

Simson, George Kuppler: 'Lytton Strachey's Use of his Sources in *Eminent Victorians*': a thesis submitted to the Faculty of the Graduate School of the University of Minnesota (unpublished), 1963.

Sitwell, Edith: *Taken Care Of*. London: Hutchinson, 1965.

Sitwell, Sir Osbert: *Laughter in the Next Room*. London: Macmillan, 1949.

Spender, Stephen: *World within World*. London: Hamish Hamilton, 1951.

Squire, Sir John: *Books Reviewed*. London: Hodder & Stoughton, 1922.

Stansky, Peter, and Abrahams, William: *Journey to the Frontier: Julian Bell and John Cornford: their lives and the 1930s*. London: Constable, 1966.

Stein, Gertrude: *The Autobiography of Alice B. Toklas*. London: John Lane, 1933.

Stephen, Adrian: *The 'Dreadnought' Hoax*. London: Leonard & Virginia Woolf, 1936.

Stone, Wilfrid: *The Cave and the Mountain*. A Study of E. M. Forster. Oxford University Press, 1966.

Strachey, Julia: *Cheerful Weather for the Wedding*. London: Leonard & Virginia Woolf, 1932.

Strachey, Lytton: *Landmarks in French Literature*. London: Williams & Norgate, 1912.

　Eminent Victorians. London: Chatto & Windus, 1918.

　Queen Victoria. London: Chatto & Windus, 1921.

　Books and Characters: French and English. London: Chatto & Windus, 1922.

　Pope (The Leslie Stephen Lecture). London: Cambridge University Press, 1925.

　Elizabeth and Essex: A Tragic History. London: Chatto & Windus, 1928.

　Portraits in Miniature and Other Essays. London: Chatto & Windus, 1931.

　Characters and Commentaries (with a preface by James Strachey). London: Chatto & Windus, 1933.

　Spectatorial Essays (with a preface by James Strachey). London: Chatto & Windus, 1964.

385

This volume contains thirty-five of the essay-reviews that Lytton wrote for the *Spectator*, less than half of his total contributions to that paper. The essays in *Books and Characters*, *Portraits in Miniature* and *Characters and Commentaries* have been regrouped into two volumes in the Chatto & Windus Uniform Edition of the Collected Works of Lytton Strachey: *Biographical Essays* and *Literary Essays*, both first published in 1948.

Ermyntrude and Esmeralda. London: Anthony Blond, 1969.

Lytton Strachey by Himself: a Self-Portrait, edited and introduced by Michael Holroyd. London: Heinemann, 1971.

Strachey, Lytton, and Fulford, Roger (eds): *The Greville Memoirs*, 8 vols. (Joint editors: Ralph and Frances Partridge.) London: Macmillan, 1937–8.

Strachey, Lytton, and Woolf, Virginia: *Virginia Woolf and Lytton Strachey: Letters*. London: Chatto & Windus, 1956.

This volume has several cuts, deletions of names, and omissions of whole letters. The present biographer has had access to the full correspondence.

Strachey, St Loe: *The Adventure of Living*. London: Nelson, 1922.

Swinnerton, Frank: *The Georgian Literary Scene*. London: Dent, 1938; rev. ed. 1951.

Figures in the Foreground: Literary Reminiscences 1917–40. London: Hutchinson, 1963.

Thurston, Marjorie: 'The Development of Lytton Strachey's Biographical Method': a dissertation submitted to the Graduate Faculty of the University of Chicago (unpublished), 1929.

Toklas, Alice B.: *What is Remembered*. London: Michael Joseph, 1963.

Trevelyan, G. M.: *Autobiography and Other Essays*. London: Longmans, 1949.

Trevor-Roper, Hugh: *Historical Essays*. London: Macmillan, 1957.

Trilling, Lionel: *E. M. Forster: A Study*. London: Hogarth Press. 1944.

Unwin, Sir Stanley: *The Truth about a Publisher*. London: Allen & Unwin, 1960.

Warburg, Fredric: *An Occupation for Gentlemen*. London: Hutchinson, 1959.

Webb, Beatrice: *My Apprenticeship*. London: Longmans, 1926.

Our Partnership. London: Longmans, 1948.

Wilson, Edmund: *Axel's Castle: A Study in the Imaginative Literature of 1870–1930*. New York: Charles Scribner's Sons, 1931.

The Shores of Light: A Literary Chronicle of the Twenties and Thirties. London: W. H. Allen, 1952.

Wood, Alan: *Bertrand Russell: The Passionate Sceptic*. London: Allen & Unwin, 1957.

Woolf, Leonard: *Sowing: An Autobiography of the Years 1880–1904*. London: Hogarth Press. 1961.

Beginning Again: An Autobiography of the Years 1911–1918. London: Hogarth Press, 1964.

Downhill All the Way: An Autobiography of the Years 1919–1939. London: Hogarth Press, 1967.

Woolf, Virginia: *The Voyage Out*. London: Duckworth, 1915.

Jacob's Room. London: Hogarth Press, 1922.

The Waves. London: Hogarth Press, 1931.

A Writer's Diary. London: Hogarth Press, 1953.

Roger Fry. London: Hogarth Press, 1940.

The Death of the Moth and Other Essays. London: Hogarth Press, 1942.

Granite and Rainbow. London: Hogarth Press, 1958.

Young, G. M.: *Victorian England: Portrait of an Age*. Oxford University Press, 1960.

'Abbé Morellet, The', *la douceur de vivre* 358
Abbotsholme 209n.
Ackerley, J.R. 339
Acton, Lord 235
'Adolescent, An' 150n.
Adventure of Living, The (St Loe Strachey) 121
'After Herrick' 63–4
'Age of Spenser, The' 346n.
Akakia (Voltaire) 157
Albany Review 81n.
   See *Independent Review*
A la Recherche du Temps Perdu (Proust): Lytton's failure to provide an Introduction to 338
Aldington, Richard: invites Lytton to write Introduction to *La Vie Privée du Maréchal, Duc de Richelieu* 338
Alençon, quoted 311
'Alexander Pope' 296n., 340–50
Ali, Hasan 225
Allen, Dr Bernard 225–7
All in Due Time (Humphry House) quoted 161
'America in Profile' 118–19
'Andrew Marvell' 114
Annan, Lord 29, 43n., 47, 107n., 168, 336n.
Antony and Cleopatra 113n., 135, 291
Apostles, The 33n., 47–8, 49, 76, 161
archy's life of mehitabel (Don Marquis) quoted 243
Arnold, Matthew 107, 148–9, 345
Art (Clive Bell) 'utter balls' 46

'Art and Indecency' 68
'Art of Biography, The' (Virginia Woolf) quoted 283
Asquith, H. H. 21
Astor, Lady 361
Athenaeum 252n.
Ayliff, Henry 333
Bacon, Anthony 297
'Bacon as a Man of Letters' 119, 324
Bacon, Francis ('the serpent') 291–2, 321–6
Bailey, J. C. 97n.
Balzac, Honoré de 136–7, 293–4
Baring, Sir Evelyn 121–6, 222, 230, 234, 235–40, 349
Baring, Maurice, quoted 124, Lytton's letters to 235n., 237n.
Barnes, T. R., quoted 105n., 294
Barrie, J. M. 112, 113
Beaverbrook, Lord quoted 281n.
Beddoes, Thomas Lovell 93–6, 348–9
Beerbohm, Sir Max quoted 33, 295
Beethoven 91
Bell, Clive: on Lytton's biographer 10; marriage to Vanessa Stephen 19, ('a wild sprightly couple') 29; considered silly by Strachey 46; at 46 Gordon Square 29, 30, 35; member of the Bloomsbury Group, 36n., 37, 39, 41 quoted 105; his respect for F.A. Simpson, 178n.; member of the Midnight Society 68n;
Bell, Julian 21
Bell, Professor Quentin 46n., 47
Bell, Vanessa. See Stephen, Vanessa

INDEX

Belloc, Hilaire 76, 98, 288
Bennett, Arnold 36, 109
Benson, E. F. quoted 209, 276
Berenson, Mary 335
Bernhardt, Sarah, acting in *Phèdre* 97
Bevan, Professor 67
Bevan, Miss in the shrubbery with Cardinal Manning 172
Biographical Essays 79n., 81n., 82n., 150n., 151n., 152n., 156n., 219n., 252n., 339n., 354n., 355n., 356n., 357n., 358n., 361n., 362n., 364n., 366n., 367n.
Birrel, Augustine: Lytton writes to 185
Black, J. B. quoted 334
Blake, William 89–92, 95
Bloomsbury Group 17–54 *pass.*, 80, 143, 218, 288
Bloomsbury Group, The (J. K. Johnstone) quoted 33, 43–4
Blunt, Wilfrid quoted 143
Boas, Guy quoted 251
Boleyn, Anne 312
'Bonga–Bonga in Whitehall' 146–7
Books and Characters 68n., 78n., 83n., 85n., 89n., 94n., 96n., 99, 151n., 152n., 156n., 252n.
Booth, Mr, his ears 297–8
Boswell, James 86, 166–7, 241, 283, 361
Bower-Shore, Clifford 245
Bray, F. E. 67n.
Brenan, Gerald 47; criticism of *Eminent Victorians* 242, 282
Brighton 363
British Museum 303
Brown, Ivor 8; quoted 282
Brown, John 254, 270–71, 281n.
Browne, Sir Thomas 55–6, 83–4, 86, 89
Browning, Robert 94, 148,
Bruckner, Ferdinand 333
Buckle, G. B. 265
Burghley, Lord 314, 327

Burke, Edmund 66
Burton, Sir Richard 225, 230, 239
Bussy, Dorothy: Lytton's letters to 18, 55, 126–7, 289, 333
Byron, Lord 74–5, 114
Cairngorms 8
Cambridge 17–18, 32, 33, 34n., 35, 49, 50, 51, 52, 53, 74, 80, 83, 104n., 105n., 114, 115, 339, 340
Cambridge Conversazione Society. See Apostles
Cambridge Review 63, 179n.
Cambridge University Press 338–9
Campbell, A. Y. quoted 133–4 Lytton writes to 135
Campbell, Roy 39; quoted 42
Campbell, R. J. 211n.
Caran d'Ache 212
'Cardinal Manning' 168, 169–91, 192, 198, 201, 209–10, 220, 231, 235
Carew, Sir George 318
'Carlyle' 362, 365–6
Carlyle, Thomas 86, 210, 212n., 362, 365–6
Carnock, Lord 227
Carrington (Dora) 261
Cavour, Count Camillo Benso 204
Cecil, Algernon 328
Cecil, Lord David, quoted 51, 277; invited by Lytton to lunch at Café Royal 287n.
Cecil, Robert ('the pygmy') 278, 291, 303, 314, 321, 326–9, 335
Chaillé-Long, Colonel 223–7
Chamberlain, Joseph 76
Characters and Commentaries 7, 71n., 77n., 79n., 81n., 82n., 84n., 85n., 105n., 115–16, 146n., 147n., 149n., 150n., 151n., 219n., 338n., 340n., 369
Chartreuse de Parme, La (Stendhal) 158
Chatto and Windus Ltd 325n., 339
Chekhov, Anton 84
Chesterfield, Lord 72, 343

Chesterton, G. K. 76, 98, 280n., 288
Civilization: an Essay (Clive Bell) 49
Clapham Sect 29
Clark, Sir Kenneth 22n., 47, 48
Clive, Lord 65, 120
Clough, Arthur: his weak ankles and solemn face 202; his enjoyable death 208; a post-office puppet 235
Clough, B. A. defends her father 202n.
Coat of Many Colours, A (Herbert Read) 284n.
Cole, Horace de Vere 30, 31, 147
Coleridge, Mary 90
Coleridge, Samuel Taylor 27, 104, 107, 373
Collected Essays (Virginia Woolf) 283n.
Collins, Professor John Churton 103, 106, 349n.
Collis, John Stewart, quoted 185, 217
'Colloquies of Senrab, The' 67, 123
Comedy of Manners, The (John Palmer) 147
'Comus at Cambridge' 87n.
Condorcet, Jean Antoine Nicolas de Caritat, Marquis of 244
Congreve, William 148
'Congreve, Collier, and Macaulay' 357n.
Connolly, Cyril 47; quoted 161
Cook, Sir Edward 11, 192–5
Cooper, Lady Diana
Duff Cooper's letters to 207, 212n.
Cooper, Duff: his criticisms of *Eminent Victorians* 207, 212n.
Cornhill Magazine 217n.
Cowper, William 73–4
Cox, Harold 118
Crane, Stephen 159
'Creighton' See 'Mandell Creighton'

Cromer, Lord. See Baring, Sir Evelyn
Cunard, Lady 361
Dangerfield, George, quoted 334
Darwin, Charles 288
Darwin, Erasmus 67n.
Davies, Sir John, partly quoted 346
Davies, Theodore Llewelyn, member of original Bloomsbury Group 32
'Death of Milo, The' 62n., 375–8
Death of the Moth and Other Essays, The (Virginia Woolf)
Desborough, Lady 361
Development of English Biography, The (Harold Nicolson) 166, 249
Dickinson, Goldsworthy Lowes 76; founds *Independent Review* 76; his influence at Cambridge 49, 51
'Diplomatist: Li Hung-Chang, A' 219, 238
Disraeli, Benjamin 270–2, 277, 295
Dobrée, Professor Bonamy 43n., 223, 234
Dobson, Austin 85, 109
Donne, John 56–7, 58, 147, 148
Dostojevsky, Fedor 115, 141, 220
Douglas, Norman praises *Elizabeth and Essex* 335
Downing College (Cambridge) 52
'Dr Arnold' 168, 207–17, 220–21
Drama and Life (A. B. Walkley) 117
Dreadnought Hoax 31, 147
Dryden, John 341
Duckworth, Stella 25
Dukes, Ashley 333
Dunciad, The (Pope) 341, 346
Dundee Advertiser 222
Edinburgh Review 151–2, 156n., 158n.
Egoist, The (Meredith) 24
Eliot, T. S.; his potential as bank manager 28; Lytton's attitude to his poetry 110; and the school of Wilson Knight 372

Elizabeth and Essex: its historical pageantry 79–80; the critical reaction from 49, 167, 278, 288, 289–337, 351–2, 365

'Elizabeth and Her Court' (G. B. Harrison and Celia Simpson) 323n.

'Elizabethan Drama' 304n.

'Elizabethanism' 114n.

Elton, Oliver, and the Chair of English Literature at Liverpool 339

Eminent Victorians: a 'pernicious' book 7; the effect of its success on Lytton 116; its militancy 117; and the Spectatorial Lord Cromer 121–6, 161–242, 243–4, 248, 250–51, 254, 260, 280n., 281–2, 287n., 296n., 299, 301, 333, 336n., 349, 359, 363, 366.

Encounter 242n.

'End of General Gordon, The' 119–28, 168–9, 217–39

Enemies of Promise (Cyril Connolly) quoted 161

'English Letter Writers' 59n., 71–5, 77, 81

Ephemera Critica (Churton Collins) 106n.

Esher, Lord: as enemy 217n.; as friend of enemy 364

Essay on Man (Pope) 345

'Ethics of the Gospels, The' 67

Eton College 213

Fall of Louis Napoleon, The (F. A. Simpson) 179n.

Familiar Faces, The (David Garnett) 43n.

Fanny Burney (Austin Dobson) 85

Father and Son (Edmund Gosse) 349

Ferrero, Guglielmo 162, 244

Fielding, Henry 148

Figures in the Foreground (Frank Swinnerton) 41n.

Firle (Sussex) 40

'First Earl of Lytton, The' 77n., 84–5

France 17, 333, 357–8

Francis, Sir Philip 66, 374

Freeman, Douglas Southall, quoted 7

'French Poetry' 116

Freud, Sigmund 10, 47, 106n., 336–7; and James Strachey 298–9; his influence on *Elizabeth and Essex* 298–300; his opinion of *Queen Victoria* 336; writes to Lytton about *Elizabeth and Essex* 336–7

'Froude' 362–5

'Fruit of the Tree, The' 57–8

Fry, Helen 143

Fry, Roger: member of the Bloomsbury Group 36n., 44, 46–7; Virginia Woolf's biography of 53; 'the last of the Victorians' 54; his Omega Workshops 144; Post - Impressionism and France 143–5, 154–5; his praise of *Queen Victoria* 249 *His letter to Lytton* 249

Fisher, H. A. L.: quoted 129; his advice on *Landmarks in French Literature* 132

Fitzroy Square, No. 29 19, 30

'Florence Nightingale' 168, 191, 192–208, 210, 219–21, 231

Fontaine, La 137–9

Fontenelle 244

Fordham, E. W., quoted 39

Forster, E. M.: biography of Goldie Dickinson 51; quoted on Cambridge 51; and the *Independent Review* 76; 'pseudoscholarship' 101; membership of Bloomsbury Group 36n., 37, 43, 46; tea and beer 39, 52; on *Elizabeth and Essex* 335

Fuller, Thomas 329

Gaige, Crosby 331n.

Garnett, David ('Bunny') his description of Vanessa Bell 22; of

Clive Bell 29; member of Bloomsbury 37; hypothetical views on Lytton's development had he lived longer 43, 49, Edwin Muir's criticism of 242n.

Lytton's letters to 55, 83–4

Garraty, John A. 195

Garsington Manor 40

Gathorne-Hardy, Robert 131n.

George V his anger over *Queen Victoria* 281n.

Gerhardie, William 27, 44, 281n.

Getting Married (Shaw) 101

'Gibbon' 362, 364, 368–9

Gibbon, Edward 162, 288, 335

Gide, André 158

Giles, Professor H. A. 47

Gladstone, William Ewart 175, 184, 222, 230, 232–4, 235n., 239n., 270, 271–2, 277

Gloriana (Benjamin Britten) 333

Goethe, Johann Wolfgang 164

Goldsworthy Lowes Dickinson (E. M. Forster) 51

Goodman, Bishop, cited on Essex and venereal disease 314n.

Gordon Square, No. 46 20, 29, 32, 35

Gosse, Sir Edmund: 83n.; bones or boys 94n.; his lack of poetic inspiration 109; on Lytton as naturalist 184; his criticism of *Eminent Victorians* 184, 349; his defence of poor Cromer 237–9; much affected 432; his appreciation of *Queen Victoria* 279–80, 350; criticism of 'Alexander Pope' 347–9

'Grandiloquence of Wordsworth, The' 119

Grant, Duncan: relationship with Lytton 18, 19; influence on Lytton's art criticism 102n.; as a member of the Bloomsbury Group 18–19, 21, 31–2, 36n., 37, 41, 46, 47; his prospects as

an Army officer 28; the Dreadnought Hoax 31; in Versailles with Lytton 130

Lytton's letters to 50, 94

Granta, The 7

Granville, Lord 235

Granville-Barker, Harley 112

Gray, Thomas 73–4

Greatness and Decline of Rome, The (Guglielmo Ferrero) 162, 244

Greaves Prize (Trinity) 65

Gregorovius, Ferdinand 235

Greville, Charles 253, 269

Greville Memoirs, The 11

Grigson, Geoffrey, his letter to *The Times Literary Supplement* 278n.

Group Psychology and the Analysis of the Ego (Freud) 299

Guedalla, Philip: his attack on F. A. Simpson 179n.; Edmund Wilson's criticism of 296n.

'Guides, The' 120

Gulliver's Travels (Swift) 246

Hall, Dr ('a rough terrier') 201

Hammond, J. L. 98, 178n., 179n.

Hans: goes to lavatory on the floor 30; blows out a match 32

Harcourt Brace Inc. 331n.

Harcourt, William 332

Hardy, Thomas 109

Harris, Frank: Lytton shocked at 287–8

Harrison, Professor G. B., quoted 302–3, 319, 322n., 323n. his letter to the author 323n.

Harrod, Sir Roy 43

Hartington, Lord 230–4, 235n.

Hassall, Christopher, his letter from Eddie Marsh 216n.

Hastings, Warren 65–6

Hawes, Ben 203, 204

Hazlitt, William 374

Hecatommithi (Cinthio) 370

'Henri Beyle' 158–60

Henry VIII 312, 318

Herbert, Sidney ('a comely, gallant creature') 177, 200–205, 208, 359
Hervey, Lord 345
Hill, Dr Birkbeck 226
'Historian of the Future, The' 68–9
History of England (G. M. Trevelyan) 303
Hitler, Adolf 40
Holland, Bernard: his biography of Spencer Compton 236; writes to Lytton 236n.
'Home Thoughts on Bloomsbury' (Roy Campbell) 42
Home University Library 129, 140
Horace (Quintus Horatius Flaccus) 353
'Horace Walpole' 11, 82
Horizon 216n.
House, Professor Humphry, quoted 161, 195
Housman, A. E. 109
Hudson, Stephen Edwin Muir's letter to 242n.
Húgel, Baron von 173
Hugo, Victor 142
Humanities (MacCarthy) 99n.
'Hume' 362, 364, 369
Hume, David 107n.
Hutchinson, Mary: Lytton writes to 281n.
Hutton, Richard Holt 111n.
Hyde Park Gate, No. 22 19, 25
Hydriotaphia (Browne) 83
'Ignotus' 110–12
Independent Review 65, 69, 76–98 pass., 151
'International Society, The' 102n.
Irvine, Canon 187–8
Italy 333
Jacob's Room (Virginia Woolf) 50
James, Henry: parody of 57–8
James Tait Black Memorial Prize: awarded to Queen Victoria 279
Jenkins, Roy 228
'John Aubrey' 356–7, 361–2

John, Augustus 31
'John Lyly' 99n.
'John Milton' 100
Johnson, Samuel 85, 89, 91, 99, 110, 166, 245–7, 283, 344, 374
Johnstone, J. K. quoted 33, 43–4, 47, 169, 221, 302; on Elizabeth and Essex 304
'Jonathan Swift' 56n.
Jones, E.B.C. See Lucas, E.B.C.
Jonson, Ben 103
Joyce, James 242, 284–6
Kallich, Professor Martin 10 quoted 299
Karim, Munshi Abdul 271
Keate, Dr 213
Keats, John 74–5, 148, 324
Kent, Duchess of 272, 273
Keynes, Maynard: his opinion of G. E. Moore 49; Vanessa Bell's remark about 22; as a member of the Bloomsbury Group 36n. 46, 48, 49; on Elizabeth and Essex 289, 314;
  Lytton's letter to 18
  His letters to Lytton 239, 289
'King Lear' 333n.
King Lear 89, 333, 373–4
King's College (Cambridge) 32, 286n.
Kingsmill, Hugh, quoted 246, 373–4
Kipling, Rudyard 109, 208
Knight, G. Wilson 372–3
Knutsford, Lord 217n.
Ladies' Home Journal: serialization of Elizabeth and Essex 332
'Lady Hester Stanhope' 360
'Lady Mary Wortley Montagu' 80–81
Lady Mary Wortley Montague and her Times (George Paston) 81
Lamb, Charles 74, 148
Lancaster Gate, No. 69 267
Landmarks in French Literature 115, 116, 129–42, 149, 151, 152, 167, 168

'L'Art Administratif' 112n.

'Last Elizabethan, The' 92

'Late Miss Coleridge's Poems, The' 90n.

Lawrence, D. H.: dislike of Bloomsbury for 38

Leathes, Sir Stanley ('Mr Stand-at-ease') 65

Leaves and Fruit (Sir Edmund Gosse) its dedication and censure 348

Leavis, Dr F. R. 44, 51, 107

Le Bas Prize 71

Lee, Sir Sidney 108

Lehmann, Rosamond 43

Lehzen, Baroness 250, 272–4

Leibniz, Gottfried Wilhelm 344

Leicester, Robert Dudley, Earl of 318, 321

Lemaître, M. 96n.

Leopold I, King 256, 273, 276

Leslie Stephen (Noël Annan) 29

Letters of Wyndham Lewis, The (W. K. Rose) 325n.

Lewis, Percy Wyndham 39–40; criticism of *Queen Victoria* 248; criticism of *Elizabeth and Essex* 325; write to Charles Prentice 325n.

Lettres Philosophiques (Voltaire) 154

Life and Letters 358n., 362n., 363, 367n.

'Life, Illness and Death of Dr North, The' 354, 356–7, 367

Listener 335n.

Literary Essays 69n., 77n., 78n., 83n. 84n. 85n. 89n. 94n. 59n. 71n., 99, 116, 147n. 149n. 150n. 96n. 338n. 340n. 357n.

'Lives of the Poets' 85, 99

Lives of the Poets (Dr Johnson) 245

Living Age 84n. 252n.

Livy (Titus Livius) 162

Lockhart, John Gibson 166–7

Lopez Dr 314–15, 317

Louis Napoleon and the Liberation of Italy (F. A. Simpson) 179n.

Louis Napoleon and the Recovery of France (F. A. Simpson) 178n., 179n.

Lucas, E.B.C. ('Topsy') 34, 331

Lucas, F. L. 34n., 52

Lytton Strachey: A Biography 18n., 33n., 61n., 96n., 209n., 345n.

Lytton Strachey by Himself 267n.

'Macaulay' 362, 365, 366–7

Macaulay, Thomas Babington 82, 86, 150, 345

'Macaulay's Marginalia' 294n.

Macbeth 374

MacCarthy, Sir Desmond: as member of the Bloomsbury Group 32, 36, 45; discharged as dramatic critic of *The Speaker* 99; as literary editor of the *New Quarterly* 98; on Lytton's morality 105; as critic of Beerbohm Tree 112; succeeds Gosse on *Sunday Times* 350;

Lytton's letter to 96n.

Mac Flecknoe (Dryden) 341

MacNiece, Louis 333

'Madame de Lieven' 358–9, 361

'Madame de Sévigné's Cousin' 357

'Mademoiselle de Lespinasse' 79–80, 151

'Madame du Deffand' 151–2, 360

Mahdi, The 221, 226

Mahler, Gustav 94

Maitland, Henry 51

Malinovsky, Bronislaw 352

Mallory, George 129

'Mandell Creighton' 362, 367–8

'Manet and the Post-Impressionists' 143

Manners, Lady Diana. See Cooper, Lady Diana

Marlborough (Wiltshire) 209

Marlborough, Duchess of 361

Marquis, Don, quoted 243

Marsh, Eddie: letter to Christopher Hassall 216n.

Martineau, Dr quoted 211

Martineau, Harriet 204

'Mary Berry' 358, 360–61

Massingham, H. W. 99

Maurois, André, quoted 9, 129–30, 245

McClelland, Vincent Alan quoted 190

McNeill, Sir John 204

McTaggart, J. E. 145

Measure for Measure quoted 244

Melbourne, Lord ('Lord M.') 256, 268–70, 275–7, 295

'Meredith, Owen'. See Lytton, Earl of

Meredith, George 148

Mérimée, Prosper, his absence 133

'Methods of Biography' 177n.

Midnight Society 56, 67

Milton, John 100

'Milton's Words' 87n.

Modern Egypt (Evelyn Baring) 238n.

'Modern Poetry' 109n., 354n.

Molière (Jean-Baptiste Poquelin) 131, 137–9

Montagu, Lady Mary Wortley 72, 345

Montgomery, Field-Marshal Lord 223

Moore, G. E. ('the Yen'): his influence on Lytton 58, 68; influence on Bloomsbury Group 37, 44, 47, 49;
  Lytton's letter to 67n.

Moorehead, Alan 223

Morrell, Lady Ottoline: introduces Lytton to W. B. Yeats 110;
  Lytton's letters to: 116, 218, 287n.

Mortimer, Raymond: his *Duncan Grant* 21n.; as member of Bloomsbury 47; on Lytton's amended opinion of Victoria's later years 265

'Mr Barrie's New Play' 112n.

'Mr Beerbohm Tree' 112n.

'Mr Creevey' 252

'Mr Granville Barker' 112n.

'Mr Walkley on the Drama' 117n.

'Mr Yeats's Poetry' 110

'Muggleton' 355–6

Muir, Edwin 242n.

My Life in Four Continents (Chaillé-Long) 226–7, 229–30

Napoleon I 151

Nash, Rosalind 197, 203

Nation, The 99

Nation and Athenaeum 339n., 351, 354n., 355n., 356n., 357n., 358n., 361n., 364n., 366n.

Neale, J. E. 315, 334

Nevinson, H. W. 223

'New History of Rome, A' 162n., 244n.

New Quarterly 77, 93, 98, 112, 116, 151

New Republic 252n., 339n., 354n., 355n., 356n., 357n., 358n., 361n.

New Statesman 39, 146, 147, 149n., 150

New Statesman and Nation 354n.

New York Times 331n.

Newman, Cardinal 170–74, 179n., 181, 183, 184, 185–8, 234, 359

Nichols, Robert 110

Nicolson, Sir Harold 166–7, 227, 249

Nineteenth Century 204n.

Norton, H.T.J.: as a member of the Bloomsbury Group 36n., 46, 48

Nutting, Anthony 229n.

Oedipus Tyrannus (Sophocles) 370

O'Faolain, Sean, quoted 185

Old Friends (Clive Bell) 20n.

Omega Workshops 46n., 144

Orlando (Virginia Woolf) 289

Othello (Shakespeare) 135, 370–74

'Othello' 108, 369–74

Oxford Book of English Prose (Arthur Quiller-Couch) 284

Oxford Movement 183
Pall Mall Gazette 224
Palmerston, Lord 269, 271, 295
Panmure, Lord ('a bison') 201, 231
Parker, Eric 118
Parr, Catherine 311
Partridge, Ralph 27, 35, 47; his B.B.C. talk 189
Paston, George 340
Pearson, Hesketh 112; on Johnson, as model 244; homosexuality and Albert 258; at the Café Royal with Lytton 286–8; his 'shocking' conversation 287–8
Peel, Robert 269–70, 277
Philip, King of Spain 301, 315, 317
Philipps, Wogan (Lord Milford) 21
Pio Nono 176–8, 180–2
Plomer, William annoys Eddie Marsh 216n.; the opera of *Elizabeth and Essex* 333; *His letter to the author* 333
'Poetry of Blake, The' 89
'Poetry of William Barnes, The' 119n.
'Pope and Mr Lytton Strachey' (Gosse) 348
Pope: His Life and Times, Mr. (George Paston) 340
Pope-Hennessy, James 157
Portraits in Miniature and other Essays 339n., 350–69
Prentice, Charles his business relationship with Lytton 325n.; on *Elizabeth and Essex* as bestseller 331; *Wyndham Lewis's letters to* 325–6 *Lytton's letters to* 313–14, 332, 351–2
'Président de Brosses, The' 354, 357–8
Principles of Literary Criticism (I. A. Richards) 46n., 50
Principia Ethica (G. E. Moore) 37, 43, 47, 68

Pritchard-Eaton, Walter 279
Progress of a Biographer, The (Hugh Kingsmill) 246n.
'Prose Style of Men of Action, The' 119
Proust, Marcel 338
Purcell, E. S., his Life of Manning 172, 177, 178, 180 190–91, 210
Putt, S. Gorley 7
Quarterly Review, The 350
Queen Elizabeth (J. E. Neale) 334
Queen Victoria 7, 167, 243–88, 291, 295, 299, 301–2, 303, 306, 333–4, 336n., 338, 347, 350, 365
Quennell, Peter as Shakespearian critic 374
Quiller-Couch, Sir Arthur ('Q'): his opinions of *Queen Victoria* 283–4; invites Lytton to write Introductions to the *New Shakespeare* 338; *His letter to Lytton* 283–4
'Rabelais' 150–51
'Racine' 92–3, 95–6, 116
Racine, Jean 95–6, 129, 134, 135–6
Rainbow Comes and Goes, The (Diana Cooper) 207n.
Raleigh, Professor Walter: on Dr Johnson 86; his Shakespearian criticism 374
Raleigh, Sir Walter ('the Fox') 291, 318, 319, 321, 329–30
Rambler, The 245
Raymond, John quoted 188, 235
Read, Conyers quoted 334
Read, Sir Herbert 284–6
Reddie, Dr Cecil 209, 214
Reign of Elizabeth, The (J. B. Black) 334
Reinach, Joseph, quoted 228
Return of William Shakespeare, The (Hugh Kingsmill), quoted 373
Richards, I. A. 46n., 50
Richardson, Samuel 289

Richmond, Sir William, versus Roger Fry 145

Rimbaud, Jean Nicolas Arthur 218

Rise of Louis Napoleon, The (F. A. Simpson) 178n.

Ritchie, Lady,
Lytton's letter to 202n.

Robert Devereux, Earl of Essex (G. B. Harrison) 302, 323n.

Roberts, S. C. 339

Robertson, A. J. 68n.

Rochefoucauld, La 78, 321

Rose, W. K. 325n.

Rothiemurchus 8

Rouge et le Noir, Le (Stendhal) 158

Rousseau, Jean-Jacques 158

Rowse, A. L., quoted 334–5

Rugby 208, 211, 213

Russell, Bertrand as militant pacifist 157

Russell, Odo 235

'Russian Humorist, A' 115

Rylands, George ('Dadie'), Lytton confesses his literary shortcomings to 286;
Lytton's letters to 335, 352n., 372

'Sad Story of Dr Colbatch, The' 339n., 355, 357, 367–8

St John, Ambrose 187

St John's College (Cambridge) 150

Sainte-Beuve, Jacques de 141

Saint-Simon, Louis de Rouvroy, Duc de 133

Saltsjöbaden (Sweden) 345

Sanders, Professor C. R. 9, 123n.

Sanger, C. P.: as member of Bloomsbury Group 32

Santayana, George, quoted 294

Saturday Review of Literature 334n., 358n., 362n.

Savage, Life of (Dr Johnson) 245

Savoy Hill 339

'Science of History' (J. B. Bury) 162n.

Scott, Gilbert 253

Scott, Sir Walter 148, 166

Scott-James, R. A., quoted 211n., 251, 257

Scott Moncrieff, C. K. 338

Scrutiny 105, 294

Second Empire, The (Philip Guedalla) 179n.

Sénancour, Étienne Pivert de 240n.

Senhouse, Roger 43n., 47;
Lytton's letter to 363–4

Serpent, Le (Paul Valéry) 338

Seward, A. C. 339

Sexual Life of Savages in North-Western Melanesia, The (Malinovsky) 352n.

Seymour, Jane 311

Seymour, Thomas 311

'Shakespeare Memorial, The' 112n.

'Shakespeare on Johnson' 90n., 99

'Shakespeare's Final Period' 108

'Shakespeare's Marriage' 102n.

Shakespeare, William 89, 92, 101, 108–9, 242, 279, 305, 369–74

Shaw, Bernard 19, 101, 112, 288

Shelley, Percy Bysshe 148, 150

Sheppard, Jack 343

Sheppard, Sir John 62;
Strachey's letters to 55, 77n.

Sherburn, Professor George 347

Shove, Gerald as member of the Bloomsbury Group 36n.

Sidgwick, Henry 51

Simpson, Celia 323n.

Simpson, Rev. F. A., his criticism of *Eminent Victorians* 176–81;
his letters to the author 178n., 179n.

Simson, Professor George Kuppler 217, 239

'Sir John Harington' 354, 356

'Sir Thomas Browne' 83–4

Sir Thomas Browne (Edmund Gosse) 83n.

Sitwell, Edith 109, 278n.

Sitwell, Sir Osbert, quoted 39, 40

Smalley, G. W. 222

Smith, Logan Pearsall 131n., 335

Smith W. F. 150–51

Souvestre, Marie 96
Sowing (Leonard Woolf) 20n.
Spain 333
Sparrow, Judge Gerald, quoted 218
Speaker, The 98–9
Spectator 18, 56n., 65, 87n., 89, 90n., 98–128 *pass.*, 162, 177n. 179, 237n., 244n., 291, 304, 315, 323n., 324, 333, 346, 354n.
Spectatorial Essays 56n., 89n., 90n., 99n., 112n., 116n., 118n. 119n., 120n., 162n., 294n., 324n,. 340n.
Spender, Stephen 45
Squire, Sir J. C. 110, 145, 280
Stamfordham, Lord 280–81
Stanley, Dean, his life of Arnold 210–12, 215
Stead, Miss 224
Stead, W. T. 222, 224
Stendhal (Henri Beyle) 141, 158–60
Stephen, Adrian 19, 30–32, 36n. 147
Stephen, Sir James Fitzjames 25, 84
Stephen, J. K. 25
Stephen, Julia 25
Stephen, Sir Leslie 19, 21, 24–5, 30, 51, 86, 150
Stephen, Thoby: relationship with Virginia Stephen 26, 27; as a member of Bloomsbury Group 32, 36n.; magnificent 66
Stephen, Vanessa: member of the Bloomsbury Group 19, 29, 36, 41; her marriage to Clive Bell 19; at 46 Gordon Square 29; description of 20–23
Lytton's letter to 217n.
Stephen, Virginia: at 29 Fitzroy Square 19, 30–32; at the death of Thoby 26; biography and description of 22–9; relationship with Lytton 27, 35; literary influence of Lytton upon 106n.; as a member of the Bloomsbury Group 19–20, 29–33, 36–9, 44, 48–50, 53–4; her biography of Roger Fry 53; in *Horizon* 216n.; not a figure of importance 242n.; on the failure of *Queen Victoria* 282–3; on its success 283; *Orlando* 289; opinion of *Elizabeth and Essex* 302, 304;
her letters to Lytton: 282, 350; *Lytton's letters to:* 93;
Sterne, Lawrence 148, 288
Stevenson, Miss Frances (Countess Lloyd George) 281n.
Stockmar, Baron 250, 272–7, 291
Strachey, Alix her influence on *Elizabeth and Essex* 298–9; on Lytton's diagnosis of Elizabeth 310n.
Strachey, Dorothy. See Bussy, Dorothy
Strachey, Evelyn John St Loe 118, 121, 323n.
Strachey, James: on Lytton's homosexuality 10; *Characters and Commentaries* 71n., 114–16; *Spectatorial Essays* 116n.; and the *Spectator* 111, 118, 124–5; at the Bloomsbury gatherings 37n.; political influence on Lytton 46; *His letters to the author:* 63n., 113n.; diagnosis hysteria formation 340; dedication of *Elizabeth and Essex* to 298; as Freud's pupil 298–9; publishes *Group Psychology and the Analysis of the Ego* 299;
His letter to Lady Strachey 281; *Lytton's letters to* 280, 336n.
Strachey, Lady (Lytton's mother): St Loe and 124, 127;
James Strachey's letter to: 281; *Lytton's letters to:* 76, 124; dedication of *Landmarks in French Literature to* 129
Strachey, Lytton:

Aphorisms: 60–62, 114–15
Appearance: 34–5, 146, 286–7
Books read: 55–9, 87
Christianity: 60, 67–8
Diary: 61
Family: 17–18, 65, 123
Friendships: 19–20, 29–30
Heterosexuality: 360
Homosexuality: 209, 218, 258–60, 307
Sense of Humour: 59–60
Style: 7–8, 9, 55–142 *pass.*, 147–60 *pass.*, 162–242 *pass.*, 243–88 *pass.*, 289–337 *pass.*, 341, 250–69 *pass.*
Verse: 8–9, 63–5
Victorianism: 37, 53–4, 161
Voice: 34–5, 40, 42
friendship with the Visigoths 19–21; Mephistopheles of Bloomsbury 51; takes shares in *Independent Review* 76; red beard and black cloak 146; lunch with Hesketh Pearson 286–8; delivers the Leslie Stephen Lecture 340; Eminent Edwardian 348; involvement in the *Elizabeth and Essex* theme 289, 307–8; appetite for punishments 396–7; fetishes 297–8; influence of Freud upon 298–300; prepares *Portraits in Miniature* 351–2; 'a thing on Othello' 369–74
Strachey, Marjorie 36n., 79n.
Strachey, Oliver 36n.
Strachey, St Loe 101, 111, 115, 116–25
Studies in Literature, Second Series (Arthur Quiller-Couch) 283n.
Sunday Essay Society (Cambridge) 67–9
Sunday Times 348, 350
Sutherland, Dr 206, 234
Sutton Court (Somerset) 123n.

Swift, Dean 55, 61, 93, 246, 251
Swinburne, Algernon 56, 89, 136, 148
Swinnerton, Frank 39, 41n.; his acceptance of F. A. Simpson's criticism of *Eminent Victorians* 178–80
Swithinbank, B. W.: Lytton's relationship with 18; *Lytton's letter to:* 55
Sydney-Turner, Saxon: member of Bloomsbury Group 36n.; member of Midnight Society 68n.
Symonds, John Addington 106n.
Tacitus, Caius Cornelius 162
Talleyrand-Périgord, Charles Maurice de 358
Tempest, The 113n.
Tener, Robert H., quoted 111n.
Tennyson, Alfred, Lord 63
Tennyson, Sir Charles 32, 47
Thackeray, William Makepeace 358
'Three New Plays' 101n.
Three Prophets (Chaillé-Long) 226, 229
Thucydides 162
Times, The 24
Times Literary Supplement, The 17, 111, 178n., 179n., 237, 278n., 279, 284, 409
Tolstoy 109
To the Lighthouse (Virginia Woolf) 24
Tom Brown's Schooldays (Thomas Hughes) 211
Tomlin, Julia. See Strachey, Julia
Tooley, Mrs Sarah 194
Townsend, Meredith 111n.
Transition (Edwin Muir) 242n.
Tree, Sir Herbert Beerbohm 110–11
Trench, Herbert 109
Trent 281n.
Trevelyan, Sir Charles 178
Trevelyan, G. M.: 76, 178n.; *His letters to Lytton:* 279n., 336;

objections to Dr Arnold 212n.; response to *Eminent Victorians* 279n.; critical appreciation of *Queen Victoria* 253, 280n.; his *History of England* 303; praises *Elizabeth and Essex* 336; foams at the mouth with rage 364

Trevelyan, R. C. ('Bob Trevy') 62, 77n.

Trevor-Roper, Professor Hugh 191, 229

Trilling, Lionel 212

Trinity College (Cambridge) 32, 56, 67n., 308, 313

Tudors, The (Conyers Read) 334

Turner, A. C. 67n.

Turner, Reggie, 280n.

'Two Frenchmen' 77-8

Ulysses (James Joyce) 286

Valéry, Paul 338

'Value of Poetry, The' 103n.

Vanbrugh, Sir John 148

Vaughan, Bishop Herbert 173

Verlaine, Paul 218

Versailles 130–31, 141, 154

Victoria of England (Edith Sitwell) 278n.

'Victorian Critic, A' 149n.

Vienna 336

Villon, François 132

Voltaire 35, 107n., 114, 130, 133, 136, 140, 145, 152–7, 166, 280n., 335, 344, 358

'Voltaire and England' 152–6

'Voltaire and Frederick the Great' 156–7

'Voltaire's Tragedies' 78

Waldman, Milton 315

Wales, Prince of (Edward VIII) 281n.

Waley, Arthur 47

Waller, A. R. 138

Walpole, Horace 73, 81–3, 152, 154, 342, 358, 360

Walpole, Sir Hugh 41

'Walpole's Letters' 11

War and Peace (periodical) 147, 219n.

Ward, Dudley 281n.

Ward, Mrs Humphry: possibilities concerning her legs 216n.; her novels in Fulham 368

Ward, W. G. 161

Ward, Wilfrid 187–8

'Warren Hastings' 65–7, 374

Wedd, Nathaniel 76

Weightman, J. G. 142

Wells, H. G. 288

What Every Woman Knows (Barrie) 113

'W. H., Mr' 108–9

Wilberforce, Henry 188

Wild Duck, The (Ibsen) 135

Wild, Jonathan 343

Wilde, Oscar 61–2, 68, 135, 313

'William Barnes' 118

Wilson, Professor John Dover, his *John Lyly* reviewed by Strachey 98; converts 'Q' 283–4; and the *New Shakespeare* 338

Wingfield-Stratford, Esmé, quoted 229

Wiseman, Cardinal 189, 231

Woburn Abbey 314

Wolseley, Lord 235

Woolf, Leonard: as a member of the Bloomsbury Group 18, 20, 36n., 37; his periodical *War and Peace* 147; against *Queen Victoria* 282; member of Midnight Society 68n.; *Lytton's letter to* 19

Woolf, Virginia. See Stephen, Virginia

Wordsworth, William 89–90, 93, 96, 136, 215

Wotton, Sir Henry 97n.

'Wrong Turning, The' 85

Yeats, W. B. 110

Words and Poetry (George Rylands) 338

Young, Hilton 42

Zobier, Rahama Pasha 236